International Criminal Justice Series

Volume 21

AF739763

Series Editors

Gerhard Werle, Berlin, Germany
Moritz Vormbaum, Münster, Germany

Series Information

The *International Criminal Justice Series* aims to create a platform for publications covering the entire field of international criminal justice. It, therefore, deals with issues relating, among others, to:

- the work of international criminal courts and tribunals;
- transitional justice approaches in different countries;
- international anti-corruption and anti-money laundering initiatives;
- the history of international criminal law.

It is peer-reviewed and seeks to publish high-quality works emanating from excellent scholars.

Editorial Office

Prof. Dr. Gerhard Werle
Humboldt-Universität zu Berlin
Faculty of Law
Unter den Linden 6,
10099 Berlin, Germany
gerhard.werle@rewi.hu-berlin.de
vormbaum@uni-muenster.de

More information about this series at http://www.springer.com/series/13470

Seada Hussein Adem

Palestine and the International Criminal Court

ASSER PRESS

Springer

Seada Hussein Adem
Alexandria, VA, USA

ISSN 2352-6718 ISSN 2352-6726 (electronic)
International Criminal Justice Series
ISBN 978-94-6265-293-4 ISBN 978-94-6265-291-0 (eBook)
https://doi.org/10.1007/978-94-6265-291-0

Library of Congress Control Number: 2019931838

Published by T.M.C. ASSER PRESS, The Hague, The Netherlands www.asserpress.nl
Produced and distributed for T.M.C. ASSER PRESS by Springer-Verlag Berlin Heidelberg

© T.M.C. ASSER PRESS and the author 2019
No part of this work may be reproduced, stored in a retrieval system, or transmitted in any form or by any means, electronic, mechanical, photocopying, microfilming, recording or otherwise, without written permission from the Publisher, with the exception of any material supplied specifically for the purpose of being entered and executed on a computer system, for exclusive use by the purchaser of the work.
The use of general descriptive names, registered names, trademarks, service marks, etc. in this publication does not imply, even in the absence of a specific statement, that such names are exempt from the relevant protective laws and regulations and therefore free for general use.

This T.M.C. ASSER PRESS imprint is published by the registered company Springer-Verlag GmbH, DE part of Springer Nature
The registered company address is: Heidelberger Platz 3, 14197 Berlin, Germany

Acknowledgements

This study was conducted within the framework of the South African-German Centre for Transnational Criminal Justice. The Centre is the result of cooperation between Humboldt-Universität zu Berlin and the University of the Western Cape. It is supported by the *Deutscher Akademischer Austausch Dienst* (DAAD) with funds from the German Federal Foreign Office. I am thankful to the DAAD and the Federal Foreign Office for fully funding my work and stay in Berlin. The study would not have come to completion without their generous financial assistance.

I am deeply indebted to various people for the unfaltering support and contribution to bring this study to fruition. My foremost gratitude goes to Prof. Dr. Gerhard Werle, my study supervisor and co-director of the Centre. Despite his busy schedule, he was able to follow my progress and give his constructive comments and constant support. I thank him not only for his excellent intellectual and academic guidance but also for being exemplary to me and many others. I am also thankful to the former co-director of the Centre Prof. Lovell Fernandez whose encouragement and support contributed greatly to the completion of the study and to the external examiner, Prof. Christian Tomuschat, whose invaluable comments considerably benefited the final draft of the study.

I am sincerely indebted to Prof. Moritz Vormbaum for his unreserved cooperation, encouragement and positive feedbacks. The work has benefited significantly from his insightful comments and tireless supervision. I also thank Prof. Chantal Meloni and Valentina Azarov for the kind material support and Dr. Boris Burghardt for editing part of the study.

I am also grateful to Anna Krey, the coordinator of the Centre, and Frau Anja Schepke as well as other members of the centre for their cooperation and invaluable administrative support throughout my stay in Berlin. I am particularly grateful to Frau Schepke who has managed all important matters pertaining to my stay in Berlin, such as university fees, health insurance, travel documents and accommodation.

Finally, yet importantly, I thank my parents, Hussein and Ansha Adem, my husband Ebrahim Kassie and my siblings Nuru and Semira Hussein whose constant prayer, support and encouragement kept me going. I also thank my friends and researchers in the Centre, Dr. Marshet Tadesse, Victoria Ojo, Marian Yankson-Mensah, Franziska Tolksdorf and Dr. Verena Zoppei. You made this journey memorable.

Above all, I say *Alhamdulilah* to the enabler, the bestower and the sustainer.

Contents

Abbreviations and Acronyms

AC	Appeals Chamber
ASP	Assembly of States Parties (of the ICC)
AU	African Union
CAR	Central African Republic
DRC	Democratic Republic of Congo
ECHR	European Court of Human Rights
EJIL	European Journal of International Law
ESCWA	United Nations Economic and Social Commission for Western Asia
FIDH	International Federation for Human Rights
HSRC	Human Sciences Research Council of South Africa
IAEA	International Atomic Energy Agency
ICAHD	Israeli Committee Against House Demolitions
ICC	International Criminal Court
ICJ	International Court of Justice
ICTR	International Criminal Tribunal for Rwanda
ICTY	International Criminal Tribunal for the Former Yugoslavia
IDF	Israeli Defence Force
ILC	International Law Commission
JICJ	Journal of International Criminal Justice
OHCHR	Office of the United Nations High Commissioner for Human Rights
OPT	Occupied Palestinian Territories
OTP	Office of the Prosecutor (of the ICC)
PA	Palestinian Authority
PLO	Palestine Liberation Organization
PTC	Pre-Trial Chamber (of the ICC)
TRC	Truth and Reconciliation Commission (of South Africa)
UNCTAD	United Nations Conference on Trade and Development

UNESCO	United Nations Educational, Scientific and Cultural Organization
UNGA	United Nations General Assembly
UNHCR	United Nations High Commissioner for Refugees
UNHRC	United Nations Human Rights Council
UNOCHA	United Nations Office for the Coordination of Humanitarian Affairs
UNOCHA-OPT	United Nations Office for the Coordination of Humanitarian Affairs—Occupied Palestinian Territory
UNRWA	United Nations Relief and Works Agency for Palestine Refugees in the Near East
UNSC	United Nations Security Council
UNSCOP	United Nations Special Committee on Palestine
WTO	World Trade Organisation

Chapter 1
Introduction and Overview

Contents

Abstract This chapter provides a general overview and an introduction. It starts by giving a background to the interaction of Palestine with the International Criminal Court followed by the objectives of the study. It also presents a discussion of the available literature on the topic. The final section of the chapter provides the limitations followed by the outline adopted to answer the main questions.

Keywords Ad hoc declaration · International Criminal Court · Israel · Israeli-Palestinian conflict · Palestine · Rome Statute

1.1 Background

When the perpetual Israeli-Palestinian conflict gives rise to yet another active hostility, with civilian casualties and damage to property, appeals for judicial interventions intensify. Interventions are called for in order to establish justice and accountability, as well as peace and stability.[1] The call for justice and accountability on the one hand, and for peace and stability on the other, stems from the fact that the conflict represents a classical case where justice and peace are highly intertwined.[2]

---

[1] Wegner 2015, p. 1.
[2] Bar-Siman-Tov 2015.

© T.M.C. ASSER PRESS and the author 2019

S. H. Adem, *Palestine and the International Criminal Court*,
International Criminal Justice Series 21,
https://doi.org/10.1007/978-94-6265-291-0_1

However, it was only in 2012 that the possibility of establishing justice was seriously contemplated for the case of Palestine.[3] Up until then, international criminal law, as a mechanism for dealing with crimes committed in international and domestic conflicts, has developed significantly. The post-World War II Nuremberg and Tokyo trials as well as the *ad hoc* for the Former Yugoslavia and for Rwanda have left a deep imprint on international criminal law.[4] These occurrences have also laid down the groundwork for the creation of the International Criminal Court (ICC), which after many decades has led to the prospect of the Court's dealing with matters arising from the situation in Palestine.

The ICC is a permanent Court established at the diplomatic conference of plenipotentiaries on 17 July 1998 for investigating and prosecuting perpetrators of the 'most serious crimes of international concern'.[5] Its founding treaty, the Rome Statute[6] entered into force on 1 July 2002.[7] The Statute is a detailed document with a comprehensive set of provisions spanning affairs relating to institutional arrangements as well as matters of both substantive and procedural law.[8] In terms of substantive criminal law, Articles 6–8 cover the core crimes of genocide, crimes against humanity, war crimes and the crime of aggression.[9]

The Court enjoys a retrospective jurisdiction if, as provided under the principle of complementarity, a State which has jurisdiction over the crime in question is genuinely 'unwilling or unable' to conduct investigation or prosecution.[10] The Court otherwise exercises jurisdiction over a crime committed on the territory of a State party to the Statute or if the accused is a national of a State party.[11] States Parties' can trigger the Court's jurisdiction for crimes committed within the jurisdiction of the Court.[12] In addition, the Security Council of the United Nations, pursuant to Chapter VII of the UN Charter,[13] is empowered to refer situations to the

3 Meloni and Tognoni 2012, p. v. Palestine remained far from the docket of any international Court after it first appeared as a focus of litigation before the Permanent Court of International Justice in 1924. See Permanent Court of International Justice, *Greece v. U.K.* (Mavrommatis Palestine Concessions), Judgment, 30 August 1924, PCIJ Series B no. 3.

4 Aksar 2004, pp. 7 et seq.; Bantekas and Nash 2010, pp. 8 et seq.; Cassese 2002, p. 3; Mettraux 2011, pp. 3 et seq.; Werle and Jessberger 2014, pp. 1–2.

5 Preamble of Rome Statute of the International Criminal Court, opened for signature 17 July 1998, 2187 UNTS 90 (entered into force 1 July 2002) (Rome Statute); Bassiouni 2013, p. 654; Scheffer 2011, pp. 67 et seq.

6 See Rome Statute, above n. 5.

7 Ibid., Preamble.

8 McGoldrick 2004, pp. 42–43.

9 Rome Statute, above n. 5, Article 5; Meron 1999, p. 48.

10 Rome Statute, above n. 5, Article 17(1)(a).

11 Ibid., Article 12(2).

12 Ibid., Article 14.

13 Charter of the United Nations, opened for signature 26 June 1945, 1 UNTS XVI (entered into force 24 October 1945); Rome Statute, above n. 5, Article 13(b).

Court, and has the power to suspend investigations or proceedings.[14] The Office of the Prosecutor of the Court has also the competence to initiate investigations on its own or by a complaint referred to the Office.[15]

Palestine's encounters with the ICC were based provisions in the Rome Statute that enable States to temporarily delegate criminal jurisdiction to the Court.[16] On 21 January 2009, Ali Khasan, the Minister of Justice of the Palestinian National Authority, submitted an *ad hoc* declaration recognizing 'the jurisdiction of the Court for the purpose of identifying, prosecuting and judging the authors and accomplices of acts committed on the territory of Palestine since 1 July 2002'. To give effect to the declaration, the document stated 'the government of Palestine will cooperate with the Court without delay or exception in conformity with chapter IX of the Statute'.[17]

In April 2012, three years after the Registrar of the Court received the Palestinian *ad hoc* declaration, the then Prosecutor of the ICC published a two page 'decision not to decide' on the declaration.[18] It detailed that the OTP was unable to commence investigation into the situation since it was not within the competence of the office to determine whether Palestine qualified to accede to the Rome Statute or to make an *ad hoc* declaration. In December 2012, the UN General Assembly, through Resolution 67/19, decided to grant Palestine a non-member observer State status.[19] In a press release dated 2 September 2014, the Office of the Prosecutor (hereafter the OTP) stated that, although this upgraded status of Palestine could not 'retroactively validate the previously invalid declaration', it was now up to the Palestinians themselves to make a new declaration or sign the Rome Statute.[20]

Be this as it may, following the 2014 Israeli military Operation dubbed 'Protective Edge'[21] and the failure of the Palestinian UN bid for the Security

[14] Ibid., Articles 13(c) and 16.

[15] Ibid., Articles 13 and 15.

[16] The provision aims to expand the jurisdictional scope of the Court by allowing non-member States to grant temporary or *ad hoc* jurisdiction to the ICC. If a crime within the scope of the Statute is committed by a non-member State on the territory of a non-member State, the latter could make a declaration on the basis of this provision. See Rome Statute, above n. 5, Article 12 (3).

[17] Palestinian National Authority 2009.

[18] OTP, Situation in Palestine, 3 April 2012, https://www.icc-cpi.int/NR/rdonlyres/C6162BBF-FEB9-4FAF-AFA9-836106D2694A/284387/SituationinPalestine030412ENG.pdf (accessed 20 November 2017).

[19] UNGA 2012.

[20] OTP, Statement of the Prosecutor of the International Criminal Court, Fatou Bensouda: The public deserves to know the truth about the ICC's jurisdiction over Palestine, 2 September 2014, https://www.icc-cpi.int/en_menus/icc/press%20and%20media/press%20releases/Pages/otp-st-14-09-02.aspx (accessed 30 July 2015).

[21] The Israeli offensive killed more than 2,000 people including 539 children. Hamas fired 3,659 rockets killing six civilians. See UNHCR 2015, pp. 18–59; Dekel 2014, pp. 13–17.

Council, which called for an urgent solution to the conflict,[22] the Palestinian Authority made another *ad hoc* declaration and signed the Rome Statute in January 2015.[23] After the receipt of the declaration, the Prosecutor opened a preliminary examination into the situation in Palestine on 16 January 2015.[24]

At the time of writing, it is premature to predict whether the preliminary examination will lead to a formal investigation and, if it does, what the scope of investigation will be. If the Prosecutor, however, decides to investigate and prosecute the alleged crimes committed in the Israel-Palestine conflict, the situation would certainly cause the Court to encounter unique legal challenges.

1.2 Objectives

In view of the foregoing background, the principal objective of the book is to examine the possible involvement of the ICC in the Israel-Palestine conflict. Given that the ICC will have to investigate not only specific and sporadic acts of violence, but also alleged long-term, structural and policy-based crimes, Palestine will present an unprecedented challenge to the Court. The statehood issue of Palestine, the unsettled boundary between Israel and Palestine, the delicacy and sensitivity of the conflict, as well as the political arrangement of Palestine, amongst others, will constitute additional challenges. Hence, in light of the Rome Statute and taking into account the substantive and procedural issues that will come into focus, this book specifically aims to:

- examine the jurisdictional and procedural challenges that the ICC will encounter in investigating and prosecuting the crimes allegedly committed by either party to the conflict;
- scrutinize, based on the facts and reports available, which crimes under the Rome Statute were committed and which are justiciable;

---

[22] The draft Resolution submitted to the UNSC insists on the necessity of an urgent solution. It demands the withdrawal of Israeli occupation forces from the West Bank and East Jerusalem by the end of 2017. The draft fell short of one vote when Nigeria and South Korea, States expected to vote in favour of the bid, abstained. See J. Goldberg, Palestinian UN bid fails by 1 vote. Was that the plan? 30 December 2014, https://forward.com/opinion/211846/palestinian-un-bid-fails-by-1-vote-was-that-the-pl/. (accessed 30 July 2015); UN News, UN Security Council action on Palestinian statehood blocked, 31 December 2014, https://news.un.org/en/story/2014/12/487342-un-security-council-action-palestinian-statehood-blocked (accessed 30 July 2015).

[23] In accordance with Article 126(2) of the Rome Statute, above n. 5, the Statute entered into force for the State of Palestine on 1 April 2015. The ICC on Palestine, https://www.icc-cpi.int/palestine?ln=en (accessed 1 August 2015).

[24] ICC, Press release: The Prosecutor of the International Criminal Court, Fatou Bensouda, opens a preliminary examination of the situation in Palestine, 16 January 2015, ICC-OTP-20150116-PR1083.

- analyse the possible significance, impact and contribution of the involvement of the ICC on the Israeli-Palestinian conflict; and
- explore the contribution of the Palestinian situation to the development of international criminal law in general and the ICC in particular.

1.3 Literature Survey

There is a wealth of literature with respect to the jurisprudence and Statute of the ICC. Similarly, the historical, political and social aspect of Palestine and Israel is well documented. Nonetheless, there is very limited academic literature that links the situation in Palestine with the ICC.

The available literature on the intervention of the ICC in the Palestine situation can be categorized, roughly, into two groups, namely pre- and post-2015. The pre-2015 category is mainly dominated by the literature addressing the 2009 *ad hoc* declaration of Palestine and the subsequent decision of the Prosecutor on the declaration. The 2009 *ad hoc* declaration gave rise to an extensive legal discussion and argument about the scope and application of *ad hoc* declarations in general and the Palestinian *ad hoc* declaration in particular.[25] The international legal status of Palestine and its statehood with regard to its ability to make such juridical acts appears central to the discussion.[26] Countering this approach, there is literature that questions the essentiality of deciding on the international legal personality or statehood of Palestine. In light of this literature, a functional interpretation of the notion 'State' for the regime of *ad hoc* declarations would make this leeway of granting jurisdiction to the Court befitting to the aims and purposes of the statute.[27] Although there is literature supporting the decision of the Prosecutor on the 2009 *ad hoc* declaration, the dominant view is that the approach employed by the Prosecutor was inconsistent with the Statute, conventional law and UN practice.[28] There is, however, a fundamental agreement amongst scholars regarding the lack of an established framework and procedure, as well as timeframe to deal with *ad hoc* declarations.[29]

Most literature dealing with the 2009 ad hoc declarations, especially that published before Palestine obtained the non-member observer State status in the UN in 2012, addressed the issue of Palestine's statehood. This relatively new development in the UN makes the issue of statehood no longer central to the Palestine-ICC

---

[25] See, among others, Ash 2009, p. 186; Azarova 2013; Dugard 2013, p. 11; El Zeidy 2014; Meloni and Tognoni 2012.

[26] See, for instance, Ash 2009, p. 186; Ronen 2012, pp. 476–480.

[27] See, for instance, Pellet 2010; Shany 2010, pp. 342−343.

[28] Dugard 2013, pp. 563–570; Quigley 2009, pp. 436–439.

[29] See, for instance, Meloni and Tognoni 2012; Schabas 2014, p. 374; Triffterer and Ambos 2016, pp. 687 et seq.

relation. Although the issue of Palestine's statehood in the abstract, according to some scholars, is not yet settled, various scholars agree that the new status of Palestine in the UN settles the issue for the purposes of the ICC.[30] Hence, most pre-2015 literature was mainly restricted to the discussion on the applicability or the scope of an ad hoc declaration in the Palestinian context.

After Palestine lodged a second ad hoc declaration and became the 123rd member of the ICC in 2015, the discussion shifted mainly towards the scope of the Court's jurisdiction over Palestine, if any, the issues of complementarity and the impact of the Court's intervention in the situation. Due to the novelty of the issue, there is a lack of literature dealing with the issue of the Court's jurisdiction in Palestine.

The possibility of establishing accountability through the ICC has given rise to an examination of Israel's judicial system in light of the principle of complementarity.[31] The conclusions in most literature, including UN Reports, indicates the deficiencies in the judicial system of Israel that help shield alleged perpetrators. The fundamental flaws in the system, according to some scholars, necessitate credible alternative avenues for establishing accountability. This restricted amount of literature on complementarity in the Palestine situation significantly focuses on the ability and willingness of Israel to address the alleged crimes. The same issue has not been dealt with in the context of Palestine's judicial system.

Some post-2015 literature addressed the commission of war crimes and crimes against humanity in the situation.[32] There is, however, a dearth of literature that is framed in a way that enables establishing individual criminal responsibility for the alleged gross crimes committed. There is also a lack of precedents regarding the prosecution of alleged crimes such as the construction of settlements and the crime of apartheid.

In the context of the situation of Palestine, some literature published since 2015 dealt with the non-legal issues associated with the relationship between Palestine and the ICC. Concerning the theories and practices of politics, this category of literature analyses the possible impact of the ICC becoming involved in the 'unresolved political conflict'.[33] Considering the Court's experience in other ongoing conflicts, some literature edified the impact of intervening in the Palestine situation on the legitimacy, reputation and effectiveness of the Court. The same is also questioned in light of the Israeli-Palestinian peace process. In this regard, the publications tend to follow two tracks. There are opponents of the Court's intervention in Palestine and the proponents. The opponents argue that by investigating the situation in Palestine, the Court is mixing up peace processes and is being used as a means to launch 'lawfare'. For others, the aims and purposes of the Court are ends in themselves that transcend politics. In any case, the literature agrees that the

30 See, for instance, El Zeidy 2014.

31 Azarova and Weill 2012, pp. 913 et seq.

32 Dugard and Reynolds 2013, p. 912; HSRC 2009.

33 Ronen 2012, pp. 491–492.

Palestinian situation is one of the most precarious situations the Court has dealt with.[34] As the context is a case in development, some of the conclusions reached in this literature is negated by new development and findings.

Apart from this literature dealing with the interaction of Palestine with the ICC and other journals, newsletters and blogs that address certain substantive issues, there is no up-to-date literature that approaches the 'Palestine and the ICC' case in a holistic way, particularly in light of the jurisprudence of the ICC and recent developments. Especially concerning the prosecution of possible cases in the situation, the Court has not obtained enough input and materials that could supplement or provide alternative viewpoints. This book, therefore, strives to provide an array of opinions and hopefully an input for the interaction of the ICC with Palestine. It also aims to assist in alleviating the dearth of literature and serve as reference material for future researchers and practitioners.

1.4 Limitation

The background of the issue that forms the subject of this book has been going on for more than a century. Similarly, the intervention of the ICC in the conflict is still an ongoing process. This necessitated a constant review and update on the points discussed in the chapters. But the facts evaluated remain mainly limited to events that happened before April 2017.

Moreover, the Israeli-Palestinian conflict is one of the most politicized and controversial conflicts of our time, which makes the obtaining of a balanced and impartial narration and portrayal of the situation especially crucial. The book, therefore, portrays an objective, fact-based and neutral perspective. Even though this study solely concerns the application of International Criminal Law to the Israeli-Palestinian conflict, for it to be sensible and pragmatic it cannot ignore the role played by geopolitics and the various stakeholders; the fact is that they matter and have to be acknowledged and discussed in one way or another.

Due to the complexity and the depth of the Israeli-Palestinian conflict, it is almost impossible to address the topic in all its dimensions. The intention is, therefore, neither to deal with the conflict in general, nor to propose an overall solution to the conflict. The book aims rather to yield an analytical legal insight, against the backdrop of the Rome Statute, into ways of addressing impunity for gross international violations perpetrated in the context of the Israeli-Palestinian conflict.

[34] Wegner 2015, p. 3.

1.5 Outline

This book comprises seven chapters. The present chapter introduces the background to the study and lays the foundation upon which subsequent chapters will be constructed. Chapter 2 addresses the historical and political background to the Israeli-Palestinian conflict. It focuses on the various incidents that gave rise to the ICC's intervention. As the intervention was necessitated not only by alleged, separate and sporadic violations, but also by the purported systematic and policy-based abuses that have been going on for many decades, the book will inevitably fall short of its goal were it to be concluded without imparting to the reader the historical and political background to the Palestinian-Israeli conflict.

Chapter 3 assesses Palestine's first *ad hoc* declaration to the ICC. It revisits Palestine's first encounter with the Court and the main issues that arose thereafter before Palestine made its second declaration and joined the ICC. It examines the decision reached by the OTP on the basis of the Rome Statute and other *ad hoc* declarations. Accordingly, the chapter addresses the issue of Palestine's statehood and determines which institutions have possible competence to decide on the statehood question.

The issues that arise during the pre-investigation stage of a situation and the criteria that need to be met for a situation to proceed to the investigation stage are included in Chap. 4. Having regard to the Palestine situation, the chapter looks into questions of jurisdiction, admissibility and the interests of justice, as provided under Article 53(1) of the Statute. Hence, it covers matters of temporal, personal and territorial jurisdiction, in addition to the complementarity and gravity criteria, as well as the countervailing consideration of the 'interest of justice'.

The criteria for selecting and prioritizing cases are dealt with in Chap. 5. Given the case at hand, the chapter offers a prospective outlook on how the OTP and the Court could go about deciding which cases to investigate and prosecute regarding the Palestine situation. The discussion focuses on the alleged gross violations committed in the Israeli-Palestinian conflict that fall within the Court's jurisdiction. The conflict has showed itself to be an arena in which numerous gross crimes have been perpetrated by actors ranging from private individuals to state machineries and institutions. Although it would be impossible to address each and every alleged perpetration of a crime, the chapter nevertheless attempts to analyse the alleged commission of crimes that may fall within the compass of the Statute and that could be prosecuted before the Court. The chapter thus ponders the elements of crimes under the Statute. It considers the criteria spelled out in Article 53 with regard to the conflict and the facts available in a manner that could help establish the individual criminal responsibility of alleged perpetrators.

The penultimate chapter analyses the possible impact and contribution of the ICC to the Israeli-Palestinian conflict. Some jurists and politicians are of the categorical view that pursuing justice for alleged crimes committed in this conflict could deter the peacemaking efforts. They contend that the ICC's involvement would contribute little, if at all, to establishing sustainable peace in the region.

Accordingly, the chapter discusses chiefly the so-called peace versus justice dilemma as it pertains to the Israeli-Palestinian conflict. Moreover, it considers the argument espoused by the Israeli government, namely, that the ICC is being hijacked as a tactic to launch 'lawfare'. Finally, the chapter yields an insight into whether criminal prosecutions, as a transitional justice accountability mechanism, would bring redress to the victims of gross human rights and humanitarian law violations, thus ultimately paving the road to peace.

Chapter 7 concludes by summarizing its major findings and by identifying and recommending measures and practices that the ICC could adopt to deal with the Palestinian situation and other similar cases.

References

Aksar Y (2004) Implementing international humanitarian law from the ad hoc tribunals to a permanent International Criminal Court. Routledge, New York.

Ash R (2009) Is Palestine a 'state'? A response to Professor John Quigley's article 'The Palestine declaration to the International Criminal Court: The statehood issue'. Rutgers Law Records 36:186–201.

Azarova V (2013) Tell it to the judge: Palestine's UN bid and the International Criminal Court. In: Qafisheh M (ed) Palestine membership in the United Nations: Legal and practical implications. Cambridge Scholars Publishing, New Castle, pp. 252–267.

Azarova V, Weill S (2012) Israel's unwillingness? The follow-up investigations to the UN Gaza conflict report and International Criminal Justice. International Criminal Law Review 12: 905–935.

Bantekas I, Nash S (2010) International criminal law, 4th edn. Hart Publishing, Oxford.

Bar-Siman-Tov Y (2015) Justice and peace in the Israeli-Palestinian conflict. Routledge, Oxon.

Bassiouni M (2013) Introduction to international criminal law, 2nd rev. edn. Martinus Nijhoff Publishers, Dordrecht.

Cassese A (2002) From Nuremberg to Rome: The international military tribunals to the International Criminal Court. In: Cassese A, Gaeta P, Jones JRWD (eds) The Rome Statute of the International Criminal Court: A Commentary. Oxford University Press, New York, pp. 3–19.

Dekel U (2014) Operation Protective Edge: Strategic and tactical asymmetry. In: Kurz A, Brom S (eds) The lessons of Operation Protective Edge. Elinir, Tel Aviv, pp. 13–20.

Dugard J (2013) Palestine and the International Criminal Court: Institutional failure or bias? JICJ 11:563–570.

Dugard J, Reynolds J (2013) Apartheid, international law, and the Occupied Palestinian Territory. EJIL 24:867–913.

El Zeidy M (2014) Ad hoc declarations of acceptance of jurisdiction: The Palestinian Situation under scrutiny. In: Stahn C (ed) The law and practice of the International Criminal Court. Oxford University Press, Oxford, pp. 179–209.

HSRC (2009) Occupation, colonialism, apartheid? A re-assessment of Israel's practices in the occupied Palestinian territories under international law. Human Sciences Research Council, Cape Town.

McGoldrick D (2004) Criminal trials before international tribunals: Legality and legitimacy. In: McGoldrick D, Rowe P, Donnelly E (eds) The permanent International Criminal Court: Legal and policy issues. Hart Publishing, Oxford, pp. 9–46.

Meloni C, Tognoni G (eds) (2012) Is There a Court for Gaza? A Test Bench for International Justice. T.M.C. Asser Press, The Hague.

Meron T (1999) Crimes under the jurisdiction of the International Criminal Court. In: von Hebel H, Lammers JG, Schukking J (eds) Reflections on the International Criminal Court: Essays in Honour of Adriaan Bos. T.M.C. Asser Press, The Hague, pp. 47–56.

Mettraux G (2011) Trial at Nuremberg. In: Schabas W, Bernaz N (eds) Routledge Handbook of International Criminal Law. Routledge, London, pp. 5–16.

Palestinian National Authority (2009) Declaration recognizing the jurisdiction of the International Criminal Court.

Pellet A (2010) The Palestinian Declaration and the jurisdiction of the International Criminal Court. JICJ 8:981–999.

Quigley J (2009) The Palestine Declaration to the International Criminal Court: The statehood issue. Rutgers Law Record 35:1–11.

Ronen Y (2012) ICC jurisdiction over acts committed in the Gaza Strip: Article12(3) of the ICC Statute and Non-state entities. In: Meloni C, Tognoni G (eds) Is There a Court for Gaza? A Test Bench for International Justice. T.M.C. Asser Press, The Hague, pp. 469–496.

Schabas W (2014) Selecting Situations and Cases. In: Stahn C (ed) The Law and Practice of the International Criminal Court. Oxford University Press, Oxford, pp. 365–381.

Scheffer D (2011) The International Criminal Court. In: Schabas W, Bernaz N (eds) Routledge Handbook of International Criminal Law. Routledge, London, pp. 67–84.

Shany Y (2010) In defence of functional interpretation of Article 12(3): A response to Yael Ronen. JICJ 8:329–343.

Triffterer O, Ambos K (eds) (2016) The Rome Statute of the International Criminal Court: A Commentary, 3rd edn. Hart Publishing, Munich.

UNGA (2012) Status of Palestine in the United Nations, UN Doc. A/RES/67/19.

UNHCR (2015) Report of the detailed findings of the independent commission of inquiry established pursuant to Human Rights Council Resolution S-21/1, UN Doc. A/HRC/29/CRP.4.

Wegner P (2015) The International Criminal Court in ongoing intrastate conflicts: Navigating the peace-justice divide. Cambridge University Press, Cambridge.

Werle G, Jessberger F (2014) Principles of International Criminal Law, 3rd edn. Oxford University Press, Oxford.

Chapter 2
Historical and Political Background of the Israeli-Palestinian Conflict

Contents

Abstract The Israeli-Palestinian conflict has a complex history. The different, often conflicting, narratives of this conflict contribute to its perpetuity. Although it is beyond the scope of this chapter to clarify the 'historical truth' in the Israeli-Palestinian conflict, it is, nevertheless, imperative to tease the common strands of the various narratives in order to reach conclusions that best reflect the facts. In light of this aim, this chapter provides a discussion of historical events ranging from the creation of the States of Palestine and Israel to military conflicts that gave rise to Palestine's delegation of jurisdiction to the International Criminal Court. The stages leading up to the interaction of Palestine with the International Criminal Court are important not only to understand the general context of

© T.M.C. ASSER PRESS and the author 2019

S. H. Adem, *Palestine and the International Criminal Court*,
International Criminal Justice Series 21,
https://doi.org/10.1007/978-94-6265-291-0_2

Palestine's resort to the Court, but also the implications of possible investigation and prosecution through the Court. Due to their importance to the general context at hand, the chapter also covers military operations that led to the 2009 and 2014 Palestinian ad hoc declarations as well as some of the peace negotiations held between the two parties.

Keywords Arab-Israel War · Occupied Palestinian Territories · Operation Cast Lead · Operation Protective Edge · Partition Plan · British Mandate for Palestine

2.1 Introductory Remarks

History shapes the present day. It sets the background against which we are able to make informed predictions. Present-day events cannot be fully explained with a narrow-minded view of what is happening on the ground. Competing and interweaving accounts of conflicts reveal the significant contribution of history in shaping the future of nations.[1] The power to narrate and simultaneously block other narrations impacts significantly on how historical facts are portrayed. Throughout history narratives have been used to mobilize people for various causes, including for purposes of colonization and decolonization of territories. In a situation involving two parties that are pitted against each other, historical narratives are constructed and documented in way that attempts to rationalise which of the contending parties holds the moral high ground.[2] This makes establishing the 'historical truth' difficult.

In the Israel-Palestine conflict it is a trite fact that historical narrations are partial and manipulated easily to justify either what appears to be an inherently unjust state of affairs, or to play the innocent victim.[3] It is hence necessary to strive to attain as comprehensive and as unprejudiced an account as possible to appraise the facts correctly.

2.2 The Origins of the Israeli-Palestinian Conflict

The Israeli-Palestinian conflict is originally a nationalistic conflict between two contending nations over the same piece of land.[4] Starting from its early days, various factors have contributed to the intensification of the conflict. Apart from clashes over borders and territory, politics, race and religion play a weighty role in

---

[1] Materu 2015, p. 16.

[2] On the significance of shaping narratives, see Said 1994, p. xiii.

[3] Berry and Philo 2006, p. vii; Kattan 2009, pp. ix–xii; Rotberg 2006, p. 1.

[4] Kattan 2009, p. 1; LeVine 2009, p. 19; Matthews 2011, p. 5.

the conflict. Outside the above-mentioned factors, the ancient histories of the two nations continue to be of momentous influence shaping the background and the justification for the genesis of the conflict.[5]

2.2.1 Pre-Israel Palestine

Palestine has been at the crossroads of major civilizations of the ancient era as well as of the three continents, namely, Asia, Europe and Africa. It is above all the *terra sancta* to the three monotheist religions.[6] Historically, Palestine and its people have been ruled by several conquerors until the conquerors were themselves either absorbed into the Palestinian population or replaced by another subjugator.[7]

Palestine was conquered by the Sultan of the Turks in 1517 and was ruled by the Ottoman Empire for 400 years.[8] The then Palestine was among the most fertile of the Assyrian provinces of the Ottoman Empire.[9] Ramallah and Jerusalem were the largest towns. Though not a defined geographic location until the 20th Century, the people of Jaffa, Haifa, Gaza, Jerusalem and the peasants in the countryside described their land as Filastin or Palestine. Despite the description, however, the Palestinians of that time did not yet appear as a 'unique nation with collective national claims'.[10]

Starting from the 1880s, various waves of Jewish migration to the land of Palestine resulted in the escalation of land purchases and settlements, which were unwelcomed by the Palestinians.[11] Due to the Ottoman Land Code of 1858, members of the upper class Ottoman landlords had registered large portions of land possessed by individual peasants, who even so often discovered that the land had never belonged to them when the absentee landlord sold it to Jewish settlers who were often funded by the Jewish National Fund.[12] Despite the increasing arrival of Jews in Palestine in the years following 1880s, there has been a huge Arab majority in the area. In 1931, for instance, 174,606 Jews and 1,033,314 Arab natives lived together in peace.[13]

---

5 LeVine 2009, pp. 3–8, 19–20; Said 1995, pp. 163–164.

6 Kapitan 1997, p. vii; Kattan 2009, p. 1; Klein 2001, p. 1.

7 People's Press Palestine Book Project 1981, pp. 8–9.

8 Kattan 2009, p. xxi; Said 1979, pp. 9–12.

9 People's Press Palestine Book Project 1981, pp. 8–9; Said 1979, pp. 9–12.

10 Bar-on 2006, p. 147.

11 Harms and Ferry 2008, pp. 61–62; Quigley 2005, p. 4.

12 Caplan 1983, p. 11; Ghandour 2010, pp. 66–70; Harms and Ferry 2008, pp. 61–62; Kayyali 1978, p. 12.

13 Laqueur 2003, p. 210; Kayyali 1978, p. 12.

As the Ottoman Empire became weaker and increasingly dependent on foreign protection, European powers established links with the population of the Empire.[14] Among others, Russia, France and Britain sought to further their respective interests in Palestine.[15] France assumed for itself the role of 'protector' of the Catholic communities of Syria, Lebanon and Palestine, while Russia anointed itself as the 'protector' of the Orthodox Christians of the region. It bears noting that, although the majority of the population in the region were Muslim, the Christians, who constituted 16% of the population were allowed to practice their religion and to exercise limited autonomy through the millet system.[16]

2.2.2 *Jewish Persecution and Zionism*

In the late 19th and early 20th century, the modernization and expansion of European Empires included the colonization of foreign lands and the forced homogenization of their population.[17] These strategic political pursuits resulted in making ethnic and religious minorities vulnerable to abuses and, in the worst cases, to their extermination and genocide. The main targets during this period were, among others, the Christians of the Black Sea and Anatolia, the Muslims of Crimea, the Balkans and Caucasus and the European Jewry.[18]

Hostility towards the European Jewry forms an important part of the Jewish modern history. Jews were subjected to vicious violence and were denied the enjoyment of the minimum civil and political rights. They were killed in pogroms and were expelled from countries.[19] Sporadic anti-Semitism and gross injustices against Jews occurred, especially in England, Spain, Portugal, Russia and Romania.[20] But the most horrific extermination of the Jews happened at the hands of the Nazis during the Holocaust, which lasted from 1939 to 1945. Jews were

---

[14] Ibid.

[15] Ibid.

[16] The Millet system was a practice which granted non-Muslim subjects a limited autonomy under the chief ecclesiastical leaders of the various religious sects. See ibid. and Shmuelevitz 1984, p. 15.

[17] Buzan and Lawson 2013, pp. 5 et seq.; Lloyd 1996; Smith 1982, p. 160; Stuchtey 2011; Zhilian and Rongqu 1980, pp. 109–113.

[18] Carmichael 2009, pp. 2–3.

[19] Grant 2002, pp. 2 et seq.; Gilbert 1987, pp. 19, 28–29; Rubinstein et al. 2002, pp. 111–112. Similar to other minorities, Jews were mainly targeted due to their religious or/and ethical uniqueness, and 'refusal to integrate' into the society they lived in. It is also argued that Jews were also targeted because of clerical anti-Semitism, which is the hatred towards Jews for the reason that they, according to the bible, killed Jesus and refused to accept him as the savior and messiah. The other origin of anti-Semitism, particular to the German Jews and as mentioned in the second volume of Hitler's *Mein Kampf*, was that Jews were considered responsible for the defeat of Germany in WWI.

[20] Berry and Philo 2006, p. 1; Kattan 2009, p. 9; Rubinstein et al. 2002, pp. 140, 159, 306.

confined to ghettos, starved and ruthlessly persecuted.[21] As part of Hitler's 'final Solution to the Jewish problem', the Nazi regime in Germany exterminated an estimated six million Jews[22] in extermination camps and gas chambers.[23]

These persecutions of the Jews in Europe, among other causes, intensified the formation of a Jewish movement aimed at safeguarding the world Jewry on the one hand, from extinction and persecution, and on the other, from disintegration and assimilation.[24] The movement, widely known as Zionism, as explained by its founder Theodor Herzl, was primarily focused on founding a Jewish State as a solution to the Jewish question.[25] Spangler argues that the Zionism ideology embodied by the current Israeli State may clash with human rights standards and this, he states, has contributed to the demonization of the ideology.[26] But he states that, as advised by Albert Einstein and Martin Buber, what early Zionists sought was a Jewish homeland and not a Jewish state. Back in 1943, Theodor Herzl, in his book titled *The Jewish State*, a book largely considered as the guideline for the creation of Israel, outlined the plan for the creation of a Jewish State as follows:[27]

> The whole plan is perfectly simple. Let the sovereignty be granted to us over a portion of the globe large enough to satisfy the rightful requirements of a nation; the rest we shall manage for ourselves. [...] The creation of a new State is neither ridiculous nor impossible. Those Jews who fall in with our idea of a State will attach themselves to the Society, which will thereby be authorized to confer and tread with governments in the name of our people. The society will thus be acknowledged in its relations with governments as a State creating power. This acknowledgment will practically create the State.

Initially, Uganda, Argentina and a territory close to the borders of Canada were discussed as possible settlement sites for the new Jewish homeland.[28] Shortly afterwards, Palestine became the new focus of the Zionist ambition due to the historical[29] and religious[30] connection the Jews had to the land of ancient

[21] Browning 2004, pp. 111 et seq.

[22] Due to lack of demographic studies at the time, the exact number of those killed in the Third Reich is not settled. See Rudolf 2003; Sanning 1983.

[23] Grant 2002, pp. 2 et seq.; Kattan 2009, p. 9; Kershaw 2008, pp. 237 et seq.

[24] Garbarini et al. 2011, pp. 27 et seq.; LeVine 2009, pp. 19–20; Kapitan 1997, pp. 4–5; Kattan 2009, p. x; Shindler 2013, p. 10.

[25] Harms and Ferry 2008, p. 53; Reich 2008, p. 16.

[26] Spangler 2015, pp. 7–8. See Herzl 1943, pp. 27–28.

[27] Ibid., pp. 27 et seq.

[28] Ibid., pp. 15, 27–28; Kapitan 1997, pp. 4–5; Rubinstein et al. 2002, pp. 111–112; Spangler 2015, pp. 7–8.

[29] Before the Kingdom of Israel was destroyed by the Assyrians and its people were exiled in the diaspora in 722 BC, albeit disputed, historical records indicate that inhabitants of the kingdom resided in the present day Northern Israel and the West Bank. See Reich 2008, p. 6.

[30] The religious claim to the land rests on the biblical narration that God promised the land to Abraham and his descendants. Pre-eminent religious Zionists argue that when the Messiah of Judaism finally descends to earth, the Holy Land should be populated by Jews so that the Messianic deliverance could take place. See, for instance, Exodus 6:8, Deuteronomy 9:1, Leviticus 20:24 and Genesis 49:10 of the Bible (of the Torah). See also Cohn-Sherbok 2008, pp. 3–4.

Palestine.[31] Arguably, it was also because of the then erroneous propaganda that the land of Palestine was uninhabited and devoid of any civilization.[32]

Consequently, the Zionist movement started to establish Jewish colonies in Palestine and waves of Jewish immigrations followed. Due to the anti-Semitism and persecution in Eastern Europe and Russia, a decade before the 'Final Solution', around 25,000 Jewish immigrants had already reached Palestine. They constituted 10% of the Palestinian population.[33]

2.2.3 The British, the Jews and the Palestinians

During the First World War, the Ottomans were allies of the Germans and Austro-Hungarians against Britain, France and Russia. Britain encouraged Arab resistance against the Ottomans in order to redirect the attention of the Ottomans away from the war to their own domestic problems, and to facilitate their downfall.[34]

In return for Sherif Hussein Ibn Ali's leadership of the resistance and in a series of ten correspondences between 1915 and 1916, Britain pledged to support the creation of an independent Arab kingdom ruled by the Sherif.[35] The Arab Kingdom was meant to comprise Palestine, Syria, Transjordan and Iraq. Britain then made another pledge in 1917. Lord Arthur Balfour, the British Foreign Minister of the time, asserted in the famous Balfour Declaration the support of Britain for the establishment of a Jewish homeland in Palestine.[36]

The Balfour Declaration is a correspondence sent from Balfour, a British government minister, to Lord Rothschild, the then representative of the Zionist

---

[31] The following statement of Herzl sums up the means and the justification behind choosing to conquer Palestine over other options: 'Palestine is our ever-memorable historic home. The very name of Palestine would attract our people with a force of marvelous potency. Supposing His Majesty the Sultan were to give us Palestine, we could in return undertake to regulate the whole finances of Turkey. We should there form a portion of a rampart of Europe against Asia, an outpost of civilisation as opposed to barbarism'. See Herzl 1943, p. 29.

[32] The quote 'A land without a people for a people without a land' was used in Zionism literature to refer to Palestine. However, the well-recognised mantra of Zionism reads 'The aim of Zionism is to create for the Jewish people a home in Palestine secured by public law'. See Caplan 1983, p. 11; Khalidi 2010, pp. 101 et seq.; Laqueur 2003, p. 210. See also Oberschall 2007, p. 131.

[33] Harms and Ferry 2008, p. 53; Matar 1996, p. 1.

[34] Holt 1970, p. 392; Mattar 2005, p. 221; Morris 2001, pp. 67 et seq.

[35] Baumann 2009, pp. 7–8; Reich 2008, p. 18.

[36] The British government declared its 'sympathy' to 'Jewish Zionist aspirations' and conveyed that it 'will use its best endeavours' to facilitate 'the establishment in Palestine of a national home for the Jewish People'. See the Balfour Declaration, http://www.icsresources.org/content/primarysourcedocs/BalfourDeclaration.pdf (accessed 31 August 2015). The principal aim of the Declaration was to obtain the support of Jews in favour of the Allied power. See Morris 2001, pp. 73 et seq.; Renton 2010, p. 17.

movement. The introductory Paragraph opens with a 'declaration of sympathy with Jewish Zionist aspirations' and concludes with a request to Lord Rothschild to bring the declaration to the attention of the Zionist Federation.[37] Evidently, the purpose of the correspondence is a 'declaration of sympathy' and support for the Zionist aspirations rather than one that gives rise to legal rights and obligations.[38] As the British government at the time had no actual or legal power over Palestine, the declaration is strictly a political declaration with no legal import.[39]

In June 1922, in the so-called Churchill white paper, the United Kingdom 'clarified' the 'ambiguities' of the contradicting pledges made to Sherif Hussein and Lord Rothschild, indicating that the correspondence did not amount to a promise to Lord Rothschild of the area that later became Israel, Gaza and the West Bank.[40] It stated 'unauthorized statements have been made to the effect that the purpose in view is to create a wholly Jewish Palestine' and that the majesty's Government have no such aim in view'.[41] In addition to such statements which appear to have placated the Palestinians, the paper also contained statements of reassurance regarding the creation of 'a Jewish National Home in Palestine'.[42]

The First World War ended with the defeat of the Ottoman Empire by the Allied Powers, and as per the terms of the Paris Peace Conference,[43] the victors divided the Middle Eastern territories of the former Ottoman Empire between Britain and France. Britain and France then created a political geography, which paid little attention to the political aspirations of the administrative units of the crumpled empire.[44] In an agreement with France and the rest of the Allies, Britain was able to maintain control of the trade route to India through the Gulf and Suez Canal to safeguard its commercial interests in the region. Palestine in particular was regarded as vital, given that its strategic location could be used to prevent further German and Turkish attempts at encroaching on the Suez Canal.[45] Palestine served also to

---

[37] Balfour Declaration, above n. 36.

[38] Loder 1923, p. 168; Silverburg 2002, p. 254.

[39] Ali et al. 2016, p. 156; Frangi 1982, p. 48; Silverburg 2002, p. 254. For more details, see Schneer 2010.

[40] British White Paper: Churchill White Paper, 3 June 1922, http://www.jewishvirtuallibrary.org/churchill-white-paper-1922 (accessed 30 November 2017); Reich 2008, p. 18.

[41] British White Paper: Churchill White Paper, above n. 40.

[42] Ibid. See also Morris 2001, pp. 75–76.

[43] Prior to the Paris Peace Conference, Britain entered into a secret agreement, called Sykes-Picot Agreement with France to carve up and control the territories of the Ottoman Empire. This agreement as well as the arrangement of the Paris Conference provided a sphere of influence over Palestine and Iraq to Britain and Syria and Lebanon to France. See Sykes-Picot Agreement, https://www.saylor.org/site/wp-content/uploads/2011/08/HIST351-9.2.4-Sykes-Picot-Agreement.pdf (accessed 23 April 2016); Morris 2001, pp. 70–71.

[44] Ibid., p. 88.

[45] It is due to this same logic that Britain planned to seize Palestine from the Ottomans in 1917. See Kattan 2009, pp. 38–39; Morris 2001, pp. 71 et seq.; Strawson 2010, p. 8.

facilitate the realization of Britain's desire to build an oil pipeline and a railway line linking Mosul to Haifa.[46]

The Paris Peace Conference did not only allocate the Ottoman territories to France and Britain, but it also established the League of Nations, which in 1922 made Palestine a British mandate territory.[47] The terms of the mandate, as enunciated by the League, contained the precise wording of the Balfour Declaration.[48] The Articles of the mandate went beyond the commitments contained in the Balfour Declaration and made the mandate authority responsible, not to facilitate, as put forth in the Declaration, for securing the establishment of a Jewish national home. The mandate, in contrast to the Balfour Declaration, is a legally binding document.[49] It stated that 'the mandatory should be responsible for putting into effect the declaration originally made on 2 November 1917, by the Government of His Britannic Majesty… in favour of the establishment in Palestine of a national home for the Jewish people…'.[50] The Britannic majesty was mandated to administer Palestine and 'safeguard the civil and religious rights of the inhabitants'.[51] It was granted 'responsibility in connection with the holy places and religious buildings or sites in Palestine'.[52] It was also responsible 'to place the country under such political, administrative and economic conditions as will secure the establishment of the Jewish national home and to facilitate Jewish immigration'.[53]

Successive tides of Jewish immigration supported by the United Kingdom (hereafter the UK) and increasing land purchases and settlements generated a Palestinian resistance and revolt,[54] which escalated into clashes with the Jews. The Palestine Royal Commission,[55] a commission established 'to ascertain the

---

46 Ali et al. 2016, p. 156; Kattan 2011, p. 12.

47 Article 22 of League of Nations, Covenant of the League of Nations, 28 April 1919; League of Nations, Mandate for Palestine (hereafter, Mandate for Palestine), 24 July 1922, https://d3n8a8pro7vhmx.cloudfront.net/truthmustbetold/pages/93/attachments/original/1448574108/Mandate_of_Palestine_.pdf?1448574108 (accessed 30 November 2017).

48 Ibid., Article 25, together with a note by the Secretary-General relating to its application to the Territory known as Trans-Jordan; Renton 2010, p. 16

49 Mandate for Palestine, above n. 47; Frangi 1982, p. 48.

50 Mandate for Palestine, above n. 47, Preamble; Gilbert 2011, p. 23; Strawson 2010, p. 8.

51 Mandate for Palestine, above n. 47, Article 2.

52 Ibid., Article 13.

53 Ibid., Articles 2 and 6.

54 From 1936–1939, an anti-colonial Palestinian revolt by the Arabs, named the Great Revolt broke out. The clash with the mandate authority caused numerous losses of lives. See Swedenburg 1999, p. 130.

55 The Commission, also called the Peel Commission, was a British Royal Commission established in 1936. After studying the causes of the disturbance, under Chapter XXII of its report to the League of Nations, it proposed the partition of Palestine as a solution. At the time, Britain rejected the proposal. See Quigley 2005, pp. 24, 27; Sinanoglou 2010, pp. 119–121.

underlying causes of the conflict', concluded that 'no further land is available which can be occupied by new immigrants without displacing the present population'.[56] Following this finding, the mandate authority restricted Jewish land purchase and immigration, a decision which severed the British-Zionist relation.[57]

In the London Conference of 1939, after discussing with the representatives of the two parties, the UK issued a 'White Paper' that specified its plan to establish an independent State with a government that represents both Arabs and Jews.[58] However, the Jewish Agency for Palestine and the American Zionist Conference contested the 'White Paper'. The latter issued the Baltimore Resolution, which stated that Palestine be reconstituted as a Jewish commonwealth.[59] The Higher Arab Committee, led by the grand mufti of Jerusalem, also rejected the 'White Paper'.[60]

2.2.4 The Partition

The United Kingdom was unable to find a solution to the competing Zionist and Arab interests, or to the escalating conflict between the two.[61] The policy of active opposition to the mandate authority adopted by the Zionist Conference in August 1945 had also made the Military Base of the UK a target of terrorist activities.[62] The intractability of the situation, therefore, compelled the UK to resort to the newly formed United Nations to come up with a permanent solution.

In response to the UK's request, the UN established the United Nations Special Committee on Palestine (UNSCOP), which investigated and recommended

---

[56] Quigley 2005, p. 19. This decision was also tabulated in the British White Paper of 1939, http://avalon.law.yale.edu/20th_century/brwh1939.asp (accessed 30 November 2017). When the independence of the state of Israel was later declared in 1948, the first decision its leaders made as a state was to rescind the White Paper. See Rubinstein et al. 2002 p. 335.

[57] Morris 2001, pp. 97 et seq.; Renton 2010, p. 36.

[58] British White Paper of 1939, above n. 56.

[59] Nakhleh 1991, p. 65; Strawson 2010, p. 71.

[60] Achcar 2009, p. 143; Cohn-Sherbok and El-Alami 2008, p. 44; Khatchadourian 2011, p. 7; Morris 2001, p. 158; Silverfarb 1986, p. 62.

[61] Morris 2001, pp. 161 et seq.; Tucker and Roberts 2008, pp. 5, 771.

[62] After World War II, the UK had announced that the immigration restriction as well as the overall policy on Palestine would remain unchanged. The decision angered those who were desperate for the creation of a State of Israel. As an active show of opposition to the British rule, the Jewish leaders ordered the Jewish Defence Force named Haganan to cooperate with the Stern gangs and the Irgun in attacking British military bases, trains, railways and bridges in Palestine. The Stern gangs and the Irgun were underground Zionist extremist organisations that among others bombed the King David Hotel and were responsible also for the Der Yassin Massacre. See Baumann 2009, pp. 17, 19; McGowan and Hogan 1999; Morris 2001, p. 181. See also Lapidot n.d., pp. 87–91.

'partition with economic union'.[63] As a result, in May 1947, as first recommended by the Palestine Royal Commission back in 1936, the UN terminated the mandate and passed a partition plan through Resolution 181.[64] The plan proposed to set up a Jewish and an Arab independent State with Jerusalem as *corpus separatum*.[65] It designated 56% of the land to the Jews and 43% to the Arabs. At the time, Jews constituted one third of the population and owned less than 10% of the land.[66] Nevertheless, the assumption was that an increasing number of Jews would migrate to the territory.

The Palestinians rejected the partition on the ground that the plan allocated too much territory to the Jews.[67] In the eye of the Palestinians and Arab leaders, the partition had no legal and moral credibility as it ignored the fundamental principles of self-determination and majority rule.[68] The opinion stemmed from the fact that the land designated to the Jewish State included 400 of the 1,000 Palestinian villages and was demographically balanced in favour of the Palestinians, i.e., 509,780 Arabs and 499,020 Jews.[69]

The Jews welcomed the partition plan. Immediately following the adoption of the partition plan and the withdrawal of the UK's troops, the Jews proclaimed the independent State of Israel in May 1948.[70] The following year, the General

---

[63] Morris 2009, p. 76; Tucker and Roberts 2008, pp. 5, 771.

[64] UNGA 1947. See also Bose 2007, pp. 219–222; Lutes 2013, pp. 368 et seq.; Ilan 2005, p. 197; Tucker and Roberts 2008, pp. 5, 771. The Partition Plan obtained 33 votes in favor, 13 oppositions and 10 abstinences. Members of the General Assembly who were financially dependent on the US later claimed that they were heavily lobbied, diplomatically intimidated or threatened with aid cuts by the US to vote in favor of the Resolution. Greece, Liberia, Haiti and the Philippines reportedly switched their votes to constitute the necessary two third majority. See Morris 2001, p. 184; Quigley 2005, p. 37.

[65] Resolution 194 places Jerusalem under the supervision and control of the UN. This plan was first recommended in Resolution 181 (II) from 1947. In 1949, UN Resolution 303 (UNGA 1949b) proposed to place Jerusalem under the administering authority of the UN Trusteeship Council. This Resolution, similar to the other Resolutions on Jerusalem, was not given any practical effect. In many Resolutions, the UN has declared illegal any action to change the international status of Jerusalem. See UNGA Resolution 194 (III) (UNGA 1948). See also Elman and Adelman 2014, pp. 3–5; Tucker and Roberts 2008, p. 771.

[66] Orgad 2015, p. 83; Söderblom 2003.

[67] Bose 2007, pp. 223, 230; Khalilieh 2016, p. 116; Lutes 2013, p. 368; Schaeffer 1999, p. 100.

[68] Lutes 2013, pp. 368 et seq.; Schaeffer 1999, p. 100; Tal 2004, p. 43.

[69] The Palestinian State would be composed of a ratio of 9,520 Jews to 749,101 Arabs. Since it was hard to find a location where the Jews were in the majority, despite the number of Palestinians, the plan allotted the more Jewish populated land to the Jews and less Jewish populated territory to the Palestinians. See Chomsky and Pappe 2010, pp. 60–66; Orgad 2015, p. 83; Quigley 2005, p. 39.

[70] See Declaration of Establishment of State of Israel,http://www.mfa.gov.il/mfa/foreignpolicy/peace/guide/pages/declaration%20of%20establishment%20of%20state%20of%20israel.aspx (accessed 23 September 2015). See also Avineri 2011, p. 42; Morris 2001, p. 215.

Assembly admitted Israel to the UN.[71] However, in contrast to the provisions of the partition plan, the Israeli proclamation of statehood equated Eretz-Israel (Hebrew for the 'land of Israel') to the whole territory of 'the British mandate Palestine'.[72] A legislative authority established by the Israeli proclamation of statehood also, as was the case with the Palestinians, rejected the British White Paper of 1939. The White Paper, in addition setting Jewish immigration restrictions, clarified that the Balfour Declaration did not provide for the conversion of the whole of Palestine into a Jewish State. Moreover, succeeding Israeli administrative ordinances, settlement policies and military orders appear inconsistent with Israeli's claim to accept the partition plan.

2.3 Occupation and Resistance

2.3.1 The Arab-Israeli Wars

Shortly after the Israeli declaration of independence, the inter-communal conflict that started when the United Nations Special Committee on Palestine (UNSCOP) published its recommendations grew to a full-fledged war between a coalition of Arab States and the new State of Israel.[73] After months of intensive fighting, the Israeli military defeated the Arab coalition which was twice its size.[74]

As a result of the 1948 Arab-Israel war (also called the War of Independence by Israelis or The Nakba/The Catastrophe by the Palestinians) Israel annexed 77% of the territory, including the areas allotted to Palestine in the Partition Plan.[75] Since then it has been the official policy of the Israeli government not only to keep in control of the annexed land, but also to reject any peace settlement that requires its

[71] Amongst the members of the General Assembly, 37 voted in favour while 12 voted against and 9 abstained. See UNGA 1949a.

[72] Declaration of Establishment of State of Israel, above n. 70. See also UNHRC 2013, p. 23. Until the Camp David agreements (1978–1979), Israel considered Palestinians as the 'Arabs of the land of Israel' with no legitimate claim of statehood. These Arabs, as per the Likud government in particular, already had more than 20 other Arab States that they could settle on. Former Prime Minister Menachem Begin was especially known for the 'revisionist Zionist goal' to incorporate mandatory Palestine to the land of Israel. See Mattar 2005, pp. 239–240.

[73] Morris 2001, p. 219; Ross 1998, p. 30; Sadeh 1994, p. 55; Tal 2004, p. 469.

[74] Other than the several guerrillas, the Palestinians as a nation were unprepared and lacked national leaders or resources to manufacture and procure arms and to mobilize the society for a war effort. The Arab coalition that was made up of Egypt, Syria, Iraq, Lebanon and Jordan was greatly divided over leadership matters, as well as over the extent and purpose of involvement in the war. On the contrary, the Hagana, although lacking in basic logistics, was able to effectively employ the short distances between the 20 brigades to its advantage. See Tal 2004, pp. 470, 475; Tucker and Roberts 2008, pp. 5, 771.

[75] Bose 2007, p. 231; LeVine 2009, p. 30.

withdrawal from the land it annexed in the war.[76] The Israeli government relies also on the armistice agreement signed between Israel and the Arab coalition at the end of the first Arab-Israeli war. The armistice line drawn in this deal, also called the Green line, has enabled Israel to retain the territory which was under its control during the war. The agreement, however, specifies that the Green lines are not international boundaries.[77]

According to the United Nations Conciliation Commission for Palestine (UNCCP), 750,000 persons who were part of the Arab population 'fled' or were 'expelled' from territories controlled by Israel during the Arab-Israel War.[78]

This part of the Israel/Palestine history is a matter of huge controversy among historians. Shindler, citing Morris, states, that the Palestinians may have fled by the orders of the local Arab leadership which wanted to build up refugee population on the borders of neighbouring Arab States to 'create a pressure' on the States to invade the Jewish State. Morris, in a book titled *The Birth of the Palestinian Refugee Problem Revisited*, argues that, although Israel did not 'enter the war with a master plan of expulsion', the exodus was triggered by 'changing military and psychological realities' and Arab strategies and tactics causing, in turn, changes in the military strategy and tactics of the Israeli Defence Force. He states further that the dire situation of Jewish Jerusalem and the Arab army's attack on Mishmar Haemek prompted the implementation of Plan Diet, which ordered the clearing out and destruction of 'the clusters of hostile or potentially hostile villages dominating vital axes'. Morris concludes that the Israeli military has reportedly executed a policy of clearing out Arab communities. Following new revelations after the recent declassification of Israeli records, Morris retracted his former statement, stating that the proportion of the expulsion and the atrocities committed are greater than the extent reflected in his earlier works.[79] Based on eye witness accounts, official UN documentation, press reports and voluminous second-hand accounts that cite declassified official Israeli government documents, Kattan, contrary to the assertion of the Israeli government, concluded that the Arabs did not flee on their own initiative, but were instead expelled from their homeland. Quigley citing the UN Observer and Red Cross reports states that the Israeli army killed hundreds of young men in execution style and expelled the rest of the population. In villages where the population was not expelled, Quigley states that men were incarcerated in prison work camps. Similar to Quigley, Mattar, citing Morris, mentions that there

[76] Efrat 2006, pp. 70–71; Morris 2009, pp. 80, 82; Quigley 2005, p. 89; Tucker and Roberts 2008, pp. 5, 771.

[77] Egyptian-Israeli General Armistice Agreement, 24 February 1949, Article 5; Lebanese-Israeli General Armistice Agreement, 23 March 1949, Articles 2–5; General Armistice Agreement between the Hashemite Kingdom of Jordan and Israel, 4 April 1949, Articles 2 and 5; Israeli-Syrian General Armistice Agreement, 20 July 1949, Articles 2–5. See also Efrat 2006, pp. 70–71; Newman 2013, p. 137; Kumaraswamy 2015, p. 34.

[78] UNCCP 1961, p. 9.

[79] Kattan 2009, pp. 170–171; Mattar 2005, p. 329; Morris 2004, pp. 4–6, 70, 166; Morris 2007, p. 49; Quigley 2005, pp. 82–85.

were two dozen massacres in which an estimated 800 Palestinian men were killed, thus prompting others to leave the villages.

Most of the evacuated villages were bulldozed and destroyed. Parts of the evacuated areas were cultivated and the rest was rebuilt as Israeli settlements to house future Jewish immigrants. The original names of the villages and roads were also changed into Hebrew names.[80] Since the 1948 Exodus, Israel has persisted in its refusal to allow the return of those Palestinians who now constitute the bigger portion of the Palestinian refugees residing in camps in Jordan, Lebanon, Syria, Gaza and West Bank.[81]

Subsequent to the first Arab-Israel War, Jordan established control of the West Bank and Egypt took control of the Gaza Strip until 1967.[82] In 1959, at the height of the cold war, Israel, assisted by British and French forces, attacked and controlled the Sinai Peninsula and briefly captured Gaza.[83] However, due to threats of sanctions and pressure from the USSR and USA, Israel withdrew from the Sinai within six months.[84]

During the 1967 Arab-Israel War,[85] also called the Six-Day War, Israel recaptured the Sinai Peninsula and the Gaza Strip as well as the West Bank, East Jerusalem and the Golan Heights.[86] It withdrew its military force from the Sinai Peninsula in compliance with the 1978 Camp David Agreement and the 1979 Peace treaty with Egypt. However, at the time of writing, Israel is still in control of the Golan Heights. The Six-Day War prompted another mass exodus of Palestinians who sought sanctuary in the Gaza Strip and the West Bank.[87]

Through Resolution 242/1967, the UN Security Council called for the 'withdrawal of Israeli armed forces from territories occupied in the recent conflict' and a 'just settlement of the refugee problem'.[88] Resolution 242 resulted in controversy because of the discrepancy between the English and French versions of the text. As one of the other working languages of the UN, French has equal status with

---

80 Ashcroft 2009, p. 83; Chomsky and Pappe 2010, pp. 63–67; Kamrava 2016, p. 77; Mattar 2005, p. 329; Morris 2001, p. 257.

81 UNRWA for Palestinian Refugees in the Near East, http://www.unrwa.org/palestine-refugees (accessed 09 September 2015).

82 UNCCP 1961, pp. 11–12. See also Kretzmer 2002, p. 4; LeVine 2009, p. 30; Quigley 2005, p. 127.

83 Bennett 2005, pp. 214 et seq.; Jabr and Berger 2016, p. 530; LeVine 2009, p. 30.

84 Berry and Philo 2006, p. 42.

85 The second Arab-Israel War was fought between Israel and Egypt, Syria, Iraq and Jordan.

86 Berry and Philo, p. 44; LeVine 2009, p. 37; Hammel 1992, p. 58; Jabr and Berger 2016, p. 530; Kretzmer 2002, p. 4.

87 UNRWA 2007, pp. 6 et seq.

88 UNSC 1967. The Resolution was adopted under chapter VI of the UN Charter that calls for 'pacific resolution of disputes'; Charter of the United Nations, opened for signature 26 June 1945, 1 UNTS 16 (entered into force 24 October 1945) (UN Charter). Chapter 6. Security Council Resolutions, as opposed to Chap. 7 Resolutions, are non-binding or recommendatory. See UN Charter, Articles 33–38 and Sams 2011, p. 51.

English.[89] During the negotiations, Arab States pushed to include the words 'all' and 'the' before the phrase 'territories occupied' but only the definitive article 'the' was included in the French version. The French version, thus reads 'withdrawal from *the* territories' while the English version says 'withdrawal from territories'. Due to this disparity Israel maintains that the Resolution does not require withdrawal from *all* territories occupied during the Six-Day War.[90] As the Resolution does not specify the extent of withdrawal necessary, some argue that Israel's withdrawal from the Sinai satisfies the terms of the Resolution.[91] The 'creative ambiguity' was crafted to get the Resolution through the Security Council.[92]

Among the Arab allies of the second Arab-Israel conflict, Egypt and Jordan accepted, but Syria rejected the Resolution until 1973. After the 1973 Arab-Israel or Yom Kippur War,[93] Syria endorsed the Resolution when it accepted Resolution 338, which called for a negotiated peace based on Resolution 242.[94] Despite its claim of complete acceptance, Israel continued to contest the withdrawal clause of the Resolution and went ahead to establish settlements in the captured territories. It also placed the controlled Palestine land under military rule.[95]

2.3.2 The Resistance: Guerrillas and Stones

After the Israeli victory in the 1967 war, Palestinians realized the futility of their reliance on the Arab States and the unity rhetoric. The division amongst the Arab coalition and the side dealings with Israel unveiled the fact that the claim by Arab

---

89 The French version reads *Retrait des forces armées israéliennes des territoires occupés lors du récent conflit.* It is the word 'des' found in the French version that is absent in the English counterpart. Both versions are http://www.securitycouncilreport.org/atf/cf/%7B65BFCF9B-6D27-4E9C-8CD3-CF6E4FF96FF9%7D/IP%20S%20RES%20242.pdf (accessed 30 November 2017).

90 Israel Ministry of Foreign Affairs, Statements clarifying the meaning of UN Security Council Resolution 242, 22 November 1967, http://www.mfa.gov.il/mfa/foreignpolicy/peace/guide/pages/statements%20clarifying%20the%20meaning%20of%20un%20security%20c.aspx. See D'Acquisto 2017, p. 7. Despite the disparity, international law no longer recognises claiming sovereignty over territory acquired through war. See also McHugo 2002, p. 851.

91 See M. Rosenne, Understanding UN Security Council Resolution 242, Jerusalem Centre for Public Affairs, http://jcpa.org/security_council_resolution_242/. Y.J. Tenembaum, A conceptual framework of analysis to interpret United Nations Security Council Resolution 242, The New Jurist, 20 December 2011; UN Security Council: The Meaning of Resolution 242, http://www.jewishvirtuallibrary.org/the-meaning-of-un-security-council-resolution-242 (accessed 27 November 2017).

92 Louis 2012, p. 235.

93 The 1973 Arab-Israeli War, also named Yom Kippur or Ramadan War, was fought between Arab allies led by Syria and Egypt on the one hand and Israel on the other. See Aker 2014; O'Ballance 1978; Rabinovich 2004.

94 UNSC 1973. See also Y.J. Tenembaum (2011), above n. 91; U.N. Security Council: The Meaning of Resolution 242, above n. 91.

95 Bennett 2005, pp. 214 et seq.; Berry and Philo 2006, p. 52; Jabr and Berger 2016, p. 530.

States' claim to fight for Palestine was primarily directed towards achieving domestic political gains rather than striving to support the aspiration of Palestinians for national liberation. Hence, Palestinian military groups took up what they called 'duty to resist'. [96]

The Palestine Liberation Organization (PLO), which was established by the Arab League in 1964, served as an umbrella group unifying the guerrilla groups, which otherwise were operating independently.[97] Fatah, a secular left wing political movement until 1954 and political party since 1965 joined the Palestine Liberation Organization and its leader, Yasser Arafat.[98]

The credibility of Fatah was boosted thanks to the many 'successful' attacks it carried out against the Israeli military and civilian objects. It was then driven out from the West Bank to Jordan by the Israeli force and later from Jordan to Lebanon by Jordan.[99] Fatah justified targeting civilian objects as an acceptable means of armed resistance to a military occupation of a territory.[100] The UN General Assembly also defended Fatah's attacks as a 'legitimate struggle or forcible self-help of colonized people' in an attempt to realize their right to self-determination and to restore their rights.[101] The attacks by the military groups did not constitute a significant existential threat to Israel. They, however, succeeded in provoking international reprisals against Israel and helped to place the Palestinian question on the agenda of the UN.[102]

In October 1974, the General Assembly invited the PLO to participate in the deliberations of the Assembly regarding issues of Palestine. Resolution 3237 further enhanced the status of the PLO to one of observer status.[103] However, the Assembly levied economic sanctions and an arms embargo on Israel, demanding that Israel to desist from its perpetual violations of Geneva Convention IV.[104]

---

[96] Saleh 2015, p. 237; Spangler 2015, p. 136.

[97] Frangi 1982, p. 99; Jabr and Berger 2016, p. 530.

[98] Frangi 1982, pp. 99 et seq.

[99] Jabr and Berger 2016, pp. 530 et seq.; Saleh 2015, pp. 239, 241.

[100] The first Fatah military operation involved blowing up bridges, mine laying and attacks on Israeli communal settlements. See Frangi 1982, p. 102.

[101] UNGA 1971a, 1985. In 1985, the GA re-defined self-defence by unequivocally condemning all acts and practices which 'endanger or take innocent human lives' be it in struggles for independence from colonial or racist regime, alien domination or any other cause. See also Quigley 2005, p. 191; Rubinstein et al. 2002, pp. 364–365.

[102] Cleveland and Bunton 2009, p. 346. The UN passed numerous resolutions calling for the end of hostilities. Resolution 2546 was most critical of Israel (UNGA 1969a). It stated that the UN was alarmed by the 'collective punishment, mass imprisonment, indiscriminate destruction of homes and other acts of oppression against the civilian population in the Arab territories occupied by Israel'. See UNGA 1967, 1969b, 1971b, 1975a.

[103] UNGA 1974a. See also Jabr and Berger 2016, pp. 530 et seq.

[104] UNGA 1974b, 1975b.

After the coming into power of the Israeli Likud Party in 1977, the construction of settlements in the occupied West Bank and Gaza Strip accelerated.[105] The estimated 4,500 West Bank and Gaza settlements grew to 16,000 by 1981.[106] In addition, the successive right-wing Likud dominated governments adopted measures to confiscate additional Arab land and demolish houses. Rampant administrative detention, arrest without warrant, incarceration without charge and the general denial of natural rights and the meting out of harsh treatment to detained Palestinians led to an uprising that lasted for five years.[107] The uprising, called Intifada, which is an Arabic word meaning 'shaking off' resorted to a form of civil disobedience and street demonstrations against the Israeli occupation and Israel's denial of the Palestinian right to self-determination. It is at this stage of the Palestinian history that stone throwing appeared as 'a symbol of Palestinian opposition'. The stone throwers clashed on numerous occasions with the Israeli army, which retaliated by firing teargas canisters and live ammunition.[108]

The Intifada began to ebb after the Palestine National Council declared the establishment of the State of Palestine on 15 November 1988.[109] The Proclamation declared 'the State of Palestine in the land of Palestine with its capital at Jerusalem'.[110] The Council stated that the State derives its legitimacy from UN General Assembly Resolution 181/1947 and that it has renounced the use of violence against citizens of Israel and recognized the State of Israel.[111] Although the declaration was silent on the question of territorial demarcation, as the mention of the Resolutions of the General Assembly indicates, the Proclamation contemplated a State of Palestine comprising the Gaza Strip and the West Bank.[112] On 15 December 1988, UN General Assembly Resolution 43/77 acknowledged the declaration of the State of Palestine, affirming that it was made in line with Resolution 181 (II) and decided to replace the designation 'Palestine Liberation Organization' with 'Palestine'.[113] The Resolution obtained an overwhelming majority, with only

---

[105] UNHRC 2009, para 176. See also Gavron 2008, p. 98.

[106] UNHRC 2009, paras 176–177; Mattar 1996, pp. 1–2.

[107] Beinin and Hajjar 2014, pp. 8–9; Jabr and Berger 2016, pp. 530 et seq.

[108] Cleveland and Bunton 2009, pp. 474–477; Gavron 2008, p. 100; Spangler 2015, p. 150; Jabr and Berger 2016, pp. 530 et seq.; Taylor & Francis Group 2004, p. 560; Kretzmer 2002, p. 2.

[109] Palestine National Council, Political communique and declaration of independence, 15 November 1988, http://nad-plo.org/userfiles/file/Document/declaration%20of%20independence%20En.pdf (accessed 11 April 2016).

[110] Boyle 1990, p. 301; Palestinian National Council, Palestinian Declaration of Independence, 15 November 1998, http://www.mideastweb.org/plc1988.htm, para 9 (accessed 15 May 2017) (hereafter, Palestinian Declaration of Independence).

[111] Palestinian Declaration of Independence, above n. 110, paras 6, 14; Kearney 2012, p. 398.

[112] Palestinian Declaration of Independence, above n. 110, para 10. See also Quigley 2005, p. 212.

[113] UNGA 1988. See also Boyle 1990, p. 301; Crawford 1990, p. 307.

two votes, the US and Israel, against it. Closely following the General Assembly's reaffirmation, 89 States recognized Palestine.[114]

Secret negotiations led to the much talked about Oslo Accords.[115] The 2000 Camp David Summit, which aimed to reach a 'permanent solution' as provided in the Oslo Accords, failed to end the occupation.[116] When the reality on the ground failed to match the expectations and promises[117] laid down in the accords, the second Intifada, also called the Al-Aqsa Intifada, broke out.[118] The misconception that the diplomatic options were exhausted caused the second Intifada to be very violent and further military options to become more seductive. The more force the Israeli Defence Force used, the more violent the demonstrations became and the higher the death toll.[119] The Oslo years and the years that followed also witnessed the emergence of out-of-control Palestinian suicide bombers, a phenomenon which increased the number of casualties on the Israeli side.[120] Between 1993 and 2007, 154 suicide bombers attacked Israeli civilians and military personnel.[121]

---

[114] UNGA 1988. See also Quigley 2012, pp. 433–434.

[115] The Oslo Accords are construed as a road map to the two-State solution, which is an interim agreement of a transitional nature that will endure until a permanent settlement is reached within the five years following the signing of the Accords. The Accords are bilateral agreements with immunity clauses and provisions dealing with allocation and transfer of power. See Interim Agreement on the West Bank and the Gaza Strip, signed 28 September 1995 (Oslo II), Article 31 (5). See also Davis and Kirk 2013, p. 253.

[116] Israel Ministry of Foreign Affairs, The Middle East Peace Summit at Camp David-July 2000, http://www.mfa.gov.il/mfa/foreignpolicy/peace/guide/pages/the%20middle%20east%20peace%20summit%20at%20camp%20david-%20july%202.aspx (accessed 27 November 2017); Malley and Hussein, Camp David: A tragedy of errors, The Guardian, 20 July 2001; Mattar 2005, p. 23; Shyovitz, 2000 Camp David Summit: background and overview, Jewish Virtual Library, http://www.jewishvirtuallibrary.org/background-and-overview-of-2000-camp-david-summit (accessed 27 November 2017).

[117] Declaration of Principles on Interim Self-Government Arrangement, signed 13 September 1993 (Oslo I). Article 1 of the Oslo I stated that the aim of the negotiations is to lead to a permanent solution based on Resolutions 242 and 338 (UNSC 1967, 1973). The Accord further stated that a free, fair and democratic election and withdrawal of Israeli forces from Gaza and Jericho Area will be conducted.

[118] Al Jazeera, The Second Intifada, 4 December 2003, http://www.aljazeera.com/archive/2003/12/20084101554875168.html (accessed 24 November 2017); Beinin and Hajjar 2014, p. 11; Norman 2010; Taylor & Francis Group 2004, p. 560.

[119] BBC News, Al-Aqsa intifada timeline, 29 September 2004, http://news.bbc.co.uk/2/hi/middle_east/3677206.stm (accessed 1 April 2017). See also Bassiouni and Ben Ami 2009, pp. 237–238; Mattar 2005, p. 23; Norman 2010.

[120] BBC News 2004, above 119; Pressman 2006. See also Taylor & Francis Group 2004, p. 560.

[121] Israel Ministry of Foreign Affairs, Suicide and other bombing attacks in Israel since the Declaration of Principles (Sept. 1993), http://www.mfa.gov.il/mfa/foreignpolicy/terrorism/palestinian/pages/suicide%20and%20other%20bombing%20attacks%20in%20israel%20since.aspx, (accessed 14 April 2016); UNHRC 2009, paras 182–183.

2.4 The Occupied Palestinian Territories

Israel's military triumph over the coalition of Arab States enabled it to conquer over 77% of ancient Palestine in the first and the remaining 22% in the second Arab-Israeli war.[122] Depending on the political views held, the seized lands are referred by various names among which 'Palestine', 'occupied territories', 'liberated territories' or 'Judea and Samaria' are frequently used. Some argue that the occupied territories are not 'normal' occupied territories since their previous status differs slightly from the 'occupation' that the negotiators of The Hague Convention and Geneva Convention IV had in mind.[123] The International Court of Justice[124] and the UN Resolutions,[125] however, determined that the conquered lands are indeed occupied territories, and have urged Israel to respect the laws of military occupation.

The Occupied Palestinian Territories (OPT) are made up of about 360 km^2 in size in the Gaza Strip and 5,860 km^2 in the West Bank and Eastern Jerusalem.[126] An estimated 4.4 million Palestinians and over 800,000 Israeli settlers (450,000 in the West Bank and 375,000 in East Jerusalem) reside in the Occupied Palestinian Territories.[127] In 2011, the average annual growth rate of the Palestinian population was 5.7%, while the settler population grows 5.3% a year compared to the 1.8% for the whole Israeli population.[128]

2.4.1 *Gaza*

Bordering Israel on the north and east, the Mediterranean Sea on the west and Egypt on the south, Gaza (the Gaza Strip) lies in the south-western corner of the former British mandate Palestine.[129] It is a territory which was subject to active Israeli

[122] Kretzmer 2002, pp. 3 et seq.

[123] Eretzy Israel, Is Israel an occupier?, http://www.eretzyisrael.org/is-israel-an-occupier.html (accessed 14 April 2017); *Israel Today*, Washington Post: There is no 'Occupied Palestine', 9 September 2014, http://www.israeltoday.co.il/NewsItem/tabid/178/nid/24913/Default.aspx (accessed 14 April 2017). See also Bregman 2014, pp. 4–8; Finkelstein 2010, p. 21. Sharon argues that the Israeli forces were withdrawn from Gaza as prescribed under the Oslo Accords. And as the continued presence of the Israeli military is agreed upon and regulated by the agreement, Israel's presence in Gaza could no longer be regarded as an occupation. See Sharon 2009, p. 3.

[124] ICJ, Advisory opinion: Legal consequences of the construction of a wall in the occupied Palestinian territory, 9 July 2004, ICJ Reports 2004 at p. 136.

[125] See UN Resolutions 3414 (UNGA 1975b) and 32/20 (UNGA 1977) and UNSC Resolution 446 (UNSC 1979).

[126] Mourad 2003, p. 138.

[127] A. Balofsky, Jewish population in Judea & Samaria growing significantly, Breaking Israel News, 5 January 2015; UNOCHA-OPT 2012b; Safty 2009, p. 228; UNHRC 2009, p. 52.

[128] UNOCHA-OPT 2012b.

[129] See Mattar 2005, p. 169.

military occupation and military rule from 1967 up to the signing of the Oslo agreements in September 1993. Although the Gaza Strip has been under a limited Palestinian autonomy since the Oslo times, Israel retains the ultimate control over Gaza.[130]

Gaza has one of the highest population densities in the world with two million people living within the 360 km^2.[131] About 72 km^2 of the strip was annexed until 2005 for the housing of 7,000 Israeli settlers.[132] In 2004, Ariel Sharon, the then Prime Minister of Israel, proposed a disengagement plan that required the withdrawal of the Israeli army and settlers from Gaza.[133] Based on this plan, Israel evacuated 21 settlements in Gaza and four settlements in the West Bank in 2005. After the implementation of the plan and the removal of the Israeli settlers and security forces, Israel still maintains exclusive control over the airspace, borders and coastline of Gaza.[134] In addition, it retains control of telecommunications, electricity, water, taxation and the population registry.[135]

Shortly after the implementation of the disengagement plan, Hamas began to gain momentum in Gaza.[136] Hamas is an offspring of the Intifada and a faction of the Muslim Brotherhood, which is an Islamist political group established by Hassan al-Banna in Egypt in 1928. Hence, it couches its 'national struggle' in religious terms.[137] In an unexpected election victory in 2006, and a subsequent military ousting of the Fatah-led Palestinian Authority from Gaza, Hamas became Gaza's ruling party. Separate from the policies of the Fatah party that has been ruling the West Bank since the 1990s and Gaza from 1968 to 2006, Hamas refuses to

---

130 In light of the nature of the administrative and military measures Israel has imposed on Gaza and despite the withdrawal of Israeli troops in 2005, Gaza is considered as 'effectively occupied' by Israel. See Article 42 of the Hague Convention (IV) Respecting the Laws and Customs of War on Land and Its Annex: Regulations Concerning the Laws and Customs of War on Land, 18 October 1907 (entered into force 26 January 1910) (Hague Regulations) and Article 6 of Geneva Convention Relative to the Protection of Civilian Persons in Time of War, signed 12 August 1949, 75 UNTS 287 (entered into force 21 October 1950) (Geneva Convention IV). See also Sects. 3.5.1.4. Palestine as an Occupied Territory and 5.3.1. Cases of War Crime.

131 Around 70–80% of Gazans are refugees of the First Arab-Israel war. See UNOCHA-OPT 2011, p. 22. See also Finkelstein 2010, p. 15; S. Khatib, Gaza Strip population said to reach 2 million, The Times of Israel, 12 October 2016.

132 UNOCHA-OPT 2011, p. 22. See also Finkelstein 2010, p. 15; Mourad 2003, p. 147.

133 Bose 2007, p. 209. Prime Minster Sharon justified the disengagement plan as an essential move to preserve and strengthen Israel's control over the West Bank settlements which, according to him, will be part of the State of Israel in future agreements.

134 UNHRC 2013, p. 7.

135 UNHRC 2009, p. 49. See also Amnesty International 2010, p. 3.

136 Cleveland and Bunton 2009, p. 476; Reuters, Timeline: key events since Hamas election victory, 20 June 2007.

137 Pina 2006, pp. 1–2.

recognise the State of Israel and it advocates the right to resist the occupation with any available means, including violent ones.[138]

Israel withheld the tax revenue it collects on behalf of the Palestinian Authority and imposed a blockade in retaliation for the election of Hamas to power.[139] The blockade cordons off Gaza with electric fences and military posts, completely cutting it off from the rest of the world.[140] Israel administers four of the five gates of Gaza to the outside world. The crossings at Erez, Karni, Kerem shalom and Sufa which connect Israel with Gaza have been under Israeli control since the blockade.[141] The Rafah crossing, on the border between Egypt and Gaza, remained mostly shut until it was closed 'indefinitely' after the Rabaa massacre.[142]

Through the crossings, Israel controls movements of goods and people in and out of Gaza. Exports from Gaza are mostly blocked and imports are restricted to what Israel considers as 'humanitarian' or vital for the survival of the population of Gaza.[143] Most of the food available to Gazans is provided by the UN and other aid organisations, thus making Gaza one the most aid reliant regions[144] in the world.[145] Moreover, give that it is in charge of the population registry, Israel is able to control entries and exits of people to and from Gaza. Palestinians are not allowed to leave Gaza without first obtaining permits, be it in urgent humanitarian cases or to meet families residing in the West Bank.[146] For non-residents, entering Gaza through the

---

138 Reuters 2007, above n. 138; Schanzer 2008, p. 107. The relationship between Hamas and Fatah has been far from harmonious and stable. The violence between these two parties and other factions has aggravated the problems in the occupied territories. Fatah and Hamas finally agreed to form a unified government in 2014, and since then there has been a relatively peaceful co-existence between them.

139 I. Kershner, Israel will release Palestinian tax revenue to Abbas government, New York Times, 25 June 2007. See also Beinin and Hajjar 2014, p. 15.

140 UNOCHA-OPT 2009, p. 2.

141 Amnesty International 2010, p. 3.

142 On 14 August 2013, the Egyptian military clashed with the supporters of ousted president Mohammed Morsi in Rabaa Al-Adawiya square in Cairo resulting in more than 1000 causalities. See Hurriyet Daily News, Protesters storm Cairo government building as death toll rises to 623 after Egypt bloodbath, 15 August 2013.

143 Goods which are prohibited from entering Gaza range from construction materials, heaters, fertilizers and livestock to stationery, musical instruments, toys, and sweets. See Gisha-Legal Centre for Freedom of Movement, http://gisha.org/UserFiles/File/HiddenMessages/ItemsGazaStrip060510.pdf (accessed 3 October 2015).

144 Around 80% of Gazans are dependent on humanitarian aid, mainly food items. Since the blockade, abject poverty has tripled, necessitating a shift in diet from Protein- rich to low-cost, high-carbohydrate foods. This shift in diet has triggered concern about the incidence of vitamin and mineral deficiencies in people. See UNHRC 2010, p. 10.

145 Amnesty International 2010, p. 3; B'Tselem 2011; Saleh 2015, pp. 40–43; UNRWA 2009.

146 United Nations Office for the Coordination of Humanitarian Affairs occupied Palestinian territory called this restriction of movement of good and people between Gaza and the West Bank part of the 'policy of separation' purposely imposed by Israeli authorities. See UNOCHA-OPT 2013, p. 1.

Israeli controlled entries is also difficult, as it requires getting a special permit from Israeli authorities.

In September 2007, Israel declared Gaza a 'hostile entity'.[147] This designation, according to the Israeli Security Cabinet, legalises the imposition of punitive measures against the 'hostile' territory in response to rockets fired into Israel.[148] The United Nations, however, condemned the blockade and the punitive measures as collective punishment against civilians.[149] As per the United Nations Conference on Trade and Development, Israel's siege and treatment of the Gaza population not only has made Gaza worse off than what it was in the 1990s, but is supposed to make Gaza a potentially uninhabitable place in the very near future.[150]

2.4.2 *The West Bank*

The West Bank forms the bulk of the Palestinian land. It borders Israel in the north, south and west, and Jordan in the east. Around 2,785,366 Palestinians and 450,000 Israeli settlers reside in the West Bank.[151] The blue print for the West Bank settlements was laid down by various master plans, which included the Alon plan (1967),[152] Drobles Plan (1978),[153] Sharon Plan (1981) and Hundred Thousand Plan (1983).[154] These plans that the Israeli government has not officially acknowledged

---

[147] Israel Ministry of Foreign Affairs, Security cabinet declares Gaza hostile territory, 19 September 2007, http://www.mfa.gov.il/mfa/pressroom/2007/pages/security%20cabinet%20declares%20gaza%20hostile%20territory%2019-sep-2007.aspx (accessed 27 November 2017).

[148] Ibid. See also B'Tselem 2007, p. 14.

[149] UN Special Rapporteur 2013.

[150] UNCTAD 2015; UN Country Team in the Occupied Palestinian Territory 2012.

[151] See A. Balofsky, Jewish population in Judea & Samaria growing significantly, Breaking Israel News, 5 January 2015; Central Intelligence Agency, The World Fact book, https://www.cia.gov/library/publications/the-world-factbook/geos/we.html (accessed 5 October 2015).

[152] The Allon Plan, which was sketched by the Israeli Defence Minister, Yigal Allon, was a plan to partition the territories occupied during the Six-Day War. The plan envisions that the West Bank be divided, that largest part of the Jordan valley be annexed, and that East Jerusalem to be 'unified' with the rest of Jerusalem under Israel's control. The plan is intended also to ensure the capture and establishment of settlements on parts of the Gaza Strip, which are not heavily populated by Palestinians. In 1981, Israel passed the Golan Heights Law and effectively annexed the areas envisioned in the Allon Plan. See Mattar 1996, p. 2; and Steinitz 2010, p. 12.

[153] The Drobless Plan also known as 'Master Plan for the Development of Settlement in Judea and Samaria, 1979–1983' modified the Alon Plan. The agenda set by the Drobless Plan was adopted by Menachem Begin's Likud Government. In the General Assembly's 36th session, the acting Chairman of the Committee on the Exercise of the Inalienable Rights of the Palestinian People condemned the Drobless plan in general and its expressed purpose in particular. The purpose of the plan as quoted by the Chairman states that 'establishing settlements and cutting off the Arab population in order to make it difficult for it to form a territorial and political continuity'. See UNGA 1981.

[154] UNHRC 2013, pp. 6–7.

as a government policy, but which it subsequently implemented, called for the annexation and settlement of areas in the West Bank, including Jerusalem as well as the northern and southern ends of Gaza. Their objective was, as reflected by the then Israeli Prime Minister Golda Meir (1969–1974), to create 'civilian security borders on strategic areas'[155] or as per Israeli Defence Minister Moshe Dayan (1953–1958) to justify the presence of the Israel Defence Force in those territories.[156] After the 1970s this 'military necessity' justification was abandoned and demolitions were ordered on grounds of civil law regulating land confiscation used under the Ottoman rule, or because the lack of required permits.[157] The confiscation and expropriation of designated Palestinian lands and the construction of new settlements on the ruins of the demolished houses has become a fixture to which the two parties have become accustomed to.[158] Between 2012 and 2014 alone, 1,867 structures owned or possessed by Palestinians were demolished to make room for new settlements.[159]

The elaborate infrastructure associated with the 149 settlements and the settlers has taken up over 43% of the West Bank.[160] There are over 522 Israeli checkpoints and roadblocks established to protect the Israeli settlers, and which at the same time severely obstruct movements of Palestinians. The settlements are maintained through a system of strict segregation between the settlers and local Palestinians, and a military law only applicable to the latter.[161] Settlements receive government funds, grants and subsidies.[162] Under the national priority scheme of the Israeli government, in addition to other benefits, the settlers receive incentives for their 'security needs and expenses'.[163]

According to the Office of the United Nations High Commissioner for Human Rights (hereafter OHCHR), due to the failure of the Israeli security forces, among other causes, settler-related violence has resulted in numerous causalities and damage to Palestinian property and land.[164] The violence has reportedly resulted in Palestinians having limited access to education, civic services and land. Moreover,

---

155 Ibid., p. 26.

156 Amnesty International 1999; Mattar 2005, p. 245; UNHRC 2013, p. 26.

157 UNHRC 2009, p. 53.

158 Spangler 2015, p. 29. See also Amnesty International 1999.

159 Palestinian Central Bureau of Statistics, Occupied Palestinian territory humanitarian needs overview, http://www.ochaopt.org/documents/hno2015_factsheet_final9dec.pdf (accessed 26 September 2015).

160 UNOCHA-OPT 2012b; UNHRC 2009, p. 52.

161 Human Rights Watch 2010, p. 43; UNHRC 2013, p. 9. See also Farsakh 2013, pp. 20–24.

162 Settlers building houses receive subsidies close to 70% of the value of the land, 50% of the development cost and additional grants to offset mortgages. In general, the Israeli government gives more subsidies and benefits to the settler community than the average Israeli despite the fact that the standard of living of the former is ten times higher than the latter. See Human Rights Watch 2010, pp. 51–55.

163 Ibid.

164 OHCHR 2013, pp. 3–6.

it has led to loss of assets and livelihoods, let alone the consequential psychosocial and mental health problems this has led to, and the risk of being displaced. Additionally, the OHCHR has stressed that the prevailing impunity for settler violence, lack of protection for the Palestinians and the absence of effective law enforcement have all combined to result in an even higher incidence and severity of settler violence over the years.[165] According to Human Rights Watch, the alleged arbitrary detention and abuse of Palestinian protesters and children as per Human Rights Watch, has created a culture of impunity and a society separate and unequal.[166]

Citing security reasons, in 2002,[167] Israel built a barrier named the 'West Bank Wall'[168] in the occupied Palestinian territory and East Jerusalem.[169] The wall severs East Jerusalem from West Bank and stretches beyond 687 kilometres in length It is three times higher than the Berlin Wall with a buffer zone of 30–100 m on each side of the wall. As the 2009 UN Fact-Finding Mission concluded, the route of the wall is determined by the main 'aim, which is more to incorporate the settlements into the Israeli side[170] than it is to inhibit alleged terrorists from endangering the safety of Israelis.

2.4.3 East Jerusalem

As discussed under Sect. 2.2.4 of this chapter, when the UN passed the partition plan in 1947, Jerusalem was given the international status of *corpus separatum*. Through various Resolutions, the UN has declared that any measure and practice directed at changing the character and status of the city is null and void.[171] Notwithstanding the UN Resolution, in 1980, Israel has proclaimed Jerusalem to be

165 Ibid.

166 Human Rights Watch 2010.

167 As justified by Israel, the wall has dramatically reduced the number of suicide bombers and illegal movements. See D. Wilkie, Security walls and suicide bombers, International Educator 15, July/August 2006, pp. 33–34.

168 The International Court of Justice in the 'Wall Opinion' employed the phrase 'West Bank Wall' to refer to the barrier. However, the names given by the Israelis and the Palestinians are 'Security Wall' and 'Apartheid Wall' respectively. See Rogers and Ben-David 2010, pp. 202 et seq.

169 Israel Ministry of Foreign Affairs, Saving lives: Israel's anti-terrorist fence-answers to questions, 1 January 2004, http://www.mfa.gov.il/mfa/foreignpolicy/terrorism/palestinian/pages/saving%20lives-%20israel-s%20anti-terrorist%20fence%20-%20answ.aspx#1 (accessed 27 November 2017). See also Barak-Erez 2006, p. 540.

170 UNHRC 2009, p. 54.

171 See, among others, UNSC Resolution 252, 21 May 1968; Resolution 267, 3 July 1969; Resolution 471, 5 June 1980; Resolution 478, 20 August 1980 and Resolution 476, 30 June 1980.

the 'complete and united' capital of Israel under its Basic Law.[172] However, the Palestinian claim to Jerusalem remains no less assertive. When in 1988 the Palestinian National Council declared Palestine to be an independent State it issued that Jerusalem is the capital city of Palestine. But Israel had captured East Jerusalem already in 1967 and passed a law incorporating the area into the 'unified city of Jerusalem'.[173] Despite the lack of consensus about the rest of Jerusalem, the overwhelming majority of the international community regards East Jerusalem as an integral part of the occupied Palestinian territory and has clarified that the laws of occupation are applicable.[174]

East Jerusalem has become a 'microcosm reflection' of the wider Israeli-Palestinian conflict and a key factor in any political settlement between the two nations.[175] Demographic factors are the primary concern of the Israeli policy in redefining the municipal boundaries of the city. Although around 293,000 Palestinians and 200,000 Israeli settlers reside in East Jerusalem,[176] the Israeli official planning documents have stated that the Palestinian population should not exceed 30% of the municipal community.[177] As stated in the European Union Heads of Mission Report, and similar to the settlements in the West Bank, settlements in East Jerusalem isolate East Jerusalem from the rest of the Occupied Palestinian Territories.[178] The Report asserts furthermore that the Israeli settlement policy attempts also to create new facts on the ground, thus effecting a demographic balance that will meet the so-called Clinton Peace Parameters. These parameters are an understanding that future negotiations will make areas that are Jewish part of Israel and those areas inhabited by Arabs part of the Palestinian State.[179]

Although much of it is an already built up area, only 13% of East Jerusalem is zoned for Palestinian constructions. Absentee landlordism, pre-1948 alleged Jewish ownership and purchase from owners are used as methods to control already built Palestinian structures and lands. On top of evictions and house demolitions for lack

---

[172] Laws of the State of Israel, Israel's Basic Law: Jerusalem, Capital of Israel, 30 July 1980 vol. 34, 5740-1979/80, 209.

[173] The Knesset amended 'The Law and Administration Ordinance (1948)' to include a section that extends 'jurisdiction and administration' of the Israeli government to cover all parts of Eastern and Western Jerusalem. See The Law and Administration Ordinance of 1948 Amendment 11, 5727-1967, 27 June 1967; and ESCWA 2017, p. 29.

[174] Members of the UN General Assembly and the high contracting parties to Geneva Convention IV have in many occasions expressed this stand. See Conference of High Contracting Parties to the Fourth Geneva Convention Declaration 17 December 2014, http://unispal.un.org/UNISPAL.NSF/0/E7B8432A312475D385257DB100568AE8 (accessed 7 September 2015); UNGA 2013.

[175] Elman and Adelman 2014, pp. 3–5; Klein 2001, p. 1; Paz-Fuchs and Ronen 2017, p. 204.

[176] UNOCHA-OPT 2012a.

[177] EU Heads of Mission in Jerusalem and Ramallah 2010, p. 2. See also UNHRC 2013, pp. 5–7.

[178] EU Heads of Mission in Jerusalem and Ramallah 2010, p. 2.

[179] Ibid.

of necessary permits, settler violence, disproportionate allocation of resources, movement and access restrictions and poverty[180] have made the life of Palestinians in East Jerusalem very challenging.[181]

2.5 Military Operations and the UN Missions

Especially after the rise of Hamas, the Israeli-Palestinian conflict has since reclaimed its status as one of the bloodiest in the world. In the last decade alone, Israel conducted eight major and many minor military operations against the military groups in Gaza, which resulted in thousands of civilian deaths and destroyed essential infrastructure used for rendering public services. Some of the more well-known are Operation Rainbow (2004), Operation Days of Penitence (2004), Operation Summer Rains (2006), Operation Autumn Clouds (2006), Operation Hot Winter (2009), Operation Cast Lead (2009) and Operation Protective Edge (2014).[182] Israel justified all these military campaigns on the grounds that they were aimed mainly at halting the firing of rockets from Gaza to Southern and the Israeli coastal areas.[183] Given the large-scale damage to property and the deaths caused by Operation Cast Lead and Operation Protective Edge, and their importance with regard to the relationship between Palestine and the International Criminal Court, these operations are discussed below.

2.5.1 Operation Cast Lead

The first phase of the 22-day operation lasted from 27 December to 3 January 2009. It consisted of both naval and aerial bombardment. According to Israeli military records, more than 100 tons of explosives were dropped in the first nine hours of the attacks. The second phase, which begun on 3 January 2009, was launched using the infantry in coordination with the Air Force and the Navy. In the last days of the operation, the Israeli force targeted already damaged units. Israel employed its Air Force, navy and ground force against the Palestinian armed groups operating in

---

[180] Around 73% of Palestinian adults and 83% of Palestinian children in East Jerusalem live in a permanent state of poverty. See Ibid., p. 8.

[181] Ibid., pp. 2–7; UNOCHA-OPT 2012a.

[182] Congressional Research Service 2009, p. 2; Journal for Palestine Studies 2009b; The State of Israel 2009, p. 15; UNHRC 2009, pp. 50–52.

[183] Ibid., p. 48. Israeli sources indicate that a total of 3,455 rockets were fired into Israel in the last decade. The majority of rockets fired into Israel have a range of up to 20 km. In recent years, however, the rockets at the disposal of many Gazan military brigades have a longer range, but lack a guidance system.

Gaza namely, Hamas, the military wing of the Popular Front for the Liberation of Palestine and the Popular Resistance Committee.[184]

In the first two phases of the operation, Israel heavily relied on drones and unmanned aerial vehicles. It has also reportedly, in some cases admittedly,[185] made use of white phosphorous (a toxic chemical substance that can be used for various military purposes),[186] Dense Inert metal explosives, depleted uranium and flechette shells that spray out thousands of tiny and potentially lethal darts.[187]

During the military operation, the UN Human Rights Council established a 'Fact-Finding Mission on the Gaza Conflict' to investigate alleged international law violations in connection with the operation. After the investigation, the Mission compiled a 600-page Report, also called the Goldstone Report, named after Richard Goldstone, a South African Jewish jurist who headed the Mission. The Report discussed and condemned Israeli policies of establishing and expanding new settlements, demolishing Palestinian houses, and constructing the wall. The Report denounced also the two-tiered road system and the overall annexation of the West Bank and East Jerusalem. In addition, it slammed Israel for closing access routes to and from Gaza, as well as the permit system and the general restrictions imposed on Gaza and the West Bank.[188]

The conclusions of the Report confirmed other reports that had implicated Israel in the commission of war crimes,[189] if not crimes against humanity in the foregoing

---

[184] Ibid., p. 86.

[185] Amnesty International 2009, pp. 27–38.

[186] The Israeli magazine called Haaretz reported that the Israeli Defence Force has admitted to having used 200 white phosphorus artillery shells. Some of these shells, as acknowledged by the force, were directed against the UNRWA school in Jabaliya. See G. Cohen, IDF to stop using shells with white phosphorus in populated areas, state tells high court, *Haaretz*, 13 May 2013; P. Wood, The explosive admission in Israel's Gaza report, *BBC News*, 1 February 2013; and Human Rights Watch 2009.

[187] Journal for Palestine Studies 2009a, pp. 186–189.

[188] UNHRC 2009, pp. 404–420. It has to be noted here that on 1 April 2011, in a commentary published in the *Washington Post*, Richard Goldstone expressed regret on some aspects of the report, especially with regard to the conclusion that Israel is potentially responsible for war crimes committed by targeting Palestinian civilians during Operation Cast Lead. He is quoted saying the following: 'If I had known then what I know now, the Goldstone report would have been a different document'. Following this statement by Justice Goldstone, also called the Goldstone Retreat, the remaining three members of the Mission accused Richard Goldstone of misrepresentation of facts and casting doubt on the 'credibility of their joint Report'. In a statement to the *Guardian*, they strongly criticized Goldstone's 'dramatic change of heart,' saying that any attempt to change the nature and purpose of the report amounted to disregarding the rights of victims and was a negation of truth and justice. They pointed out the contentions mentioned in Goldstone's *Washington Post* Commentary and implied that he had 'bowed to intense political pressure'. See R. Goldstone, Reconsidering the Goldstone Report on Israel and war crimes, Washington Post, 1 April 2011; H. Jilani et al., Goldstone report: statement issued by members of UN mission on Gaza war, The Guardian, 14 April 2011.

[189] Human Rights Watch 2009; Amnesty International 2009.

attack.[190] The Report made no bones about the fact that the military attack was an extension and continuation of Israel's policies on Gaza and other Palestinian territories—policies which are or result from violations of international human right and humanitarian law. Notwithstanding Israel's justification of the attack as a necessary response to and an exercise of the right to self-defence against to Palestinian rocket attacks, the Fact-Finding Mission found that the operation was at least partially directed against the people of Gaza as a whole.[191] The mission has also strongly criticized Palestinian armed groups for their failure to take all feasible precautions to protect civilians and civilian objects and for their indiscriminate rocket and mortar attacks, which could qualify as war crimes or crimes against humanity.[192]

The Fact-Finding Mission emphasized that there was a need to hold people accountable and criminally responsible as a prerequisite for establishing sustainable peace. Given the existing structural flaws, the lack of effective and independent domestic investigations and prosecutions, the Mission encouraged national courts of States Parties of the Geneva Conventions to relay on Universal jurisdiction to investigate and prosecute the alleged crimes. Without an impartial investigation and prosecution by the parties to the conflict, the Mission recommended the UN Security Council to refer the situation in Gaza to the ICC in line with Article 13(b) of the Rome Statute of the International Criminal Court.[193]

2.5.2 *Operation Protective Edge*

Operation Protective Edge was conducted in the summer of 2014. It resulted in one of the highest number of causalities. Unlike Operation Cast Lead, this attack was the result of a chain of events.[194] On 12 June 2014, three Israeli teenagers were abducted and later shot dead. Israel accused Hamas of the murder of the teens and conducted an intensive investigation, which involved home searches and widespread arrests and detentions.[195] On 2 July 2014, in what appeared to have been a revenge attack, a Palestinian youth was abducted and burned to death. This incident unleashed violent Palestinian demonstrations which escalated into firing rockets towards Israel.[196] However, as was the case regarding other similar attacks, the

190 UNHRC 2009, p. 99.

191 Ibid., p. 406.

192 Contrary to popular belief, the mission concluded that Hamas or its affiliates did not committed perfidy and did not purposely expose civilians to attacks. See ibid., p. 420; and Amnesty International 2009, pp. 48–50.

193 UNHRC 2009, p. 424. See also Falk 2012, pp. 94–96.

194 Operation Protective Edge: A Timeline, http://deadclydeside.wordpress.com/2014/07/18/operation-protective-edge-a-timeline/ (accessed 9 October 2015).

195 Ibid.

196 Ibid.

Israeli government justified Operation Protective Edge as a defensive measure against escalating Palestinian rocket attacks, and as an action aimed destroying military infrastructure and tunnels attributable to Hamas and other groups.[197]

Israel launched 6,000 airstrikes, including targeted attacks on residential buildings. This attack resulted in 2,134 fatalities, among which were 1,473 civilians and 501 children. Palestinian armed groups in turn fired 3,659 unguided rockets, of which about 735 were intercepted by Israel's sophisticated Iron Dome defence system. Of the total of rockets fired by the Palestinians, 224 hit built-up areas and killed six Israeli civilians.[198] The operation caused an international outcry which called for justice for the victims and a permanent solution to the century-old conflict.

After Palestine became a State party to the Rome Statute in 2015, following its failed attempt to delegate jurisdiction to the Court in 2009,[199] another UN Human Rights Council Independent Commission mandated to investigate alleged crimes committed during Operation Protective Edge, has also published its Report.[200] The report accuses both parties to the conflict of possible commission of war crimes during and in the context of the operation. It underscored the fact that impunity for international human rights and humanitarian law violations continues to prevail for Israelis, be it for the alleged crimes committed during the 2009 or 2014 hostilities, or in the context of other circumstances. The Report stated that, despite the concerns registered and the recommendations made by the *Goldstone Report* or other similar reports, nothing has been done to rectify the long-standing impunity. Moreover, it lauded the ongoing efforts of the ICC and called for Israel to accede to the Rome Statute.[201]

2.6 Peace Negotiations

Due to the unyielding background of rampant impunity for crimes committed throughout the Israeli-Palestinian conflict and the extent of its geo-political impact, to name but one reason, the conflict has been deliberated upon and discussed at numerous peace conferences and negotiation tables. From the Madrid Peace Conference in 1999, up to the 'Camp David' negotiation of 2000,[202] the early history of this conflict evidences several, yet futile, negotiations.

---

197 See UNHRC 2015 and UNOCHA-OPT 2014.

198 UNHRC 2015, pp. 18–59; UNOCHA-OPT 2014, p. 2; FIDH 2014, pp. 9–13.

199 See Chap. 3.

200 UNHRC 2015.

201 UNHRC 2015.

202 The Madrid Peace Conference was the first public negotiation between Israel and the Arab States, and a Palestinian delegation. Two years later, secret negotiations led to the signing of the first Oslo Accord. The Paris Agreement, the 'Gaza-Jericho Agreement and the 'Taba' Agreement were signed in April 1994, May 1994 and September 1995, respectively. Between 1997 and 2000, a total of four rounds of negotiations were conducted between the then President of the Palestinian Authority, Yasser Arafat, and Benjamin Netanyahu of Israel.

The highly speculated and talked about Oslo Accords[203] did not result in any tangible and feasible changes on the ground.[204] Even if the actions of parties to the Oslo Accords were not in strict compliance with the terms of the Accords, the provisions of the agreement were considered valid until the President of the State of Palestine in an address to the General Assembly on 30 September 2015 made a declaration of unilateral withdrawal from the Accords. He said the withdrawal was because of Israel's failure to abide by the agreement and to act in pursuit of the two-state solution.[205]

Since the turn of the 21st century, there have been five more rounds of negotiations. These were the Arab Peace Initiative or Beirut Summit, the Annapolis conference,[206] the peace talks of 2013–2014[207] and the Abbas Peace plan.[208] None of them resulted in any significant change. The peace deals have been usually disrupted by issues such as Israel's refusal to withdraw to the 1967 borders, the refugees' right to return, the evacuation of settlements, the status of Jerusalem and resource sharing.

Amongst the considered peace deals, the Arab Peace Initiative is perceived as a 'lost strategic opportunity of historic proportions' and one of the most attractive peace deals to date.[209] The initiative, which was proposed by Saudi Arabia, called for a full withdrawal of Israel from Arab territories occupied in 1967, for the

---

[203] Declaration of Principles on Interim Self-government Arrangement of 1993 (Oslo I) and the Israeli-Palestinian Interim Agreement on the West Bank and the Gaza Strip of 1995 (Oslo II) were sponsored by the United States. Many attribute the failure of the Oslo Peace Accords to the following: the unwillingness of the parties to make the necessary concessions to bring about peace and stability; the avoidance of a discussion on important topics such as the right to return of Palestinian refugee; and the thorny issue of settlements.

[204] Bar-Siman-Tov 2013, pp. 178–179; Qurie 2008, pp. 1–3.

[205] J. Lauria, Abbas says Palestinians no longer are bound by Oslo Accords, Wall Street Journal, 30 September 2015.

[206] The 2007 Annapolis Peace Conference is also another symbolic conference. The conference failed to yield any concrete results due to the power split in Palestine between Hamas and Fatah, and the refusal of Israel to allow the right to return of refugees and to engage in discussions on issues related to settlement construction. See P. Wood, Still talking: Annapolis one year on, *Global Policy Forum*, 27 November 2008.

[207] The 2013–2014 peace talks were facilitated by the then US Secretary of State, John Kerry. The talks collapsed as both parties failed to reach any compromise. The Palestinian side blamed Israel for the failure of the peace talks as Israel approved 1,200 new settlements while the negotiation was underway. Israel agreed to release 104 prisoners and to transfer of bodies of Palestinians buried in Israeli cemeteries. See Goldenberg 2015; H. Sherwood, Israelis and Palestinians meet for peace talks, The Guardian, 14 August 2013.

[208] The 2014 Abbas plan presented matters related to borders, freezing of settlement construction and end of occupation within three years. President Abbas threatened to go to the ICC if Israel and the US do not agree with the plan. See J. Khoury, Abbas' peace plan: Israeli withdrawal from West Bank within three years, Haaretz, 2 September 2014.

[209] Centre for the Renewal of Israeli Democracy, The Arab peace initiative: Israel's strategic loss and historic opportunity, http://www.molad.org/images/upload/files/The-Arab-Peace-Initiative-Final.pdf (accessed 21 August 2016).

implementation of Resolutions 242 and 338 of the UN Security Council and a 'just solution to the Palestinian Refugee problem' based on Resolution 194 of the UN General Assembly.[210] In return, it offered Israel 'normal relations' and a 'comprehensive peace' with 21 Arab countries, and recognition of its legitimate right to exist 'in peace and good neighbourliness'.[211] The Israeli government did not accept the deal owing to the terms dealing with retraction from occupied land and because of the stipulation that it agree to right of refugees to return.[212]

Another peace attempt that seems to have outlived its decade-long involvement and utility in respect of the Israel-Palestine peace process goes by the name of the Middle-East Quartet. The Quartet has brought together four of the most powerful players in the Middle East, namely, the United States, Russia, the United Nations and the European Union. It was formed as an *ad hoc* informal broker between the two nations following the collapse of the Oslo Accords and the eruption of the second Intifada in early 2001. Up on its formation, it has a conflict resolution and crisis management missions. It was aimed also to play a less formal role of a forum through which the other three could lobby the US to re-engage in the Israeli-Palestinian peace process. However, the Quartet has not only failed to make any meaningful progress, but it has also been relegated to the status of a political bystander.[213]

The *Goldstone Report* rightly recommends the ensuring of respect for human rights, international law and that rule of law play a central role in peace negotiations.[214] Given a frame of mind characterised by recurrent lack of commitment and willingness to strike compromises, the peace process would still be arduous even if making these basic requisites are made to be negotiable. Progress can be made only if settling the conflict is centred on achieving a sense of justice and accountability. Hence, at least in the Israeli-Palestinian situation, as Falk[215] rightly puts it, the opposite of war is not just peace, but also justice.

2.7 Chapter Summary

This chapter has discussed most of the events pivotal to the conflict and the current state of affairs by examining alternative narrations and multiple perspectives of the various parties involved. It has covered the origins of the conflict and the role

---

210 See Text of Arab peace initiative, http://www.europarl.europa.eu/meetdocs/2009_2014/documents/empa/dv/1_arab-initiative-beirut_/1_arab-initiative-beirut_en.pdf (accessed 21 August 2016).

211 Ibid.

212 Al-Kadi 2010, pp. 15–16; Centre for the Renewal of Israeli Democracy, above n. 209.

213 Elgindy 2012, pp. 1–8.

214 UNHRC 2009, pp. 382–383.

215 Falk 2012, p. 102.

played by States and international institutions as well as their impact on the current Israeli-Palestinian conflict. To the extent that the status of the Occupied Palestinian Territories is crucial for the contents of subsequent chapters of this study, this chapter has also sketched geo-social and political background of the territories under discussion, as well as their position in relation to the State of Israel. As UN reports are excellent source documents for information on the region, a brief description of some of the findings of these reports is also included. In spite of efforts to make objective sense of the facts garnered from this veritable wealth of reference materials, the mere fact that the conflict continues unabated at the time of writing makes it difficult to appraise an unfolding state of affairs in an accurate, detailed and comprehensive manner.

References

Achcar G (2009) The Arabs and the Holocaust: The Arab-Israel War. Metropolitan Books, New York.

Aker F (2014) October 1973-The Arab Israeli War, 1st edn. Design Publishing, Inc., Sarasota.

Ali A, Thian I, Taleb YA (eds) (2016) The different aspects of Islamic culture: Islam in the world today. United Nations Educational, Scientific and Cultural Organisation, Place de Fontenoy.

Al-Kadi A (2010) The Arab peace initiative: An instrument for peace. The International Center for the Study of Radicalisation and Political Violence, London.

Amnesty International (1999) Amnesty International Israel and the Occupied Territories: Demolition and Dispossession: The Destruction of Palestinian Homes. Amnesty International Publications, London.

Amnesty International (2009) Israel/Gaza, Operation 'Cast Lead': 22 days of death and destruction. Amnesty International Publications, London.

Amnesty International (2010) Suffocating: The Gaza Strip under Israeli blockade. Amnesty International, London.

Ashcroft B (2009) Caliban's Voice: The Transformation of English in Post-Colonial Literatures. Routledge, New York.

Avineri S (2011) Self-determination and Israel's declaration of independence. In: Baker A (ed) Israel's rights as a nation-state in international diplomacy. Jerusalem Center for Public Affairs, Jerusalem, pp. 35–44.

Barak-Erez D (2006) Israel: The security barrier between international law, constitutional law, and domestic judicial review. Oxford Journals 4:540–552.

Bar-on M (2006) Conflicting narratives of a conflict or narratives of a conflict, can the Zionist and Palestinian narratives of the 1948 War be bridged? In: Rotberg R (ed) Israeli and Palestinian narratives of conflict, history's double helix. Indiana University Press, Bloomington, pp. 142–173.

Bar-Siman-Tov Y (2013) Justice and fairness as barriers to the resolution of the Israeli-Palestinian conflict. In: European Commission (ed) JAD-PBP Project Justice and Durable Peace by Piece. Jerusalem Institute for Israel Studies, Jerusalem, pp. 253–271.

Bassiouni C, Ben Ami S (2009) A Guide to documents on the Arab-Palestinian/Israeli conflict: 1897–2008. Martinus Nijhoff Publishers, Leiden.

Baumann M (2009) Crisis in the Middle East: Israel and the Arab States 1945–2007. Hodder Education, Oxon.

Beinin J, Hajjar L (2014) Palestine, Israel and the Arab-Israeli conflict: A primer. Middle East Research and Information Project 1–15.

Bennett C (2005) Muslims and modernity: Current debates. MPG Books Ltd, London.
Berry M, Philo G (2006) Israel and Palestine, competing histories. Pluto Press, Berry.
Bose S (2007) Contested lands: Israel-Palestine, Kashmir, Bosnia, Cyprus, and Sri Lanka. Harvard University Press, Cambridge.
Boyle F (1990) The creation of the State of Palestine. EJIL 1:301–306.
Bregman A (2014) Cursed victory: A history of Israel and the Occupied Territories. Allen Lane, London.
Browning C (2004) The Origins of the Final Solution: The evolution of Nazi Jewish policy 1939–1942. University of Nebraska Press, Lincoln.
B'Tselem (2007) Human rights in the Occupied Territories. The Israeli Information Center for Human Rights in the Occupied Territories, Jerusalem.
B'Tselem (2011) Dispossession and exploitation: Israel's Policy in the Jordan Valley and Northern Dead Sea. The Israeli Information Center for Human Rights in the Occupied Territories, Jerusalem.
Buzan B, Lawson G (2013) The global transformation: The nineteenth century and the making of modern international relations. International Studies Quarterly 57(3): 620–634.
Caplan N (1983) Futile diplomacy: Early Arab-Zionist negotiation attempts, 1913–1931. Routledge, New York.
Carmichael C (2009) Genocide before the Holocaust. Yale University Press, New Haven, Connecticut.
Chomsky N, Pappe I (2010) Gaza in crisis, reflections on Israeli's war against the Palestinians. Haymarket Publishing, London.
Cleveland W, Bunton M (2009) A history of the modern Middle East, 4th edn. West View Press, Boulder, Colorado.
Cohn-Sherbok D (2008) A Jewish perspective. In: Cohn-Sherbok D, El-Alami D (eds) The Palestine-Israeli conflict: A beginner's guide. One World Publications, Oxford, pp. 3–128.
Cohn-Sherbok D, El-Alami D (2008) The Palestine-Israeli conflict: A beginner's guide. One World Publications, Oxford.
Congressional Research Service (2009) Israel and Hamas: Conflict in Gaza (2008–2009). CRS Report 40101.
Crawford J (1990) The creation of the State of Palestine: Too much too soon? (1990) EJIL 1:307–313.
D'Acquisto G (2017) A linguistic analysis of diplomatic discourse: UN resolutions on the question of Palestine. Cambridge Scholars Publishing, New Castle.
Davis R, Kirk M (eds) (2013) Palestine and the Palestinians in the 21st century. Indiana University Press, Bloomington.
Efrat E (2006) The West Bank and Gaza Strip: A geography of occupation and disengagement. Routledge, New York.
Elgindy K (2012) The Middle East quartet: A post mortem. Brookings Publications, Washington, DC.
Elman M, Adelman M (2014) Knowing Jerusalem through disciplinary conflict and cooperation. In: Elman M, Adelman M (eds) Jerusalem: Conflict and cooperation in a contested city. Syracuse University Press, New York, pp. 1–46.
ESCWA (2017) Israeli practices towards the Palestinian people and the question of apartheid, UN Doc. E/ESCWA/ECRI/2017/1.
EU Heads of Mission in Jerusalem and Ramallah (2010) EU Heads of Mission Report on East Jerusalem.
Falk R (2012) The Goldstone Report and the Goldstone Retreat: Truths told by law and reviled by geopolitics. In: Meloni C, Tognoni G (eds) Is There a Court for Gaza? A Test Bench for International Justice. T.M.C. Asser Press, The Hague, pp. 83–104.
Farsakh L (2013) Colonial occupation and development in the West Bank and Gaza: Understanding The Palestinian Economy Through The Work of Yusif Sayigh. In: Davis R, Kirk M (eds) Palestine and the Palestinians in the 21st century. Indiana University Press, Bloomington, pp. 35–59.

FIDH (2014) Trapped and punished: The Gaza civilian population under Operation Protective Edge. FIDH, Gaza.

Finkelstein N (2010) This time we went too far: Truth and consequences of the Gaza invasion. OR Books, New York.

Frangi A (1982) The PLO and Palestine. Zed Books Ltd, London.

Garbarini A, Kerenji E, Lambertz J, Patt A (2011) Jewish responses to persecution: 1938–1940. AltaMira Press, Plymouth, UK.

Gavron D (2008) Holy Land mosaic: Stories of cooperation and coexistence between Israelis and Palestinians. Rowman & Littlefield Publishers, Lanham, Maryland.

Ghandour Z (2010) A discourse on domination in Mandate Palestine: Imperialism, property and insurgency. Routledge, Oxon.

Gilbert M (2011) An overwhelmingly Jewish state: From the Balfour Declaration to the Palestine Mandate. Jerusalem Center for Public Affairs, Jerusalem.

Gilbert M (1987) The Holocaust: The Jewish tragedy. Fontana/Collins, Glasgow.

Goldenberg I (2015) Lessons from the 2013–2014 Israeli-Palestinian final status negotiations. Centre for New American Security, Washington, DC.

Grant R (2002) Genocide: The final solution to the Jewish question. Trafford Publishing, Victoria, British Columbia.

Hammel E (1992) Six days in June: How Israel won the 1967 Arab-Israeli War. Scribner's, New York.

Harms G, Ferry T (2008) The Palestine Israel conflict: A basic introduction, 2nd edn. Pluto Press, London.

Herzl T (1943) The Jewish state: An attempt at a modern solution of the Jewish question. Scopus Publishing Company, New York.

Holt P (1970) The Later Ottoman Empire in Egypt and the Fertile Crescent. In: Holt PM, Lambton AKS, Lewis B (eds) The Cambridge history of Islam: The Central Islamic lands from pre-Islamic times to the First World War. Cambridge University Press, Cambridge, pp. 374–393.

Human Rights Watch (2009) Rain of fire: Israel's unlawful use of white phosphorus in Gaza. Human Rights Watch, New York.

Human Rights Watch (2010) Separate and unequal: Israel's discriminatory treatment of Palestinians in the occupied Palestinian territories. Human Rights Watch, New York.

ICJ (2004) Concerning legal consequences of the construction of a wall in the occupied Palestinian territory, advisory opinion of 9 July 2004. ICJ Reports 2004.

Ilan A (2005) Withdrawal without recommendations: Britain's decision to relinquish the Palestine Mandate, 1947. In: Kedourie E, Haim S (eds) Zionism and Arabism in Palestine and Israel. Routledge, New York, pp. 183–209.

Journal for Palestine Studies (2009a) The Israeli Arsenal deployed against Gaza during Operation Cast Lead. Journal of Palestine Studies 38(3):38–53.

Journal for Palestine Studies (2009b) Israeli Military Operations against Gaza, 2000–2008. Journal of Palestine Studies 38(3):122–138.

Jabr S, Berger E (2016) The Survival and well-being of the Palestinian people under occupation. In: Tiliouine H, Estes R (eds) The State of social progress of Islamic societies: Social, economic, political and ideological challenges. Springer International Publishing, Switzerland, pp. 529–546.

Kamrava M (2016) The impossibility of Palestine: History, geography and the road ahead. Yale University Press, New Haven.

Kapitan T (ed) (1997) Philosophical perspectives of the Israeli-Palestinian conflict. Routledge, London.

Kattan V (2009) From coexistence to conquest: International law and the origins of Arab-Israel conflict 1891–1949. Pluto Press, London.

Kattan V (2011) International law and the origins of the Israel-Palestine conflict: New approaches, new findings. Institute of Law Palestine and International Law: New approaches: Proceedings of the conference held at Birzeit University on 24–26 September 2010. Birzeit University, West Bank, pp. 1–12.
Kayyali A (1978) Palestine: A modern history. Croom Helm, Kent.
Kearney M (2012) Why Statehood Now: A Reflection on the ICC's Impact on Palestine's Engagement with International Law. In: Meloni C, Tognoni G (eds) Is There a Court for Gaza? A Test Bench for International Justice. T.M.C. Asser Press, The Hague, pp. 391–408.
Kershaw I (2008) Hitler, the Germans and the Final Solution. Vail-Ballou Press, New York.
Khalidi R (2010) Palestinian identity: The construction of modern national consciousness. Columbia University Press, New York.
Khalilieh S (2016) Diaspora and VFR: An exploratory study. In: Isaac RK, Hall CM, Higgins-Desbiolles F (eds) The politics and power of tourism in Palestine. Routledge, New York, pp. 113–123.
Khatchadourian H (2011) The quest for peace between Israel and the Palestinians. Wipf & Stock Publishers, Eugene, Oregon.
Klein M (2001) Jerusalem: The contested city. C. Hurst & Co. Ltd., London.
Kretzmer D (2002) Occupation of justice: The Supreme Court of Israel and the occupied territories. State University of New York Press, Albany, New York.
Kumaraswamy P (20150) Historical Dictionary of the Arab-Israeli conflict. Rowman & Littlefield, London.
Lapidot Y (n.d.) The Irgun: A short history. http://www.daat.ac.il/daat/vl/theirgun/theirgun01.pdf. Accessed 3 September 2015.
Laqueur W (2003) A history of Zionism. Tauris Parke Paperbacks, New York.
LeVine M (2009) Impossible peace: Israel/Palestine since 1989. Zed Books Ltd., London.
Lloyd T (1996) The British Empire, 1558–1995. Cambridge University Press, Cambridge.
Loder J (1923) The truth about Mesopotamia, Palestine and Syria. George Allen & Unwin Ltd., London.
Louis R (2012) Britain: The ghost of Suez and Resolution 242. In: Louis R, Shlain A (eds) The 1967 Arab-Israeli War: Origins and consequences. Cambridge University Press, Cambridge, pp. 219–236.
Lutes S (2013) Chronology. In: Peters J, Newman D (eds) Routledge handbook on the Israeli-Palestinian conflict. Routledge, Oxon, pp. 366–377.
Matar I (1996) Jewish settlements, Palestinian rights and peace. Pennsylvania State University, Philadelphia.
Materu S (2015) The post-election violence in Kenya: Domestic and international legal responses. T.M.C. Asser Press, The Hague.
Mattar I (1996) Jewish settlements, Palestinian rights, and peace. Pennsylvania State University, State College, Pennsylvania.
Mattar P (ed) (2005) Encyclopaedia of the Palestinians. Facts on File, Inc., New York.
Matthews EG (ed) (2011) The Israel-Palestine Conflict: Parallel discourses. Routledge, London.
McGowan D, Hogan M (1999) The saga of Deir Yassin: Massacre, revisionism and reality. The University of Michigan, Ann Arbor.
McHugo J (2002) Resolution 242: A legal reappraisal of the right-wing Israeli interpretation of the withdrawal phrase with reference to the conflict between Israel and the Palestinians. International and Comparative Law Quarterly 51(4): 851–881.
Morris B (2001) Righteous victims: A history of the Zionist-Arab conflict, 1881–2001. Vintage Books, New York.
Morris B (2004) The birth of the Palestinian refugee problem revisited. Cambridge University Press, Cambridge.

Morris B (2007) Revisiting the Palestinian exodus of 1948. In: Rogan E, Shlaim A (eds) The war for Palestine, rewriting the history of 1948, 2nd edn. Cambridge University Press, Cambridge, pp. 37–59.
Morris B (2009) One state, two states resolving the Israel/Palestine conflict. Yale University Press, New Haven.
Mourad K (2003) Our sacred land, voices of the Palestine-Israeli conflict. The University of Michigan, Ann Arbor.
Nakhleh I (1991) Encyclopaedia of the Palestinian problem, Vol. 1. Intercontinental Books, New York.
Newman D (2013) Territory and Borders. In: Peters J, Newman D (eds) Routledge handbook on the Israeli-Palestinian conflict. Routledge, Oxon, pp. 135–144.
Norman J (2010) The Second Palestinian Intifada: Civil Resistance. Routledge, Oxon.
O'Ballance E (1978) No victor, no vanquished: The Arab-Israeli War, 1973. Presidio Press, New York.
Oberschall A (2007) Conflict and peace building in divided societies: Responses to ethnic violence. Routledge, Oxon.
OHCHR (2013) Update on settler violence in the West Bank, including East Jerusalem. United Nations High Commissioner for Human Rights, Geneva.
Orgad L (2015) The Cultural defense of nations: A liberal theory of majority rights. Oxford University Press, Oxford.
Paz-Fuchs A, Ronen Y (2017) Integrated or segregated? Israeli-Palestinian employment. In: Handel A, Allegra M, Maggor E (eds) Normalizing occupation: The politics of everyday life in the West Bank settlements. Indiana University Press, Bloomington, pp. 172–192.
People's Press Palestine Book Project (1981) Our roots are still alive: The story of the Palestinian people. Institute for Independent Social Journalism, New York.
Pina A (2006) Fatah and Hamas: The New Palestinian factional reality. CRS Report RS22395.
Pressman J (2006) The Second Intifada: Background and causes of the Israeli-Palestinian Conflict. The Journal of Conflict Studies 23:1715–5673.
Quigley J (2005) The Case for Palestine: An International Law Perspective. Duke University Press, Durham, North Carolina.
Quigley J (2012) The Palestine declaration to the International Criminal Court: The statehood issue. In: Meloni C, Tognoni G (eds) Is There a Court for Gaza? A Test Bench for International Justice. T.M.C. Asser Press, The Hague, pp. 429–439.
Qurie A (2008) Beyond Oslo, the Struggle for Palestine: Inside the Middle East Peace Process from Rabin's Death to Camp David. I.B. Tauris & Co. Ltd., London.
Rabinovich A (2004) The Yom Kippur War: The epic encounter that transformed the Middle East. Schocken Books, New York.
Reich B (2008) A brief history of Israel, 2nd edn. Facts on File, Inc., New York.
Renton J (2010) Flawed Foundations: The Balfour Declaration and the Palestine Mandate. In: Miller R (ed) Britain, Palestine and Empire: The Mandate Years. Ashgate Publishing, London, pp. 15–38.
Rogers R, Ben-David A (2010) Coming to terms: A conflict analysis of the usage, in official and unofficial sources, of 'security fence', 'apartheid wall' and other terms for the structure between Israel and Palestinian territories. Media, War & Conflict 2:202–229.
Ross S (1998) Causes and consequences of the Arab-Israeli conflict. Evans Brothers Limited, London.
Rotberg R (2006) Building legitimacy through narrative. In: Rotberg R (ed) Israeli and Palestinian narratives of the conflict: History's double helix. Indiana University Press, Indianapolis, pp. 1–18.
Rubinstein HL, Cohn-Sherbok D, Edelheit AJ, Rubinstein WD (2002) The Jews in the modern world: A history since 1750. Arnold, London.
Rudolf G (ed) (2003) Dissecting the Holocaust: The growing critique of 'truth' and 'memory'. Theses & Dissertations Press, Chicago.

Sadeh E (1994) Militarization and state power in the Arab-Israeli conflict: Case study of Israel, 1948–1982. Dissertations.com.
Safty A (2009) Might over right, how the Zionists took over Palestine. Garnet Publishing Limited, Reading, UK.
Said E (1979) The question of Palestine. Times Books, New York.
Said E (1994) Culture and imperialism. Vintage Books, London.
Said E (1995) Peace and its discontents: Essays on Palestine in the Middle East peace process. Knopf Doubleday Publishing Group, New York.
Saleh M (2015) History of Palestine, a methodical study of the Palestinian struggle. Al-Falah Foundation, Cairo.
Sams K (2011) IHL obligations of the UN and other international organisations involved in international missions. In: Odello M, Piotrowicz R (eds) International military missions and international law. Martinus Nijhoff Publishers, Boston, pp. 45–72.
Sanning W (1983) The dissolution of the Eastern European Jewry. University of Michigan, Ann Arbor.
Schaeffer R (1999) Severed states: Dilemmas of democracy in a divided world. Rowman & Littlefield Publishers, Lanham, Maryland.
Schanzer J (2008) Hamas vs. Fatah: The struggle for Palestine. Palgrave Macmillan, New York.
Schneer J (2010) The Balfour Declaration: The origins of the Arab-Israeli conflict. Bloomsbury Publishing Plc., London.
Sharon A (2009) Why is Israel's presence in the territories still called "occupation"? Jerusalem Centre for Public Affairs, Jerusalem.
Shindler C (2013) A History of Modern Israel, 2nd edn. Cambridge University Press, Cambridge.
Shmuelevitz A (1984) The Jews of the Ottoman Empire in the late fifteenth and sixteenth centuries: Administrative, economic, legal and social relations as reflected in the responsa. E. J. Brill, Leiden.
Silverburg S (ed) (2002) Palestine and international law: Essays on politics and economics. Mcfarland & Company Inc., Jefferson, North Carolina.
Silverfarb D (1986) Britain's informal empire in the Middle East: A case study of Iraq, 1929–1941. Oxford University Press, Oxford.
Sinanoglou P (2010) The Peel Commission and partition, 1936–38. In: Miller R (ed) Britain, Palestine and empire: The mandate years. Ashgate Publishing, London, pp. 119–140.
Smith W (1982) European Imperialism in The Nineteenth And Twentieth Centuries. Nelson-Hall, Chicago.
Söderblom J (2003) A state of inequity: The UN Partition Plan of 1947. The Terrorism Intelligence Center, Canberra.
Spangler E (2105) Understanding Israel/Palestine - Race, Nation and Human Rights in the Conflict, vol 3. Sense Publishers, Rotterdam.
The State of Israel (2009) The operation in Gaza, 27 December 2008 – 18 January 2009: Factual and legal aspects. Ministry of Foreign Affairs, Jerusalem.
Steinitz Y (2010) Defensible borders in a historical context. Jerusalem Center for Public Affairs, Jerusalem.
Strawson J (2010) Partitioning Palestine: Legal fundamentalism in the Palestinian Israeli conflict. Pluto Press, London.
Stuchtey B (2011) Colonialism and imperialism, 1450–1950. http://www.ieg-ego.eu/stuchteyb-2010-en. Accessed 23 April 2017.
Swedenburg T (1999) The role of the Palestinian peasantry in the Great Revolt (1936–9). In: Pappe I (ed) The Israel/Palestine Question. Routledge, New York, pp. 129–168.
Tal D (2004) War in Palestine, 1948, Strategy and Diplomacy. Routledge, London.
Taylor & Francis Group (2004) The Middle East and North Africa 2004, 50th edn. Europa Publications, London.
Tucker S, Roberts P (eds) (2008) The Encyclopedia of the Arab-Israeli conflict: A political, social, and military history. ABC-CLIO Inc., Santa Barbara, California.

UNCCP (1961) Historical survey of efforts of the United Nations Conciliation Commission for Palestine to secure the implementation of Paragraph 11 of General Assembly Resolution 194 (III), UN Doc. A/AC.25/W/81/Rev.2.
UNCTAD (2015) Report on UNCTAD Assistance to the Palestinian people: Developments in the economy of the occupied Palestinian territory, UN Doc. TD/B/62/3.
UN Country Team in the Occupied Palestinian Territory (2012) Gaza in 2020: A liveable place? Office of the United Nations Special Coordinator for the Middle East Peace Process, Jerusalem.
UNGA (1947) Resolution 181 (II), UN Doc. A/RES/181(II).
UNGA (1948) Resolution 194 (III), UN Doc. A/RES/194 (III).
UNGA (1949a) Resolution 273, UN Doc. A/RES/273 (III).
UNGA (1949b) Resolution 303 (IV), UN Doc. A/RES/303 (IV).
UNGA (1967) Resolution 2254, UN Doc. A/RES/2254.
UNGA (1969a) Resolution 2546, UN Doc. A/RES/2546.
UNGA (1969b) Resolution 2569, UN Doc. A/RES/2569.
UNGA (1971a) Resolution 2787 (XXVI), UN Doc. A/RES/2787.
UNGA (1971b) Resolution 2851 (XXVI), UN Doc. A/RES/2851.
UNGA (1974a) Resolution 3237 (XXIX), UN Doc. A/RES/3237.
UNGA (1974b) Resolution 3240 (XXIX), UN Dec. A/RES/3240.
UNGA (1975a) Resolution 3379, UN Doc. A/RES/3379.
UNGA (1975b) Resolution 3414 (XXX), UN Doc. A/RES/3414.
UNGA (1977) Resolution 32/20, UN Doc. A/RES/32/20.
UNGA (1981) Letter dated 19 June 1981 from the Acting Chairman of the Committee on the exercise of the inalienable rights of the Palestinian people to the Secretary-General, UN Doc. A/36/341-S/14566.
UNGA (1985) Resolution 4060, UN Doc. A/RES/40/61.
UNGA (1988) Resolution 43/177, UN Doc. A/RES/43/177.
UNHRC (2009) Human Rights in Palestine and Other Occupied Arab Territories: Report of the United Nations Fact-Finding Mission on the Gaza Conflict, UN Doc. A/HRC/12/48.
UNHRC (2010) Report of the international fact-finding mission to investigate violations of international law, including international humanitarian and human rights law, resulting from the Israeli attacks on the flotilla of ships carrying humanitarian assistance, UN Doc. A/HRC/15/21.
UNHRC (2013) Report of the independent international fact-finding mission to investigate the implications of the Israeli settlements on the civil, political, economic, social and cultural rights of the Palestinian people throughout the Occupied Palestinian Territory, including East Jerusalem, UN Doc. A/HRC/22/63.
UNHRC (2015) Human rights situation in Palestine and other occupied Arab territories: Report of the detailed findings of the independent commission of inquiry established pursuant to Human Rights Council resolution S-21/1, 22 June 2015, UN Doc. A/HRC/29/CRP.4.
UNOCHA-OPT (2009) Locked in: the humanitarian impact of 2 years of blockade on the Gaza Strip. UNOCHA-OPT, East Jerusalem.
UNOCHA-OPT (2011) Easing the blockade: assessing the humanitarian impact on the population of the Gaza Strip. UNOCHA-OPT, East Jerusalem.
UNOCHA-OPT (2012a) East Jerusalem: Key Humanitarian Concerns. UNOCHA-OPT, East Jerusalem.
UNOCHA-OPT (2012b) The humanitarian impact of Israeli settlement policies, update December 2012. UNOCHA-OPT, East Jerusalem.
UNOCHA-OPT (2013) The Gaza Strip: The humanitarian impact of movement restriction on people and goods. UNOCHA-OPT, East Jerusalem.
UNOCHA-OPT (2014) Occupied Palestinian territory: Gaza emergency situation report. UNOCHA-OPT, East Jerusalem.
UNRWA (2007) The United Nations and Palestinian Refugees. UNRWA, East Jerusalem.
UNRWA (2009) Briefing Paper: Poverty in the occupied Palestinian territory 2007. UNRWA, East Jerusalem.

UNSC (1967) Resolution 242, UN Doc. S/RES/242.
UNSC (1968) Resolution 252, UN Doc. S/RES/252.
UNSC (1973) Resolution 338, UN Doc. S/RES/338.
UNSC (1979) Resolution 446, UN Doc. S/RES/446.
UN Special Rapporteur (2013) Collective punishment in Gaza must end: Israel's blockade enters its 7th year. OHCHR, Geneva.
Zhilian Z, Rongqu L (1980) Reflections on colonialism and modernisation. Research Institute for History 4:109–113.

Chapter 3
The 2009 Palestinian *Ad hoc* Declaration

Contents

Abstract In 2009, the Palestine Authority lodged an *ad hoc* declaration to the International Criminal Court accepting the jurisdiction of the Court for crimes committed since 2002. Almost three years later, the Office of the Prosecutor decided not to open an investigation on the situation in Palestine until the Assembly of States parties of the Court or the United Nations gives clarification on the statehood issue of Palestine. This chapter analyses the *ad hoc* declaration legal regime and the decision of the Office of the Prosecutor on Palestine's declaration. It examines the route the Prosecutor employed in reaching the decision not to proceed followed by an alternative route that the author argues fits the provisions of the Rome Statute and the Practice of the United Nations. In addressing the statehood issue of Palestine, which the Prosecutor argued is a determining factor, the chapter discusses some key historical events that shed light on Palestine's statehood, the elements of the Montevideo Convention and the theories of State recognition. The chapter also provides a functional approach or a practical route to deal with issues regarding *ad hoc* declarations in light of the aims and purposes of the Rome Statute.

Keywords *Ad hoc* declaration · Jurisdiction · *Kompetenz-Kompetenz* · Office of the Prosecutor · Rome Statute · Statehood of Palestine

© T.M.C. ASSER PRESS and the author 2019

S. H. Adem, *Palestine and the International Criminal Court*,
International Criminal Justice Series 21,
https://doi.org/10.1007/978-94-6265-291-0_3

3.1 Introductory Remarks

The first attempt to refer the situation in Palestine to the International Criminal Court occurred in 2009 following Operation Cast Lead. In what appeared to be a reaction to the Operation, on 22 January 2009, four days after the end of the Operation, the Palestinian Minister of Justice lodged an *ad hoc* declaration with the Registrar of the ICC pursuant to Article 12(3) of the Rome Statute.[1] The relevant part of the declaration recognised the jurisdiction of the Court for 'the purpose of identifying, prosecuting and judging the authors and accomplices for acts committed on the territory of Palestine since 1 July 2002'.[2] On 3 April 2012, the then Prosecutor of the Court, Luis Moreno Ocampo, removed the embargo on the Palestinian *ad hoc* declaration. He outsourced the decision on the matter to the UN and the Assembly of the States Parties (ASP) of the ICC.[3]

After providing a legal background on *ad hoc* declarations, this chapter analyses the manner in which former Prosecutor Ocampo dealt with the 2009 Palestinian *ad hoc* declaration. It first examines available avenues that are better equipped to address the matter and further analyses the main reasons behind the decision by employing the prosecutor's approach. Subsequently, it provides a different approach in dealing with the issue at hand.

3.2 The Legal Regime of *Ad hoc* Declarations

In a situation where neither the country of commission nor citizenship is a party to the Statute and in the absence of a UN Security Council referral of the situation to the OTP, the ICC can exercise jurisdiction if the non-party State lodges a declaration. This declaration is lodged pursuant to Article 12(3) of the Statute[4] and with the aim to cover crimes committed on the territory or by a national of the accepting State.[5] Although the provision was adopted envisaging the possibility of a non-party State to accept the jurisdiction of the Court, States parties to the Statute can also employ the provision to draw the Court's attention to a specific situation within the temporal jurisdiction of the Court.[6]

---

1 Palestinian National Authority 2009.

2 Ibid., para 1.

3 OTP, Situation in Palestine, 3 April 2012, https://www.icc-cpi.int/NR/rdonlyres/C6162BBF-FEB9-4FAF-AFA9-836106D2694A/284387/SituationinPalestine030412ENG.pdf (accessed 20 November 2017).

4 Rome Statute of the International Criminal Court, opened for signature 17 July 1998, 2187 UNTS 90 (entered into force 1 July 2002) (Rome Statute), Article 12(3); Ambos 2016, pp. 248 et seq.; Guilfoyle 2106, pp. 108 et seq.

5 Rome Statute, above n. 4, Articles 12(2), (3).

6 Ambos 2016, p. 249; Schabas 2014, p. 374; Triffterer and Ambos 2016, p. 686.

Contrary to the mechanisms for triggering jurisdiction under Article 13 of the Statute, *ad hoc* declarations do not oblige the Prosecutor to open an investigation where, in light of Article 53, she/he decides not to proceed.[7] However, in receipt of the declaration, the Prosecutor is required to open a preliminary examination on the situation.[8] The channel for *ad hoc* declarations to provide temporary jurisdiction have been employed by Côte d'Ivoire, Uganda, Palestine, Egypt and Ukraine.[9] Though there is a lack of explicit procedure for *ad hoc* declarations, the Prosecutor has consistently used the *proprio motu* procedure[10] to deal with *ad hoc* declarations.[11]

Despite the principle of non-retroactive application of jurisdiction provided for in the Statute, *ad hoc* acceptance of jurisdiction allows States to provide a precise time clause that may go as far back as July 2002.[12] The first ever *ad hoc* declaration was lodged by Côte d'Ivoire on 18 April 2003.[13] It gave the Court jurisdiction for 'acts committed on Ivorian territory since the events of 19 September 2002' valid for an 'unspecified period of time'.[14] The declaration was reconfirmed in December 2011.[15] Côte d'Ivoire signed the Rome Statute on 30 November 1998 but ratified it only in 2013. Upon request of the Prosecutor, the Pre-Trial Chamber granted authorisation to proceed to investigation and to broaden the temporal scope of investigation covering events that occurred since 19 September 2002.[16] This precedent shows that *ad hoc* declarations have both prospective and retroactive application.[17] It is, in particular, the retroactive application that makes this provision important for States parties to the Statute.

---

[7] OTP 2013, para 76; Triffterer and Ambos 2016, p. 686.

[8] Rome Statute, above n. 4, Article 53; Schabas 2010, p. 657.

[9] ICC, Declarations of Article 12(3), https://www.icccpi.int/en_menus/icc/structure%20of%20the%20court/registry/Pages/declarations.aspx (link no longer active; accessed 11 April 2016); Triffterer and Ambos 2016, p. 686.

[10] Article 15(1) of the Rome Statute empowers the Prosecutor to initiate a preliminary examination *proprio motu* on the basis of information or communication she received. After conducting the examination, the Prosecutor has to obtain a Pre-Trial Chamber authorisation to proceed to investigation. See Rome Statute, above n. 4, Articles 15(1–2) and 53(1). On *proprio motu* procedures see Materu 2015, p. 180.

[11] Ambos 2016, p. 264; Triffterer and Ambos 2016, p. 686. See also Stegmiller 2011, p. 85.

[12] Rome Statute, above n. 4, Articles 11 and 12(3); Triffterer and Ambos 2016, p. 686.

[13] Stegmiller 2011, p. 85.

[14] Republic of Côte d'Ivoire 2003.

[15] Republic of Côte d'Ivoire 2010; Triffterer and Ambos 2016, p. 686.

[16] ICC, Situation in the Republic of Côte d'Ivoire, Decision Pursuant to Article 15 of the Rome Statute on the Authorization of an Investigation into the Situation in the Republic of Côte d'Ivoire, ICC-02/11-14, 3 October 2011, para 15; ICC, Situation in the Republic of Côte d'Ivoire, Decision on the Prosecution's Provision of Further Information Regarding Potentially Relevant Crimes Committed Between 2002 and 2010, 22 February 2012, ICC-02/11-36, para 37.

[17] Triffterer and Ambos 2016, p. 686.

The second *ad hoc* declaration was made by Uganda, delegating the Court jurisdiction for crimes committed as of 1 July 2002.[18] Uganda signed the Statute on 14 July 2002 and it entered into force for Uganda in September 2002. The Prosecutor indicated that 'the temporal jurisdiction extends back to 1 July 2002'.[19] Hence, the declaration helped to backdate and extend the Court's jurisdiction up to the date of entry into force of the Statute with the aim to cover incidents that occurred when the Court had no automatic jurisdiction over Uganda.

The *ad hoc* declaration made by Ukraine on 17 April 2014 stipulated a specific crime, namely crimes against humanity.[20] Different from a referral by a State party or by the Security Council, the exercise of jurisdiction contemplated under Article 12(3) of the Statute may appear as encompassing specific crime/crimes within the jurisdiction of the Court. The wording of the Statute—'the State may … accept the exercise of jurisdiction by the Court with respect to the crime in question'—may purport to denote that the accepting State could consent to the jurisdiction of the Court with regard to one or more of the crimes under the Statute instead of a situation.[21]

This (narrow) interpretation would result in a selective exercise of jurisdiction or 'asymmetric liability', which an accepting State could exploit to target an opposing party in a conflict.[22] In order to mend this possible one-sided manipulation of the provision, the Assembly of States Parties, through the Rules of Procedure and Evidence[23] specified that, notwithstanding its *ad hoc* nature, an *ad hoc* consent to the Court's jurisdiction has the same consequence as a referral of a situation except for its unique *ad hoc* nature.[24] In *Prosecutor v. Gbagbo*, the Pre-Trial Chamber I has also ruled that the scope of *ad hoc* declarations is predetermined by the legal framework of the Court.[25] The Court noted Rule 44 of the Rules of Procedure and

---

[18] See the letter of the Prosecutor annexed to Decision Assigning the Situation in Uganda to Pre-Trial Chamber II, Situation in Uganda, ICC-02/04, 5 July 2004. See also The Republic of Uganda, Referral of the Situation Concerning the Lord's Resistance Army, 16 December 2003, https://www.icc-cpi.int/Pages/item.aspx?name=president+of+uganda+refers+situation+concerning+the+lord_s+resistance+army+_lra_+to+the+icc (accessed 13 February 2016).

[19] See the letter to the president of the ICC (17 June 2004), annexed to Decision Assigning the Situation in the Democratic Republic of Congo to Pre-Trial Chamber I, 8 July 2004, ICC-01/04-1. See also ICC, Situation in Uganda, Decision Assigning the Situation in Uganda to Pre-Trial Chamber II, ICC-02/04-1, 5 July 2004.

[20] ICC, Press release: Ukraine accepts ICC jurisdiction over alleged crimes committed between 21 November 2013 and 22 February 2014, 17 April 2014, https://www.icc-cpi.int/Pages/item.aspx?name=pr997 (accessed 21 April 2017).

[21] Schabas 2011, pp. 85–86; Triffterer and Ambos 2016, p. 684.

[22] Kaul 2002, p. 611.

[23] See ICC, Rules of Procedure and Evidence, adopted 9 September 2002, ICC-ASP/1/3 part II.A (Rules of Procedure and Evidence), Rule 44.

[24] Schabas 2010, p. 288; Triffterer and Ambos 2016, p. 685.

[25] ICC, *Prosecutor v. Laurent Gbagbo*, Decision on the 'Corrigendum of the challenge to the jurisdiction of the International Criminal Court on the basis of Articles 12(3), 19(2), 21(3), 55 and

Evidence and stated that the rule is adopted for the purpose of ensuring that non-party States do not engage the Court 'opportunistically'.[26]

The Ukrainian declaration also limits the Court's jurisdiction to senior officials who were in office from 21 November 2013 to 22 February 2014.[27] The declaration is carefully tailored to ensure that only one side of the conflict is investigated. In her 2014 annual report on Preliminary Examination Activities, the Prosecutor tacitly disregarded these *ratione materiae* and *ratione personae* restrictions and treated the declaration as only providing jurisdiction to the Court for the relevant time.[28] On 8 September 2015, Ukraine lodged a second *ad hoc* declaration with regard to alleged crimes committed on its territory from 20 February 2014 onwards.[29] Due to this submission, the Prosecutor extended the temporal scope of the preliminary examination that started on 25 April 2014 to include alleged crimes committed after February 2014.[30] Hence, this practice suggests that while setting a temporal limitation is acceptable, a declaring State cannot effectively set a limit on the subject matter.

Since declarations do not oblige the Prosecutor to proceed to investigate, if the Prosecutor decides that 'there is a reasonable basis to proceed to an investigation, following a preliminary examination of the situation, she or he has to obtain authorisation from the Pre-Trial Chamber of the Court.[31] Although the *ad hoc* declaration regime allows the accepting State to limit the specific duration or the *ratione temporis* of the situation, the 'time-frame' of the investigation on the situation is, nevertheless, determined by the Pre-Trial Chamber of the Court upon the request of the Prosecutor.[32] Moreover, during the receipt of the declaration of acceptance, the Registrar of the Court is duty bound to remind the accepting States that framing the situation to be investigated is within the discretion of the Court.[33]

Two Article 12(3) declarations, namely, those of Palestine and Egypt, gave rise to discussions on the capacity of the declaring party or the *locus standi* necessary to enable an *ad hoc* delegation of jurisdiction. The first Palestinian *ad hoc* declaration

59 of the Rome Statute filed by the Defence for President Gbagbo (ICC- 02/11-01/11-129)', 15 August 2012, ICC-02/11-01/11-212 (*Laurent Gbagbo* 2012), para 59.

[26] Ibid. See also Ambos 2016, p. 258; Triffterer and Ambos 2016, p. 688.

[27] ICC, Press release: Ukraine accepts ICC jurisdiction over alleged crimes committed between 21 November 2013 and 22 February 2014, 17 April 2014, https://www.icc-cpi.int/Pages/item.aspx?name=pr997 (accessed 21 April 2017); Note verbale of the Acting Minister for Foreign Affairs of Ukraine, Mr. Andrii Deshchytsia, 16 April 2014, https://www.icc-cpi.int/itemsDocuments/997/UkraineMFAdocument16-04-2014.pdf (accessed 07 December 2015).

[28] OTP 2014. See also Triffterer and Ambos 2016, p. 688.

[29] Declaration by Ukraine lodged under Article 12(3) of the Statute, 8 September 2015, https://www.icc-cpi.int/iccdocs/other/Ukraine_Art_12-3_declaration_08092015.pdf#search=ukraine (7 December 2015).

[30] OTP 2015, p. 18.

[31] Rome Statute, above n. 4, Article 53(2).

[32] Ibid., Article 15. See also Triffterer and Ambos 2016, p. 686.

[33] *Laurent Gbagbo* 2012, above n. 25, para 59. See Triffterer and Ambos 2016, pp. 685–686.

(discussed in detail under Sect. 3.3) was rejected due to the uncertainty surrounding the legal personality/Statehood of Palestine and its 'inability' to make the declaration.[34] In the case of Egypt, lawyers representing the Egyptian Freedom and Justice Party, a political party led by former President Mohamed Morsi until it was banned and dissolved in 2014, submitted an *ad hoc* declaration with regard to alleged crimes committed in Egypt since 1 June 2013.[35] In May 2014, the Prosecutor announced that since the parties do not exercise 'full power' to represent the State of Egypt they 'lacked *locus standi* to seize the Court's Jurisdiction pursuant to Article 12 para 3 of the Statute'.[36] Hence, the Prosecutor stated that the submission would be treated as a communication as per Article 15 of the Statute. In justifying his decision, the Prosecutor averred that the new government 'appointed' in July 2013 under the El-Sisi leadership, rather than the Morsi led party, was treated by the UN member States as representative of the State of Egypt.[37] Thus, in light of these practices, parties representing the population in question and recognised as such by the international community have the *locus standi* to submit or to delegate jurisdiction to the Court.

3.3 Decision of the Prosecutor on the 2009 Palestinian Declaration

In his decision on the Palestine's declaration the Prosecutor expounded that as per Article 15 of the Statute his office has conducted the necessary examinations to make sure whether there is a reasonable basis to proceed to an investigation. He announced that it is not within the competence of his office, but rather up to the 'competent organs of the UN or the Assembly of States Parties of the Court', to make a legal determination if 'Palestine qualifies as a State for the purpose of the Statute'.[38] He cited Article 125 of the Rome Statute and noted that 'where it is controversial or unclear whether an applicant (to accession) constitutes a "State", it is the practice of the Secretary General to follow or seek the General Assembly's directives on the matter'.[39] The main part of the Prosecutor's decision reads:[40]

> The issue that arises, therefore, is who defines what is a "State" for the purpose of article 12 of the Statute? In accordance with article 125, the Rome Statute is open to accession by "all States", and any State seeking to become a Party to the Statute must deposit an instrument

[34] OTP 2012, above n. 3. This issue is analysed in detail below.

[35] OTP 2014, Press release: The Determination of the Office of the Prosecutor on the Communication Received in Relation to Egypt, 8 May 2014, ICC-OTP-20140508-PR1003.

[36] Ibid.; Triffterer and Ambos 2016, p. 686.

[37] OTP 2014, above n. 35.

[38] OTP 2012, above n. 3.

[39] Ibid., paras 5, 6.

[40] Ibid.

of accession with the Secretary General of the United Nations. In instances where it is controversial or unclear whether an applicant constitutes a "State", it is the practice of the Secretary General to follow or seek the General Assembly's directives on the matter. This is reflected in General Assembly resolutions which provide indications of whether an applicant is a "State". Thus, competence for determining the term "State" within the meaning of article 12 rests, in the first instance, with the United Nations Secretary General who, in case of doubt, will defer to the guidance of General Assembly. The Assembly of States Parties of the Rome Statute could also in due course decide to address the matter in accordance with article 112(2)(g) of the Statute.

The Prosecutor employed the procedure for determining statehood in the case of accession to the Statute to determine the status of an entity making an *ad hoc* declaration. In light of this, the issue that need to be pondered is whether determinations of statehood in the case of *ad hoc* declarations on the one hand and accession to the Statute on the other are one and the same thing. The issue that is closely linked to this one is identifying the organ that can decide whether a given entity is capable of accepting jurisdiction. The following section discusses these two issues respectively.

3.4 Determination of Statehood for the Purpose of the ICC Jurisdiction

Accession and *ad hoc* delegation of jurisdiction are different juridical acts giving rise to different rights and responsibilities under the Statute. Unless otherwise provided, up on acceding to a treaty, a State is bound by all the terms of the treaty. Among other things, it is required to observe and enforce the terms of the treaty in good faith.[41] In the case of *ad hoc* declarations, however, the declaring party only temporarily bequeaths one of the main facets of sovereignty with no reciprocal rights.[42] In the case of accessions, the UN Secretary General is the depository of the Statute while the Registrar of the Court receives *ad hoc* declarations.[43]

If an entity whose statehood is unclear wants to accede to a treaty, paras 79–81 of the Summary of Practice of the Secretary General as Depositary of Multilateral Treaties provide a solution.[44] In regard to those treaties that expressly welcome

[41] Article 26 of Vienna Convention on the Law of Treaties, concluded at Vienna on 23 May 1969, 1155 UNTS 331 (entered into force 27 January 1980) (Vienna Convention).

[42] See S. Adem, Palestine and the ICC: a critical appraisal of the decision of the Office of the Prosecutor on the Palestine ad hoc declaration (Unpublished thesis, University of the Western Cape, 2015).

[43] Rome Statute, above n. 4, Articles 12(3) and 125(2); Treaty Section of the Office of Legal Affairs 1999, p. 23.

[44] Ibid., pp. 22–23.

members of the specialised agencies of the UN—in addition to member States of the UN and signatories of the Statute of the International Court of Justice, among others—the Secretary General does not face difficulties.[45] This approach, named the Vienna formula, aims to include those States that the international community recognizes as States but is unable to join the UN due to political opposition of a veto wielding member of the Security Council.[46]

However, most treaties such as the Rome Statute and the Convention on the Suppression and Punishment of the Crime of Apartheid are open to participation by 'all States' or 'any State' without any further specification.[47] When an instrument of accession for such instruments is received from entities whose statehood is unclear, it would fall outside the competence of the Secretary General of the UN to give a decision. As the decision would be, in most cases, highly political and controversial, the practice of the Secretary General, under para 81, states that a decision could be reached only if the General Assembly provides a complete list of States falling within the 'all States' or 'any State' formula.[48]

Had Palestine signed the Rome Statute in 2009, instead of lodging an *ad hoc* declaration, the Secretary General, who is the depository of the Statute, would have employed the 'all States' route. Although this route could be followed in case of accessions to the Statute, no such mechanism or particular organ of the Court is expressly designated in case of *ad hoc* declarations. As signing the Statute on the one hand and lodging an *ad hoc* declaration on the other are separate juridical acts, it would be unfitting to employ the one route to the other. Hence, in accordance with possible interpretation of the Rome Statute and conventional law, it is imperative to establish if this competence rests within the Court, in contrast to other organs such as the UN, and, if so, to determine the particular organ of the Court competent for this purpose.

---

[45] For instance, Article 81 of the Vienna Convention, above n. 41, expressly provides:

> The present Convention shall be open for signature by all States Members of the United Nations or of any of the specialized agencies or of the International Atomic Energy Agency or parties to the Statute of the International Court of Justice, and by any other State invited by the General Assembly of the United Nations to become a party to the Convention…

See also Treaty Section of the Office of Legal Affairs 1999, p. 22.

[46] Ibid., p. 22.

[47] Rome Statute, above n. 4, Article 125(1); International Convention on the Suppression and Punishment of the Crime of Apartheid, opened for signature 30 November 1973, 1015 UNTS 243 (entered into force 18 July 1976), Article 13; Convention on the Prevention and Punishment of Crimes against Diplomatic Agents and Other Internationally Protected Persons, opened for signature 14 December 1973, 1035 UNTS 167 (entered into force 20 February 1977), Article 16.

[48] Treaty Section of the Office of Legal Affairs 1999, p. 23.

3.4.1 *'Kompetenz-Kompetenz'*

International Courts and Tribunals are governed by a fundamental jurisprudential principle named the principle of *Kompetenz-Kompetenz*. The principle is a pre-requisite for judicial function[49] as it vests an international Court or Tribunal with the inherent authority to define the limits of its own jurisdiction.[50] The International Court of Justice has on different occasions[51] stressed that, as per its Statute and settled jurisprudence, it is bound to interpret its own Statute and to answer issues related to its own jurisdiction. In the *Tadić* judgement, the Appeals Chamber of the International Criminal Tribunal for the Former Yugoslavia (ICTY) has also stated it:[52]

> is part, and indeed a major part, of the incidental or inherent jurisdiction of any judicial or arbitral Tribunal, consisting of its "jurisdiction to determine its own jurisdiction". It is a necessary component in the exercise of the judicial function and does not need to be expressly provided for in the constitutive documents of those Tribunals.

Similarly, the ICC has also adopted this jurisprudence and established this principle on various decisions.[53] It has also emphasised that the Court has the 'primary role as well as the final say on the interpretation, construction and application of the provisions of the Statute'.[54] In the decision on the Confirmation of Charges Pursuant to Article 61(7)(a) and (b) of the Statute on *Ruto, Kosgey and Sang* case the Pre-Trial Chamber II ruled that[55]

---

[49] Amerasinghe 2003, p. 154; Gaillard and Savage 1999, p. 396.

[50] Aksar 2004, pp. 35–36; Ambos 2016, p. 247; Chazournes 2011, pp. 1027–1034.

[51] ICJ, Fisheries Jurisdiction (*United Kingdom of Great Britain v. Iceland*), Judgement, 2 February 1973, ICJ Reports 1973 at p. 3, para 12; ICJ, *Lichtenstein v. Guatemala*, Judgment, 18 November 1953, ICJ Reports 1953 at p. 111, para 119. See also El Zeidy 2015, p. 189.

[52] ICTY, *Prosecutor v. Dusko Tadić*, Decision on the defence motion for interlocutory appeal on jurisdiction, 2 October 1995, IT-94-1-AR72 (*Tadić* 1995), para 18. A similar decision has also been issued by the Special Tribunal for Lebanon. See Special Tribunal for Lebanon, In the Matter of El Sayed, Decision on Appeal of Pre-Trial Judge's order Regarding Jurisdiction and standing, 10 November 2010, CH/AC/2010/02, para 43.

[53] ICC, *Prosecutor v. Joseph Kony et al.*, Decision on the Admissibility of the Case under Article 19(1) of the Statute, 10 March 2009, ICC-02/04-01/05-377, para 46; ICC, *Prosecutor v. Jean-Pierre Bemba Gombo*, Decision Pursuant to Article 61(7)(a) and (b) of the Rome Statute on the Charges of the Prosecutor Against Jean-Pierre Bemba Gombo, 15 June 2009, ICC-01/05-01/08-424, para 23.

[54] El Zeidy 2015, p. 189; Vagias 2014, pp. 84–85.

[55] ICC, *Prosecutor v. Ruto, Kosgey and Sang*, Decision on the Confirmation of Charges Pursuant to Article 61(7)(a) and (b) of the Rome Statute, Situation in the Republic of Kenya, 23 January 2012, ICC-01/09-01/11-373, para 24. A similar ruling was held in the situation of Uganda. See ICC, *Prosecutor v. Dominic Ongwen*, Decision on the Prosecutor's Application that the Pre-Trial Chamber Disregard as irrelevant the submission filed by the registry on 5 December 2005, 9 March 2006, ICC-02/04-01/15-53-Red, paras 22–23.

> [r]egardless of the mandatory language of Article 19(1) of the Statute, which requires an assessment of whether the Court has the competence to adjudicate the case sub judice, any judicial body has the power to determine its own jurisdiction, even in the absence of an explicit reference to that effect.' This is an essential component in the exercise of any judicial body of its functions and is derived from the well-recognized principle of la compétence de la compétence.

Notwithstanding this established jurisprudence, interpretation and application of the Statute would still exclusively fall on the institutions of the ICC pursuant to Article 1 and Article 21(1)(a) of the Statute. The first provision provides that the provisions of the Statute govern the functions of the Court and Article 21 provides other sources of law that the Court could apply. El Zeidy rightly argues that in its second and third Paragraphs the latter provision 'makes it clear that the interpretation of the law is an inherent and an integral function of the Court'.[56] Thus, he states, the interpretation of any provision, including Article 12, which is a jurisdictional provision, falls within the interpretative judicial powers of the Court. Since an interpretation of the word 'State' under Article 12(3) is a question of 'legal determination' as admitted by the Prosecutor under para 6 of his decision, El Zeidy concludes that the determination about *ad hoc* declaration is left to one of the four organs of the Court.[57]

Instead, in the Palestine situation, the former Prosecutor of the Court vigorously argued that the competence to determine whether Palestine qualifies to lodge the *ad hoc* declaration and to interpret what a 'State' is rests with the UN General Assembly or the Assembly of States Parties. However, as per the above analysis and the principle of *Kompetenz-Kompetenz*, it is in fact the ICC which has the power, as well as the obligation, to decide on its own competence to entertain matters before its organs as well as to interpret, construe and apply its own Statute.[58]

3.4.2 Possible Avenues to Determine the Statehood Issue

After establishing the duty of the Court to interpret the word 'State' for the purpose of Article 12(3), what then naturally follows is to identify which particular organ of the Court is the most appropriate to make such determination. The Rome Statute does not provide a specific organ or procedural regime that should be employed for *ad hoc* declarations let alone for an interpretation of ambiguous terms within this

[56] El Zeidy 2015, p. 190.

[57] Rome Statute, above n. 4, Article 34. See Azarova 2013, p. 262; El Zeidy 2015, p. 190.

[58] Ibid., p. 189.

legal regime. Since the procedure employed for *ad hoc* declarations is *proprio motu*,[59] it is plausible to discuss an interpretation of the term in light of this procedure.

In his decision, the former Prosecutor forwarded to the UN and ASP the duty to decide on what is admittedly a legal question.[60] Indeed, 'recognition' of the existence of a State, albeit arguable, could be made by these institutions, as these are political bodies made up of representatives of political entities. One could argue that the Prosecutor's approach could be backed by the practice followed by the International Atomic Energy Agency (IAEA) General Conference when Namibia tried to accede to the IAEA Statute while its statehood was still doubtful. The IAEA General Conference, which is composed of member States of the Statute, approved Namibia's accession following the Depository State's request for clarification on the statehood issue. The problem in adopting this normatively authoritative precedent, as some did in a similar instance,[61] is that, in the case at hand, the issue is not concerned with accession but with interpretation of the Statute. And, in light of the Vienna Convention on the Law of Treaties,[62] the *lex specialis*, namely the Rome Statute, rather than a general UN practice, shall be adopted.[63]

Article 119 of the Statute provides two routes to settle disputes. Paragraph 1 provides that 'dispute concerning the judicial functions of the Court shall be settled by the decision of the Court'.[64] The second Paragraph mandates the Assembly of States Parties to settle other 'disputes between two or more States parties relating to the interpretation and or application of the Statute' when parties fail to settle the matter after three months of negotiation. Although the phrase 'interpretation and or application of the Statute' may appear to refer to matters of purely substantive nature, the fact that the ASP is called to settle the matter defeats the literal interpretation of the phrase. Making a legal determination is beyond the competence of the assembly when the nature of the dispute involves analysis of questions of law and fact. This is further supported by the reference to 'disputes concerning judicial functions', under 119(1), to the Court as opposed to the ASP. Hence, it would be

[59] Rome Statute, above n. 4, Articles 15 and 53(1). See also the approach followed by the Prosecutor on preliminary examination of situations that arise from *ad hoc* declarations. Available https://www.icc-cpi.int/en_menus/icc/structure%20of%20the%20court/office%20of%20the%20prosecutor/comm%20and%20ref/reports/Pages/default.aspx (accessed 12 April 2016). See also Materu 2015, p. 180.

[60] OTP 2012, above n. 3, para 5.

[61] R. Howse, Howse reply to letter to the editor, *Just Security*, 8 January 2015.

[62] Vienna Convention, above n. 41, Article 77(2).

[63] N. Karin, The establishment of the International Criminal Tribunal for Palestine (Part I), *Just Security*, 21 January 2015.

[64] Rome Statute, above n. 4, Article 119(1).

unsound to call up on the assembly of States parties of the ICC to settle a purely judicial issue.[65]

Article 119(1), however, explicitly refers to 'judicial functions' that deal with, among others, interpretation of the pre-conditions to exercise jurisdiction, matters of jurisdiction and admissibility or definition of crimes.[66] As interpretation of the word 'State' under Article 12(3) falls under the heading of the preconditions to exercise jurisdiction', it is concluded that the matter concerns 'the judicial function' of the Court. Therefore, as per para 1, it shall be settled by the Court, which could ultimately create a precedent for subsequent cases.[67] One has to determine, however, the procedure leading up to the determination of the issue by the Court and the particular branch of Court that could settle the matter.

The Pre-Trial of the Court could be one of the most competent organs and a viable avenue to rule on the validity of a declaration in general and the interpretation of the word 'State' under Article 12(3) in particular.[68] The Chamber is empowered to carry out judicial functions that need to be executed before the beginning of a trial.[69] On the situation in Côte d'Ivoire, the Pre-Trial Chamber III ruled on the validity of the *ad hoc* declaration.[70] The fact that the Chamber addressed issues related to the validity of the *ad hoc* declaration makes it similar to the Palestinian case, even if issues related to interpretation were not raised in the Côte d'Ivoire or previous *ad hoc* declarations.

Although interpretation of the Statute is best suited to a Chamber equipped with legal experts, the Chamber has to first be seized with the matter. To seize on a matter related to *proprio motu* procedures—as *ad hoc* declarations follow a *proprio motu* procedure—the Pre-Trial Chamber has to be approached by the Prosecutor.

After conducting a preliminary examination of a situation, the Prosecutor has to decide whether or not there is 'a reasonable basis to proceed with an investigation'.[71] The responsibility of the Prosecutor at this stage involves 'determining

---

[65] Amnesty International 2012; Azarova 2013, p. 262; C. Meloni, Palestine and the ICC: some notes on why it is not a closed chapter, 25 September 2012, http://opiniojuris.org/2012/09/25/palestine-and-the-icc-some-notes-on-why-it-is-not-a-closed-chapter/ (accessed 13 February 2016); W. Schabas, Palestinian statehood and the International Criminal Court: a curious condition from Whitehall, 27 November 2012 http://humanrightsdoctorate.blogspot.com/2012/11/palestinian-statehood-and-international.html (accessed 13 February 2016).

[66] Triffterer and Ambos 2016, p. 2276.

[67] Ibid., pp. 2276–2277.

[68] Boas argues that it is of considerable importance for Courts to have an active role at the Pre-Trial Stage of the proceeding. For more on the advantages see Boas 2007, p. 279; Meloni 2012, above n. 65; Schabas 2012.

[69] Rome Statute, above n. 4, Article 19(6) states: 'prior to the confirmation of the charges, challenges to the admissibility of a case or challenges to the jurisdiction of the Court shall be referred to the Pre-Trial Chamber'. See Smet 2009, p. 405; Triffterer and Ambos 2016, p. 1421.

[70] ICC, Situation in the Republic of Côte d'Ivoire, Decision Pursuant to Article 15 of the Rome Statute on the Authorization of an Investigation into the Situation in the Republic of Côte d'Ivoire, 15 November 2011, ICC-02/11-14, paras 14–22, 186–187.

[71] Rome Statute, above n. 4, Article 15.

whether a situation meets the legal criteria established by the Statute to warrant investigation by the ICC'.[72] And these legal criteria pursuant to Article 53(1)(a)–(c) of the Statute involve an analysis of issues of jurisdiction, admissibility and interest of justice. Questionably, the Prosecutor, in the case at hand, created a sequence between the examination of the pre-conditions under Article 12 and the requirements set under Article 53(1) so as to avoid making an explicit determination that could have either rested under Article 15(3) or 15(6).[73]

In the absence of the Prosecutor's request, the Court would not review either the validity of the declaration or the decision of the Prosecutor unless the decision not to proceed is made on the basis of interest of justice or the Prosecutor concludes there is a reasonable ground to proceed to an investigation and requests the Pre-Trial Chamber for authorisation (which was not the case in the Palestine situation).[74] Hence, the Court could not, on its own initiative, rule on the validity of the Palestinian *ad hoc* declaration or pass a ruling on whether Palestine qualifies to lodge the declaration.

However, had the Prosecutor not disposed the case as he did, he could have made a decision on the matter and request the Pre-Trial Chamber for any additional legal analysis or ruling on the jurisdiction and admissibility of the situation. With regard to the ICC, the *Kompetenz-Kompetenz* could be easily argued for on the basis of Article 19 of the Statute. Article 19 states that the Court 'shall satisfy itself that it has jurisdiction in any case brought before it'.[75] The International Law Commission's (ILC) commentary on Article 24 of the ILC Draft Statute, which is the provision considered as the origin of Article 19, states that each of the organs of the Court has an *ex officio* responsibility to determine on the matter before it.[76] Given the duty of the Court that arises from Article 19 of the Statute and its *Kompetenz-Kompetenz*, the OTP, as one organ of the Court, is duty bound to satisfy itself that it has jurisdiction over the matter. In addition, as per Article 19(3) of the Statute, the Prosecutor is entitled to 'seek a ruling from the Court regarding a question of jurisdiction or admissibility'.[77] Hence, had the Prosecutor decided on the matter and subsequently sought a ruling from the Chamber, the latter could have provided an interpretation of the term in light of the legal and factual background of the situation.

---

72 OTP 2013.

73 OTP 2012, para 3. See also El Zeidy 2015, p. 190; Schabas 2012.

74 Rome Statute, above n. 4, Articles 15(3) and 53(1).

75 Ibid., Article 19(1).

76 International Law Commission, Draft Statute for an International Criminal Court with Commentaries, 1994, http://legal.un.org/ilc/texts/instruments/english/commentaries/7_4_1994.pdf, p. 45; Triffterer and Ambos 2016, p. 853.

77 Rome Statute, above n. 4, Article 19(3).

3.5 The Palestine Statehood Issue

After establishing the competence of the Court to determine the statehood of an entity for its own purposes, what then follows is what issues constitute the details of the determination.

Although the Prosecutor outsourced the duty to decide on the eligibility of the entity making a declaration, he has raised some considerations on substantive issues related to the statehood of Palestine. Under para 7 of his decision, he touched upon the status of Palestine in the UN and UN bodies and the bilateral State recognitions, further reflecting his stand that the determining factor for the effectiveness of the declaration is the abstract statehood question of Palestine. As the decision is premised on the 'uncertain status' of Palestine based on the Prosecutor's cursory and undetailed historical and political analysis, it is necessary to deal with the statehood issue in light of the approach adopted by the Prosecutor. In support of a teleological approach of dealing with the matter, the section that follows analyses the statehood issue for the specific purpose of *ad hoc* declarations.

3.5.1 The Statehood of Palestine: General Considerations

There is no unanimity over what a complete and contemporary legal definition of statehood is.[78] In fact, the issue is contingent upon the historical, political and legal outlay of the time necessitating an examination of various considerations. The following section examines the declaration of statehood of Palestine, the criteria of the Montevideo Convention, theories of State recognition and the occupied status of Palestine to reach a conclusion on Palestine's statehood.

3.5.1.1 Palestine's Declaration of Statehood

As shown in Chap. 2, after the Palestine National Council declared the statehood of Palestine in 1988, the UN General Assembly Resolution 43/77 acknowledged the declaration and replaced the designation 'Palestine Liberation Organization' with 'Palestine'.[79] Following the affirmation, 89 States recognised Palestine.[80] In doing so, the Palestine Liberation Organisation, arguably, agreed to the two State solution and consented to a peaceful settlement.

Hence, as a result of the declaration of statehood and the wide recognition worldwide, it is possible to argue that a Palestinian State existed since 1988. The absence of any denunciation of the declaration as a violation of the territorial rights

---

78 Azarova 2013, p. 262.

79 UNGA 1988; Boyle 1990, p. 301; Crawford 1990, p. 307.

80 Quigley 2012, pp. 433–434.

of Israel also supports this conclusion.[81] Alternatively, on the basis of the Preamble Paragraph of the declaration, it could also be argued that the 1988 declaration was not a declaration of a new State but rather an affirmation of an already existing State.[82] Expressly quoting the League of Nations Covenant, the declaration states:[83]

> The international community, in Article 22 of the Covenant of the League of Nations of 1919 … recognized that the Palestinian Arab People was no different from the other Arab peoples detached from the Ottoman State and was a free and independent people (…).

Palestine, as seen in Chap. 2, was one of the class A mandates under the British administration. As a system devised to provisionally administer territories until they become 'independent nations' capable of administering their affairs,[84] the ultimate goal of the mandate system was guaranteeing the right to self-determination and independence of the people in question.[85] Although it was receiving administrative advice and assistance from the mandate authority, Palestine has separately concluded League of Nations registered treaties with other States and organisations,[86] and its inhabitants were considered nationals of Palestine rather than Britain or Ottoman Turkey.[87] Moreover, the 'existing sovereignty' was reflected in the 1947 partition plan which ended the British mandate and envisioned the two-State solution,[88] and on which both Israel and Palestine base the legitimacy of the declaration of their respective statehood.[89]

However, after the declaration of independence, Palestine's move to accede to international treaties such as the Geneva Conventions and attempts to join international bodies such as the World Trade Organisation (WTO) and the United Nations Educational, Scientific and Cultural Organization (UNESCO), were unsuccessful on the ground that the status of Palestine as a State was 'unclear'.[90]

---

[81] Quigley 2002, p. 44.

[82] Palestine National Council 1988.

[83] Ibid. See also Quigley 2012, p. 437.

[84] League of Nations, Covenant of the League of Nations, 28 April 1919, http://www.refworld.org/docid/3dd8b9854.html, Article 22.

[85] ICJ, Advisory opinion: The Legal consequences for States of the continued presence of South Africa in Namibia (South West Africa) notwithstanding Security Council Resolution 276 (1970), 21 June 1971, para 31. See also Gowlland-Debbas 2012, p. 518; Quigley 2016, p. 50.

[86] International Agreement for the Establishment of an International Bureau of Intelligence on Locusts, (1926). See also Agreement Regarding Reciprocal Enforcement of Judgements with Egypt, (1929); Agreement Concerning the Exchange of Postal Parcels with Switzerland (1929); Agreement Concerning the Exchange of Postal Parcels with Italy (1931); Agreement Concerning the Exchange of Postal Parcels with France (1936); Agreement Concerning the Exchange of Postal Parcels with Greece (1936).

[87] Quigley 2012, p. 438.

[88] UNGA 1947. See also Quigley 2016, p. 50.

[89] Gowlland-Debbas 2012, p. 519.

[90] Although Palestine has not yet joined the WTO, after obtaining the 'non-member observer State' status at the UN, it has signed the Geneva Conventions on 2 April 2014 and it joined UNESCO on 23 November 2011. See Embassy of Switzerland, Note of Information sent to the

Another account for the then unclear status of Palestine in the international arena was the record of Palestine in a specially devised category of 'other organisations', at the United Nations Diplomatic Conference of Plenipotentiaries for the Establishment of the International Criminal Court.[91] In subsequent meetings of the States Parties of the ICC, Palestine was grouped amongst 'Entities, intergovernmental organizations, and other Entities'.[92] Similarly, in the 2004 advisory opinion on the wall, the International Court of Justice treated the statehood of Palestine as a status that should materialise in the near future.[93]

In light of the foregoing ambivalent stand, it is difficult to reach a definite conclusion on the statehood of Palestine on a mere reliance on the declaration of independence and the engagement of Palestine with international law and organisations. Hence, it necessitates further analysis of other considerations.

3.5.1.2 The Montevideo Convention

The Montevideo Convention of 1933 is the most widely accepted source regarding the definition of statehood.[94] It provides the traditional normative set of qualifications of what a State should possess. Generally put, the four distinct features of a State provided under Article 1 of the Convention are permanent population, defined territory, government and capacity to enter into relations with other States. It has to be noted that the Convention was ratified only by 15 American States,[95] and its criteria were not subsequently promoted. Taking into account various practices, these criteria are not only outdated, but are also over and under inclusive as they itemise features not critical to and leave out criteria necessary to statehood.[96] Some of the criteria are pre-requisites for while others are consequences of statehood. Despite its deficiencies, it is baffling that the Convention and its criteria are widely quoted. Granting a State of Palestine does not automatically emerge or cease to exist due to the mere satisfaction of the Montevideo criteria but considering the criteria still influence international practice as a policy guideline, discussion of the elements is necessary.

High Contracting Parties to the Geneva Conventions, 13 September 1989; Boyle 1990, p. 301; Crawford 1990, p. 307; Kearney 2012, p. 398.

[91] See UN Diplomatic Conference of Plenipotentiaries on the Establishment of an International Criminal Court 2002, p. 44.

[92] ASP 2009. See also Ash 2009, p. 194.

[93] ICJ, Advisory opinion: Legal Consequences of the Construction of a Wall in Occupied Palestinian Territory, 9 July 2004, ICJ Reports 2004 at p. 136 (ICJ Advisory opinion 2004), para 162. See also Kearney 2012, p. 399.

[94] Grant 1999, p. 403.

[95] The countries that ratified the Montevideo Convention are Brazil, Chile, Colombia, Cuba, Dominican Republic, Ecuador, El Salvador, Guatemala, Haiti, Honduras, Mexico, Nicaragua, Panama, United States and Venezuela.

[96] Grant 1999, p. 453.

Permanent Population: The first qualification necessitates a community inhibiting a habitable territory on permanent basis.[97] With regard to this criterion, putatively, there is a distinguishable population of Palestinians inhabiting the disputed land for centuries with the intention to reside there permanently.

Defined Territory: States are territorial entities. As Jessup[98] rightly argued 'one cannot contemplate a State as a kind of disembodied spirit'.[99] A State may exist despite a contending territorial claim by another. There could be claims over an entire territory or only its boundaries. The first category of claim was raised when admission to the UN was discussed with regard to Israel, Kuwait and Mauritania.[100] Needless to note that claims related to undefined frontiers cannot affect territorial rights[101] and that there is no minimum rule on the size of land inhabited. The State of Tuvalu and Nauru, for instance, are respectively seven and 21 km^2 in size.[102] Hence, the fact that the Palestinian territory is not fully defined or delimited, as is the case with a substantial part of the Israeli border, does not challenge the fulfilment of this criterion.

Government: One of the pre-conditions of statehood is the existence of an 'institutionalized, political administrative and organisational machinery for the purpose of regulating relations in the community and charged with the task of upholding the rules'. Such authority shall be capable of exercising State authority over the population and territory.[103] Similar to the territorial delimitations, as a pre-requisite for statehood, government—be it an actual exercise of authority or the right or title to exercise power—is also relative.[104] Moreover, this requirement of effective government does not have an authoritative application to entities emerging from secessionist movements, colonialism, or military occupation. As such, it is unfeasible, as was clear to the international community, to expect States such as the Congo, East Timor, the Baltic States or States that broke up from the former Yugoslavia to have an effective government from the outset.[105] Nonetheless, as a minimum precondition, a 'government' in control of a certain portion of the territory is vital.

---

[97] Raic 2002, pp. 58–59.

[98] As the delegate of the United States to the UN at the 383th meeting of the Security Council, Philip C. Jessup argued as such in favor of admission of Israel to UN. See UNSC 1948, p. 41.

[99] Ibid. See also Crawford 1977, p. 112.

[100] Ibid.; Raic 2002, pp. 60–61.

[101] ICJ, North Sea Continental Shelf Cases (*Federal Republic of Germany/Denmark; Federal Republic of Germany/Netherlands*), 20 February 1969, ICJ Reports 1969 at p. 3 (North Sea Continental Shelf Cases), para 46. More than 50% of international boundaries are undefined. See Schabas 2011, p. 83.

[102] Raic 2002, p. 60.

[103] Ibid., p. 62.

[104] Crawford 1977, pp. 117, 119.

[105] Mendes 2010.

Palestine has an authority that discharges legislative, executive and judicial duties. It also has undisputed power to administer Gaza and parts of the West Bank. From 1988 onwards, the PLO, led by Yasser Arafat and then later on by Mahmud Abbas, served as a government. This political body administered portion of the occupied Palestine as well as the whole populace of the territory and provided social and administrative services. After the political split within the Palestine Liberation Organisation, Hamas unilaterally ruled occupied Gaza from 2007 until it signed a reconciliation agreement to form a unified government with Fatah in 2014.[106] For the most part of the Palestinian history, the Palestinian leadership did not have control over external security and full foreign diplomatic autonomy. However, lack of power over these areas does not necessarily defeat statehood.[107]

Capacity to Enter into Relations: There is a debate whether this last criterion for statehood is evidence or a consequence of statehood, or rather a criterion or a condition for statehood.[108] In any case, this capacity could not be one of the significant criteria since treaty-making competence, as one of the main manifestation of this capacity, is also held by international organisations.[109] In *Calgar and others v. Billingham*[110] it was held as follows:

> If the existence of (diplomatic) relations with other States is mandatory for the existence of statehood, this would necessarily imply that without such relations the entity is not a State. This in turn would mean that under such circumstances the recognition of that entity (for the purpose of establishing relations) would be premature and without object. It is clear that such reasoning (which is in its foundations nothing more than a plea in favour of the constitutive theory on recognition) leads to a vicious circle because it confuses a condition for statehood with a (most likely) consequence of statehood. It must, therefore, be rejected.

Since the declaration of Palestine's independence up to the time the 2009 *ad hoc* declaration was made, more than 90 States have recognised Palestine.[111] One of the legal functions of recognition—the first being the evidential value of statehood discussed under this chapter—is its 'constitutive' result of furnishing a background for the establishment of diplomatic relations and treaty making power. Palestine

---

[106] Although the first official reconciliation agreement between the two political parties was signed in April 2014, an effective unification deal between Fatah and Hamas was made in October 2017. See P. Beaumont, Palestinian unity government of Fatah and Hamas sworn in, The Guardian, 2 June 2014; M. Hossain, Are Fatah and Hamas United for the Sake of Peace?, The Jerusalem Post, 30 October 2017.

[107] Worster 2010, p. 1168.

[108] Grant quotes Crawford who writes 'Capacity is not a criterion but rather a consequence of Statehood and one which is not constant but depends on the status and situation of a particular States'. On a similar note, he refers to Detter's argument that notes that capacity is a criterion rather than a condition of Statehood. See Crawford 1990, p. 309; Grant 1999, p. 435.

[109] Ibid.

[110] United Kingdom Special Commissioners of Income Tax, *Caglar v. Billingham (Inspector of Taxes) and related appeals*, Special Commissioner's Decision, [1996] STC (SCD) 150, 7 March 1996, para 182. See also Warbrick 1996.

[111] Crawford 1990, p. 309.

was admitted to the League of Arab States[112] and has signed several international instruments. Trade and investment treaties with the United States and the European Union are some of them. Treaties on rail way and maritime cooperation were also accepted for deposit by the UN Secretary General,[113] indicating an organisational machinery 'capable of and authorized to' sign binding international legal documents.[114]

On the contrary, Palestine was denied admission to the Food and Agriculture Organization, World Health Organization and other UN agencies.[115] Similarly, following Palestine's application for UN membership, the Security Council failed to recommend Palestine to the General Assembly due to the US's opposition.[116] Even if these aforementioned restrictions on 'capacity to enter into relation' do not totally refute the international legal personality of Palestine, they make its status, under the criteria of the Montevideo Convention, slightly uncertain.

3.5.1.3 Theories of State Recognition

State practice has so far shown that entities have been recognised as States notwithstanding the non-satisfaction of the Montevideo criteria. Bosnia Herzegovina, for instance, has been recognised although it did not meet the criteria.[117] On the other hand, Somaliland's recognition has been withheld though it satisfied the criteria. On the basis of this and other examples, some scholars suggest that the Montevideo criteria possess only of limited degree of influence compared to the effects of recognition on emerging States.[118]

Concerning the legal nature and effects of recognition, there are two irreconcilable positions. On the one side there are those who hold the view that recognition

---

[112] BBC News, Timeline: Arab League, 15 November 2011.

[113] Worster 2010, pp. 1169–1172.

[114] Raic 2002, p. 74.

[115] WHO 1989a, p. 1; WHO, State of Palestine Application for Membership in the World Health Organization, 1 April 1989, UN Doc. WHA42.1. See also WHO 1989b.

[116] With regard to admission of States to the UN, the ICJ has ruled that political considerations should not be criteria for judgment, and that decisions should not be conditional on intentions unrelated to the issue under consideration. Such stance amounts to an abuse of power and a breach to the legal obligation as the responsible State is 'not juridically entitled to make its consent to the admission dependent on conditions not expressly provided' under the UN Charter. See Security Council Fails to Adopt Text Demanding That Israel Halt Settlement Activity as Permanent Member Casts Negative Vote, SC/10178, Security Council 6484th Meeting, 18 February 2011, http://www.un.org/press/en/2011/sc10178.doc.htm (accessed 23 April 2016). See also ICJ, Advisory opinion: Conditions of Admission of a State to Membership in the United Nations (Article 4 of the Charter), 28 May 1948, para 57; and Al Zoughbi 2013, p. 166.

[117] Turk 1993, p. 69.

[118] Crawford 1990, p. 309; Vidmar 2013, p. 241.

by other States is simply a declaration of the recognising State's willingness to engage in diplomatic relations with the emerging State, which should meet the factual objective statehood criteria (declaratory theory). And on the other, there are those who take the view that it is recognition that constitutes or creates new States and without which any entity could not be considered as such by other States (constitutive theory).[119]

As a yardstick to determine statehood, the declaratory theory comprises the Montevideo established normative guidelines and the retroactive recognition by other States of the confirmation of those guidelines. On the basis of this theory, concluding that a Palestinian State exists may not, in view of the accounts discussed above, pose a significant challenge as the generally accepted factual elements as well as the grants of recognition are satisfied.

With regard to the application of the constitutive theory as well, due to the significant number of States recognising Palestine, one could affirmatively conclude that Palestine qualifies for statehood. Crawford, however, rightly argues that the constitutive theory leads to an inescapable 'extreme subjectivity in the notion of the State'.[120] International law does not provide a rule that makes the recognition of the majority of the international community binding on third States. Although over 100 States have recognised Palestine until 2012, in the absence of such a rule, he argues that those States which do not recognise Palestine, such as United States and Israel, could not be bound by the 'statehood' of Palestine 'created' by the majority's recognition. Despite the inconsistencies that may follow, as the issue at hand focuses on the abstract statehood of Palestine, the theory could be applied to reflect the stance of the majority of States on the statehood of Palestine.[121]

In another sense of the term, although other States' recognition of Palestine does not bind Israel, it could be argued that Israel, on another occasion, has tacitly recognised a Palestinian State. On the basis of the premise that recognition is an international acceptance of the existence of a State by another, it could be concluded that Israel would not have asked for Palestine's recognition of Israel's statehood as a pretext for negotiations had Israel not considered Palestine as an entity with an international legal personality.[122] Despite the stance of Israel, the fact that more than 100 States recognised Palestine by 2012[123] supports the abstract statehood of Palestine.[124]

---

[119] Crawford 1990, p. 309; Raic 2002, p. 28; Quigley 2002, pp. 42 et seq.

[120] Crawford 1990, p. 309; Raic 2002, pp. 28 et seq.

[121] Crawford 1990, p. 309; Quigley 2002, p. 42.

[122] Crawford 1990, p. 309.

[123] The discussion is limited to the State recognitions made by 2012 mainly because the Prosecutor's decision on the *ad hoc* declaration and its implied ruling on Palestine's statehood relied on events that happened on and before 2012.

[124] Quigley 2002, pp. 42 et seq.

3.5.1.4 Palestine as an Occupied Territory

Consequent to the second Arab-Israel war (see Sect. 2.3.1), Israel is considered as occupying the Palestinian territories. Under international humanitarian law, a belligerent occupation is presumed in the context of an occupation of the territory of a Sovereign State.[125] In December 2001, the contracting parties to Geneva Convention IV have also confirmed unanimously the applicability of the Convention to the Palestinian occupied territory.[126] In light of the rules of the Geneva Convention, Israel has also proclaimed its intention to apply the humanitarian provisions of the laws of occupation in the occupied territories. Israel does not officially claim sovereignty over the occupied territories and Palestinians domiciled in the occupied Palestinian territories are not considered nationals of Israel.[127] If a sovereign nation was absent in the occupied territories, there would have been no issue of belligerent occupation.[128] Thus, as occupation does not affect sovereignty, it would be difficult to conclude that international law allowed an anomalous position of 'occupied but stateless territory'.[129]

3.5.1.5 Conclusion on the Abstract Statehood of Palestine

The historical and political background of Palestine does not warrant a conclusive stance on its statehood. Based on the declaration of independence and State

[125] Common Article 2 of Geneva Convention Relative to the Protection of Civilian Persons in Time of War, signed 12 August 1949, 75 UNTS 287 (entered into force 21 October 1950) (Geneva Convention IV) states '… [T]he Convention shall also apply to all cases of partial or total occupation of the territory of a High Contracting Party, even if the said occupation meets with no armed resistance…'. Article 42 of Hague Convention (IV) Respecting the Laws and Customs of War on Land and Its Annex: Regulations Concerning the Laws and Customs of War on Land, 18 October 1907 (entered into force 26 January 1910) (Hague Regulations) states, '[T]erritory is considered occupied when it is actually placed under the authority of the hostile army…the occupation extends only to the territory where such authority has been established and can be exercised'. See also S. Adem (2015), above n. 42.

[126] The Geneva Conventions and the Israeli occupation of Palestine, Fact Sheet Series no. 1 (2004) 1, https://d3n8a8pro7vhmx.cloudfront.net/cjpme/pages/2110/attachments/original/1470164694/01-En-Conventions-Factsheet.pdf?1470164694 (accessed 22 April 2016).

[127] Quigley 2002, p. 46. In February 2017, the Israeli Knesset passed a bill named 'The Regularization Law' or 'The Expropriation Law'. The bill is the first of its kind to retroactively legalize the expropriation of Palestinian-owned land. It aims to legitimize the land already occupied by settlers in parts of the West Bank. So far, it has not obtained endorsements from the Israeli Attorney General or the Prime Minister. Nonetheless, the bill remains one of the first laws that show Israel's effort to exercise sovereignty over parts of the OPT. See J. Reed, New Israeli law Retroactively Legalises Settlements, Financial Times, 6 February 2017.

[128] S. Adem (2015), above n. 42.

[129] Quigley 2002, p. 46; R. Sherman, Caught in limbo: the Palestinian Authority and the misunderstood state in international law (Unpublished thesis, University of Otago, 2005), pp. 52–53. For an opposing view, see Ash 2009, p. 199.

recognition, as well as the legal status of Palestine as an occupied State, one could reach the conclusion that Palestine enjoys at least an international legal personality similar to any other State. Nonetheless, the fact that there are some uncertainties in regard to Palestine's satisfaction of the Montevideo criteria and that up to the time the Registrar of the ICC received the *ad hoc* declaration certain international organisations, including in the negotiations of plenipotentiaries of the Rome Statute, failed to treat it as a State indicates the otherwise.

3.5.2 The Functional Approach: Statehood for the Purposes of Ad hoc *Declarations*

Apart from general considerations on the statehood of Palestine, the question of statehood in the context of the ICC is decisive for this study. The Palestinian declaration was lodged pursuant to Article 12(3) of the Rome Statute headed 'pre-conditions to the exercise of jurisdiction'.[130] Considering the object and purpose of the Statute in general and the provision in particular, at the stage of preliminary examination, it is crucial to examine whether the statutory requirements or the conditions necessary for exercising the Court's jurisdiction are fulfilled. The ICC functions on a delegated jurisdiction. This necessitates a determination on the international legal personality of Palestine and its ability or inability to temporarily delegate a criminal jurisdiction to the ICC. Since criminal jurisdiction is an inherent exhibit of sovereignty and the resultant statehood, an interpretation of the word 'State' for the purpose of the Court is essential.

According to Article 31(1) of the Vienna Convention on the Law of Treaties, 'a treaty shall be interpreted in good faith in accordance with the ordinary meaning to be given to the terms of the treaty in their context and in light of its object and purpose'. The word 'State' under the Rome Statute has no clear definition in public international law. Hence, it requires an interpretation most suited to fulfil the object and purpose of the Statute. This teleological approach or functional interpretation is frequent in many international Conventions, and is expressed with phrases such as 'for the purpose of this Convention' or 'for the present Convention'.[131] In contrast to the generic ones, such functional approaches are most favoured since they ensure broad and effective implementation of the instruments and help actualize the object and purpose of the same.

---

[130] Rome Statute, above n. 4, Article 12(3).

[131] See, among others, Article 1 of UNGA, Convention on the Law of the Sea, 10 December 1982, 1833 UNTS 3 (entered into force 16 November 1994); and Article 2 of Vienna Convention, above n. 41. See also Pellet 2012, p. 412.

In the case *French Republic v. Commission*,[132] entertained by the European Court of Justice, the Advocate General stated:

> The concept of the State has to be understood in the sense most appropriate to the provision in question and to their objectives; the Court rightly follows a functional approach, basing its interpretation on the scheme and objective of the provisions within which the concept features.

In the decision 'Reparation for Injuries Suffered in the Service of the UN', the ICJ has used a similar approach.[133] Dealing with the issue of legal personality of the UN to claim reparations for damages caused, the Court argued as follows:

> [T]he subjects of the law ... are not necessarily identical in their nature or in the extent of their right ... Throughout its history, the development of international law has been influenced by the requirements of international life and the progressive increase in the collective activities of States has already given rise to instances of action upon the international plane by certain entities which are not States. But to achieve the ends (of the entities)... attribution of international personality is indispensable.

In light of the ICJ's stance on legal personality as reflected in the 'reparations case', Palestine was allowed to participate and submit written contributions in the ICJ Wall case. The Court employed a functional approach as the ascertainment of the entities statehood was viewed irrelevant for the functions of the institution and the case at hand.[134]

Similarly, in the *Tadić* case the Appeals Chamber of the ICTY indicated that due to the absence of an integrated judicial system and the self-containment of Tribunals in the international field, unlike in the domestic law context, a narrow concept of jurisdiction may not exist in international law.[135] As can be gathered from the opinion of the Court, the development of international law necessitates granting legal personalities to entities that may not qualify as States in the traditional sense.[136] On this point Dupuy states that due to this opinion of the Court 'various entities can be granted personality without this constituting a crime against sovereignty'.[137]

The Rome Statute was adopted in order to establish individual criminal liability for 'the most serious crimes of concern to the international community'.[138] As a treaty body, the Court functions on a consent based delegated jurisdiction with the resolve of ending impunity and guaranteeing international justice. Taking into consideration the Court's vocation for universality, Article 12(3), in particular, was

---

[132] The European Court, *French Republic v. Commission of the European Communities*, Opinion of the Advocate General, 13 December 2001, C-482/99, paras 55–56. See also Pellet 2012, p. 413.

[133] ICJ, Advisory opinion: Reparation of Injuries Suffered in Service of the UN, 11 April 1949, ICJ Reports 1949 at p. 174, para 178.

[134] ICJ Advisory opinion 2004, above n. 93; Shany 2012, p. 502.

[135] *Tadić* 1995, above n. 52, para 11. See also Aksar 2004, p. 35.

[136] See also Ibid.

[137] See Dupuy as quoted in Pellet 2012, p. 412.

[138] Rome Statute, above n. 4, Preamble, para 10.

adopted to set the statutory requirements for extending the jurisdictional outreach of the Court.[139] As such, the extension of jurisdiction is dependent on the sovereign discretion of a 'State' that is capable of delegating criminal jurisdiction to the Court. With this object and purpose in mind, the pertinent question is whether Palestine could effectively delegate a criminal jurisdiction to the ICC and satisfy the Statehood requirement for the purposes of the *ad hoc* declaration.

Although the decision of the Prosecutor did not raise the effects of the Oslo Accords on Palestine's ability to delegate criminal jurisdiction, much has been said about the restrictive effects of the Accords.[140] Shany, who otherwise has argued in favour of a flexible and functional interpretation of the term 'State', argues, based on the Oslo Accords, that the Palestinian Authority's attempt to delegate criminal jurisdiction to the Court in excess of the legal power it possesses is an act of *ultra vires*.[141] Similarly, Shaw concludes that the Palestinian Authority does not have all the 'rights and competences' it purports to delegate to the ICC, hence, it 'lacks the capacity to lodge declarations'.[142]

As a matter of fact, Article 1 of the 1995 Interim Accords (Oslo II) limits the Palestinian Authority's criminal jurisdiction to offences committed by 'Palestinians and/or non-Israelis' and excludes criminal jurisdiction over offences committed by Israeli nationals and over crimes committed in Area C in the West Bank.[143] Furthermore, Article IX(5) restricts the Palestinian Authority's power to engage in foreign relations only to economic, cultural, scientific and educational matters. The vagueness of the provisions and the frequent violations of the Accords by the two parties may give rise to issues on the authority of the Accords to create legal obligation. However, evidently, the Palestinian Authority's legal powers were first 'created and defined' by the Accords.[144] It follows that, be it a representative of a State or a quasi-State, the Palestinian Authority could not effectively delegate power it willingly forgone to Israel in an international agreement.[145] The reading of Article 98 of the Rome Statute, moreover, suggests the need to act in consistent to and in compliance with international law, 'State or diplomatic immunity of a person or property of a third State' and obligations under international agreements.[146] Based on these premises, one may argue that the Palestinian Authority cannot validly delegate jurisdiction to the ICC.

139 Triffterer and Ambos 2016, p. 684.

140 Kontorovich 2013, p. 1; Shany 2012, pp. 506–509.; Shaw 2011, pp. 319–320.

141 Shany 2012, pp. 506–509.

142 Shaw 2011, pp. 319–320.

143 Interim Agreement on the West Bank and the Gaza Strip, signed 28 September 1995 (Oslo II).

144 See Oslo II, above n. 143, Articles 1–9. It has to be noted that the Palestinian Authority constitutes members authorized by the PLO and was led by the head of the PLO, Yasser Arafat.

145 Shany 2012, pp. 506–509.

146 See Rome Statute, above n. 4, Article 98.

Nevertheless, provisions of international agreements cannot stand in contravention of customary international law, much less *jus cogens*.[147] The core crimes under the Rome Statute are serious breaches of international humanitarian law that also fall within the grave breaches regime of the Geneva Conventions. They are offences the prohibitions of which constitute a rule of *jus cogens* and their prosecution or extradition mandatory (principle of *Aut Dedere Aut Judicare*).[148] The implication of their status as *jus cogens* is that the duty to either prosecute or extradite cannot be abrogated by bilateral or multilateral treaties.[149] Palestine, as a holder of a territorial title over the territories within the 1967 borders and Israel as a signatory to the Geneva Conventions and the UN Charter, have duties under these legal regimes. Hence, the Accords could not be raised against a delegation of a criminal jurisdiction to the possible prosecution of these international crimes.

The Gaza Strip, arguably until the 2005 disengagement of Israel,[150] East Jerusalem and the West Bank are internationally recognised as occupied territories within the ambit of Geneva Convention IV.[151] As stipulated under Article 64 of Geneva Convention IV and Article 43 of the Hague Regulations, Israel as an occupying power may only administer the occupied land in the context of the existing laws and in light of rules of international human rights protection. The occupying power shall not enact rules not justified by military security or public order and could not repeal the national laws or its penal jurisdiction unless there is a

---

[147] Article 53 of the Vienna Convention reads:

> A treaty is void if, at the time of its conclusion, it conflicts with a peremptory norm of general international law. For the purposes of the present Convention, a peremptory norm of general international law is a norm accepted and recognized by the international community of States as a whole as a norm from which no derogation is permitted and which can be modified only by a subsequent norm of general international law having the same character.

Furthermore, Article 64 makes void any treaty that is in contravention of peremptory norm. See Vienna Convention, above n. 41, Articles 53 and 64; and North Sea Continental Shelf Cases, above n. 101, para 182. See also Kearny and Dalton 1970, pp. 495, 535; Linderfalk 2011, pp. 360 et seq.; McGregor 2006, p. 437.

[148] With regard to the use of customary international law to interpret the core crimes of the ICC Statute see Grover 2014, p. 221.

[149] Bassiouni and Wise 1995, p. 52.

[150] Israel Minister of Foreign Affairs, Israel's Disengagement from Gaza and North Samaria (2005), http://mfa.gov.il/MFA/AboutIsrael/Maps/Pages/Israels%20Disengagement%20Plan-%202005.aspx (accessed 12 April 2016); J. Morley, Israeli Withdrawal From Gaza Explained, The Washington Post, 10 August 2005; Peters 2010, p. 33.

[151] See UNSC 1967, 1973. See also Geneva Convention IV, above n. 125, Common Article 2. In December 2001, the contracting parties to Geneva Convention IV reaffirmed the applicability of the convention to the Palestinian Territories occupied by Israel. See ICRC, Press release: Conference of High Contracting Parties to the Fourth Geneva Convention, 5 December 2001, https://www.icrc.org/eng/resources/documents/statement/57jrgw.htm.

threat to the security of the occupying power.[152] Article 47 of Geneva Convention IV, in particular, provides that the occupying power could not in any manner deprive the occupied people the benefits of the Convention by introducing new changes or 'by any agreement concluded between the authorities of the occupied territories and the occupied power'.[153] Hence, considering these established principles of the Convention, many of the important provisions of the Oslo Accords, including those that limit the criminal jurisdiction of Palestine as well as its foreign relations, are in violation of these provisions and consequently *void ab initio*.[154]

The Palestinian *ad hoc* declaration was lodged by an authority that exercises criminal jurisdiction over the relevant territories. There is no competing sovereignty claim or prosecutorial conflict between Israel and Palestine on territories under the administration of the Palestinian Authority.[155] Thus, having in mind the undisputed territorial jurisdiction over these territories, and in the absence of any prohibitive rule of international law to exercise jurisdiction,[156] the Palestinian Authority can effectively delegate its criminal jurisdiction to the ICC.

Furthermore, State centrism in international law is mainly employed on the assumption that all non-State entities are represented directly or indirectly.[157] An approach which may leave certain categories of people in a 'legal void' shall not be upheld. In the ICJ case of *Portugal v. Australia*,[158] concerning the necessity for the representation of East Timor, Judge Weeramantry argued that:[159]

> [a]ny other view would result in the anomalous situation of the current international system leaving a territory and a people, who admittedly have important rights opposable to all the world, defenceless and voiceless [...]

Viewing the concept of the State as an abstract entity—especially in international instruments dealing with human rights, humanitarian law and in this particular case, international criminal law—conceals the 'real nature of the State as an institution of society' and individuals as the ultimate subjects of the law.[160] Hence,

---

152 Geneva Convention IV, above n. 125, Article 64; The Hague Regulations above n. 125, Article 43. See also Gasser 1995, p. 27.

153 Geneva Convention IV, above n. 125, Article 47. See also Gowlland-Debbas 2012, p. 524.

154 Resolution 34/70 of the General Assembly has also stated that any 'partial agreement or separate treaty which purports to determine the future of the Palestinian territories occupied by Israel since 1967 in violation of their rights to self-determination' would not have any valid effect. See UNGA 1979, Gowlland-Debbas 2012, p. 524.

155 Quigley 2002, pp. 44–46.

156 Permanent Court of International Justice, *S.S. Lotus, France v. Turkey*, Judgment, 7 September 1927, 1927 PCIJ Series A no. 10, paras 45–47.

157 Sherman 2005, above n. 129, p. 54.

158 ICJ, Case Concerning East Timor (*Portugal v. Australia*), Judgment, 30 June 1995, [1995] ICJ Rep 90 (Case Concerning East Timor).

159 Case Concerning East Timor, above n. 158, Judge Weeramantry, Separate Opinion, para 181.

160 Sherman 2005, above n. 129, p. 54.

the functional interpretation of the provision, as well as the jurisprudence surrounding the issue, supports the interpretation of the term to include Palestine as qualifying to submit *ad hoc* declarations.

3.6 Subsequent Developments

In December 2012, seven months after the decision of the then Prosecutor on the first Palestine *ad hoc* declaration was made public, the UN General Assembly granted Palestine a non-member observer State status.[161] With regard to this 'accrued status', Prosecutor Bensouda published an op-ed in the British daily newspaper The Guardian, indicating that while this new status could not 'retroactively validate the previously invalid 2009 declaration, Palestine could now join the Rome Statute'.[162] The statehood of Palestine appears to be settled, at least, for the purposes of the Court. Nonetheless, Ocampo's approach to the 2009 declaration and what appears to be an endorsement of that decision by Prosecutor Bensouda shows a precedent in development. Such a precedent, as argued in this chapter, may not be inclusive of social realities, the aims of establishing justice and advancing human dignity, and may not attain the essence and purpose of the statute in general.

3.7 Chapter Summary

The 2009 Palestinian *ad hoc* declaration has given rise to discussions on the legal regime governing the temporary delegation of jurisdiction. Although an abstract determination on the statehood of the entity making the declaration is not indispensable, the discussions on the 2009 Palestinian *ad hoc* declaration have mainly focused on the Palestinian statehood. Even if a determination of statehood involves political considerations, there is no procedure in the Rome Statute or the Rules of Evidence and Procedure that suggests calling on the UN and the Assembly of States Parties. The route the prosecutor has taken and the decision he reached disregard the legal aspects of the issue that could be settled within the institutions of the Court. In the absence of any other State claiming to represent a certain entity and when the issue concerns the protection of human rights and humanitarian law, an entity does not necessarily have to possess the traditional abstract 'qualities' of a State. A general exclusion of such entities from the international arena is contrary not only to the egalitarian understanding of international law in general, but also to the

[161] UNGA 2012.

[162] F. Bensouda, The truth about the ICC and Gaza, *The Guardian*, 29 August 2014.

specific purposes of these instruments. Hence, focus should rest on the approach which best serves the purposes of the instruments in question, and the overriding human and democratic values.

References

Aksar Y (2004) Implementing international humanitarian law: From the ad hoc tribunals to a permanent International Criminal Court. Routledge, London.

Al Zoughbi (2013) The de jure State of Palestine under belligerent occupation: Application for admission to the United Nations. In: Qafisheh M (ed) Palestine membership in the United Nations: Legal and practical implications. Cambridge Scholars Publishing, New Castle, pp. 162–186.

Ambos K (2016) Treaties on international criminal law: International criminal procedure, vol. 3. Oxford University Press, Oxford.

Amerasinghe C (2003) Jurisdiction of international tribunals. Kluwer Law International, The Hague.

Amnesty International (2012) Amnesty International's response to the ICC Office of the Prosecutor's statement that it cannot investigate crimes committed during the Gaza conflict. https://www.amnesty.ca/news/news-item/ai039s-response-to-icc-prosecutor039s-decision-not-to-investigate-crimes-during-gaza-. Accessed 17 February 2016.

Ash R (2009) Is Palestine a 'state'? A response to Professor John Quigley's article 'The Palestine declaration to the International Criminal Court: the statehood issue'. Rutgers Law Records 36:182–201.

ASP (2009) Delegations to the second resumption of the seventh session of the Assembly of States Parties to the Rome Statute of the International Criminal Court, 9–13 February 2009, UN Doc. ICC-ASP/7/INF.1/Add.2.

Azarova V (2013) Tell it to the judge: Palestine's UN bid and the International Criminal Court. In: Qafisheh M (ed) Palestine membership in the United Nations: Legal and practical implications. Cambridge Scholars Publishing, New Castle, pp. 252–267.

Bassiouni M, Wise E (1995) Aut dedere aut judicare: The duty to extradite or prosecute in international law. Martinus Nijhoff Publishers, Dordrecht.

Boas G (2007) The Milosevic trial: Lessons for the conduct of complex international criminal proceedings. Cambridge University Press, Cambridge.

Boyle F (1990) The creation of the state of Palestine. EJIL 1:301–306.

Chazournes L (2011) The principle of compétence de la compétence in international adjudication and its role in an era of multiplication of courts and tribunals. In: Arsanjani M et al (eds) Looking to the future: Essays on international law in Honor of W. Michael Reisman. Martinus Nijhoff Publishers, Boston, pp. 1027–1064.

Crawford J (1977) The criteria for statehood in international law. British Yearbook of International Law 48(1): 93–182.

Crawford J (1990) The creation of the state of Palestine: Too much too soon? EJIL 1:307–313.

El Zeidy M (2015) Ad hoc declarations of acceptance of jurisdiction: The Palestinian situation under scrutiny. In: Stahn C (ed) The law and practice of the International Criminal Court. Oxford University Press, Oxford, pp. 179–209.

Gaillard E, Savage J (eds) (1999) Fouchard, Gaillard, Goldman on international commercial arbitration. Kluwer Law, The Hague.

Gasser H (1995) Protection of the civilian population. In: Fleck D (ed) The handbook of humanitarian law in armed conflicts. Oxford University Press, Oxford, pp. 209–292.

Gowlland-Debbas V (2012) Note on the legal effects of Palestine's declaration under Article 12(3) of the ICC Statute. In: Meloni C, Tognoni G (eds) Is There a Court for Gaza? A Test Bench for International Justice. T.M.C. Asser Press, The Hague, pp. 513–524.
Grant T (1999) Defining statehood: The Montevideo Convention and its discontents. Columbia Journal of Transnational Law 37:403–457.
Grover L (2014) Interpreting crimes in the Rome Statute of the International Criminal Court. Cambridge University Press, Cambridge.
Guilfoyle D (2106) International criminal law. Oxford University Press, Oxford.
Kaul H (2002) Preconditions for the exercise of jurisdiction. In: Cassese A, Gaeta P, Jones JRWD (eds) The Rome Statute of the International Criminal Court: A commentary, vol 1. Oxford University Press, Oxford, pp. 583–616.
Kearney M (2012) Why statehood now: A reflection on the ICC's impact on Palestine's engagement with international law. In: Meloni C, Tognoni G (eds) Is There a Court for Gaza? A Test Bench for International Justice. T.M.C. Asser Press, The Hague, pp. 391–407.
Kearny R, Dalton R (1970) The treaty on treaties. American Journal of International Law 64:495–561.
Kontorovich E (2013) Jurisdiction over Israeli settlement activity in the International Criminal Court. Northwestern Law & Econ Research Paper 13–10.
Linderfalk U (2011) The creation of jus cogens – Making sense of Article 53 of the Vienna Convention. Max Planck Institute for Comparative Public Law and International Law 71:359–378.
Materu S (2015) The post-election violence in Kenya: Domestic and international legal responses. T.M.C. Asser Press, The Hague.
McGregor L (2006) State immunity jus cogens. ICLQ 55:437–446.
Mendes E (2010) Statehood and Palestine for the purposes of Article 12(3) of the ICC Statute: A contrary perspective. https://www.icc-cpi.int/NR/rdonlyres/D3C77FA6-9DEE-45B1-ACC0-B41706BB41E5/281876/OTPErrolMendesNewSTATEHOODANDPALESTINEFORTHEPURPOS.pdf. Accessed 17 February 2016.
OTP (2013) Policy paper on preliminary examinations.
OTP (2014) Policy paper on preliminary examinations.
OTP (2015) Policy paper on preliminary examinations.
Palestinian National Authority (2009) Declaration recognizing the jurisdiction of the International Criminal Court.
Palestine National Council (1988) Political communique and declaration of independence.
Pellet A (2012) The effects of Palestine's recognition of the International Criminal Court's jurisdiction. In: Meloni C, Tognoni G (eds) Is There a Court for Gaza? A Test Bench for International Justice. T.M.C. Asser Press, The Hague, pp. 409–428.
Peters J (2010) The Gaza disengagement: Five years later. Israel Journal of Foreign Affairs 3:33–44.
Quigley J (2002) Palestine: The issue of statehood. In: Silverburg S (ed) Palestine and international law: Essays on politics and economics. McFarland & Company, Inc., Jefferson, North Carolina, pp. 37–54.
Quigley J (2012) The Palestine declaration to the International Criminal Court: The statehood issue. In: Meloni C, Tognoni G (eds) Is There a Court for Gaza? A Test Bench for International Justice. T.M.C. Asser Press, The Hague, pp. 429–439.
Quigley J (2016) Palestine is a state so the consent declaration is a valid basis for investigation by the ICC. In: Steinberg R (ed) Contemporary issues facing the International Criminal Court. Brill Nijhoff, Boston, pp. 39–50.
Raic D (2002) Statehood and the law of self-determination. Kluwer Law International, The Hague.
Republic of Côte d'Ivoire (2003) Declaration accepting the jurisdiction of the International Criminal Court. https://www.icc-cpi.int/NR/rdonlyres/57B00915-8FDF-4532-9BDE-8AF338E3E364/279844/ICDEENG7.pdf. Accessed 13 February 2016.

Republic of Côte d'Ivoire (2010) Confirmation de la declaration de reconnaissance [confirmation of the declaration of jurisdiction]. https://www.icc-cpi.int/NR/rdonlyres/498E8FEB-7A72-4005-A209-C14BA374804F/0/ReconCPI.pdf. Accessed 13 February 2016.
Schabas W (2010) The International Criminal Court: A Commentary on the Rome Statute. Oxford University Press, Oxford.
Schabas W (2011) An introduction to the International Criminal Court, 4th edn. Cambridge University Press, Cambridge.
Schabas W (2014) Selecting situations and cases. In: Stahn C (ed) The law and practice of the International Criminal Court. Oxford University Press, Oxford, pp. 365–381.
Shany Y (2012) In defence of functional interpretation of Article 12(3): A response to Yael Ronen. In: Meloni C, Tognoni G (eds) Is There a Court for Gaza? A Test Bench for International Justice. T.M.C. Asser Press, The Hague, pp. 497–511.
Shaw M (2011) The Article 12(3) Declaration of the Palestinian Authority, the International Criminal Court and International Law. JICJ 9:319–324.
Smet S (2009) A structural analysis of the role of the Pre-Trial Chamber in the fact-finding process of the ICC. In: Stahn C, Sluiter G (eds) The emerging practice of the International Criminal Court. Martinus Nijhoff, Boston, pp. 405–440.
Stegmiller I (2011) The pre-investigation stage of the ICC: Criteria for situation selection. Duncker & Humblot, Berlin.
Triffterer O, Ambos K (eds) (2016) The Rome Statute of the International Criminal Court, 3rd edn. Hart Publishing, Munich.
Turk D (1993) Recognition of states: A comment. EJIL 4:66–74.
UN Diplomatic Conference of Plenipotentiaries on the Establishment of an International Criminal Court (2002) Summary records of the plenary meetings and of the meetings of the committee of the whole, vol. 2. United Nations, New York.
UNGA (1947) Resolution 181 (II), UN Doc. A/RES/181(II).
UNGA (1979) Resolution 34/70, UN Doc. A/RES/34/70.
UNGA (1988) Resolution 43/177, UN Doc. A/RES/43/177.
UNGA (2012) Resolution 67/19, UN Doc. A/RES/67/19.
UNSC (1948) Official Records, 383rd Meeting, 2 December 1948, UN Doc. S/PV.383.
UNSC (1967) Resolution 242, UN Doc. S/RES/242.
UNSC (1973) Resolution 338, UN Doc. S/RES/338242.
Vagias M (2014) The Territorial Jurisdiction of the International Criminal Court. Cambridge University Press, Cambridge.
Vidmar J (2013) Democratic statehood in international law: The emergence of new states in post-Cold War practice. Hart Publishing, Oxford.
Warbrick C (1996) Unrecognized states and liability for income tax. International and Comparative Law Quarterly 45:954–960.
WHO (1989a) 42nd World Health Assembly, Geneva, 8–19 May 1989: Resolutions and decisions, annexes. WHO, Geneva.
WHO (1989b) Request of Palestine for admission as a member of the World Health Organization, A 42/Conf. Paper No. 1 Rev. 1, World Health Organization, 11 May 1989.
Worster W (2010) The exercise of jurisdiction by the International Criminal Court over Palestine. American University International Law Review 26:1153–1209.

Chapter 4
Pre-Investigation Considerations

Contents

Abstract Following the submission of the second Palestinian ad hoc declaration in 2014, the Office of the Prosecutor opened a preliminary examination into the situation in Palestine. During preliminary examinations, the Prosecutor employs a four-tier filtering mechanism to determine whether the examination could proceed into investigation or not. The examination on the situation in Palestine, similar to others, requires a determination on issues of jurisdiction, admissibility and interest of justice. This chapter, therefore, examines these issues in light of, among others, the practice of the Office of the Prosecutor and the Rome Statute. In view of the situation in Palestine, it covers temporal, material, territorial and personal jurisdiction, followed by a discussion of the fundamental concepts of complementarity and gravity to determine the admissibility of potential cases before the International Criminal Court. Similar to other considerations, the chapter concludes that the last pre-investigation consideration, namely 'interest of justice', is also satisfied in the context of Palestine.

Keywords Admissibility · complementarity · interest of justice · temporal jurisdiction · preliminary examination · situation in Palestine

© T.M.C. ASSER PRESS and the author 2019

S. H. Adem, *Palestine and the International Criminal Court*, International Criminal Justice Series 21,
https://doi.org/10.1007/978-94-6265-291-0_4

4.1 Introductory Remarks

On 31 December 2014, Palestine lodged its second *ad hoc* declaration and accepted the jurisdiction of the ICC for alleged crimes committed in the Occupied Palestinian Territory, including East Jerusalem, since 13 June 2014.[1] In addition, it also deposited an instrument of accession to the Rome Statute.[2] The respective representatives of the two international bodies, i.e., the Registrar of the ICC and the Secretary General of the UN, acknowledged the moves.

Upon the receipt of the declaration, the Office of the Prosecutor opened a preliminary examination to establish whether there is a reasonable ground to open an investigation into the situation in Palestine.[3] In her reports on preliminary examination activities, the Prosecutor has indicated that her office is 'in the process of conducting a thorough factual and legal assessment of the information available' to 'establish whether there is a reasonable basis to believe that crimes within the jurisdiction of the Court have been or are being committed'.[4]

In earlier precedents, the enabling Statutes for prosecuting crimes under international law, namely the International Military Tribunal at Nuremberg and Tokyo, had a pre-determined focus and target, namely the major war criminals of the Axis power.[5] Similarly, in the case of the International Criminal Tribunal for the Former Yugoslavia and the International Criminal Tribunal for Rwanda and other Tribunals such as the Special Court for Sierra Leone, the Extraordinary Chambers in Cambodia and the Special Tribunal for Lebanon, choosing the specific cases for prosecution within the limited territorial jurisdiction of the specific Court was left to the discretion of the Prosecutor.[6]

Different from these experiments, the constituting material of the ICC does not on its own serve as 'trigger'.[7] The jurisdiction of the Court has to be triggered by one of the following three mechanisms: State party referral, Security Council referral or a *proprio motu* decision by the Prosecutor.[8] Once jurisdiction is triggered,

---

[1] ICC, Press release: Palestine declares acceptance of ICC jurisdiction since 13 June 2014, 9 May 2017, ICC-CPI-20150105-PR1080; Kittrie 2016, p. 218.

[2] ICC, Press release: The state of Palestine accedes to the Rome Statute, 7 January 2015, ICC-ASP-20150107-PR1082.

[3] ICC, Press release: The prosecutor of the International Criminal Court, Fatou Bensouda, opens a preliminary examination of the situation in Palestine, 16 January 2015, ICC-OTP-20150116-PR1083; Kittrie 2016, p. 219.

[4] OTP 2015a, p. 17.

[5] Askin 1997, p. 202; Bantekas 2010, p. 389; Glaser 2008, pp. 55 et seq.; Kelsen 2008, pp. 274 et seq.; Olásolo 2005, p. 35; Smith 2012, p. 80; Werle and Jessberger 2014, p. 5.

[6] Bantekas 2010, pp. 412, 445, 450; Bassiouni 2013, pp. 742, 756, 762, 771; Werle and Jessberger 2014, pp. 114, 121–127.

[7] Guilfoyle 2016, pp. 105, 130 et seq.; Kuczyńska 2015, pp. 117–118; Schabas 2011, p. 157.

[8] Rome Statute of the International Criminal Court, opened for signature 17 July 1998, 2187 UNTS 90 (entered into force 1 July 2002) (Rome Statute), Article 13; Ambos 2016, p. 255; Bantekas 2010, p. 426; Werle and Jessberger 2014, p. 110.

the Prosecutor is obligated to open a preliminary examination of the situation to make sure that the situation merits an investigation and ultimately a prosecution of those most responsible.

The preliminary analysis that could lead to the decision to open a formal investigation involves legal analysis and examination of available materials to determine whether jurisdictional and gravity requirements, issues of complementary and interest of justice are met.[9] In contrast to the discretion of the Prosecutors of the *ad hoc* Tribunals, who were not empowered to decide against investigation, the Prosecutor of the ICC, after conducting the preliminary examination, has the discretion to decide to proceed to investigation.[10] This is given the Prosecutor is convinced that there is a reasonable basis to proceed to investigation and, when the statute requires, has obtained an authorisation to investigate from the Pre-Trial Chamber.[11]

This chapter analyses the main considerations that the Prosecutor examines before making a decision whether the situation in Palestine merits opening a formal investigation. In the sequence of the criteria provided under Article 53(1) of the Statute, it analyses the legal and jurisprudential background of pre-investigation considerations in the ICC with regard to the situation in Palestine. It starts by discussing the statutory criteria: jurisdiction (temporal, either territorial or personal, and material), admissibility (complementary and gravity), and the interests of justice. It also addresses other practical considerations in conducting preliminary examinations.

4.2 Preliminary Examination: An Overview

Preliminary examinations have a great significance in the practice of the ICC. Although the examinations manifest the functional independence of the Prosecutor, the nature of the analysis necessitates making difficult choices.[12] The broad discretion of the Prosecutor and the wide range of choices result in the uncertainty of the decision that may be reached, which in turn give preliminary examinations more leverage than investigations.[13] It puts pressure on the State under examination to better its judicial system in compliance with international standards

[9] Rome Statute, above n. 8, Article 53(1); ICC, Rules of Procedure and Evidence, adopted 9 September 2002, ICC-ASP/1/3 part II.A (Rules of Procedure and Evidence), Rule 104.

[10] Jalloh 2014, p. 14; Jurdi 2011, p. 95; Kuczyńska 2015, pp. 117–118; Stigen 2008, p. 349.

[11] OTP 2013b, pp. 3–6. Triffterer and Ambos 2016, p. 1368. See also Peschke 2011, p. 198; Kuczyńska 2015, pp. 117–118.

[12] Caban 2011, pp. 200–201.

[13] L. Louman, Report: Preliminary examination and legacy/sustainable exit: reviewing policies and practices—part 1, 26 October 2015, http://postconflictjustice.com/report-preliminary-examination-and-legacysustainable-exit-reviewing-policies-and-practices-part-1/ (accessed 31 March 2016); Kuczyńska 2015, pp. 117–118.

(positive complementarity)[14] and to look into other transitional justice mechanisms to properly deal with the atrocities committed. The 'unsettled' focus of the Prosecutor making any scenario within the Court's jurisdiction a target and susceptible to examination contributes to the prevention of crimes and has a deterrent effect.[15]

The Prosecutor has devised a four-tier 'filtering process' to determine whether a situation warrants a formal investigation. Despite the analytical considerations peculiar to each phase, the Prosecutor claims a 'holistic approach' throughout the examination.[16] Phase one (pre-filter mechanism) involves an initial analysis and verification of the information received under Article 15 to 'filter out' information on crimes which do not fall within the Court's jurisdiction.[17] In phase two, for communications that passed phase one and for information that arose from State party referrals, Security Council referrals, *ad hoc* declarations and testimonies obtained at the seat of the Court,[18] the Prosecutor examines whether the preconditions under Article 12 and the 'reasonable basis' criterion are satisfied. The second phase is considered as the 'formal commencement of the preliminary examination' since the legal and factual analysis conducted will give rise to the identification of possible cases within the Court's jurisdiction. Phase three deals with admissibility matters and the fourth phase focuses on interest of justice.[19]

Information gathered in each phase is measured against the 'reasonable basis' criterion. In light of Rules 48 and 104 of the Rules of Procedure and Evidence, it could be argued that the 'reasonable basis' standard under Articles 15(3–4) and 53 (1) is interpreted the same way. Stegmiller argues that at the pre-investigation stage, the 'reasonable basis' standard has a lower threshold than that of 'sufficient basis' to commence investigation in Article 53(2), the 'reasonable grounds' to issue warrant of arrest in Article 58(1)(a) or the 'substantial grounds' to confirm charges under Article 61(7)'.[20] The Pre-Trial Chamber has interpreted the phrase to mean 'a sensible or reasonable justification for a belief that a crime falling within the jurisdiction of the Court has been or is being committed'.[21] The less stringent

[14] Cryer et al. 2010, p. 75; Stone 2015, p. 291.

[15] OTP 2015b, p. 20. Schabas and Bernaz argue that there is empirical proof that a mere threat of prosecution may prevent conflict and to end wars more quickly. See Schabas and Bernaz 2011, p. 454.

[16] OTP 2013b, p. 18; Ellis 2014, p. 38.

[17] Stegmiller 2013, p. 487.

[18] On the basis of Article 15(2) and Rule 104(2), the procedure provided in Rule 47 allows the Prosecutor to receive oral and written testimonies at the seat of the Court. Rules of Procedure and Evidence, above n. 9, Rules 47 and 104(2); Rome Statute, above n. 8, Article 15(2). Stegmiller 2011, p. 224.

[19] OTP 2013b, p. 19; Ellis 2014, p. 38.

[20] Stegmiller 2011, p. 230; Triffterer and Ambos 2016, p. 1370

[21] ICC, Situation in the Republic of Kenya, Decision pursuant to Article 15 of the Rome Statute on the Authorization of an investigation into the situation in the Republic of Kenya, 31 March 2010, ICC-01/09-19 (Situation in the Republic of Kenya 2010), para 35; Triffterer and Ambos 2016, p. 1371.

threshold helps to avoid protracted examinations before Pre-Trial Chamber supervision is possible. It also helps to limit the gathering of information to what is 'sufficient enough' to seek authorisation confidently.[22]

Moreover, throughout the preliminary examination stage, the Prosecutor has neither 'investigative powers'[23] nor benefits of State cooperation (part 9 of the Statute).[24] Hence, the office assesses information from reliable sources, mainly 'States, organs of the UN, intergovernmental and non-governmental organizations'.[25] Up on completion of the four phases, the Prosecutor can decide: (1) not to proceed to investigation, (2) to gather additional information, (3) proceed to an investigation, (4) to continue to assess the relevant national proceedings.[26] In the case of Security Council and State referrals, there is an assumption that the Prosecutor would proceed to investigations. It is only when the Prosecutor does not do so that she has to present her justification to the Pre-Trial Chamber, which could overrule her decision if it is made on 'interest of justice' grounds. In *proprio motu* situations, however, the Prosecutor has to prove before the Chamber the existence of 'reasonable basis'[27] to proceed to investigation.[28] Nonetheless, regardless of the type of trigger mechanism, the same procedure and criteria are employed in dealing with situations under preliminary examinations.

The following sections deal with the possible factors that may come into consideration in the preliminary examination of the situation of Palestine. The first part of the discussion follows the sequence outlined in the 2013 policy paper on preliminary examinations of the OTP.[29] As the examination of the situation of Palestine arose from an *ad hoc* declaration, the assessment focuses on matters of jurisdiction: admissibility and interest of justice to the exclusion of the initial assessment under phase one.

---

[22] Stegmiller 2011, pp. 230–231.

[23] Rome Statute, above n. 8, Article 54(2).

[24] Pursuant to Article 86, States parties have a general obligation to cooperate with the Court. However, the provision explicitly refers to 'investigation and prosecution', which do not include pre-investigation activities. On what appears to be a result of concerns from States sensitive to the broad power of the Prosecutor, State party cooperation becomes obligatory after a confirmation decision from the Pre-Trial Chamber. The Prosecutor could, however, seek voluntary cooperation. For more on cooperation see Stegmiller 2011, p. 228; and Kuczyńska 2015, pp. 117–118.

[25] Rules of Procedure and Evidence, above n. 9, Rule 104(2).

[26] OTP 2013b, p. 21. See also Pellegrino 2014, p. 7.

[27] Stegmiller 2011, p. 212; Olásolo 2005, pp. 35 et seq.

[28] Rome Statute, above n. 8, Article 15(4); Ambos 2016, p. 264; Stegmiller 2011, p. 212; Stone 2015, p. 219.

[29] OTP 2013b. The Policy Paper provides the criteria employed in assessing situations under Preliminary Examination. It details the raison d'être of the standard employed and the policy behind the criteria in light of the Statute and other policy documents.

4.3 Jurisdiction

Be it in its legal or political sense, the jurisdictional range of the ICC is one of the most complicated aspects of the Statute.[30] Varieties of opinions and concerns were entertained at the Rome conference during the negotiation of the provisions dealing with jurisdiction. Ultimately, delegates—not only concerned with the establishment but also the exercise of jurisdiction—delimited the temporal (Article 11), material (Article 5), personal (Articles 12 and 26) and territorial (Articles 12 and 13(b)) parameters of the Court's jurisdiction.[31] Pursuant to Article 53(1)(a), similar to other cases, the Prosecutor must determine that the information available gives rise to a reasonable basis to believe that all the latter jurisdictional requirements are fulfilled in the situation in Palestine.[32]

4.3.1 Ratione temporis

Contrary to its predecessors, which were mainly established to prosecute crimes *ex post facto*, the ICC does not enjoy a retroactive jurisdiction prior to the date of the coming into force of its Statute.[33] Article 11(1) of the Statute expressly provides an absolute bar on the temporal scope of the Court, stating that the Court enjoys jurisdiction only on 'crimes committed after the entry into force of this Statute'.[34] For States acceding to the Statute after 1 July 2002, para 2 provides that the temporal threshold applicable is the date the Statute came into force for the acceding State. That is the 'first day of the month after the 60th day following the deposit' of the instrument of 'ratification, acceptance, approval or accession'.[35]

Yet, as an exception to this prospective stance and without prejudice to the absolute bar provided under Article 11(1), para 2 recalls the legal regime of Article 12(3) that allows the retroactive acceptance of jurisdiction open to States and non-States parties.[36] This limitation on the temporal scope of jurisdiction provided under Article 11 is affirmed by the fundamental principle of non-retroactivity enshrined under Article 24(1) and closely linked with the principle *nullum crime sine lege* under Article 22(1).[37] Any exercise of criminal jurisdiction is required to

---

[30] Wagner 2003, p. 412.

[31] Ambos 2016, pp. 242–243; Calvo-Goller 2006, pp. 181 et seq.; Guilfoyle 2016, pp. 105 et seq.; Knoops 2014, pp. 77 et seq.; Vagias 2014, pp. 47–60; Werle and Jessberger 2014, pp. 96 et seq.

[32] OTP 2013b, p. 9.

[33] See generally Knoops 2014, pp. 77 et seq.; Werle and Jessberger 2014, pp. 96 et seq.

[34] Triffterer and Ambos 2016, p. 657.

[35] Rome Statute, above n. 8, Article 126(2).

[36] Triffterer and Ambos 2016, p. 658.

[37] Bougon 2002, p. 549; Schabas 2011, p. 73; Triffterer and Ambos 2016, pp. 658–660.

be in line with these general principles of criminal law.[38] The principles are exclusively concerned with the protection of the accused at the time of establishing his or her individual liability. Due to the explicit prohibition under Article 24,[39] it is not a matter for consideration whether the individual has or could have reasonably appreciated the criminal nature of the conduct.[40]

Palestine's instrument of accession was deposited in January 2015 and the instrument came into force for Palestine on 1 April 2015. Nonetheless, the preliminary examination that commenced on 16 January 2014 was the result of the second Palestinian *ad hoc* declaration to the Court and provides a temporal scope that started from 13 June 2014. Hence, in light of the above principles, the examination targets alleged crimes committed after 13 June 2014.

The issue that follows is whether this temporal bar disallows investigation into continuing and permanent crimes that started to occur before 13 June 2014. Such conducts of continuing nature could be envisaged in the case of, among others, enforced disappearances,[41] using, conscripting and enlisting children[42] or unlawful confinement.[43] The Pre-Trial Chamber in the decision authorising an investigation into the situation in the Republic of Côte d'Ivoire stated that insofar as the contextual elements of the continuing crimes are the same as those that fall within the scope provided in the *ad hoc* declaration and 'involve the same actors' and were 'committed within the context of …the same attacks…or conflicts', the extent of the temporal scope could cover those crimes.[44] This precedent could be used to assert that where the nature and context of an act within the temporal scope of the *ad hoc* declaration is the same as those outside the scope—but within the absolute temporal

---

[38] Van Schaack 2011, p. 101.

[39] This is not the case for the *ad hoc* Tribunals. The prohibition of retroactive criminalisation under the Rome Statute is different from the ad hoc Tribunals and national war crimes Trials that were established to deal with crimes that were committed before their establishment. The issue of *Nullum Crimen* was not considered relevant as the violations were considered a violation of international criminal law. See Boot 2002, p. 372.

[40] The Rome Statute provides non-retroactivity also in respect to crimes that the ad hoc Tribunals retroactively prosecuted. See, for instance, ICTY, *Prosecutor v. Delalić et al.*, Trial Chamber ICTY, 16 November 1998, IT-96-21-T, para 293. See also Boot 2002, p. 372; Nissel 2004, p. 676.

[41] The question of enforced disappearance as a continuing crime has been established in various case laws including IACHR, *Rio Negro Massacres v. Guatemala,* Judgment, 4 September 2012; IACHR, *Velasquez Rodriguez v. Honduras,* Judgment, 29 July 1988; Human Rights Committee, *Ibrahima Gueye et al. v. France,* Communication No. 196/1985, 3 April 1989, UN Doc. CCPR/C/35/D/196/1985 (1989) (Human Rights Committee 1989). See also Triffterer and Ambos 2016, pp. 664–667.

[42] Rome Statute, above n. 8, Article 8(2)(e)(viii).

[43] Ibid., Article 8(2)(a)(vii).

[44] Situation in the Republic of Côte d'Ivoire 2011, above n. 44, paras 179–180.

bar—the Court enjoys jurisdiction.[45] However, as the Chamber's assertion in the case of Côte d'Ivoire is limited to crimes committed after 1 July 2002, the issue requires further scrutiny.

Issues on continuing or permanent crimes came to light during the negotiation of Article 24(1), namely the principle of non-retroactivity.[46] The provision, which is framed as 'No person shall be criminally responsible under this Statute for *conduct* prior to the entry into force of the Statute', avoided words such as committed, occurred or completed.[47] Due to lack of agreement on issues of continuous crimes that start to be committed before 1 July 2002, the construction of this provision was left intentionally ambiguous, in so doing opening it to the interpretation of the Court.[48]

The Pre-Trial Chamber dealt with a continuing or permanent crime in the *Lubanga* case.[49] In addressing the crime of enlisting and conscripting children into the Union of Congolese Patriots, which was rightly framed a continuous crime, the Pre-Trial Chamber focused on the perpetuity of the crime after the coming into effect of the Statute as opposed to the date of the first commission. It argued that the time of enlisting and conscripting a child is not decisive as long as the child remains a member of the armed force during the time the Court has jurisdiction over the matter.[50] As per the elements of the crime, the child is considered conscripted or enlisted in the armed group or used to participate in hostilities on daily basis as long as he is in the armed group.[51] The Court enjoys jurisdiction as long as the child remains a member of the armed group after 1 July 2002. The commission of the crime ceases only when the child soldier turns 15 years of age or leaves the armed group.[52] As the violation persists and the *actus reus* of the crime continues to be committed even after the coming into effect of the Statute, this approach to permanent or continuous crimes does not violate the principle of non-retroactivity or the temporal bar of the Statute.

Footnote 24 of the elements of the crime of enforced disappearances appears to be in line with this interpretation. It provides that the crime falls within the jurisdiction of the Court only if all the *actus reus* of the crime occurred within the

---

[45] See ibid. The ad hoc Tribunals have also adopted a similar approach. See, for instance, ICTR, *Prosecutor v. Simon Bikindi,* Judgement, 2 December 2008, ICTR-01-72-T, para 27; ICTR, *Prosecutor v. Nahimana et al.*, Judgement, 28 November 2007, ICTR-99-52-A, paras 41, 315.

[46] Triffterer and Ambos 2016, pp. 662 et seq.

[47] Rome Statute, above n. 8, Article 24(1). See also Boot 2002, p. 372.

[48] Schabas 2011, pp. 75 et seq.; Triffterer and Ambos 2016, p. 662.

[49] ICC, *Prosecutor v. Thomas Lubanga Dyilo,* Decision on the confirmation of charges, 29 January 2007, ICC-01/04-01/06-803-tEN (*Lubanga* 2007), para 248.

[50] Ibid.; ICC, *Prosecutor v. Thomas Lubanga Dyilo*, Judgment pursuant to Article 74 of the Statute, 14 March 2012, ICC-01/04-01/06-2842 (*Lubanga* 2012), para 618. See also Human Rights Committee 1989, above n. 41, para 10; and Triffterer and Ambos 2016, p. 665.

[51] ICC, Elements of Crimes, 2002, ICC-ASP/1/3 part II.B (Elements of Crimes), Article 8(2)(e)(vii).

[52] See ibid., Article 8(2)(b)(xxvi).

temporal jurisdiction of the Court.[53] This clarification is provided only for the crime of enforced disappearances. One could argue that the special treatment accorded to enforced disappearance was given to obtain the consent of South American States during the negotiation of the Rome Statute. Considering the widely reported enforced disappearance cases in South American States, this path to retroactive prosecution would have opened those States to judicial scrutiny.[54] In light of this premises, one could conclude that footnote 24 is an exception provided only to cases of enforced disappearance and that the Statute has left the matter open with regard to other continuing crimes.

Although this argument may have some merits, the criterion under footnote 24 for the crime of enforced disappearances, which is that the *actus reus* shall be committed or continue to be committed within the Court's temporal scope, is consistent with the approach the Pre-Trial Chamber followed in the *Lubanga* case.[55] The common required element in both continuing crimes (conscripting and enlisting children and enforced disappearances) is that the elements of the *actus reus* of the crimes continue to be committed after 1 July 2002.[56] Thus, despite the date the commission of the crime commenced, if the material elements of any continuous crime, in the Palestine context, continue to occur within the temporal jurisdictional scope of the Court, the crime falls within the jurisdiction of the Court.

In light of the Pre-Trial Chamber's stance,[57] as well as the above argument, crimes committed between 1 July 2002 and 13 June 2014 would be within the jurisdiction of the Court if the nature and context of an act committed after 13 June 2014 is the same as those committed after 1 July 2002. In the same vein, regardless of the date of commission, if the material element of a crime (re)occurred after 13 June 2014, the crime also falls within the jurisdictional parameters of the Court.

Another issue unique to Palestine with regard to continuing or permanent crimes is the fact that the OTP considers Palestine to have standing before the Court only after the General Assembly passed Resolution 67/19 of 2012.[58] Accordingly, the

---

[53] The crime of enforced disappearance is treated as a continuing crime in various judgements, among others, see IACHR, *Case of Blake v. Guatemala*, Judgment, 2 July 1996, IACHR Series C no. 27, paras 35–39, 29–40; IACHR, Case of *Blake v. Guatemala*, Judgment, 24 January 1998, IACHR Series C no. 36, para 130; ECHR, *Cyprus v. Turkey*, Judgment, 10 May 2001, Application No. 25781/94, paras 40, 132. Various human right instruments have also prohibited the conduct. See Declaration on the Protection of All Persons from Enforced Disappearance, 1992, A/RES/47/133, Article 17(1); Inter-American Convention on the Forced Disappearance of Persons, OAS Treaty Series no. 68, entered into force 28 March 1996, Article 3. See also Nissel 2004, pp. 664, 668.

[54] Boot 2002, p. 371; and Nissel 2004, p. 687.

[55] *Lubanga* 2007, above n. 49, para 248; *Lubanga* 2012, above n. 50, para 618.

[56] Although the initial attack referred under footnote 24 occurred earlier than the date the Statute came into force, as far as the attack is continuing past the latter date, the Court enjoys jurisdiction. See Nissel 2004, p. 670.

[57] See *Lubanga* 2007, above n. 49, para 248; Situation in the Republic of Côte d'Ivoire 2011, above n. 44, paras 179–180.

[58] OTP 2015a, p. 12.

question that comes to mind is whether the ICC enjoys jurisdiction for continuing crimes that started to occur before 2012.

Prosecutor Bensouda's stance on the first Palestinian *ad hoc* declaration is an endorsement of the decision of the former Prosecutor.[59] The latter's decision on the matter indicated that a clarification on the status of Palestine shall be obtained from the General Assembly or the Assembly of States Parties of the ICC. Palestine's statehood did not emanate from Resolution 67/19.[60] The Resolution, as the decision of the former Prosecutor discerned, only clarified or affirmed the statehood of Palestine.[61] As concerns regarding the principle of non-retroactivity cannot be raised in this case, the technicality of when the General Assembly chose to clarify the issue of Palestine's statehood cannot be used to avoid investigation of grave crimes that started to be committed before 2012.

4.3.2 *Ratione materiae*

As stressed under para 4 of the preamble of the Statute, the subject matter jurisdiction of the ICC is limited to 'the most serious crimes of concern to the international community'. Article 5 of the Statute comprises the same phrase and an additional 'operative part' listing the specific crimes considered 'atrocity crimes', namely the crime of genocide, crimes against humanity, war crimes and the crimes of aggression. The international dimension and the heinous nature of these crimes dictate prosecution since humanity as a whole is considered a victim.

The crimes under Article 5 are prosecutable if they fulfil the international element and the threshold built in under their specific provision, i.e. the intent to destroy 'a group or part of a group' for the crime of genocide, the 'widespread and systematic attack on a civilian population' for crimes against humanity and the 'armed conflict'[62] requirement for war crimes.[63] These thresholds not only focus

---

[59] ICC, Press release: The prosecutor of the International Criminal Court, Fatou Bensouda, opens a preliminary examination of the situation in Palestine, 16 January 2015, ICC-OTP-20150116-PR1083.

[60] OTP, Situation in Palestine, 3 April 2012, https://www.icc-cpi.int/NR/rdonlyres/C6162BBF-FEB9-4FAF-AFA9-836106D2694A/284387/SituationinPalestine030412ENG.pdf (accessed 30 July 2015, para 5.

[61] Ibid., paras 5–8.

[62] Some argue that in contrast to the other two crimes, the definition of war crimes under the Statute has no quantitative dimension. The introductory paragraph of the crime could be read as a guidance to focus the jurisdiction of the Court on situations with a threshold similar to what is provided to other definitions. See OTP, Letter of the Prosecutor on the situation in Iraq, 9 February 2006, https://www.icc-cpi.int/NR/rdonlyres/04D143C8-19FB-466C-AB77-4CDB2FDEBEF7/143682/OTP_letter_to_senders_re_Iraq_9_February_2006.pdf (accessed 25 May 2005); Schabas 2011, p. 94.

[63] Werle and Jessberger 2014, p. 170.

the attention of the Court to the prosecution of 'the most serious crimes' and criminals, but also help limit the discretion of the Prosecutor.[64]

For the purposes of preliminary examinations, the Prosecutor has to analyse the available information with regard to the subject matter of the Court. She has to consider factors related to the 'contextual circumstances', 'the pattern of similar conducts' and 'the *de jure* and *de facto* role of the individual, group or institution and their link with the alleged crimes, and the mental element'.[65] Since a full-fledged investigation is inconceivable at this stage, an outright conclusion on the alleged crimes is not expected.

Concerning the first preliminary examination on Palestine, the former Prosecutor did not pay any regard to the Goldstone Report[66] or other publicly available documents as he avoided dealing with any of the substantive matters.[67] Given the current credence on the status of Palestine, the second preliminary examination would most certainly consider the conclusions published by the UN Human Rights Council, information submitted by individuals and States as well as other independent organs. Of particular importance would be reports on alleged 'collective punishment' of the population of Gaza, punitive house demolitions by Israel and alleged torture, summary and extra-judicial killings and other war crimes committed by both Hamas and Israel.[68]

In the 2015 report on preliminary examination activities, the Prosecutor has indicated that her office has accepted 66 communications about crimes under international law allegedly committed in Palestine since 13 June 2014 and that the office 'has taken steps to analyse and verify the seriousness of information received, including through a rigorous and independent source evaluation process'.[69] Without prejudice to other alleged crimes that may be identified later, the office has published a preliminary finding on the commission of alleged crimes. In particular, the war crime of indiscriminate attacks by both parties to the conflict, summary execution by Hamas, settlements and settlement related violence, confiscation, appropriation and demolition of the property of Palestinians and systematic and institutionalized ill treatment of children by Israel are identified.[70]

Notwithstanding other statutory criteria in preliminary examinations, the alleged crimes recognised by the Prosecutor and those not yet recognised but are reportedly committed give rise to a reasonable ground to believe that crimes within the subject-matter jurisdiction of the Court have been committed in the situation in Palestine.

---

[64] Schabas 2011, p. 94.

[65] OTP 2013b, pp. 9–10.

[66] UNHRC 2009.

[67] OTP 2012, above n. 60.

[68] Abrams 2015; Erakat 2014; UNHRC 2015, paras 668–675; Human Rights Watch, Israel/Palestine, https://www.hrw.org/middle-east/n-africa/israel/palestine (accessed 11 April 2016).

[69] OTP 2015a, pp. 11, 16.

[70] Ibid., pp. 14–16.

4.3.3 *Ratione loci or personae*

To complete the second phase of a preliminary examination, the Prosecutor has to show that there are reasonable grounds to believe that crimes within the jurisdiction of the Court were committed either on the territory or by a national of the State party or the declaring State under consideration.[71] To date investigations and prosecutions tend to rely on territory. It bears noting that prosecutions concerning the Republic of Congo, Sudan, Kenya Central African Republic, Côte d'Ivoire and Uganda as well as the Security Council referrals on Sudan and Libya focused on territory rather than on nationality.[72] The former Prosecutor contemplated a possible prosecution of a case based on *ratione personae* in the situation of Iraq, which, at the time of writing, is once again under preliminary examination.[73] In the Iraq situation, the inquiry focuses on nationals of a State party (the United Kingdom) for crimes allegedly committed on the territory of a non-party State (Iraq). Considering the context of the situation in Palestine, it is unlikely that the Prosecutor may employ an either or approach. Crimes committed in the territory of Palestine by nationals of both Israel and Palestine are likely prone to investigation and prosecution. The Court, however, cannot enjoy jurisdiction over purported perpetrators of the crime of aggression and use of certain prohibited weapons as specific ratification of the amendment is required.[74]

Having in mind the lapsed Jordanian claim to sovereignty over the West Bank, Israel's claim over an undivided Jerusalem as its capital and the 'redrawing' of the 1967 boundaries, one of the most contentious issues with regard to territorial jurisdiction on the situation on Palestine is the territorial delimitation.[75] Although the General Assembly is not empowered to delimit boundaries, given the decision of the Prosecutor to open the Preliminary Examination relied on Resolution 67/19, it is plausible to use the same Resolution for delimiting the territorial scope of the examination.

Recalling Resolution 181 (II) of 1947, Resolutions 242 (1967) of 1967 and 338 (1973), the General Assembly Resolution 67/19 recognizes Palestine in territories

[71] Rome Statute, above n. 8, Article 12(2). See also Ambos 2016, p. 244; Calvo-Goller 2006, pp. 181 et seq.; Knoops 2014, pp. 77 et seq.; Vagias 2014, pp. 47–60; Triffterer and Ambos 2016, p. 683; Werle and Jessberger 2014, pp. 96 et seq.

[72] Schabas 2011, p. 77; Triffterer and Ambos 2016, pp. 683–684.

[73] OTP 2016, p. 18; Kittrie 2016, p. 220.

[74] Similarly, the Court would not be able to investigate and prosecute minors and UN personnel. See Rome Statute, above n. 8, Articles 26, 121(5). See also ICC, Negotiated Relationship Agreement between the International Criminal Court and the United Nations, entered into force 4 October 2004, ICC-ASP/3/Res.1, Article 19. Palestine signed the Kampala amendments in 2016. However, the ASP activated the jurisdiction in 2017 and allowed the Prosecutor to prosecute the crime effective July 2018.

[75] Ash 2009, pp. 12–13.

occupied since 1967, including East Jerusalem. Hence, crimes allegedly committed in Gaza, the West Bank and East Jerusalem fall under the Court's jurisdiction.[76] The OTP has also adopted this reading as the 2015 report on Preliminary Examination activities dealt with alleged crimes committed on those territories.[77]

4.4 Admissibility

In the second phase of the examination of the situation, once the Prosecutor reaches a preliminary determination that the legal criteria for the Court's operation are met, the third phase requires an assessment whether the matter within the Court's jurisdiction should be litigated before the Court.[78] Admissibility, as provided under Article 17(1) of the Statute, requires an examination of complementarity and gravity.[79] In the wording of the provision, the exceptions to admissibility or the four factors that need to be examined to determine the question of admissibility are whether:

- A State having jurisdiction is investigating or prosecuting the case;
- After an investigation and prosecution the State has concluded that there is no ground to prosecute;
- The alleged perpetrator has already been tried for the same conduct;
- The gravity of the case is insufficient to be brought before the Court.[80]

As provided under Article 53(1)(b), before determining to open an investigation, the Prosecutor has to examine if 'the case is or would be admissible as per Article 17'. Despite Article 17's reference to 'case' instead of 'situation', the Prosecutor and the Pre-Trial Chambers have clarified that the consideration under this phase of examination will deal with 'potential cases' likely to be investigated,

[76] Different from the first *ad hoc* declaration, the territorial and political fragmentation between the West Bank and Gaza do not affect the territorial jurisdiction of the Court. The *de facto* governing body of Gaza, Hamas, has given consent to the intervention of the Court, although the Palestinian Authority in the West Bank made the declaration. See Reuters, Hamas Voices Support for Membership of 'Palestine' in ICC, The Jerusalem Post, 23 August 2014. For a comparative perspective regarding the same issue on the first *ad hoc* declaration See S. Adem, Palestine and the ICC: a critical appraisal of the decision of the Office of the Prosecutor on the Palestine ad hoc declaration (Unpublished thesis, University of the Western Cape, 2015), pp. 24–25.

[77] OTP 2015a, pp. 14–16.

[78] OTP 2013b, p. 10; Ambos 2016, pp. 266 et seq.; Schabas 2011, p. 188.

[79] Cameron 2004, p. 83.

[80] Rome Statute, above n. 8, Article 17(1). See also ICC, *Prosecutor v. Germain Katanga and Mathieu Ngudjolo Chui,* Judgment on the Appeal of Mr. Germain Katanga against the Oral Decision of Trial by Chamber II of 12 June 2009 on the admissibility of the case, 25 September 2009, ICC-01/04-01/07 (*Katanga* and *Chui* 2009), para 78.

as opposed to a clearly 'identified set of incidents, suspects and conducts'.[81] As the assessment at this stage is merely preliminary, the decision on admissibility as well as the identification of potential cases is without prejudice to conclusions that may be reached on the same matter at a later stage.[82]

In the Lubanga case, the Pre-Trial Chamber approached the admissibly issue as having only two parts, namely issues of complementarity (Article 17(1)(a)–(c)) and gravity (Article 17(1)(b)).[83] Although the principle *ne bis in idem* is crucial, due to the specific reference of 'the person concerned' under Article 17(1)(c) and the context at hand, a detailed analysis of the principle is only feasible at a later stage. Hence, this section discusses the two main parts of admissibility consecutively.

4.4.1 Complementarity

The first part of the admissibility test, complementarity, provides a procedure to allocate a forum when there are competing jurisdictions. Complementarity is one of the pivotal principles of the Statute regulated under Article 17 and reiterated under Article 1 and para 10 of the preamble. Analogous to the approach adopted by international human rights bodies, which require the applicant to prove the exhaustion of local remedies,[84] the ICC functions as a fall back and secondary jurisdiction to be employed when a national jurisdiction is unwilling or unable to investigate and prosecute.[85] By providing an exception to the presumption in favour of domestic prosecution,[86] the principle reinforces the primary obligation of States to prosecute crimes under international law. In a sense, a State's failure to live up to

[81] Situation in the Republic of Kenya 2010, above n. 21, paras 50, 182, 188; Situation in the Republic of Côte d'Ivoire 2011, above n. 44, paras 190–191, 202–204; ICC, Situation in the Republic of Kenya, Request for authorization of an investigation pursuant to Article 15, 26 November 2009, ICC-01/09-3, paras 51, 107. See also Ambos 2016, pp. 268, 282 et seq.; OTP 2013b, p. 11.

[82] Ibid.

[83] ICC, *Prosecutor v. Thomas Lubanga Dyilo*, Decision on the Prosecutor's application for a warrant of arrest, Article 58, 10 February 2006, ICC-01/04-01/06-8 (*Lubanga* 2006), para 29; Ambos 2016, pp. 282 et seq.; El Zeidy 2008, p. 160.

[84] International Covenant on Civil and Political Rights, opened for signature 16 December 1966, 999 UNTS 14668 (entered into force 23 March 1976), Article 41(1)(c); American Convention on Human Rights, signed 22 November 1969, 1144 UNTS 123 (entered into force 18 July 1978), Article 46; African Charter on Human and Peoples' Rights, adopted 27 June 1981, 1520 UNTS 217 (entered into force 21 October 1986), Articles 50 and 56(5). See also European Court of Human Rights, *Demopoulos and Others v. Turkey*, Decision as to the Admissibility of app no. 46113/99, 1 March 2010, paras 50–57; IACHR, *Velasquez Rodriguez v. Honduras*, Judgment on preliminary objections, 26 June 1987, IACHR Series C no. 1, paras 87–88.

[85] Guilfoyle 2016, pp. 109 et seq.; El Zeidy 2008, p. 159 ; Kleffner 2008, pp. 248 et seq.; Schabas 2011, p. 191; Stone 2015, p. 288.

[86] El Zeidy 2008, p. 160.

its obligations momentarily deprives it of its sovereign prerogative over its own jurisdiction.[87] The principle also relies on the practical consideration that the forum with better efficiency and effectiveness investigates and prosecutes, thereby contributing to the betterment of international justice and the fight against impunity.[88] The territorial State is the preferred forum not only due to ease of access to evidence and witnesses, but also because national prosecutions create greater 'sense of local ownership' compared to prosecutions before international organs.[89]

In light of the criteria set up under Articles 53(1)(b) and 17(1)(a)–(c) of the Rome Statute, the assessment on complementarity is approached in the following order: First, the Prosecutor assesses if there are any ongoing investigations or prosecutions or if there were investigations in the past that the State decided not to prosecute; and, second, she examines the State's unwillingness or inability in its decision regarding investigation or prosecution. In the absence of an affirmative response to the first assessment, it would be putting the cart before the horse to consider the question of unwillingness and inability.[90] Provided the gravity threshold has been met, inaction to investigate or prosecute on the part of the State having jurisdiction also renders the assessment on unwillingness and inability trivial.

In the *Lubanga* and *Kushayb* cases, the Pre-Trial Chamber I has ruled that 'it is a *conditio sine quo non* for a case arising from the investigation of a situation to be inadmissible that national proceedings encompass both the person and the conduct which is the subject of the case before the Court'.[91] The assessment is 'case specific' or rather 'potential case' specific for this stage of the examination.[92] Even if a State having jurisdiction has conducted or is conducting investigations or prosecutions, the examination should 'encompass the same persons for the same conduct as that which forms the basis of the proceedings before the Court'.[93] With regard to the determination of what constitutes 'the same persons for the same

[87] Mégret 2006, p. 37.

[88] Cryer et al. 2010, p. 153; Stone 2015, p. 288; Triffterer and Ambos 2016, pp. 793–798.

[89] Jones 2015, p. 102.

[90] *Katanga* and *Chui* 2009, above n. 80, para 78.

[91] *Lubanga* 2006, above n. 83, paras 31, 37; ICC, *Prosecutor v. Ahmad Harun & Ali Kushayb*, Decision on the Prosecution Application under Article 58(7) of the Statute, 27 April 2007, ICC-02/05-01/07-1, paras 24–25.

[92] Since the Prosecutor may not identify specific cases at the preliminary examination stage, her assessment could not necessarily be case specific. See Cryer et al. 2010, p. 154.

[93] ICC, *Prosecutor v. William Samoei Ruto, Henry Kiprono Kosgey and Joshua Arap Sang*, Judgment on the appeal of the Republic of Kenya against the decision of Pre-Trial Chamber II of 30 May 2011, 30 August 2011, ICC-01/09-01/11-307, para 1, 47; ICC, *Prosecutor v. Saif Al-Islam Gaddafi and Abdullah Al-Senussi*, Decision on the Admissibility of the Case against Abdullah Al-Senussi, 11 October 2013, ICC-01/11-01/11-466 (*Gaddafi* 2013), para 66; *Lubanga* 2006, above n. 83, para 37. In the latter case Lubanga was in custody in Democratic Republic of Congo for crimes of Genocide and crimes against humanity. The ICC, however, argued that he is not charged with the crime of recruiting child soldiers, for which the Chamber issued an arrest warrant. See also OTP 2013b, p. 12.

conduct', the Pre-Trial Chamber has stated that this 'will vary according to the concrete facts and circumstance of the case' and, therefore, requires a case-by-case analysis.[94] Moreover, as addressed above, the material jurisdiction of the Court demands the focus of the preliminary examination to rest on those most responsible for the most serious crimes of concern to the international community.

In dealing with the first assessment of complementarity, particularly whether Israeli or Palestinian Courts are conducting or have conducted investigations and prosecutions or their inactivity to prosecute, the emphasis is on the aforementioned scope of material jurisdiction.

Be that as it may, the assessment on complementarity does not aim to judge the national judicial system as a whole. It aims to examine it only with regard to its dealing with the specific case at hand, based on 'concrete facts as they exist at the time', as opposed to 'hypothetical proceedings'.[95] This, however, does not mean that the legislative and judicial framework on which the investigation and prosecution rely would not be called into question, especially with regard to their effectiveness, transparency, impartiality, thoroughness and independence.[96] Lack of conformity with international standards of the legal system impugns the willingness and ability of the State to conduct investigations and prosecutions genuinely.

4.4.1.1 Israel's Accountability Mechanism

Israeli authorities do not have any official statistics regarding the prosecution of crimes in the context of the Israeli-Palestinian conflict. The Reports on the investigation and accountability mechanisms of Israel are infused with accounts of lack of compliance with international standards.[97] International human rights bodies, as well as the Israeli Turkel commission,[98] have identified numerous structural, procedural and substantive limitations that impair Israel's ability to fulfil its duty to investigate international crimes.[99] The Israeli Information Centre for Human Rights in the Occupied Territories, B'Tselem, goes to the extent of stating that 'there is currently no official body in Israel capable of conducting independent investigations

---

94 *Gaddafi* 2013, above n. 93, para 66. See also OTP 2013b, p. 12.

95 OTP 2013b, p. 12. See also OTP 2005, pp. 3–4.

96 UNHRC 2010, paras 21–25; Schmitt 2011, pp. 35–48.

97 UNHRC 2015, paras 618–651; UNHRC 2010, paras 35–64; UNHRC 2009, paras 1815–1835; Yesh Din 2011.

98 The Commission is officially known as the Public Commission to Examine the Maritime Incident of 31 May 2010. It was established on 14 June 2010 by the government of Israel with a mandate to investigate the Gaza flotilla incident of 31 May 2010 and the naval blockade imposed on Gaza. It was headed by a former Supreme Court judge named Jacob Turkel. At the end of the investigation, the commission published two reports on the mechanisms of Israel to deal with violations of law of armed conflicts. The official page of the commission is http://www.turkel-committee.gov.il/index-eng.html (accessed 05 April 2016). See also Weill 2012, p. 110.

99 UNHRC 2015, para 618.

of suspected violations of international humanitarian law' and has further stated that 'Israel's law enforcement system, in its present form, cannot adequately address suspicions'.[100] Leading Israeli human rights NGO in monitoring investigations, Yesh Din, together with B'Tselem, has also issued a statement in September 2014 stating that due to the fundamental structural flaws of the investigative system and the difficulty to conduct professional investigations, they have abstained from lending any assistance.[101]

The UN Committee of Experts has repeatedly noted the dual role played by the Military Advocate General (MAG), who is the legal advisor to the military authorities as well as the head of criminal investigation and prosecution in the military, as the central problem of the investigation system.[102] The Military Advocate General provides legal advice for military operations and participates in policy decisions directly affecting his ability to conduct independent and impartial investigations.[103] The overall policy and operational decisions in the military are obtained from senior political officials with equivalent or higher rank to the military advocate general.[104] The UN Human Rights Council has opined that in situations of breach of international law there is no mechanism in place to investigate policy-level decisions and possible liability of political officials and military commanders.

Nonetheless, pointing out the reports by the Turkel Commission, the UN Human Rights Council has taken note of the efforts of Israel to bring its accountability mechanism in line with international standards, and its attempt to implement the 18 Recommendations the commission issued.[105] In line with Recommendation 5 of the Commission, a Fact-Finding Assessment mechanism (FFA) is established with the purpose of conducting a fact-finding assessment.[106] Until 2014 the Military Advocate General used operational debriefing, which was primarily aimed 'to serve the operational needs of the military', to conduct fact-finding assessments.[107] The

---

[100] B'Tselem, Israeli authorities have proven they cannot investigate suspected violations of international humanitarian law by Israel in the Gaza Strip, 5 September 2014, http://www.btselem.org/accountability/20140905_failure_to_investigate (accessed 17 March 2016).

[101] UNHRC 2015, para 610; Israeli human rights organizations B'Tselem and Yesh Din: Israel is unwilling to investigate harm caused to Palestinians, 4 September 2014, http://www.btselem.org/press_releases/20140905_failure_to_investigate (accessed 21 March 2016).

[102] UNHRC 2015, para 619; UNHRC 2009, para 1792.

[103] Weill 2012, p. 110.

[104] B'Tselem, Israeli authorities have proven they cannot investigate suspected violations of international humanitarian law by Israel in the Gaza Strip, 5 September 2014, http://www.btselem.org/accountability/20140905_failure_to_investigate (accessed 17 March 2016).

[105] The 18 recommendations of the commission do not offer a solution to the dual role of the MAG and do not specify the circumstances that necessitate investigation of civilian deaths. See Adalah 2015, p. 12.

[106] Turkel Commission 2013, p. 382.

[107] Ibid.; UNHRC 2015, paras 620 et seq.

Fact-Finding Assessment is thus mandated to conduct fact-finding tasks and inform the Military Advocate General whether a certain incident merits an investigation. Ultimately, however, the decision to open investigation rests with the Military Advocate General.

Although there are few prosecutions for suspected breaches of military orders by low-ranking military personnel, the Council has concluded that the number and nature of cases giving rise to indictments 'raise serious questions regarding the effectiveness of the current mechanisms to hold to account those responsible for the most serious alleged crimes'.[108]

With regard to alleged unlawful killings and other human rights violations in the Occupied Palestinian Territories, there is a procedure that allows Palestinians to lodge complaints against Israelis in Israeli Courts. However, according to Amnesty International, such complaints have, in practice, little if any chance of resulting in investigations and prosecutions.[109] From 2011 to 2015, for instance, there had been only two indictments and one conviction following 36 investigations over the killing of Palestinians in the West Bank.[110] According to Yesh Din, more than 97% of investigations of alleged crimes committed against Palestinians do not result in indictments.[111]

The claim of complementarity, could not, however, be raised as a bar to the ICC's investigation regarding State-sponsored alleged crimes. Alleged crimes such as construction of settlements, appropriation of land, perpetrating crime of apartheid and persecution are reportedly backed by State policies and laws. Up to the time of writing, no Israeli Court has dealt with these State polices in a way that could alter the policies and practices. In this sense, the Israeli Supreme Court decision upholding the Anti-boycott Law and a decision that upheld a law that allows racial segregation through the denial of residency to Palestinians on the ground of 'social suitability' and 'cultural fabric' are exemplary.[112] Hence, regarding these crimes particularly, Israel does not have any compelling complementarity claim.

---

108 See UNHRC 2015, paras 650–651; and Yesh Din, Data Sheet, September 2014 http://www.yesh-din.org/userfiles/file/datasheets/YeshDin%20-%20DataSheet%20Metzach%209_14%20-%20Eng%20(1)%20(1).pdf (accessed 21 March 2016).

109 Amnesty International 2009, p. 90.

110 UNHRC 2015, paras 650–651; Yesh Din 2014, above n. 108.

111 Ibid.

112 Supreme Court of Israel, *Avneri v. The Knesset*, Decision, HCJ 5239/11, 15 April 2015; the decision of the Court on Admittance committees Law is published in Hebrew, https://www.adalah.org/uploads/oldfiles/Public/files/Hebrew/Legal_Advocacy/Decisions/Decision_on_community_towns_september_2014.pdf (accessed 29 March 2017). See Human Rights Watch 2015a. See also Adalah, Israeli Supreme Court upholds "Admissions Committees Law" that allows Israeli Jewish communities to exclude Palestinian Arab citizens, 17 September 2014, https://www.adalah.org/en/content/view/8327 (accessed 23 May 2016); and B'Tselem 2016.

4.4.1.2 Palestine's Accountability Mechanism

On the Palestinian side, the UN Human Rights Council has repeatedly indicated that there is a lack of concerted effort to conduct credible investigations of international law violations.[113] The absence of an effective presence of the Government of National Consensus in the Gaza Strip, as well as the difficulty of unifying the parallel judicial systems operating in Gaza and the West Bank are noted as obstacles to conduct proper investigations.[114] Although Palestinian Courts may ideally prosecute Israeli citizens on the ground of territoriality and passive personality principles, exercising legal jurisdiction on a belligerent occupation setting against the citizens of an occupying power is almost impossible.

With regard to the investigation of Palestinians, however, the issue is more of unwillingness than inability. The Council has pointed out that other than the establishment of the Palestinian Independent Investigation Commission by the Palestinian Authority, there is no available information on efforts to investigate, let alone prosecute, alleged extrajudicial killings of collaborators[115] or indiscriminate rocket and mortar attacks against Israel.[116] In relation to the latter, Hamas, instead, allegedly promotes these conducts *during periods* it is not committed to maintaining ceasefires.[117]

Concerning the overall judicial structure of the State, the system in general requires basic structural reforms to create and maintain an independent judiciary with improved operational capacity. In addition to the need to reconstruct the law enforcement physical infrastructures destroyed by war, the judiciary, the police, prosecutors and prison officials require training in order to discharge their respective functions properly.[118]

Therefore, in light of these factors, both Israeli and Palestinian investigatory and prosecutorial mechanisms fail to meet the required standard. Hence, as things stand at the time of the Prosecutor's examination and in the absence of any improvement in the available mechanisms, domestic measures cannot bar prosecution before the ICC.

---

[113] UNHRC 2015, paras 652–657; UNHRC 2009, paras 1838, 1840.

[114] UNHRC 2015, paras 652–657; UNHRC 2009, paras 1838, 1840. See also Gompert et al. 2005, p. 50.

[115] The investigations and prosecutions conducted with regard to incidents of killings and torture within the Gaza Strip in the context or in connection with Military operation, as per the authorities, are rather 'family revenge cases or individual revenge cases'. UNHRC 2009, para 1840.

[116] UNHRC 2015, paras 652–657.

[117] Amnesty International 2009 p. 90

[118] Abdelbaqi 2006, p. 9; Gompert et al. 2005, pp. 49–51.

4.4.2 Gravity

Apart from the gravity-driven inclusion of crimes within the material jurisdiction of the Court[119] and the emphasis on the 'most serious crimes of concern to the international community',[120] an additional threshold of gravity is provided under Article 17(1)(d) of the Statute. In the words of the former Prosecutor, gravity is not just 'a characteristic of the crime but also an admissibility factor'.[121] Hence, despite the fulfilment of the complementarity criteria, a case may be ruled inadmissible if it does not satisfy the second limb of admissibility, namely the gravity element.

As per the Pre-Trial Chamber, this element furnishes the Court an 'additional safeguard' to prevent it from dealing with 'peripheral cases'.[122] Ambos and Stegmiller argue that this 'special' gravity provided under Articles 53(1)(b) and 17 (1)(d) should be read as a 'legal gravity' in contrast to, what they characterise, as the 'relative gravity' criterion under Article 53(1)(c).[123] On the other hand, Lattanzi states that in the context of preliminary examinations, evaluation of gravity as an admissibility factor is not necessary. She argues that gravity should be treated as an 'autonomous element of the reasonable basis, together with the interests of the victims'.[124]

The Court, however, has developed adequate jurisprudence on the assessment of gravity in the context of preliminary examinations. Decisions not to initiate investigations in the situation of Iraq[125] and in the situation on Registered Vessels of the Comoros, Greece and Cambodia[126] as well as North Korea were made on the

---

[119] ICC, Situation in the Democratic Republic of the Congo, Decision on the Prosecutor's Application for Warrant of Arrest, Article 58, 10 February 2006, ICC-01/04-520-Anx2, para 46.

[120] Rome Statute, above n. 8, Preamble, para 9.

[121] OTP, Statement by Luis Moreno-Ocampo, Prosecutor of the International Criminal Court: Informal meeting of Legal Advisors of Ministries of Foreign Affairs, 24 October 2005, https://www.icc-cpi.int/NR/rdonlyres/9D70039E-4BEC-4F32-9D4A-CEA8B6799E37/143836/LMO_20051024_English.pdf, pp. 8–9.

[122] Situation in the Republic of Kenya 2010, above n. 21, para 56.

[123] Ambos 2010, pp. 48–50; Ambos 2016, pp. 284 et seq.; Stegmiller 2011, pp. 332–335.

[124] Lattanzi 2010, p. 197.

[125] OTP 2006, above n. 62, p. 9. On his response the Prosecutor stated that the situation did not meet the necessary threshold in the Statute as the alleged crimes committed in Iraq do not qualify 'as part of a plan or policy or as part of a large-scale commission'. He also pointed out that the number of victims is small compared to other situations under examination. Following the receipt of additional information on alleged crimes committed in Iraq, the OTP has reopened the preliminary examination on the situation of Iraq on 13 May 2014. See OTP, Statement: Prosecutor of the International Criminal Court, Fatou Bensouda, re-opens the preliminary examination of the situation in Iraq, 14 May 2014, https://www.icc-cpi.int/en_menus/icc/press%20and%20media/press%20releases/Pages/otp-Statement-iraq-13-05-2014.aspx (accessed 22 March 2016). See also Kittrie 2016, p. 220.

[126] OTP 2014, para 142. On 16 July 2015, following an application for review by the Union of Comoros, the Pre-Trial Chamber requested the Prosecutor to reconsider her decision. See ICC, Decision on the request of the Union of the Comoros to review the Prosecutor's decision not to

basis of gravity. The same parameter was used to focus the investigation in the situation of Uganda on the Lord's Resistance Army (LRA) rather than on Uganda People's Defence Force (UPDF).[127] Hence, in contrast to Lattanzi's argument, the jurisprudence of the Court provides for generic assessment of the gravity of 'potential cases'.[128]

At the examination stage, the first assessment is whether the object of the investigation on the 'potential cases' lies on the alleged perpetrators who are likely to bear the greatest responsibility for the commission of the crimes.[129] The 'senior leader' requirement adopted by the Pre-Trial Chamber in the *Ntaganda* case was overturned by the Appeals Chamber, which rejected the formalistic and rigid interpretation that, it notes, hampers 'the preventive or deterrent role of the Court'.[130]

Certainly, factors such as seniority, level and position of the alleged perpetrators have a determinative factor on the role played with regard to the commission of the crime. Yet the decision remains within the prosecutorial strategy and has to be made on a case-by-case basis. Needless to say, military commanders and political leaders of Israel as well as Hamas and other armed groups operating in Gaza would most certainly be within the remit of the Court.

The second assessment in light of the Israeli-Palestinian conflict is a generic assessment of the qualitative and quantitative factors in view of the scale, nature, manner of commission and the resultant impact of the alleged crimes as similarly provided in Regulation 29(2) of the Regulations of the Office of the Prosecutor, and 'any aggravating circumstance'.[131]

Notwithstanding other admissibility challenges, in light of the threshold in Article 53(1)(b), there is no issue concerning the satisfaction of the gravity element on the situation in Palestine. The 2015 preliminary examination report on the situation has highlighted the number of victims and the extent of socio-economic

initiate an investigation, Situation on the Registered Vessels of the Union of the Comoros, the Hellenic Republic and the Kingdom of Cambodia, 16 July 2015, ICC-01/13-34.

127 OTP, Statement by Chief Prosecutor Luis Moreno-Ocampo, 14 October 2005, https://www.icc-cpi.int/NR/rdonlyres/9AC37606-6662-448F-8689-7317E341E6D7/277305/Uganda_LMO_Speech_141020091.pdf (accessed 25 May 2017), p. 3; Schabas 2009, p. 232.

128 The Pre-Trial Chamber has defined the term 'potential cases' to include the groups of people involved and the crimes within the jurisdiction of the Court that are likely to be the object of investigation. See Situation in the Republic of Kenya 2010, above n. 21, paras 58–60.

129 Ibid., paras 188–9; ICC, Situation in the Republic of Côte d'Ivoire, Decision Pursuant to Article 15 of the Rome Statute on the Authorization of an Investigation into the Situation in the Republic of Côte d'Ivoire, 15 November 2011, ICC-02/11-14-Corr, para 204; OTP 2013b p. 15; Triffterer and Ambos 2016, p. 1373

130 ICC, Situation in the Democratic Republic of Congo, Judgment on the Prosecutor's Appeal against the decision of Pre-Trial Chamber I entitled 'Decision on the Prosecutor's Application for Warrants of Arrest, Article 58', 13 July 2006, ICC-01/04-169, paras 68–82. See also Triffterer and Ambos 2016, p. 813.

131 Situation in the Republic of Kenya, above n. 21, paras 61–62; OTP 2013b, p. 15. Triffterer and Ambos 2016, p. 1373.

and environmental damages caused due to the alleged violations of international humanitarian and human rights law during Operation Protective Edge.[132] Be it in the case of the creation and maintenance of the Israeli settlement activity, the alleged systematic and institutionalised ill-treatment of incarcerated Palestinian children or the reported summary execution of collaborators by Hamas,[133] one can reach the conclusion that the degree to which the alleged crimes were systematic, their execution planned and organized and the perpetual duration would satisfy the gravity element for this stage of the proceeding.

4.5 The 'Interest of Justice' Consideration

Interest of justice is a 'potentially countervailing consideration' that may provide a reason not to proceed to investigations even if the positive requirements of jurisdiction and admissibility are satisfied.[134] There is no duty on the part of the Prosecutor to establish that an investigation serves the interest of justice unless there are convincing reasons to believe that an investigation would go against the interest of justice.[135] Upon the satisfaction of the other criteria, Article 53(1)(c) of the Statute disallows the Prosecutor from starting an investigation if 'taking into account the gravity of the crime and the interest of victims, there are nonetheless substantial reasons to believe than an investigation would not serve the interest of justice'.[136]

There are no clear guidelines in the Rome Statute on how to interpret and apply this element. The lack of a clear guideline and definition on the exact content of the term is, however, slightly complemented by a system of Pre-Trial Chamber review. The Prosecutor has to substantiate her decision not to investigate when the decision is reached on the grounds of interest of justice.[137] The Policy Paper on Interest of Justice published in 2007 adopts an approach that appears to exclusively favour the demands of justice in contrast to the demands of peace.[138] It states that matters of international peace and security are not within the ambit of responsibility of the Prosecutor. Hence, as per the Prosecutor's view, political, security or peace-making efforts do not sway decisions to investigate and prosecute, as it is these initiatives

[132] As a result of the indiscriminate attacks on civilians and civilian objects, it is reported that over 1,000 Palestinians and six Israelis were killed, and 11,000 Palestinians and 1,600 Israelis were injured. Various reports have also indicated the incalculable damage incurred to the extent of making Gaza uninhabitable in the near future. See OTP 2015a, pp. 14–16; and FIDH 2014; Human Rights Watch 2015b; and UNCTAD 2015.

[133] OTP 2015a, pp. 14–16.

[134] OTP 2013b p. 16; OTP 2007, p. 2.

[135] Ibid., pp. 2–3; Peschke 2011, pp. 198 et seq.

[136] Rome Statute, above n. 8, Article 53(1)(c). See Peschke 2011, p. 198.

[137] Rome Statute, above n. 8, Article 53(2).

[138] OTP 2007.

that should be made to comply with the legal framework of the Court.[139] The 2013 Policy Paper on Preliminary Examinations also states that the provision should not be construed as a 'conflict management tool' and the Prosecutor as 'a mediator in political negotiations'. This outcome, as per the Policy Paper, would 'run contrary to the explicit judicial functions of the Office and the Court as a whole'.[140] Seemingly, the sense of justice the Prosecutor has favoured is purely retributive and judicial, different from the broader restorative or transitional type. So far, the Prosecutor has not reached a decision not to investigate on the ground of interest of justice and points out that such decisions are meant to be highly exceptional.[141]

The narrow interpretation of interest of justice, even if it could be 'a self-imposed commitment device' and a strict limitation on the Prosecutorial discretion,[142] may strengthen the 'bargaining position' of the Prosecutor, which could be beneficial in situations as politically charged as Palestine. In light of the strict interpretation of the phrase, it can be argued that in situations where an investigation or prosecution endangers international peace and security and when political considerations are crucial, a UN Security Council deferral could be a suitable gateway.[143]

Be that as it may, considering the political environment in which the Court functions, pragmatic considerations related to interest of peace have an inevitable impact on the effectiveness of the prosecutorial strategy.[144] The haste to prosecute Omer Al-Bashir[145] and Muammar Gaddafi[146] has, arguably, negatively impacted the prospects of a negotiated peace, the duration of the bloodshed and the image of the Court in general.[147] When arrest warrants were issued against Al-Bashir, who

---

139 Ibid., p. 4. See also Kleffner 2008, p. 291.

140 OTP 2013b, pp. 16–17.

141 Ibid., p. 17. See also Kleffner 2008, pp. 254 et seq.

142 Mnookin 2013, p. 148.

143 Rome Statute, above n. 8, Article 16; Stegmiller 2011, p. 367.

144 Rashid 2013, p. 62.

145 The situation in Sudan Darfur was a result of a Security Council referral to the prosecutor in 2005. In the history of international criminal Tribunals, Al-Bashir became the first sitting head of State to be indicted. The Pre-Trial Chamber issued an arrest warrant against Al-Bashir in March 2009. See ICC, Situation in Darfur, Sudan, Warrant of Arrest for Omar Hassan Ahmad Al Bashir, 4 March 2009; Security Council Resolution 1593, ICC-02/05-01/09, 31 March 2005; UNSC 2005. See also Werle and Jessberger 2014, p. 110.

146 In June 2011, the Pre-Trial Chamber issued an arrest warrant against the then leader of Libya, Muammar Gaddafi. The prosecutor began the investigation in Libya following a UN Security Council referral of the situation in February 2011. Arrest warrants were also issued against Gaddafi's son, Saif Al-Gaddafi and the chief of the secret service of Libya, Abdullah Al-Senussi. See ICC, Situation in the Libyan Arab Jamahiriya, Warrant of Arrest for Muammar Mohammed Abu Minyar Gaddafi, 27 June 2011, ICC-01/11-13; UNSC 1970. See also Werle and Jessberger 2014, p. 111.

147 After the arrest warrant against Gaddafi was issued, the African Union published a Statement indicating that none of its member States would execute the Arrest warrant. See African Union, Decision on the Implementation of the Assembly Decisions on the International Criminal Court:

still remains at large, in retaliation, he suspended aid groups from reaching hundreds of thousands of people in dire situations in Darfur.[148] Similarly, the indictment against Muammar Gaddafi was claimed to be at the expense of political solutions, as it allegedly cornered Gaddafi to fight to the end than to relinquish power.[149] This should not, however, be construed to mean that the Court should allow 'conditional amnesty' to those most responsible when the interest of peace requires.

It can be argued that flexibility in timing indictments and regard to diplomatic options may in most cases reduce the number of victims and their suffering.[150] With regard to unstable situations and where investigations would threaten peace talks, Rashid praises the strategy adopted by the former Prosecutor of ICTY and ICTR, Richard Goldstone, in dealing with the prosecution of Slobodan Milosević.[151] In developing a strategy to prosecute perpetrators of the Srebrenica massacre, Goldstone indicted Karadzic[152] and Mladic[153] but excluded Milosević who was, at the time, indispensable to the Dayton Peace Agreement.[154] Milosević later faced trial on 66 counts after the completion of NATO's Kosovo intervention and when any hostile response from his side could no more be dangerous.[155] Such an approach does not only protect the interest of victims and would likely result in successful investigations and prosecutions, but it also helps the Prosecutor avoid entrapping herself in politics. Although not conventionally, the Prosecutor has resorted to stalling the preliminary examination of situations to give leeway to other

---

Doc. EX.CL/670(XIX), 1 July 2011, Assembly/AU/Doc.366 (XVII), para 6. See also Mnookin 2013, p. 149.

148 Al Jazeera, Mixed reaction to Bashir Warrant, 5 March 2009, http://www.aljazeera.com/news/africa/2009/03/2009357272395326.html (accessed 29 March 2016).

149 Hayner 2013; S. Tisdall, This arrest warrant could make Gaddafi more dangerous, The Guardian, 27 June 2011.

150 For more on timing of indictments see Mnookin 2013, p. 159.

151 Rashid 2013, p. 62. Boas, on the other hand argues that the Prosecution of Milosević is far from 'best practice'. He States, the prosecution strategy is reactive, not well planned and executed. The structure, scope and nature of the indictments, in addition to the Court and Milosević himself could be blamed for the way the trial run the way it did. See Boas 2007, pp. xvii, 1, 79.

152 In 1997, the Prosecutor Charged Karadzic for the Srebrenica massacre. The Trial Chamber of ICTY acquitted Karadzic of the first count of Genocide in June 2012. The decision was later reversed by the Appeals Chamber of the Tribunal. See ICTY, *Prosecutor v. Radovan Karadzic*, Judgment, 11 July 2013, IT-9S-SI18-AR98bis.l.

153 Mladic was initially indicted on 25 July 1995. The operational indictment was issued in December 2011 after he was arrested in May 2011 and transferred to the Tribunal.

154 The Dayton Agreement signed in December 1995 in Paris ended the worst conflict in the history of Europe since WWII. It was signed between the then Presidents of Bosnia, Serbia and Croatia, Iztbegov, Milosević and Tudjman, respectively. Orentlicher 2010, p. 26. See also Werle and Jessberger 2014, p. 115.

155 Boas 2007, p. 1; Rashid 2013, p. 62. Milosević died on 11 March 2006 before the completion of the trial.

mechanisms for addressing situations in the situation of Palestine[156] and other situations such as Afghanistan[157] and Colombia.[158] Especially in the latter case, for more than ten years, the Prosecutor has closely monitored the Peace negotiations (Israeli-Palestinian), the legal process and the transition in Colombia and has displayed regard for the local realties of the situation.[159]

However, in the case of Palestine, peace and diplomatic options have proved futile. There has not been any worthwhile peace negotiation between the two parties since the Oslo Accords back in the 1990s. Neither the soft diplomacy since the 90s nor the vegetative stance of the Palestinian Authority has halted the escalating level and intensity of violence and alleged illegal actions. Hence, the intervention of the ICC could hardly jeopardise the interest of justice. In addition, having in mind the calls from the victims and the international community for ICC's intervention, it is in the interest of not only Palestinian and Israeli victims but also the international community as a whole to see the interest of justice served in the conflict.

4.6 Governing Principles

Preliminary examinations of situations, or any task of the Prosecutor for that matter, are governed by the principles of impartiality, independence and objectivity.[160] The principle of impartiality requires an unbiased and consistent application of the criteria provided regardless of where or on whom the examination is focused. In light of the 2013 Policy Paper on Preliminary Examination, the Prosecutor is not expected to apportion blame between the two States under examination.[161] A focus on crimes allegedly committed by either the Palestinian or Israeli side, does not necessitate an examination of the other side to 'balance-off perceptions of bias'.[162] Nonetheless, in the situation at hand, such perceptions are hard to avoid despite the level of impartiality the Prosecutor may display.

Impartial justice does not only require independence from the other organs of the Court, but also freedom from altering one's decision for the desires of any party or anticipated repercussions.[163] The independence of the Prosecutor while dealing with the situation in Palestine should not also be influenced by the persistence of

---

156 As discussed in Chap. 3, former Prosecutor Ocampo took more than three years to reach a decision on the first Palestinian *ad hoc* declaration.

157 The Prosecutor has kept the situation in Afghanistan under Preliminary Examination since 2007. See OTP 2015a, p. 26; Mnookin 2013, pp. 163–164.

158 See also Murithi 2014, pp. 183–185.

159 The Colombian judiciary has prosecuted thousands of perpetrators during this period. For more see Seils 2014.

160 See OTP 2013a.

161 OTP 2013b, pp. 7–8.

162 Ibid.

163 Rome Statute, above n. 8, Article 42; OTP 2013b, p. 7; Triffterer and Ambos 2016, p. 1270.

Israel not to cooperate with the Court.[164] Israel's non-cooperation may greatly affect the proceedings that may follow the examination.[165] A complete access to the occupied territories is only possible with the cooperation of Israel, giving Israel a considerable leverage over the investigations.[166] Despite the ever-changing stance of Egypt regarding the opening of the Rafah crossings,[167] entry to Gaza through Egypt could be possible unless Egypt, which is not a State party to the Rome Statute, refuses to cooperate. Moreover, bearing in mind the amount of information already available and the ICC-friendly Israeli human rights bodies that are willing to assist in investigation, Israel's non-cooperation should not, on its own, inhibit either the proceedings or the functional independence of the Prosecutor.

Similar to the Romano-Germanic legal tradition, Article 54(1) broadens the investigative role of the Prosecutor to look into both 'incriminating and exonerating circumstances'.[168] Such an objective approach does not only help to establish the truth and assist the Court in the search for justice, but it also facilitates in the solicitation of evidence, especially to address the resource imbalance between the Prosecutor and the potential suspects.[169] Since the Prosecutor does not gather her own evidence during the preliminary examination stage, the principle of objectivity is crucial in evaluating the seriousness and credibility of available sources. In the interest of fairness, the policy paper also provides for the need to give all relevant

---

[164] Israel announced that it has reversed its policy towards the ICC and has decided to open for dialogue on 9 July 2015, only to clarify later on that the aim of the dialogue was to explain that the Court has no authority to entertain Palestinian complaints. See B. Ravid, Exclusive: Israel decides to open dialogue with ICC over Gaza Preliminary examination, Haaretz, 9 July 2015.

[165] The deleterious effect of non-cooperation on collecting evidence and apprehending suspects has been seen in the practice of *ad hoc* Tribunals, notably in the *Barayagwiza* case in the ICTR and the *Blaškić* case in the ICTY. See ICRC, *Jean-Bosco Barayagwiza v. The Prosecutor*, Decision, 3 November 1999, ICTR-97-19; and *Blaškić* 2000, above n. 150. See also Cryer 2009, p. 201.

[166] Refusal to allow entry to the Prosecutor may not be a smart political decision to the Israeli officials bearing in mind the bad publicity that it may risk, and also considering the agreement of Russia, which is in a similar situation as Israel, to cooperate with the Court for the investigation on the situation of Ukraine and Georgia. Russia is now within the target of the Court for the second time. With regard to the Situation in Ukraine, Russia could possibly argue that the Court does not have jurisdiction over Crimea, an argument similar to the one raised by Israel and its allies in relation to Palestine. See Radio Free Europe Radio Liberty, Russia Says Will Cooperate with ICC Georgia War Probe, 5 April 2016, http://www.rferl.org/content/russia-says-will-cooperate-with-icc-probe-of-war-crimes/27520262.html (accessed 5 April 2016).

[167] Following the agreement between Egypt and the PA to open the Rafah crossings, the outlet was giving passage to Palestinians in 2015. After the coming to power of the Al-Sisi government in Egypt, the Rafah crossings are, reportedly closed indefinitely. J. Khoury, Egypt, the PA Agree on Re-opening Rafah Crossing, Fatah Official Says, HAARETZ, 17 November 2015. See also P. Strickland and E. Zanoun, Palestinians in Gaza mass for rare Rafah border opening, Aljazeera, 13 February 2016.

[168] Rome Statute, above n. 8, Article 54(1)(a); ICC, Regulations of the Office of the Prosecutor, entered into force 23 April 2009, ICC-BD/05-01-09, Regulation 34(1).

[169] Triffterer and Ambos 2016, pp. 1382–1383. See also OTP 2013b, p. 8.

parties an opportunity to submit information. Until the time of writing, the State of Palestine has submitted files related to alleged crimes.[170]

In line with the principle of transparency, the OTP also publishes reports on preliminary examinations. So far, it has published regular updates on more than 21 situations since 2011. In the 2015 and 2016 reports, for instance, the Prosecutor published an annual update on nine situations including on the situation in Palestine. In the latter case, the report only dealt with matters related to material jurisdiction as an assessment on matters of admissibility and interest of justice has not been made yet. The publication of such information at any preliminary stage, as the 2013 Policy Paper indicates, greatly contributes to prevention of crimes and to positive complementarity. The commencement of the examination could mitigate or deter violent confrontations between the two parties.[171] The prospect of discomfiture that an ICC indictment could bring and the popular support for one's plight causes parties to watch their behaviours.

In the introductory section of the 2015 Report on Preliminary Examination Activities, it was maintained that 'geographical and regional balance' is not taken into consideration in determining to proceed to an examination.[172] Rightly so, there is no statutory framework necessitating the maintenance of a regional balance. However disputable the justification behind the recent shift in the focus of the Court from Africa to the other part of the world may be, the possibility of Israel, 'an upstanding member of the Western civilization',[173] to be before a Court known to prosecute African dictators and war lords may bring a significant change in outlooks.

As mentioned elsewhere, there is no time frame for preliminary examinations.[174] The absence of a time frame does not, however, imply that the examination could continue indefinitely.[175] Although not prescribed in the Statute, the Prosecutor has a duty to decide on preliminary examinations within a reasonable period. In relation to the situation in the Central African Republic, the Pre-Trial Chamber decided that regardless of the complexity of the situation, preliminary examinations should be

---

170 RT, 'ICC Credibility Test': Palestinians submit first war crimes evidence against Israel, 25 June 2015, https://www.rt.com/news/269803-palestinians-submit-evidence-icc/ (accessed 31, March 2016). As per the OTP's 2015 Report on Preliminary examination activities, Palestine has submitted communications to the office on 25 June, 3 August and 30 October 2015. The Israeli government has also published a report on the 'factual and legal aspects' of the 2014 conflict in Gaza. See OTP 2015a, pp. 16–17.

171 Israel is looking into possible 'large-scale prosecution' of the heads of the PA in the US. See BBC News, Will ICC membership help or hinder the Palestinians' cause? 1 April 2015, http://www.bbc.com/news/world-middle-east-30744701 (accessed 1 April 2016).

172 OTP 2015a, p. 3. See also OTP 2013b, p. 8; Kuczyńska 2015, p. 76; Kittrie 2016, p. 219.

173 D. Li, Palestine and the ICC, MERIP, http://www.merip.org/palestine-icc (accessed 1 April 2016).

174 Regulation 19(4) of the OTP provides that preliminary Examinations should continue 'as long as the situation remains under investigation'.

175 El Zeidy 2015, p. 185; Stegmiller 2011, p. 230.

completed 'within a reasonable time'.[176] Comparing the duration of the examination in the Central African Republic, which was in its second year to that of the situation in Uganda and the Democratic Republic of Congo, which only took two to six months, the Chamber requested the Prosecutor to furnish a report on the status of the examination.[177]

Leaving aside the discussion on whether the matter is susceptible to judicial review or the pros and cons of such a review,[178] restricting preliminary examinations to a certain time frame or 'reasonable time' in disregard of the complexity of the situation, has serious downsides. In situations as intricate as Palestine, an exhaustive assessment of the vast available information, probing domestic judicial alternatives or obtaining the vital State cooperation may not be possible within 'the reasonable time' typical for other situations. Although the Prosecutor may be justified in taking a longer time to examine, needless to say, she has to consider factors such as the interest of justice and the interest of victims in timing the examination.

4.7 Chapter Summary

The situation in Palestine is not only a situation most deserving of the attention of the ICC, it is also a situation that satisfies the statutory criteria established by the Statute. The discussion above has shown that the Court enjoys jurisdiction in the situation. There are reasonable grounds to believe that no domestic judicial body is investigating and prosecuting crimes within the purview of the Statute. On the face of it, therefore, the situation appears admissible and in line with the interest of justice criterion of the Statute. Despite the conclusion the Prosecutor may reach at the end of the preliminary examination, the fact that the conflict is brought before an international justice mechanism would ideally play a role in facilitating and shaping the agenda of peace efforts, promoting complementarity,[179] deterring potential crimes and change the dynamics of the conflict in general.

---

[176] The Chamber stated that in many parts of the Statute terminologies such as 'reasonable time', 'without delay', 'promptly' and 'in an expeditious manner' are used with regard to the many functions of the Court. It appears that the Court has derived the 'reasonable time' standard for preliminary examinations from such provisions. See ICC, Situation in the Central African Republic, Decision Requesting Information on the Status of the Preliminary Examination of the Situation in the Central African Republic, 30 November 2006, ICC-01/05-06 (Situation in the Central African Republic 2006), para 4. See also Kuczyńska 2015, p. 76; Nouwen 2011, p. 229.

[177] Situation in the Central African Republic 2006, above n. 176, para 4; and Kuczyńska 2015, p. 76.

[178] For a discussion on the supervisory role of the PTC at the pre-investigation stage, see Stahn 2009, p. 276; Stegmiller 2011, pp. 232–236.

[179] The impact of ICC intervention is a catalyst to complementarity as Israel has made efforts to better its judicial framework following the Gaza flotilla incident. See Sect. 4.4.1.1.

References

Abdelbaqi M (2006) Introduction to the Palestinian criminal justice system. Max Planck Institute for Foreign and International Criminal Law 1–56.

Abrams E (2015) Amnesty International, Human Rights Watch, and the question of Hamas, Gaza, and Israel. https://www.cfr.org/blog/amnesty-international-human-rights-watch-and-question-hamas-gaza-and-israel. Accessed 20 September 2016.

Adalah (2015) Report to The United Nations Independent Commission of Inquiry on the 2014 Gaza Conflict. Adalah, Haifa.

Ambos K (2010) The Colombian peace process and the principle of complementarity of the International Criminal Court: An inductive situation based approach. Springer, Berlin.

Ambos K (2016) Treaties on international criminal law: International criminal procedure, vol. 3. Oxford University Press, Oxford.

Amnesty International (2009) Operation 'Cast Lead': 22 days of death and destruction. Amnesty International Publications, London.

Ash R (2009) Is Palestine a 'state'? A response to Professor John Quigley's article 'The Palestine declaration to the International Criminal Court: the statehood issue'. Rutgers Law Records 36:186–201.

Askin D (1997) War crimes against women: Prosecution in international war crimes tribunals. Martinus Nijhoff Publishers, Dordrecht.

Bantekas I (2010) International criminal law, 4th edn. Bloomsbury Publishing, London.

Bassiouni M (2013) Introduction to international criminal law, 2nd rev. edn. Martinus Nijhoff Publishers, Leiden.

Boas G (2007) The Milosevic trial: Lessons for the conduct of complex international criminal proceedings. Cambridge University Press, Cambridge.

Boot M (2002) Nullum crimen sine lege and the subject matter jurisdiction of the International Criminal Court: Genocide, crimes against humanity and war crimes. School of Human Rights Research, Utrecht.

Bougon S (2002) Jurisdiction ratione temporis. In: Cassese A, Gaeta P, Jones J (eds) The Rome Statute of the International Criminal Court: A Commentary. Oxford University Press, Oxford.

B'Tselem (2016) The Occupation's fig leaf: Israel's Military law enforcement system as a whitewash mechanism. B'Tselem, Jerusalem.

Caban P (2011) Preliminary examinations by the Office of the Prosecutor of the International Criminal Court. CYIL 2:199–216.

Calvo-Goller N (2006) The trial proceedings of the International Criminal Court: ICTY and ICTR precedents. Martinus Nijhoff Publishers, Leiden.

Cameron I (2004) Jurisdiction and admissibility issues under the ICC statute. In: McGoldrick D, Rowe P, Donnelly E (2004) The permanent International Criminal Court: Legal and policy issues. Hart Publishing, Oxford.

Cryer R (2009) Means of gathering evidence and arresting suspects in situations of state's failure to cooperate. In: Cassese A (ed) The Oxford companion to international criminal justice. Oxford University Press, Oxford, pp. 201–207.

Cryer R, Friman H, Robinson D, Wilmshurst E (2010) An introduction to international criminal law and procedure, 2nd edn. Cambridge University Press, Cambridge.

El Zeidy M (2008) The principle of complementarity in international criminal law: Origin, development and practice. Martinus Nijhoff Publishers, Leiden.

El Zeidy M (2015) Ad hoc declaration of acceptance of jurisdiction: the Palestinian situation under scrutiny. In: Stahn C (ed) The law and practice of the International Criminal Court. Oxford University Press, Oxford, pp. 179–209.

Ellis M (2014) Sovereignty and justice: Balancing the principle of complementarity between international and domestic war crimes tribunals. Cambridge Scholars Publishing, Newcastle.

Erakat N (2014) Humanitarian law and Operation Protective Edge: A survey of violations and remedies. https://www.files.ethz.ch/isn/183320/738d0446fdfbae889f723f019683c6b3.pdf. Accessed 20 September 2016.
FIDH (2014) Trapped and punished: The Gaza civilian population under Operation Protective Edge. FIDH, Gaza.
Glaser S (2008) The charter of the Nuremberg Tribunal and new principles of international law. In: Mettraux G (ed) Perspectives on the Nuremberg trial. Oxford University Press, Oxford, pp. 55–71.
Gompert D, Shine K, Robinsons G, Neu CR, Green J (2005) Building a successful Palestinian state. Rand Corporation, Santa Monica, California.
Guilfoyle D (2016) International criminal law. Oxford University Press, Oxford.
Hayner P (2013) Libya: The ICC enters during war. https://www.ecfr.eu/ijp/case/libya. Accessed 20 September 2016.
Human Rights Watch (2015a) Dispatches: Israeli Supreme Court upholds ‘anti-boycott law’. Human Rights Watch, New York.
Human Rights Watch (2015b) World Report 2015: Israel/Palestine. Human Rights Watch, New York.
Jalloh C (ed) (2014) The Sierra Leone Special Court and its legacy: The impact for Africa and international criminal law. Cambridge University Press, New York.
Jones A (2015) Tailoring justice for mass atrocities: The constraints of international law and the ICC’s complementarity regime. In: Saul M, Sweeney J (eds) International Law and Post-Conflict Reconstruction Policy. Routledge, Oxon, pp. 95–116.
Jurdi N (2011) The International Criminal Court and national courts: A contentious relationship. Routledge, Oxon.
Kelsen H (2008) Will the judgment in the Nuremberg Trial constitute a precedent of international law? In: Mettraux G (ed) Perspectives on the Nuremberg Trial. Oxford University Press, Oxford, pp. 274–289.
Kittrie O (2016) Lawfare: Law as a weapon of war. Oxford University Press, New York.
Kleffner J (2008) Complementarity in the Rome Statute and national criminal jurisdictions. Oxford University Press, New York.
Knoops G (2014) An introduction to the law of international criminal tribunals: A comparative study, 2nd edn. Brill Nijhoff, Leiden.
Kuczyńska H (2015) The accusation model before the International Criminal Court: Study of convergence of criminal justice systems. Springer, New York.
Lattanzi F (2010) Concurrent jurisdictions between primacy and complementarity. In: Belleli R (ed) Law and Practice from the Rome Statute to its review. Routledge, Oxon.
Mégret F (2006) Why would states want to join the ICC? A theoretical exploration based on the legal nature of complementarity. In: Kleffner J, Kor G (eds) Complementary views on complementarity: Proceedings of the International Roundtable on the complementary nature of the International Criminal Court, Amsterdam, 25/26 June 2004. T.M.C. Asser Press, The Hague.
Mnookin R (2013) Rethinking the tension between peace and justice: The international criminal prosecutor as diplomat. Harvard Negotiation Law Review 18:147–174.
Murithi T (2014) Between political justice and judicial politics: Charting a way forward for the African Union and the International Criminal Court. In: Werle G, Vormbaum M (eds) Africa and the International Criminal Court. T.M.C. Asser Press, The Hague, pp. 179–194.
Nissel A (2004) Continuing crimes in the Rome Statute. Michigan Journal of International Law 25:653–689.
Nouwen S (2011) Fine-tuning complementarity. In: Brown B (ed) Research handbook on international criminal law. Edward Elgar Publishing Limited, Gloucestershire, pp. 206–231.
OTP (2005) First report of the Prosecutor of the International Criminal Court, Mr Luis Moreno Ocampo, to the Security Council pursuant to UNSCR 1593 (2005). https://www.icc-cpi.int/NR/rdonlyres/71FC0D56-11FC-41B9-BF39-33FC54F2C2A1/223633/ICCOTPST20080605ENG6.pdf.

OTP (2007) Policy paper on interests of justice. https://www.icc-cpi.int/NR/rdonlyres/772C95C9-F54D-4321-BF09-73422BB23528/143640/ICCOTPInterestsOfJustice.pdf. Accessed 20 September 2016.
OTP (2013a) Code of conduct for the Office of the Prosecutor. https://www.icc-cpi.int/iccdocs/PIDS/docs/Code%20of%20Conduct%20for%20the%20office%20of%20the%20Prosecutor.pdf. Accessed 20 September 2016.
OTP (2013b) Policy paper on preliminary examinations. https://www.icc-cpi.int/iccdocs/otp/OTP-Policy_Paper_Preliminary_Examinations_2013-ENG.pdf.
OTP (2014) Situation on registered vessels of Comoros, Greece and Cambodia: Article 53(1) Report. https://www.icc-cpi.int/iccdocs/otp/OTP-COM-Article_53(1)-Report-06Nov2014Eng.pdf. Accessed 20 September 2016.
OTP (2015a) Report on preliminary examination activities. https://www.icc-cpi.int/iccdocs/otp/OTP-PE-rep-2015-Eng.pdf. Accessed 20 September 2016.
OTP (2015b) Strategic plan: 2016–2018. https://www.icc-cpi.int/iccdocs/otp/EN-OTP_Strategic_Plan_2016-2018.pdf. Accessed 20 September 2016.
OTP (2016) Report on preliminary examination activities https://www.icc-cpi.int/Pages/item.aspx?name=161114-otp-rep-PE. Accessed 20 September 2016.
Olásolo H (2005) The triggering procedure of the International Criminal Court. Martinus Nijhoff Publishers.
Orentlicher D (2010) That someone guilty be punished: The impact of the ICTY in Bosnia. Open Society Justice Initiative, New York.
Pellegrino A (2014) The International Criminal Court through the lens of international relations: The politics of law. Centro de Direito Internacional 1–21.
Peschke K (2011) The ICC investigation into the conflict in northern Uganda: Beyond the dichotomy of peace versus justice. In: Brown B (ed) Research handbook on international criminal law. Edward Elgar Publishing Limited, Gloucestershire, pp. 178–205.
Rashid F (2013) The interests of justice under the ICC Prosecutor power: Escaping forward. In: Esin C, Johanssen J, Lake C, Schwartz P, Tamboukou M, Rashid F (eds) Crossing conceptual boundaries. University of East London, London, pp. 53–69.
Schabas W (2009) Prosecutorial discretion and gravity. In: Stahn C, Sluiter G (eds) The emerging practice of the International Criminal Court. Martinus Nijhoff Publishers, Boston, pp. 229–246.
Schabas W (2011) An introduction to the International Criminal Court, 4th edn. Cambridge University Press, Cambridge.
Schabas W, Bernaz N (2011) Routledge handbook of international criminal law. Routledge, London.
Schmitt M (2011) Investigating violations of international law in armed conflict. Harvard National Security Journal 2:31–84.
Seils P (2014) Intolerance of impunity does not make ICC an enemy of peace. https://www.opendemocracy.net/openglobalrights/paul-seils/intolerance-of-impunity-does-not-make-icc-enemy-of-peace.
Smith C (2012) The rise and fall of war crimes trials: From Charles I to Bush II. Cambridge University Press, Cambridge.
Stahn C (2009) Judicial review of prosecutorial discretion: Five years on. In: Stahn C, Sluiter G (eds) The emerging practice of the International Criminal Court. Martinus Nijhoff Publishers, Boston, pp. 247–280.
Stegmiller I (2011) The pre-investigation stage of the ICC: Criteria for situation selection. Duncker & Humblot, Berlin.
Stegmiller I (2013) The International Criminal Court and Mali: Towards more transparency in international criminal law investigations? Criminal Law Forum 24:475–499.
Stigen J (2008) The relationship between the International Criminal Court and national jurisdictions: The principle of complementarity. Martinus Nijhoff Publishers, Leiden.
Stone C (2015) Widening the impact of the International Criminal Court: The Prosecutor's preliminary examinations in the larger system of the international criminal justice. In:

Minow M, True-Frost CC, Whiting A (eds) The first global prosecutor: Promise and constraints. University of Michigan Press, Ann Arbor.
Triffterer O, Ambos K (eds) (2016) The Rome Statute of the International Criminal Court, 3rd edn. Hart Publishing, Munich.
Turkel Commission (2013) Israel's mechanisms for examining and investigating complaints and claims of violations of the laws of armed conflict according to international law (2nd report). Turkel Commission, Israel.
UNCTAD (2015) Report on UNCTAD assistance to the Palestinian people: Developments in the economy of the Occupied Palestinian Territory. UNCTAD, Geneva.
UNHRC (2009) Human rights in Palestine and other occupied Arab territories: Report of the United Nations Fact-Finding Mission on the Gaza conflict, UN Doc. A/HRC/12/48.
UNHRC (2010) Human rights situation in Palestine and other occupied Arab territories, UN Doc. A/HRC/15/50.
UNHRC (2015) Human rights situation in Palestine and other occupied Arab territories: Report of the United Nations Fact-Finding Mission on the Gaza Conflict, UN Doc. A/HRC/29/CRP.4.
UNSC (1970) Resolution 1970, UN Doc. S/RES/197.
UNSC (2005) Resolution 1593, UN Doc. S/RES/1593.
Vagias M (2014) The territorial jurisdiction of the International Criminal Court. Cambridge University Press, Cambridge.
Van Schaack B (2011) The principle of legality in international criminal law. Santa Clara University Legal Studies Research Paper 10-08. https://ssrn.com/abstract=1657999.
Wagner M (2003) The ICC and its jurisdiction- myths, misconceptions and realities. Max Planck UNYB 7:409–512.
Weill S (2012) The follow up to the Goldstone Report and its legal impact in Israel and BEYOND. In: Meloni C, Tognoni G (eds) Is There a Court for Gaza? A Test Bench for International Justice. T.M.C. Asser Press, The Hague, pp. 105–120.
Werle G, Jessberger F (2014) Principles of international criminal law, 3rd edn. Oxford University Press, Oxford.
Yesh Din (2011) Alleged investigation: The failure of investigations into offenses committed by IDF Soldiers against Palestinians. https://www.yesh-din.org/en/alleged-investigation-the-failure-of-investigations-into-offenses-committed-by-idf-soldiers-against-palestinians. Accessed 25 May 2017.

Chapter 5
Case Selection and Crimes Under the Rome Statute

Contents

Abstract Once a preliminary examination proceeds to investigation, the Office of the Prosecutor has the task of selecting and prioritising potential cases that could surface before the Court. This chapter examines the criteria for case selection and prioritisation followed by a discussion of possible charges that could be prosecuted before the International Criminal Court in the context of the Israeli-Palestinian conflict. The scope of the preliminary examination is limited by various jurisdictional parameters. As this study deals with the same issue in light of the Rome Statute, the Elements of Crimes, the criteria for case selection, it does not examine all possible cases that may emanate from the situation in Palestine. It rather discusses alleged crimes that represent 'the true extent of criminality' and 'the scale and impact' of the alleged crimes in the situation that fall within the jurisdiction of Court. Amongst the core crimes of the Statute, the study examines possible war crimes and crimes against humanity allegedly committed in the Palestine situation, emphasising cases with legal issues unique to the situation.

Keywords Crimes against humanity · selection of cases · situation in Palestine · crime of apartheid · International Criminal Court · war crimes

© T.M.C. ASSER PRESS and the author 2019

S. H. Adem, *Palestine and the International Criminal Court*, International Criminal Justice Series 21,
https://doi.org/10.1007/978-94-6265-291-0_5

5.1 Introductory Remarks

A decision on whom and what offences to prosecute creates one of the major distinctions between international and domestic prosecutions. In the domestic setting, all cases that pass the *de minimis* threshold are prosecutable, yet such is not the case in the international context.

Prosecution of a case before the ICC involves an analysis of 'ill-defined and complex' criteria and a broad range of prosecutorial discretion.[1] Investigations and prosecutions of the ICC necessitate dealing with the thorny issue of case selection and prioritisation.[2] Selecting situations to investigate and cases to prosecute is necessary as it is impractical for the Court to prosecute each and every alleged conduct and perpetrator,[3] and goes against the complementarity principle of the Rome Statute.[4] A cautious approach to case selection helps avoid overburdening the machinery of justice with cases having low prospects of successful prosecution, thereby contributing to the maintenance of the quality and integrity of the proceedings. The Rome Statute, the Rules of Procedure and Evidence, the Policy Paper on Case Selection and Prioritisation, among others, guide the prosecutor on how to come up with specific charges to pursue.

This chapter addresses the issues that are taken into consideration in coming up with cases to pursue before the Court. It analyses the criteria for case selection and prioritisation. In light of the Rome Statute, the Elements of Crimes and the criteria for case selection, the chapter is mainly aimed at examining possible cases that could be brought before the Court in regard to the situation in Palestine. It therefore examines possible war crimes and crimes against humanity within the jurisdictional scope of the Court. It particularly focuses on those cases that are often raised in regard to the situation in Palestine.

5.2 Strategy for Case Selection

Case selection is an indispensable practice of the Prosecutor's discretion. The discretion grants her the power to decide on the subjects and objects of the investigation and prosecution, which is, however, susceptible to procedural and practical limitations.[5] The procedural limitations, in particular, were introduced to

[1] Schabas 2008, p. 735. See also Peschke 2011, p. 198.

[2] See Article 53(1) of the Rome Statute of the International Criminal Court, opened for signature 17 July 1998, 2187 UNTS 90 (entered into force 1 July 2002) (Rome Statute); Rules 48 and 104 of ICC, Rules of Procedure and Evidence, adopted 9 September 2002, ICC-ASP/1/3 part II.A (Rules of Procedure and Evidence); Stegmiller 2011, pp. 209 et seq.

[3] Guariglia and Rogier 2015, p. 352.

[4] OTP 2016, p. 4.

[5] Côte 2005, p. 167.

strike a balance between the interests of what Brubacher calls the liberalist and realist categories of the Preparatory Committee of the Rome Statute.[6] The liberalists lobbied for a Prosecutor capable of initiating proceedings *ex officio*. The realists, on the other hand, pressed for a limited prosecutorial discretion out of fear of political manipulation and abuse of power.[7]

One of the provisions that reflect the compromise reached is Article 53 of the Rome Statute. When a situation satisfies the 'reasonable basis' standard and proceeds from preliminary examination to investigation the standard to graduate an investigation to a prosecution is of 'sufficient basis'.[8] The decision of the Prosecutor, on any of the above, is open to a Pre-Trial Chamber review either on the request of the Security Council or the State that made the referral or on the Chamber's own initiative.[9] Similarly,the Prosecutor has a broad discretion not only to employ 'gravity' and 'interest of justice' as a ground for her decision to investigate and prosecute,[10] but also to 'define' the terms both theoretically and practically. Ultimately, despite the judicial oversight, the decision to investigate and prosecute rests with the discretion of the Prosecutor as the Chamber could only request the Prosecutor to reconsider the decision.[11] Hence, in the absence of an established formal law or guideline for case selection and considering the broad Prosecutorial discretion available, disparities in case selection criteria are difficult to avoid.[12]

The sensitivity towards decisions concerning which conduct and perpetrator to prosecute, at times, gives rise to controversies. For instance, the 'seniority' of *Thomas Lubanga* and the charges brought against him, the decision not to investigate British soldiers in Iraq in 2006, the prosecution of only the rebel leaders in Uganda and DRC and the lesser attention on sexual and gender based crimes

---

[6] Brubacher 2004, pp. 72–73.

[7] Ibid., Steinke provides a detailed analysis of the stance taken and the policy justification behind the idealist and realist groups at the negotiations for the Rome Statute. Focusing on the legal arguments presented by Germany, he states how Germany gathered support for judicial independence of the prosecutor (the idealist vision), pushed for a reduced influence of the UN Security Council and how it influenced the resulting establishing treaty. See Steinke 2012, pp. 92 et seq.

[8] As an ILC report indicates, decisions of 'no sufficient basis' standard could be reached if: first 'there is no indication of a crime within the jurisdiction of the Court'; second, despite the fact that the crime falls within the Court's jurisdiction, the available evidence do not warrant a conviction; third, the case would probably be inadmissible pursuant to Article 53 of the Statute. See International Law Commission, Draft Statute for an International Criminal Court with Commentaries, 1994, http://legal.un.org/ilc/texts/instruments/english/commentaries/7_4_1994.pdf, p. 93. See also Stegmiller 2011, p. 243.

[9] Rome Statute, above n. 2, Articles 13(b), 14 and 53(3)(a)(b).

[10] Côte asserts that 'gravity' and 'interest of justice' involve 'some degree of subjective determination with moral and political dimensions'. See Côte 2005, pp. 168–169; Schabas 2008, p. 735.

[11] Rome Statute, above n. 2, Article 53.

[12] For an overview of the discretionary nature of case selection see Schabas 2015, pp. 375–380.

(especially in the first decade of the Court)[13] are some of the selectivity decisions that generated much controversy.

On 15 September 2016, the OTP released a Policy Paper on Case Selection and Prioritisation. The policy paper has the stated purpose of ensuring that prosecutorial discretion is 'guided by sound, fair and transparent principles and criteria'.[14] It details considerations in exercising prosecutorial discretion for case selection and prioritisation of investigations and prosecutions.[15] It also analyses the policy and practice of the Court with regard to 'the process of choosing the incidents, persons and conducts to be investigated and prosecuted within a given situation and across different situations'.[16] Due to their close correlation, the policy paper also derives principles and criteria included in the Policy Paper for Preliminary Examinations (discussed under Sect. 4.2).[17]

Before delving deep into an analysis of possible cases that could be brought before the Court in the situation of Palestine, it is imperative to establish the framework for selecting cases. Hence, the following section discusses the legal and substantive case selection criteria of the OTP in light of the Policy Paper on Case Selection and Prioritisation and the OTP's Strategic Plan for 2016–2018.

5.2.1 Legal Criteria

Decisions to initiate an investigation and selections of cases for investigation involve analysis of three legal criteria embodied in Article 53 of the Rome Statute. Both involve evaluation of the jurisdiction of the Court in light of the information available and the alleged conducts,[18] the admissibility of the matter in reference to the principle of complementarity and gravity[19] and necessitate the Prosecutor to

---

[13] ICC, *Prosecutor v. Thomas Lubanga Dyilo*, Decision on Sentence Pursuant to Article 76 of the Statute, 10 July 2012, ICC-01/04-01/06-2901, para 60; Hayes 2015, p. 826. See also Moreno-Ocampo 2013, p. 154. The indictment and conviction of Mr Jean-Pierre Bemba for sexual and gender related war crimes has, however, proved the increasing commitment of the Prosecutor on the fight against these specific crimes. See OTP, Statement of the Prosecutor of the International Criminal Court, Fatou Bensouda, regarding the conviction of Mr Jean-Pierre Bemba: "This case has highlighted the critical need to eradicate sexual and gender-based crimes as weapons in conflict" https://www.icc-cpi.int/Pages/item.aspx?name=otp-stat-bemba-21-03-2016 (accessed 18 May 2016).

For an institution that thrives on legitimacy and credibility in the view of its audiences, criticisms on case selection and debates on the motivation behind the decisions are disparaging. See DeGuzman 2012, pp. 266–268.

[14] OTP 2016, p. 4.

[15] OTP 2016. See also Kuczyńska 2015, pp. 117–118.

[16] OTP 2016, p. 3.

[17] Ibid., p. 4.

[18] Rome Statute, above n. 2, Articles 19 and 58(1).

[19] Ibid., Article 17.

make sure that investigation/prosecution of the case would not go against the interest of justice.[20] The policy paper emphasises that the criteria and analysis published in the policy paper for preliminary examinations are *mutatis mutandis* applicable to case selection.[21] However, the latter requires a more rigorous analysis and stricter test than the selection of situations.[22]

Article 53(1) establishes a duty to investigate unless 'there is no reasonable basis to proceed'. Paragraph 2 requires the Prosecutor to proceed to prosecution unless there is 'no sufficient basis' for prosecution. One has to assess the 'reasonability threshold' of the two legal phrases to identify the standard of proof necessary for each stage of the proceedings.

5.2.1.1 Determination of the 'Reasonable Basis to Proceed' Standard

Althoughthe 'reasonable basis' standard is found in few places in the Statute—Articles 15, 53 and 58—the Statute does not provide a definition.[23] The three provisions are applicable between the stages of preliminary examination and opening of an investigation. Hence, as the Pre-Trial Chamber II stated in its decision in the situation in Kenya, the reasonability threshold applicable is essentially the same for the above three.[24] Since the information available at this stage is not expected to be comprehensive or conclusive, 'the reasonable basis' standard is lower at the preliminary stage than at the completion of the investigation' or the standard for starting a prosecution.[25] In analysing the 'reasonable basis' test, the PTC has stated that:[26]

> [T]he Chamber must be satisfied that there exists a sensible or reasonable justification for a belief that a crime falling within the jurisdiction of the Court 'has been or is being committed'. A finding on whether there is a sensible justification should be made bearing in mind the specific purpose underlying this procedure.

[20] Ibid., Article 53(2); ICC, Policy Paper on Case Selection and Prioritisation (2016), p. 8.

[21] OTP 2016, p. 8. See also Schabas 2015, pp. 375–380.

[22] OTP 2016, p. 8.

[23] Stegmiller 2011, p. 252; Peschke 2011, p. 198; Triffterer and Ambos 2016, p. 1369.

[24] ICC, Situation in Kenya, Request for authorization of an investigation pursuant to Article 15, November 2009, ICC-01/09-3, paras 37, 104.

[25] Materu argues, and rightly so, that the Rome Statute, above n. 2, provides four different evidentiary standards namely the 'reasonable basis to proceed' under Articles 15 and 53, 'reasonable grounds to believe' under Article 58, 'sufficient evidence' under Article 61 and 'proof beyond reasonable doubt' under Article 63. Out of these four standards, the 'reasonable basis to proceed' requires a lower threshold of proof. See Materu 2015, p. 180; Triffterer and Ambos 2016, p. 1369.

[26] ICC, Situation in Kenya, Request for authorization of an investigation pursuant to Article 15, 26 November 2009, ICC-01/09-3, para 104.

Stegmiller argues that the 'reasonable basis' test requires an even lesser proof than the '*prima facie* case' requirement[27] which could be equivalent to the 'reasonable grounds' in Article 58(1)(a). Conceding that the terms have to be interpreted in a similar fashion throughout the Statute, he argues that the standard of specificity shall advance when a situation progresses to investigation.[28] He further proposes, rightly so, that a reasonable basis should be deemed to exist 'if initial suspicion is presumed by the Prosecutor and could realistically lead to specific cases for prosecution'.[29]

5.2.1.2 Determination of the 'Sufficient Basis' Standard

In Article 53(2) the focus shifts from investigation to prosecution, hence from 'situation' to 'case'. For the 'sufficient basis' standard to be satisfied, similar to the *prima facie* test, the available evidence should provide a ground for conviction. When making a decision whether to proceed to prosecution or not, the criteria listed under Article 53(2)(a) to (c) shall be examined in light of this 'sufficiency' standard.[30] In contrast to the 'reasonable basis' standard, there should be a higher threshold, increased degree of specificity and certainty towards the selected cases. This threshold should, therefore, be deemed satisfied 'if specific cases for prosecution have been identified and potentially lead to a conviction if not successfully rebutted during Trial'.[31]

5.2.2 Selection of Cases

Unlike the selection of situations to investigate, where all situations that satisfy the reasonable basis standard will be investigated, there is no presumption that all investigated cases will be prosecuted.[32] Amongst hundreds of possible cases within a situation, the Prosecutor has to single out, in light of the established criteria, those few cases that meet the threshold of criminality necessary for prosecution.[33] After identifying the alleged crimes or incidents, alleged perpetrators are identified and alternative case theories are examined.[34] The Prosecutor conducts an 'in-depth, open ended' investigation on the alternate case hypothesis to test case theories

27 Stegmiller 2011, p. 254.
28 Ibid., p. 253.
29 Ibid., p. 256.
30 Triffterer and Ambos 2016, p. 1374.
31 Stegmiller 2011, p. 256.
32 Schabas 2015, p. 377.
33 Guariglia and Rogier 2015, p. 377.
34 OTP 2015, p. 15.

against both incriminating and exonerating evidence.[35] The approach makes decision making on selection and prioritisation of cases easier. Such a decision, according to the policy paper, has to consider the following three criteria: gravity, degree of responsibility of the alleged perpetrator and the potential charges.[36]

5.2.2.1 Gravity as a Criterion for Case Selection

Gravityplays an overarching dual role both in the selection of situations and in the selection and prioritisation of cases within a situation.[37] In selecting the situation in Palestine, as discussed in Chap. 4, the Prosecutor has to make sure that the situation satisfies the gravity criterion provided under Articles 53(1)(b) and 17(1)(d) of the Statute.[38]

As a criterion for case selection, gravity helps guide the Prosecutor's strategy in focusing its investigations and prosecutions, 'in principle, on the most serious crimes within the situation'.[39] Although the office may employ a higher threshold than applied for the 'admissibility test' in selecting the situation, the policy paper states that the assessment of gravity for case selection is similar to the one used for selection of situations.[40] As Regulation 29(2) provides, the assessment is conducted taking into consideration the 'scale, nature, manner of commission, and impact of the crimes'.[41]

The scale of the crime is determined in light of the number of victims, and the extent of the damage resulted, including the 'geographical and temporal' intensity of the crime.[42] In the latter case, the office considers crimes committed with high intensity over a short period or those committed with low intensity in an extended period of time.[43] With regard to the nature of the crime, the specific factual elements of the crimes may be of particular concern. Such crimes include 'killings, rape and other sexual or gender-based crimes, crimes against or affecting children', persecution, or the imposition of conditions of life on a group calculated to bring about its destruction'.[44]

---

[35] Ibid., See also Guilfoyle 2016, p. 126.

[36] OTP 2016, pp. 12–15.

[37] Guariglia and Rogier 2015, p. 359.

[38] Ibid.

[39] OTP 2016, pp. 12–13.

[40] Ibid., p. 13.

[41] ICC, Regulations of the Office of the Prosecutor, entered into force 23 April 2009, ICC-BD/05-01-09 (Regulations of the Office of the Prosecutor), Regulation 29(1). See also Ambos and Stegmiller 2013, p. 423; OTP 2016, p. 12.

[42] Guariglia and Rogier 2015, p. 360; OTP 2016, p. 13.

[43] Ibid.

[44] Ibid., p. 13.

As to the manner of commission, the policy paper outlines ‘particularly aggravating aspects’.[45] For this purpose, the means employed, the degree of participation, the intent of commission, the systematic nature of commission, the existence of a plan or organised policy, as well as those that were committed in contravention of the duty to protect, are emphasised.[46] Similarly those that display ‘particular cruelty’ such as crimes against defenceless victims or those committed with motives of discrimination and those that aim to destroy groups using ‘rape and sexual or gender-based violence’ are of particular concern to the office.[47] The resultant effect of the crime on affected individuals, communities and the environment, and their susceptibility is taken into consideration in assessing ‘the impact of the crime’.[48]

The assessment regards both qualitative and quantitative factors.[49] Previous practices also show comparisons of the gravity of different situations and cases as one reason for decisions to or not to proceed, indicating the OTP’s broader understanding of gravity and discretionary application. Ambos and Stegmiller rightly argue that the Prosecutor has to make a clear distinction if decisions on case selection were made on the basis of Articles 53(2)(b), 17(d) of the Statute or/and Article 53(2)(c) of the Statute.[50] If a decision bases on Article 53(2)(b) and Article 17(d), it is a legal determination on admissibility. Hence, similar to decisions on the ground of jurisdiction and complementarity, if a decision not to proceed is made, the Pre-Trial Chamber—up on the application of the Security Council or the State making the referral—could only request the Prosecutor to reconsider the decision. If, however, the gravity assessment resulted in a decision not to proceed on the basis of Article 53(2)(c), the decision could only be effective if it obtains a confirmation from the Pre-Trial Chamber. Thus, as the ultimate decision to proceed may depend either on the Prosecutor or the Pre-Trial Chamber, subject to the provision employed, it is imperative that the Prosecutor specifies the provision on which the gravity assessment is based.

5.2.2.2 Degree of Responsibility of Alleged Perpetrators

In contrast to the general gravity assessment at the ‘situation’ stage, case selection requires an assessment of the gravity of a ‘case’ focused not only on the gravity of the crimes but also on the degree of responsibility of the perpetrators.[51] There is a long history of international criminal prosecutions focusing on those who bear the

---

[45] Guariglia and Rogier 2015, p. 360; OTP 2016, p. 13.

[46] Ibid.

[47] Ibid., pp. 13–14.

[48] Ibid., p. 14.

[49] Regulations of the Office of the Prosecutor, above n. 41, Regulation 29(1). See also Ambos and Stegmiller 2013, p. 423; OTP 2016, pp. 12–14.

[50] Ambos and Stegmiller 2013, pp. 423–425.

[51] Guariglia and Rogier 2015, p. 361.

greatest responsibility.[52] The post-WWII prosecutions, the UN *ad hoc* Tribunals, the Special Court for Sierra Leone, the Extraordinary Chambers in the Courts in Cambodia have, among others, limited their prosecutions to senior leaders and those most responsible.[53] However, the precise scope of the extent of responsibility is not clearly specified in their respective Statutes. Nevertheless, in light of the practice of international prosecutions, the position of the accused, the form of participation, the motive behind the crime and the manner of commission are indicators of the extent of responsibility and the role of the alleged perpetrator of the identified crime.[54]

The early policy stance of the Prosecutor focused on those 'who bear the greatest responsibility for the most serious crimes'. Regulation 34 (1) of the Regulations of the Office, the Policy Paper and the Prosecution's Strategic Plan all lead towards ensuring that charges are directed against those most responsible.[55] As the phrase 'who bear the greatest responsibility for the most serious crimes' is not explicitly included under Article 53 of the Statute,[56] the possibility of prosecuting low to mid-level perpetrators could not be completely ruled out.[57] This assertion is substantiated by the Appeals Chamber decision on *Lubanga* and *Ntaganda* case, which overturned the Pre-Trial Chamber's decision.[58] The Chamber argued that 'sufficient gravity' is an obligatory legal threshold limiting cases only to 'senior leaders'.[59] Using a teleological interpretation, the Pre-Trial Chamber asserted that the gravity criterion could maximize the deterrent effect of the Court if it is interpreted to focus only on 'the most senior leaders' and those 'most responsible'.[60] The Chamber's rigid interpretation, as later argued by the Appeals Chamber and the Prosecutor,

---

[52] Stigen 2008, p. 90.

[53] Aranburu 2010, pp. 2–6.

[54] Stegmiller 2011, p. 428.

[55] OTP 2016, pp. 14–15.

[56] Ambos and Stegmiller argue that a statutory ground for the Prosecutor's policy to focus on those 'who bear the greatest responsibility for the most serious crimes' could be derived from Article 53(2)(c). The provision provides *inter alia* 'gravity of the crime', and 'role in the alleged crime' as grounds for determination which cover the main idea behind the phrase. This, however, does not provide a 'free standing discretionary policy' as the fact that the decision was based on Article 53(2)(c) would make it prone to a review by the PTC. See Ambos and Stegmiller 2013, p. 426. See also Guilfoyle 2016, p. 130.

[57] A general idea to the 'most responsible to the most serious crimes' could however be derived from Articles 5 and 17 of the Statute. See Stegmiller 2011, p. 430.

[58] ICC, *Prosecutor v. Thomas Lubanga Dyilo*, Decision on the Prosecutor's application for a warrant of arrest Article 58, 10 February 2006, ICC-01/04-01/06-8 (*Lubanga* 2006), para 41 et seq.

[59] Ambos and Stegmiller 2013, p. 424.

[60] ICC, Situation in the Democratic Republic of Congo, Judgment on the Prosecutor's Appeal against the decision of Pre-Trial Chamber I entitled 'Decision on the Prosecutor's Application for Warrants of Arrest, Article 58', 13 July 2006, ICC-01/04-169 (Situation in the Democratic Republic of Congo 2006), para 73 et seq.; *Lubanga* 2006, above n. 58, paras 41 et seq. See Ambos and Stegmiller 2013, p. 424.

instead hampers the deterrent effect of the Court, as most perpetrators would be excluded from the outset.[61] When reversing the Chamber's decision, the Appeals Chamber did not, however, go beyond revoking the assessment of the PTC.

Considering the flexibility necessary in choosing alleged perpetrators, employing this criterion as part of the strict legal gravity under Article 53(2)(b) does not only raise practical difficulties but also possible challenges on personal jurisdiction and admissibility.[62] The 'most responsible' criterion, although is related to gravity, is a notion that should be assessed on its own right. For the purposes of case selection and prioritisation, the 'most responsible' criterion should be analysed in discretionary terms contingent on the policy of the Prosecutor and availability of evidence.[63] Hence, although the focus should still be on those most responsible, when choosing cases for prosecution in the situation in Palestine, the Prosecutor has to also look into cases that involve low to mid-level perpetrators. As indicated in the office's strategic plan, the prosecutor has to focus on mid and high level perpetrators to establish an 'evidentiary foundation' for cases against those most responsible.[64] The 'building-upward strategy' or the 'pyramid' helps the Office to have 'a reasonable prospect of conviction' against those most responsible.

As for the Prosecutor's plan, where a conduct is deemed exceptionally grave and has 'extensive notoriety', the office also considers prosecuting low-level perpetrators.[65] Pursuant to the policy paper, the degree of responsibility of the alleged perpetrator, is assessed in light of 'the nature of the unlawful behaviour; the degree of their participation and intent; the existence of a discriminatory motive; and any abuse of power or official capacity'.[66] Hence, despite the targeted person's *de jure* hierarchical position in the Israeli or Palestinian leadership structure, he or she could be 'most responsible'. This indicates that the application necessitates an evidence-oriented and case-by-case analysis.[67]

5.2.2.3 Charges

Since the adoption of the 2012–15 strategic plan, the prosecutorial policy has abandoned 'focused investigation' in favour of in-depth and open ended investigations.[68] Focused investigation was one of the guiding principles of the prosecution strategy.[69] It allows the Prosecutor limited flexibility because of electing to

---

[61] Situation in the Democratic Republic of Congo 2006, above n. 60, paras 73 et seq.

[62] Ambos and Stegmiller 2013, p. 426.

[63] Guariglia and Rogier 2015, p. 361.

[64] OTP 2015, p. 16.

[65] Ibid.

[66] OTP 2016, p. 14.

[67] Ibid.

[68] Ibid., p. 16. See also Guariglia and Rogier 2015, p. 361; and Guilfoyle 2016, p. 130.

[69] Ambos and Stegmiller 2013, pp. 418–419.

focus on those bearing the greatest responsibility for the most serious crimes. The Prosecutor selects alleged perpetrators for prosecution from the highest echelon of State hierarchy while others are left to domestic prosecution.[70] Selection of few grave incidents focusing on those most responsible has the aim of expediting investigations and prosecutions.[71]

According to the open ended approach, however, the office first identifies alleged crimes for investigation within the wide range of incidents and identifies alleged perpetrators based on the available evidence. The in-depth approach requires the office to collect evidences to support the alternative case hypotheses. The hypotheses have to be examined based on the available evidence so as to reach decisions on prosecution.[72]

Nonetheless, the fact that a case is 'trial ready' does not necessarily mean that it will be prosecuted. Even amongst trial ready cases, which satisfy the criteria provided under Article 53(1)(a) to (c) of the Statute, the Prosecutor has to prioritise.[73] The office has to choose cases that are representative of 'the true extent of criminality', the 'most prominent form of victimization', the 'scale and impact' of the crime and the affected community in the situation in Palestine.[74] Moreover, as the examination in the Palestine context is being conducted in an on-going conflict, practical considerations such as safety and security of witnesses and the staff of the Prosecutor's office and the availability and accessibility of evidence may also affect the decision on the choice of cases.[75]

5.3 Potential Cases Under the Rome Statute

Having established the criteria for case selection and prioritisation, what follow is the potential cases that may surface in the Palestine situation. In light of the policy of the Prosecutor, the following section focuses on potential cases that may reflect 'the true extent of criminality' and 'the scale and impact' of the alleged crimes in the situation. Although, admittedly, there are other cases with an equivalent degree of gravity and seriousness, the section focuses on the following cases mainly due to the specific legal issues they give rise to. The scope of this section does not also extend to addressing individual responsibility as ascertaining individual responsibility and participation requires discovery of factual evidences to tie the alleged perpetrator to the specific criminal conduct. Nonetheless, issues that have to be addressed regarding the material and mental element of the crimes and substantive

---

[70] Ibid.; Guilfoyle 2016, pp. 129 et seq.

[71] Ambos and Stegmiller 2013, pp. 418–419.

[72] OTP 2015, p. 16.

[73] Regulations of the Office of the Prosecutor, above n. 41, Regulation 33.

[74] Regulations of the Office of the Prosecutor, above n. 41, Regulation 34(2); OTP 2016, p. 14.

[75] Guariglia and Rogier 2015, pp. 361–362.

and procedural challenges that may transpire regarding the identified incidents and conducts are examined. Pursuant to Article 21, in addition to the Rome Statute and elements of the crimes, other conventional laws and the jurisprudences behind the crimes are consulted.

The section focuses first on cases of war crimes due to their preponderance and prevalence in the conflict followed by cases of crimes against humanity. These crimes are addressed to the exclusion of the crime of aggression and the crime of genocide. Any scrutiny on the crime of aggression is avoided *a priori* as the Court lacks jurisdiction in the situation at hand.[76] Concerning the crime of genocide, no credible source has shown the commission of the crime in the Palestine context. Hence, as there is no reasonable ground to believe that the crime is committed, an examination of the case does not appear necessary.

5.3.1 Cases of War Crime

War crimes in the Israeli-Palestinian conflict are the most widely documented and reoccurring commissions. Although the call for the intervention of the ICC in the conflict intensifies during military operations, the fact that a significant number of the alleged crimes are also committed in the context of military occupation makes this category of crime one of the central justifications behind the intervention of the Court.

War crimes are violations of International Humanitarian Law (IHL) that are specifically criminalised by international law.[77] For a conduct to qualify as a war crime, a breach of the laws and customs of armed conflict and a criminalization of the specific conduct under the treaty or customary international law are required.[78]

The laws and customs of armed conflict applicable today, *aka* international humanitarian law are mainly enshrined in the law of Geneva and the law of The Hague.[79] The four Geneva Conventions of 1949, the two Additional Protocols of 1977 and customary international law, among others, constitute the law of Geneva. This body of humanitarian law is primarily aimed to protect those who are not (civilians) or no longer (prisoners of war) taking part in armed conflicts.[80] On the

[76] On 26 June 2016, Palestine has become the 30th States Party of the ICC to ratify the Kampala amendment to the definition of aggression. Nonetheless, in principle, the temporal scope does not cover Palestine, as the alleged crime of aggression has to be committed one year after the required 30 ratifications are obtained so as to fall within the Court's jurisdiction. The ASP's decision that the ICC can prosecute the crime becomes effective on 17 July 2018. See S. Maupas, After 15 years, ICC states still debating crime of aggression, *JusticeInfo.Net*, 15 February 2017.

[77] Schwarz 2017, p. 1307; Werle and Jessberger 2014, p. 403.

[78] Triffterer and Ambos 2016, p. 303.

[79] Salmón 2015, p. 1136;

[80] Ibid.; Schwarz 2017, pp. 1311–1312; Triffterer and Ambos 2016, p. 303.

other hand, the law of The Hague, which constitutes various legal instruments[81] including the Hague Regulations of 1899 and 1907, prohibits particularly atrocious means and methods of warfare. Hence, international humanitarian law has the main purpose of mitigating the harsh effects of armed conflicts by establishing principles that aim to strike a balance between 'military necessity and humanitarian considerations'.[82] Nowadays, there is a growing consensus that the principles established in the law of Geneva and The Hague have reached a customary international law status.[83] Of particular significance are the cardinal principle of distinction,[84] proportionality and prohibition of causing superfluous injury or unnecessary suffering.

On the other hand, as the Geneva Conventions call for domestic criminal justice only for grave breaches, not every violation of international humanitarian law committed in the context of an armed conflict may amount to war crime.[85] Although the prohibition of certain impermissible behaviours in armed conflict is widely established and codified, the endeavours to hold individuals responsible for violation of international humanitarian law emerged after the WWI.[86]

In 1919, the Versailles Peace Treaty criminalised violations of humanitarian law and provided for the prosecution of war crimes of German war criminals.[87] However, the Nuremberg Tribunal established what is now considered as a generally accepted notion of establishing individual criminal liability under international law.[88] The paradigm shift brought about by the Nuremberg Charter surpasses

---

[81] Of particular importance are the Convention for the Protection of Cultural Property in the Event of an Armed Conflict of 14 May 1954, the Convention on the Prohibition of the Development Production and Stockpiling of Bacteriological and Toxin Weapons and on their Destruction of 10 April 1972 and the Convention on the Prohibition of the Use, Stockpiling, Production and Transfer of Anti-Personnel Mines and on their Destruction of 18 September 1997.

[82] Henckaerts and Doswald-Beck 2005; ICRC 2009, pp. 11, 79; Triffterer and 2016, pp. 305 et seq.

[83] International Military Tribunal, Judgment of the International Military Tribunal of Nuremberg, 30 September and 1 October 1946, in Trial of the Major War Criminals before the International Military Tribunal (Nuremberg Trial Proceedings), vol. 22, para 65; ICJ, Advisory opinion: Legal Consequences of the Construction of a Wall in the Occupied Palestinian Territory, 9 July 2004, ICJ Reports 2004 at p. 136 (ICJ Advisory opinion 2004), para 89; ICJ, Advisory opinion, Legality of the Threat or Use of Nuclear Weapons, 8 July 1996, ICJ Reports 226 (ICJ Advisory opinion 1996), para 75. See also Bedi 2007, p. 345; Bouchet-Saulnier 2007, p. 2011; Dinstein 2004, p. 33; Mégret 2015, pp. 669 et seq.; Schwarz 2017, p. 1304; Tomuschat 2014, p. 349; Werle and Jessberger 2014, p. 398.

[84] See ICJ Advisory opinion 1996, above n. 83; Salmón 2015, p. 1136.

[85] Article 49 of Convention for the Amelioration of the Condition of the Wounded and Sick in Armed Forces in the Field, signed 12 August 1949, 75 UNTS 31 (entered into force 21 October 1950) (Geneva Convention I); Schwarz 2017, pp. 1305 et seq.

[86] Werle and Jessberger 2014, p. 402.

[87] Ibid.; Triffterer and Ambos 2016, p. 303.

[88] The Tribunal coined the concept as 'crimes against international law are committed by men, not by abstract entities, and only by punishing individuals who commit such crimes can the provisions of international law be enforced'. See Nuremberg Trial Proceedings, above n. 83, 30 September 1946, vol. 22, para 465; Triffterer and Ambos 2016, p. 307.

the traditional concepts of 'acts of State', State immunity and the concept of absolute State sovereignty in making individuals liable to criminal responsibility in an international Court.[89] The Nuremberg Charter, in particular Article 6(b), enabled the prosecution of the major war criminals of the Axis power for breaches of the laws and customs of war under international law.[90]

Decades later, the Yugoslavia and Rwanda *ad hoc* Tribunals considerably developed the jurisprudence of the law of war crimes through prosecutions of war crimes on the basis of international law.[91] In one of the landmark decisions of the Yugoslavia Tribunal, the *Tadić* decision, the Tribunal dealt with, among other issues, the distinction between situations of armed conflict and situations of internal disturbances and tensions caused by acts of terrorism.[92] The distinction is significant as it determines whether international humanitarian law is applicable to a situation or not. Using the discretion provided under Article 3 of its Statute,[93] the Tribunal has also extended not only the rules of international armed conflict to non-international armed conflicts but also the extent of customary law applicable to armed conflict.[94] Although it made a significant contribution to the law of war on its part, the Statute of the Rwanda Tribunal limited the discretion—as well as the contribution—of the Tribunal (for war crimes) only to common Article 3 of the Geneva Conventions and Additional Protocol II.[95] At the time the Statute was adopted, the latter two bodies of law were considered exhaustive of the law for non-international armed conflict.[96]

Article 8 of the Rome Statute provides a close-ended exhaustive list of war crimes.[97] Paragraph 1 of the provision provides the Court jurisdiction over war crimes 'in particular when committed as part of a plan or policy or as part of a large-scale commission'.[98] The 'plan, policy or large-scale' requirement is not a required element of the crimes, but rather a 'practical guideline' to indicate which crimes deserves the attention and the limited resources of the Court.[99] Without

89 Mettraux 2011, p. 8.

90 Werle and Jessberger 2014, p. 402.

91 Ibid., p. 403.

92 ICTY, *Prosecutor v. Dusko Tadić*, Decision on the defence motion for interlocutory appeal on jurisdiction, 2 October 1995, IT-94-1-AR72 (*Tadić* 1995), paras 66–70; Olasolo 2008, p. 38.

93 Article 3 of the Statute of the ICTY (adopted 25 May 1993, UN Doc. S/RES/827 (1993)) enumerates serious violations of customary law of armed conflict, which give rise to individual criminal responsibility. Due to the illustrative nature of the provision, the Tribunal was granted the right to determine customary international law of armed conflict at least for the purposes of the Tribunal. See Cryer 2005, pp. 264–266.

94 *Tadić* 1995, above n. 92, paras 66–70; Werle and Jessberger 2014, pp. 407, 430.

95 See Articles 1 and 4, Statute of the ICTR, adopted 8th November 1994, UN Doc. S/Res/955 (1994).

96 Ibid.; Cryer 2005, p. 267.

97 Ibid., p. 268.

98 Rome Statute, above n. 2, Article 8(1).

99 Ambos 2013, pp. 283–284; Schabas 2011, p. 94; Triffterer and Ambos 2016, pp. 321–322.

prejudice to issues of gravity and admissibility, a single conduct may amount to a war crime.

Article 8(2)(a) includes lists of grave breaches of the Geneva Convention, which are customarily considered criminal in the context of international armed conflict.[100] Paragraph b consists of 'serious violations of the laws and customs applicable in international armed conflict, within the framework of international law'.[101] Despite being frequently ignored in contemporary conflicts and at times controversial,[102] the set of crimes under Article 8(2)(b) are also crimes with customary law status applicable in the context of international armed conflict.[103] Separate from situations of internal disturbances and tensions, Paragraph c and e of Article 8(2) provide lists of 'serious violations of the laws and customs of war applicable in armed conflicts not of an international character'. The set of crimes applicable in both types of armed conflicts are categorised based on their threshold, as violations of common Article 3 of the Geneva Convention (Paragraph a and c) and violations of general international humanitarian law (Paragraph b and e).[104]

The interpretation and application of the elements of war crimes takes into consideration the 'established framework of international law',[105] the 'principles of the international law of armed conflict',[106] as well as 'internationally recognised human rights'.[107] Also in light of these instruments, for a certain conduct to constitute war crime within the ambit of the Statute, material contextual elements and a specific mental element have to be satisfied.

With regard to the general mental element, different from the elements of the specific conducts of war crime, awareness of the factual circumstances is taken into consideration.[108] The context of the commission or the notion of armed conflict, the geographical and temporal scope in light of the applicability of the law of war crimes, the nexus between the prohibited act and the armed conflict and the protected status of the target constitute the contextual elements. Hence, before delving into a discussion of the specific alleged conducts of war crimes committed in the situation in Palestine, it is necessary to put into perspective, whether the situation,

---

100 Öberg 2009, pp. 170–171.

101 Rome Statute, above n. 2, Article 8(2)(b).

102 See, for example, the negotiation history of Article 8(2)(b)(iii), (iv) and (viii) in Triffterer and Ambos 2016; and ICC Case Matrix, https://www.casematrixnetwork.org/icc-case-matrix/ (accessed 2 September 2016). See also Cryer 2005, pp. 270–273.

103 Schwarz 2017, pp. 1304 et seq.

104 Bothe 2002, p. 386; Triffterer and Ambos 2016, p. 318.

105 Rome Statute, above n. 2, Article 8(2)(b).

106 These principles include The Hague Conventions on the Laws and Customs of War on Land of 1899 and 1907 and their annexed Regulations and the Geneva Conventions of 1949 and their two additional protocols of 1977.

107 Rome Statute, above n. 2, Article 21(3).

108 See ICC, Elements of Crimes, 2002, ICC-ASP/1/3 part II.B (Elements of Crimes), Article 8, introduction, para C.

on the face of it, satisfies the general objective elements to warrant an assumption that conducts of war crimes were committed.

The existence of a situation of *de facto* armed conflict needs to be established for the provisions of war crimes to take effect.[109] Neither the Geneva Conventions, nor the Rome Statute provides a clear definition of armed conflict. Common Article 2 of the Geneva Conventions, however, states that all four Conventions shall apply to all cases of:

> [d]eclared war or of any other armed conflict which may arise between two or more of the High contracting parties, even if the state of war is not recognized by one of them. The Convention shall also apply to all cases of partial or total occupation of the territory of the high contracting party, even if the said occupation meets with no armed resistance.

The commentary of the Geneva Conventions reads as follows:[110]

> Any difference arising between two States and leading to the intervention of armed forces is an armed conflict within the meaning of (common) Article 2, even if one of the parties denies the existence of a state of war. It makes no difference how long the conflict lasts, or how much slaughter takes place.

In its decisions in the *Bemba* and *Lubanga* cases, the ICC has endorsed the definition of armed conflict adopted by the ICTY Appeals Chamber's decision.[111] The Chamber stated that 'an armed conflict exists whenever there is a resort to armed force between States or protracted armed violence between governmental authorities and organised armed groups or between such groups within a State'.[112] The magnitude or intensity of the use of force is, therefore, immaterial particularly in international armed conflicts which makes humanitarian law and the provisions of war crimes applicable even to 'minor clashes' and violations of the 'internationally protected territory of another State'.[113]

Israel and Palestine are parties to the Geneva Conventions since 1951 and 2014, respectively. Regardless of how the two parties to the conflict characterise the

---

[109] Schwarz 2017, p. 1313; Triffterer and Ambos 2016, p. 312.

[110] Pictet 1952, p. 32. See also *Tadić* 1995, above n. 92, paras 66–70;

[111] See ibid., para 70; ICC, *Prosecutor v. Jean-Pierre Bemba Gombo*, Decision Pursuant to Article 61(7)(a) and (b) of the Rome Statute on the Charges of the Prosecutor Against Jean-Pierre Bemba Gombo, 15 June 2009, ICC-01/05-01/08 (*Bemba* 2009), paras 229 et seq.; ICC, *Prosecutor v. Thomas Lubanga Dyilo*, Judgment pursuant to Article 74 of the Statute, 14 March 2012, ICC-01/04-01/06-2842, paras 531 et seq.; ICTR, *Prosecutor v. Akayesu,* Judgement, 2 September 1998, ICTR-96-4-T (*Akayesu* 1998), para 620 See also Werle and Jessberger 2014, p. 410.

[112] *Tadić* 1995, above n. 92, para 70; Werle and Jessberger 2014, p. 410.

[113] Ibid., p. 412.

conflict,[114] an armed conflict is assumed to exist as both parties have employed their armed forces.[115] As enshrined in Article 1(4) of Additional Protocol I of the Geneva Conventions and the second Paragraph of common Article 2 to the Geneva Conventions, the term armed conflict covers the fight against alien occupation in the exercise of the right to self-determination and all cases of partial and total occupation.[116] Hence, despite the intensity of the armed conflict—and the 2005 disengagement of Israel from Gaza—the fact that the phrase 'occupied Palestine territories' is internationally recognised as including the Gaza Strip, in addition to the West Bank and East Jerusalem, makes the situation a perpetual state of military occupation and therefore an armed conflict.[117]

Be that as it may, proponents of the 'Gaza is not occupied' assertion often raise the European Court of Human Rights (ECHR) judgment in *Chiragov and Others v. Armenia* and *Sargsyan v. Azerbaijan*.[118] The Court used Article 42 of the 1907 Hague Regulation and reached the conclusion that for a belligerent occupation to exist the occupying power must exercise actual authority or effective control over the occupied territory. In light of this judgment, one may argue that in the absence of 'boots on the ground' Gaza could not be considered occupied.

Israel's 2005 disengagement from Gaza could amount to partial withdrawal, yet still occupation, as Gaza's air space, naval and border crossings are still under Israel's control. In a situation where the occupying power, in the words of the Trial Chamber of the ICTY, could 'send troops within a reasonable time to make the authority of the occupying power felt', physical presence of an army is immaterial

---

[114] As established under Article 13(3) of Geneva Convention I, above n. 85 and Geneva Convention II (Convention for the Amelioration of the Condition of Wounded, Sick and Shipwrecked Members of Armed Forces at Sea, 75 UNTS 31), Article 4A(3) of Geneva Convention III (Convention on Prisoners of War, 75 UNTS 135) and Article 43(1) of Additional Protocol I (Protocol Additional to the Geneva Conventions of 12 August 1949, and relating to the Protection of Victims of International Armed Conflicts, opened for signature 8 June 1977, 1125 UNTS 3 (entered into force 7 December 1978)), it is irrelevant to the application of IHL whether or not parties in an armed conflict recognised each other as States or not.

[115] Greenwood 2008, p. 48; Triffterer and Ambos 2016, p. 312.

[116] See Greenwood 2008, p. 48. The wider application of this provision also covers groups attempting to secede from a parent State. In regard to the universality and customary status of most of the Geneva rules see Mégret 2015, pp. 669 et seq.

[117] The Israeli Supreme Court has acknowledged—while discussing the 2005 disengagement of Israel from the Gaza Strip—that Israel is in belligerent occupation of the Gaza Strip. However, following the disengagement, Israel does not claim to be occupying the Gaza Strip any longer. On the other hand, the UN and the US consider Gaza as part of the occupied territories. See the Gaza Disengagement case: Supreme Court of Israel, *The Regional Council of Gaza Coast et al. v. The State of Israel et al*, Judgment, 9 June 2005, HCJ 1661/05, para 80. See also J. Levs, Is Gaza 'occupied' territory?, *CNN*, 6 January 2009; and Sect. 3.5.1.4 above.

[118] The cases deal with access to property and the right to return of individuals displaced by the Nagorno-Karabakh conflict between Azerbaijan and Armenia. See ECHR, *Sargsyan v. Azerbaijan*, Judgment, 16 June 2015, 40167/06, paras 93, 143 et seq.; ECHR, *Chiragov and Others v. Armenia*, Judgment, 16 June 2015, 13216/05, paras 96 et seq.

to assume occupation.[119] Moreover, for one to derive end of occupation from the 2005 disengagement, there has to be proof that the local administration has regained full and free sovereignty over the territory, which is not the case in the Gaza situation.[120]

The ECHR's categorical conclusion on the concept overlooks vital considerations. The primary aim of the law of occupation is humanitarian, which makes the concept reliant on facts on the ground.[121] The 1907 Hague Regulation's 'boots on the ground' requirement appears obsolete in the view of technological and military advancements that allow effective control in the absence of 'boots on the ground'.[122] The judgment did not also consider the broader notion of occupation recognised under common Article 2 of the Geneva Conventions and that of Geneva Convention IV. In light of Article 6 of the Geneva Convention, particularly when the issue under consideration is protection of individuals, the term is given a broader meaning.[123] This interpretation is also adopted in the *Naletilić* decision.[124] Thus, the occupying power should not necessarily have effective control as much as the application of the law of occupation concerns protection of individuals.[125]

At this juncture, it is paramount to establish the character of the armed conflict in the Palestine situation for the purposes of the Court. Considering Resolution 67/19 of 2012 confirmed the statehood of Palestine and the Prosecutor's subsequent treatment of Palestine as a State, the conflict can be safely grouped as an international armed conflict.[126] However, one could question if the conflict, prior to Resolution 67/19, could be categorised as an international armed conflict in light of the Prosecutor's stance on the matter. Having in mind the position of the Prosecutor

---

[119] ICTY, *Prosecutor v. M. Naletilić and V. Martinović*, Judgment, 31 March 2003, IT-98-34-T (*Naletilić and Martinović* 2003), para 217.

[120] Ability of the foreign troops to exercise authority or 'potential effective control' reduces the 'full and free sovereignty' the local government could enjoy. See Ferraro 2012, p. 150; ICRC, Occupation and international humanitarian law: questions and answers, 4 August 2004, https://www.icrc.org/eng/resources/documents/misc/634kfc.htm (accessed 30 May 2017).

[121] *Naletilić and Martinović* 2003, above n. 119, para 211; UN War Crimes Commission 1949, p. 55. See Ferraro 2012, p. 134. Ferraro asserts that 'the existence of an occupation – as a species of international armed conflict – must be determined solely on the basis of the prevailing facts'. This view is widely held in the international jurisprudence and State military manuals.

[122] See Sassòli 2015, p. 1190.

[123] Common Article 2 refers to both partial and total occupation, as well as occupation in the absence of armed resistance and does not make distinction in regard to the application of Geneva Convention IV (Convention Relative to the Protection of Civilian Persons in Time of War, 75 UNTS 287). See Common Article 2 of the Geneva Conventions. See also Ferraro 2012, pp. 135–136.

[124] *Naletilić and Martinović* 2003, above n. 119, paras 211 et seq. A similar approach was also taken by the International Arbitral Awards of the Eritrea-Ethiopia Claims Commission. See Eritrea-Ethiopia Claims Commission, *The State of Eritrea v. The Federal Democratic Republic of Ethiopia*, Partial Award Regarding Western Front, Aerial Bombardment and Related Claims-Eritrea's Claims 1, 3, 5, 9–13, 14, 21, 25 & 26, 19 December 2005, para 27.

[125] Ferraro 2012, pp. 138, 150; Shany 2005, pp. 374–376 et seq.

[126] *Tadić* 1995, above n. 92, para 70; ICRC 2002a, p. 23.

that a State of Palestine exists following Resolution 67/19, categorising the Israeli-Palestinian conflict prior to Resolution 67/19 as a traditional international armed conflict would be challenging. The conflict would not also fall within the non-international armed conflict category as it is not contained within the boundaries of either State.

Article 1(4) of Additional Protocol I categorises 'fighting against colonial domination and alien occupation and against racist regimes in the exercise of their right of self-determination' as an international armed conflict.[127] These conflicts do not qualify as international armed conflict in the traditional dichotomy of conflicts as they are not conducted between two sovereign States. In addressing this issue, the Supreme Court of Israel quoted Cassese and stated that 'an armed conflict which takes place between an Occupying Power and rebel or insurgent groups – whether or not they are terrorist in character – in an occupied territory, amounts to an international armed conflict'.[128]

Although humanitarian law provides this expansion on the concept of international armed conflict, a similar approach is not adopted in the Rome Statute. In resolving this matter Werle and Jessberger rightly establish that since the law of war crimes is aimed at enforcing international humanitarian law, it is preferable to treat such situations as international armed conflicts for the purposes of war crimes law.[129] This approach is also in line with the reading of Article 21(1)(b) of the Rome Statute that allows the Court to apply, *inter alia* 'established principles of the international law of armed conflict'.[130] Hence, for the purposes of the Rome Statute, the Israeli-Palestinian conflict prior to Resolution 67/19 can also be grouped as an international armed conflict.

Moreover, not every crime committed during an armed conflict amounts to a war crime. The conduct under scrutiny has to be committed 'in the context of' the armed conflict or it should be one 'associated with' the armed conflict.[131] Hence, in the absence of this nexus, the conduct qualifies only as an ordinary crime

[127] Additional Protocol I, above n. 114, Article 1(4); ICJ Advisory opinion 2004, above n. 83, para 118. There is no issue that post 1967 Israeli-Palestinian conflict is mainly a conflict arising from the occupation of the Palestinian territories. In 1974, the UN has also affirmed the right to self-determination of the Palestinian people. The General Assembly has also stated the same. See UNSC 1974 and UNGA 2003.

[128] Supreme Court of Israel, *The Public Committee against Torture in Israel v. Government of Israel*, Judgment, 13 December 2006, HCJ 769/02, para 18; Cassese 2005, p. 420.

[129] Werle and Jessberger 2014, p. 414. See also Triffterer and Ambos 2016, p. 939.

[130] Rome Statute, above n. 2, Article 21(1); Triffterer and Ambos 2016, p. 939.

[131] For instance, the elements of war crimes provided in the Rome Statute for attacks directed against civilians and civilian objects or disproportionate attacks all require such nexus. See Rome Statute, above n. 2, Articles 8(2)(b)(i) and (ii), 8(2)(e)(i), and 8(2)(b)(iv). The nexus requirement also has a strong precedent see, for instance, ICTR, *Prosecutor v. Rutaganda,* Judgment, 26 May 2003, ICTR-96-3-A, para 557; ICTR, *Prosecutor v. Kamuhanda*, Judgment, 22 January 2004, ICTR-95-54A-T, para 733; ICTR, *Prosecutor v. Akayesu,* Judgment, 1 June 2001, ICTR-96-4-A, paras 438, 807. See also Olasolo 2008, p. 53; and Schwarz 2017, p. 1310.

committed in the time of war. [132] As to the Appeals Chamber of the ICTY, a close relation to the armed conflict or a proof that the existence of the conflict has influenced the commission of the conduct suffices.[133] Endorsing the above case law, the Appeals Chamber of the ICC has stated that it is sufficient that the existence of the armed conflict played a substantial role in the decision to perpetrate, the ability or the way it was executed.[134] This, however, does not require that the perpetrator shall have a combatant status or a status of those taking an active part in hostilities.[135] Hence, the nexus would still exist if the perpetrator is a member of a rebel group, an armed force or a civilian.

Particularly for the cases discussed below, the link to an armed conflict emanates from two scenarios, i.e., the existence of active armed conflict and the continuing military occupation. The alleged violations of the laws of armed conflict such as that of attack on civilians and civilian objects and use of human shields were committed in active military engagement between the military wings in Gaza and the Israeli Defence Force during Operation Protective Edge. As indicated above, the fact that the Operation qualifies as an armed conflict or a military engagement fulfilling the required intensity is not disputed by either party. With regard to other alleged war crimes such as construction of settlements, as discussed in the above section, the fact that the alleged crime is committed in the context of military occupation creates the required linkage with an armed conflict.

However, for a conduct to constitute a war crime, the prohibited action or omission must affect or target a protected person or object.[136] The Rome Statute criminalises targeting those protected under the four Geneva Conventions: the sick, wounded, shipwreck and religious and medical personnel, prisoners of war, civilians in the hands of the adverse party or an occupying power. The Statute, read in line with provisions of the Geneva Conventions,[137] also covers medical units,

---

[132] Ambos 2013, p. 286. The nature of the required link is not, however, clear. The jurisprudence of the *ad hoc* Tribunals sheds some light on the matter. The Appeals Chamber of the Tribunals indicate that the nexus between the forbidden conduct and the armed conflict does not necessarily have to be direct in the sense that the conduct should not necessarily have to happen in the wartime and amidst the warzone.

[133] *Tadić* 1995, above n. 92, para 70; ICTR, *Prosecutor v. Milorad Kunarac*, Appeal Judgment, 12 June 2002, IT-96-23 and IT-96-23/1-A (*Kunarac* 2002), para 58.

[134] ICC, *Prosecutor v. Thomas Lubanga Dyilo*, Decision on the Confirmation of the Charges, 29 January 2007, ICC-01/04-01/06-803-tEN, para 287. See also *Kunarac* 2002, above n. 133, para 58.

[135] Olasolo 2008, p. 54.

[136] Ibid., p. 61; Schwarz 2017, p. 1311.

[137] Geneva Convention I, above n. 85, Articles 15, 19, 20, 21, 33–37; Geneva Convention II, above n. 114, Articles 18 22–25, 27, 39, 40; Geneva Convention IV, above n. 123, Articles 16, 18, 19 21–23, 53, 57, 97. See Rome Statute, above n. 2, Article 21(1)(b); ICRC, Customary IHL Database: Rule 7—The Principle of Distinction between Civilian Objects and Military Objectives (ICRC Customary IHL Database: Rule 7), https://ihl-databases.icrc.org/customary-ihl/eng/docs/v1_cha_chapter2_rule7 (accessed 28 November 2016).

establishments and vehicles, aid societies and other private or public property located in an occupied territory.[138]

In the words of the Statute, targeting civilian population and objects[139] in general and 'personnel, installations, material units or vehicles involved in a humanitarian assistance and peace keeping mission',[140] 'undefended towns villages dwellings or buildings'[141] and those rendered *hors de combat,* in particular is a criminal act.[142] In addition, establishments aimed for 'religion, education, art, science or charitable purposes, historic monuments, hospitals and places where the sick and wounded are collected' are also protected'.[143]

Even so, following the coming into power of Hamas, the Israeli Security Cabinet, on 19 September 2007, has declared the Gaza Strip as a 'hostile territory'.[144] Once declared hostile, an enemy force could engage force without any display of hostile intent or act on the part of the party declared hostile.[145] This would give the impression that any individual within the perimeters of the 'hostile territory' could be killed without regard to the reasonableness of lethality in contrast to the conduct of the 'hostile party'. The phrase 'hostile territory', unlike 'hostile party', which is a developing concept in international law,[146] has no root in the jurisprudence of armed conflict. Hence, the unilateral declaration on the part of Israel could not strip off the protected status of civilians and civilian objects in the territory declared hostile.

Geographically, as the protection of international humanitarian law extends throughout the territory of the belligerent States, war crimes could be committed even in areas that are not the vicinity of the armed conflict.[147] The scope, however, depends on the specific war crime under consideration and the applicable norm,[148] as some war crimes are considered as such if committed at the scene and time of the armed conflict.

The notion of armed conflict, as discussed above, includes partial and total occupation of a territory by a foreign power. In addition to Operation Protective

---

[138] Henckaerts and Doswald-Beck 2005, pp. 12 et seq.; ICRC 2009, p. 74; Olasolo 2008, p. 62.

[139] Rome Statute, above n. 2, Article 8(2)(b)(i) and (ii).

[140] Ibid., Article 8(2)(b)(iii).

[141] Ibid., Article 8(2)(b)(v).

[142] Ibid., Article 8(2)(b)(vi).

[143] Ibid., Article 8(2)(b)(ix). See ICRC 2009, p. 74.

[144] The decision of the cabinet reads 'Hamas is a terrorist organization that has taken control of the Gaza Strip and turned it into hostile territory'. See The Israel Ministry of Foreign Affairs, Security Cabinet declares Gaza hostile territory, http://www.mfa.gov.il/mfa/pressroom/2007/pages/securitypercent20cabinetpercent20declarespercent20gazapercent20hostilepercent20territory percent2019-sep-2007.aspx (accessed 11 July 2016).

[145] Maxwell 2012, p. 32.

[146] Ibid.

[147] *Tadić* 1995, above n. 92, para 68; ICTY, *Prosecutor v. Dario Kordić and Mario Čerkez,* Judgment, 26 February 2001, IT-95-14/2-T (*Kordić* and *Čerkez* 2001), para 829; *Kunarac* 2002, above n. 133, para 57. See Werle and Jessberger 2014, p. 421.

[148] Ibid.

Edge in Gaza, where the two sides were engaged in active hostility, the existence of occupation in the sense provided under Common Article 2 of the Geneva Convention extends the geographical scope to the Gaza Strip, the West Bank and East Jerusalem.

Other than providing that the forbidden conduct has to take place 'in the context of' or 'associated with' armed conflict, the elements of crimes do not provide a scope to the armed conflict.[149] According to established jurisprudence,[150] a state of war is presumed to exist starting from the time the first bullet was fired up to the time when a general state of peace is reached.[151] However, the laws of war would still be applicable until those civilians or prisoners of war (if any) detained in connection with the armed conflict are released or an occupied territory is freed. Hence, without prejudice to other jurisdictional limitations, crimes committed under Israeli occupation and those committed in active hostilities such as during Operation Protective Edge fall within the jurisdictional scope of the Court.

Another important issue is with respect to making a distinction between breaches of the law of war and acts of terrorism. The Israeli government pleads that it is at war with Hamas, which it considers is 'a terror group' running the Gaza Strip.[152] Separate from non-State actors such as Al-Qaeda, Hamas, which is the elected governing body of Gaza, identifies itself with the State of Palestine and enunciates its armed struggle as a national liberation resistance against a foreign occupation. The Israeli-Palestinian conflict is an international armed conflict involving some of the governing bodies of Palestine and the State of Israel.[153] Hence, breaches of the laws of armed conflict shall be treated as war crimes rather than acts of terrorism. Once the existence of armed conflict is established, for war crime cases, the issue of 'just cause' *aka jus ad/contra bellum* is irrelevant.

In an armed conflict, the moral and legal necessity of respecting the laws of armed conflict subsists despite the moral judgment regarding the existence of a 'just cause'.[154] However, this is different from State-sponsored terrorist activities allegedly committed by either party to the conflict that deliberately aim to terrorise civilians.[155] The ICC does not deal with the crime of terrorism *stricto sensu* and there is no consensus on the definition of the term. Yet, the particular conducts of terrorism may satisfy the material aspects of war crimes (and crimes against humanity). Similar to any war crime, however, the existence of an armed conflict

---

[149] See Elements of Crimes, above n. 108, Article 8(2)(b)(I) and (II).

[150] *Tadić* 1995, above n. 92, para 70; ICTY, *Prosecutor v. Dusko Tadić*, Opinion and Judgment, 7 May 1997, IT-94-1-T (*Tadić* 1997), paras 561–566; ICTY, *Prosecutor v. Blaškić*, 3 March 2000, IT-95-14-T (*Blaškić* 2000), para 63.

[151] With regard to initiation and cessation of armed conflict see Dinstein 2000; Olasolo 2008, p. 50; Werle and Jessberger 2014, p. 421.

[152] See the Israeli Defence Force blog, https://www.idfblog.com/facts-figures/rocket-attacks-toward-israel/ (accessed 04 October 2016).

[153] *Tadić* 1995, above n. 92, para 70. See ICRC 2002a, p. 23.

[154] French 2003, pp. 39–44.

[155] Ibid.

with the required intensity threshold and in the sense discussed above shall be established.[156]

Before delving into the discussion on the concrete cases in the situation, it is imperative to establish the necessary mental element for prosecuting cases of war crimes. Individual liability for war crimes entails the satisfaction of intent and knowledge as provided under Article 30 of the Statute.[157] A range of crimes under Article 8(2)(b) such as (i), (ii), (iii), (iv) and (ix) expressly provide for intentional commission. Unlike other core crimes, this express mention indicates that intention, where it is expressly provided, is required not only for the conduct but also for the consequences of the same, i.e., if the perpetrator has knowledge that a given conduct would in ordinary course of events result in a certain prohibited consequence.[158] Hence, war crimes such as direct attacks on civilians and civilian objects require 'purposefulness' not only in dropping the bomb but also in hitting the civilian object.[159]

To satisfy the mental element, as the Elements of Crimes provides, a perpetrator has to be aware of the 'existence of an armed conflict'.[160] Such awareness could justify the particular blameworthiness of war crimes in contrast to ordinary crimes.[161] However, the perpetrator is required to be aware of neither the factual nor the legal aspects of the conflict that are considered to characterize the conflict as international or non-international.[162] With regard to the status of the protected, the perpetrator is expected to be aware of the factual circumstances.[163]

5.3.1.1 Attacks on Civilians and Civilian Objects

Attacks directed against civilians and civilian objects and those disproportionate to the military gain anticipated constitute the core components of the principle of

[156] Van der Wilt and Braber 2014, pp. 4–9.

[157] Bothe 2002, p. 389

[158] Ibid.

[159] Ibid.

[160] Elements of Crimes, above n. 108, introduction to Article 8. The awareness element is common to the crimes listed under Article 8(2)(a) and (b). See ICC, *Prosecutor v. Germain Katanga*, Decision on the Confirmation of Charges, 30 September 2008, ICC-01/04-01/07-717 (*Katanga* 2008), para 244.

[161] Ambos 2013, pp. 284–285. For more on equating moral blameworthiness with criminal liability or the so called principle of culpability see Brown 2011, p. 6

[162] ICRC 2002a, p. 15. Werle and Jessberger argue that in events where the international character of the conflict is decisive for individual guilt, awareness of the international character of the conflict is necessary. See Werle and Jessberger 2014, p. 426. For an alternative view, see Ambos 2013, p. 287.

[163] Ibid., p. 285.

distinction and proportionality.[164] Parties are required to distinguish between civilians and civilian objects on the one hand and military objectives on the other, as any use of force should only aim to totally or partially destroy, capture or neutralise the enemy force.[165] Hence, in light of these principles, attacks shall be directed against military objectives and should be conducted with precautionary measures with the aim to salvage civilians or civilian objects or to reduce the collateral damage. Parties are not allowed to employ prohibited weapons or cause disproportionate and excessive damage.[166] This, however, does not mean that civilian and civilian objects enjoy absolute immunity when they are at the scene of and during an armed conflict. Considering the unavoidability of incidental civilian damage in armed conflicts, Additional Protocol I declares that incidental damage is tolerable if States conduct hostilities with utmost care necessary to reduce such damage.[167]

In light of the laws and customs of war, the Rome Statute and the Elements of Crimes, the following discussion addresses alleged violations of the principles of armed conflict in the Israeli-Palestinian conflict. It discusses specific conducts that are in contravention of the principle of distinction, proportionality and duty to take precaution, and are criminalised under the Rome Statute. The section does not aim to give a comprehensive analysis of all the alleged war crimes in the situation in Palestine. It only addresses the most apparent alleged crimes within the jurisdictional range of the Court.

Intentional Attacks on Civilians and Civilian Objects

Distinct from indiscriminate attacks, which are not specifically aimed to harm civilians, the target of intentional attacks on civilians and civilian objects are civilians and civilian objects themselves.[168] Purposefully causing harm to civilians and civilian objects is prohibited under Articles 51 and 52 of Additional Protocol I.

---

[164] Additional Protocol I, above n. 114, Article 52(2). These principles are one of the cornerstones of international humanitarian law that aim to regulate how parties to a conflict conduct hostilities regardless of the nature and type of armed conflict. See ICJ Advisory opinion 1996, above n. 83, para 78; ICRC Customary IHL Database: Rule 7, above n. 137. See also Salmón 2015, pp. 1136 et seq.; and Kittrie 2016, p. 215.

[165] Additional Protocol I, above n. 114, Articles 48 and 52(2); Article 13 of Additional Protocol II (Protocol Additional to the Geneva Conventions of 12 August 1949, and relating to the Protection of Victims of Non-international Armed Conflicts, opened for signature 8 June 1977 (entered into force 7 December 1978)); ICRC 2009, p. 4; Solis 2010, p. 520.

[166] For a detailed discussion of the core principles of armed conflict see ibid., pp. 250 et seq.

[167] Additional Protocol I, above n. 114, Articles 48, 51(2) and 57(2)(a). The nature of the violation and the interests Articles 51(2) and 48 of Additional Protocol I aim to guard are similar regardless of the nature of the armed conflict. See also Olasolo 2008, p. 14.

[168] Schwarz 2017, p. 1315.

Regardless of harm, the acts constitute war crimes pursuant to Article 8(2)(b)(i)(ii) (iii), (ix) and (xxiv) of the Rome Statute.[169]

Allegations of intentional attacks on civilians and civilian objects were consistently made with regard to Operation Protective Edge. The large number of civilian causalities,[170] corroborated with testimonies, documents and other submission examined by the 2015 UN Fact-Finding mission indicate that the attacks were purportedly directed towards civilians and civilian objects.[171]

Under Paragraph 26 of its findings, the mission has indicated, among others, Israel's attacks on 'residential buildings resulting in death of entire families', ground operation that razed urban neighbourhoods and the Palestinian armed groups' reliance on 'attack tunnels' as new patterns in the 2014 hostilities.[172]

In respect to Palestinian armed groups, rockets and mortars fired towards southern Israel, according to official Israeli sources, have resulted in civilian causalities and damage to civilian objects.[173] However, the commission's report does not provide conclusive information on the armed groups' intent to target those protected.[174] Nonetheless, for the purposes of prosecution, each case is dealt with individually and with regard to the specific intent for the specific attack.[175] In light of the commission's report, the conflicting statements of the armed groups[176] coupled with the incapacity of the rockets and mortars to be directed towards a

[169] *Katanga* 2008, above n. 160, para 270. The first case of the Court has dealt with such war crimes against the leaders of the Lord Resistance Army (Kony and four high ranking members). See ICC, *Prosecutor v. Joseph Kony et al.*, Warrant of arrest for Joseph Kony issued on 8th July 2005 as amended on 27 September 2005, 13 October 2005, ICC-02/04-01/05-53, para 38; Warrant of arrest for Vincent Otti, 13 October 2005, ICC-02/04-01/05-54, para 38; Warrant of arrest for Raska Lukwiya, 13 October 2005, ICC-02/04-01/05-55, para 26; Warrant of arrest for Okot Odhiambo, 13 October 2005, ICC-02/04-01/05-56, para 28; Warrant of arrest for Dominic Ongwen, PTC II, 13 October 2005, ICC-02/04-01/05-10, para 26. Regarding Article 8(2)(b)(i), see Ambos 2013, pp. 174–175; and Werle and Jessberger 2014, p. 277.

[170] See Sect. 2.5 for details on causality and damage to civilian objects. See also Human Rights Watch 2015.

[171] UNHRC 2015a, paras 26 et seq.

[172] Ibid., para 26. The commission has not focused on attacks on UN shelters, medical facilities and other infrastructures as these patterns, pursuant to the commission, are 'recurring realities' in the region. With regard to the latter, therefore, other reports, notably, reports by Human Rights Watch and Amnesty International are considered.

[173] Ibid., para 21; ICRC 2009, p. 76.

[174] UNHRC 2015a, paras 21 et seq.

[175] Rome Statute, above n. 2, Article 8(1).

[176] There are instances in which Palestinian armed groups release statements announcing their intention to target Israeli civilians and population centres and on other instances, the groups warn Israeli civilians from imminent rocket attacks. For instance, on 20 August, the Al-Qassam Brigades gave warning to Israeli citizens near Gaza to take or remain in shelters. On 26 August, the same Brigades took responsibility for a mortar attack against Kibbutz Nirim, an Israeli city about 2 km from Gaza, which killed two Israeli civilians.

specific military objective, may suggest that the 'primary purpose' of the attack was rather aimed to 'spread terror' within the civilian population.[177]

In light of the elements of crimes, direct attack on civilians and civilian objects require, on the part of the perpetrator, the intention to make civilians and civilian objects the object of the attack.[178] Targeting civilians and civilian objects is a war crime in the absence of a clear evidence that: first, those protected have lost their protection due to their active participation in hostilities or their military usage, second, the damage to the civilian object is collateral which is proportional to an anticipated military advantage or third, that the attack could be justified by military necessity.[179] Even in the presence of a military objective in or close to the civilians and civilian object, the attack needs to be examined in light of the principle of proportionality and humanity.[180] Despite the motive behind the attacks—be it to spread terror or an act of reprisal[181]—as long as a specific attack has civilian population and objects as the object of attack, in the absence of any of the above possible defences, one could infer the perpetrator's intent in targeting a civilian object. The Prosecutor has to establish also that there is an awareness or expected awareness on the part of the accused that those targeted have a protected status.[182]

One could also argue that considering their military capacity and in instances that the armed groups made efforts to target mortars towards military objectives,[183] they could be considered as satisfying the necessary precautionary requirement. Despite that, employing means of warfare that are inherently incapable of discriminating between civilians and civilian objects and military objectives is outlawed. The prohibition is regardless of the limits of the military arsenals of the group or precautionary measures taken. In light of the case laws of the *ad hoc* Tribunals, such an attack is tantamount the direct targeting of civilians and civilian objects. In the *Blaŝkić* case, for instance, the Trial Chamber has ruled that employing 'home-made mortars' which are difficult to guide, with non-linear and irregular trajectory, is evidence that the perpetrators had wanted to make civilians a

177 UNHRC 2015a, paras 21 et seq.

178 Elements of Crimes, above n. 108, Article 8(2)(b)(i) War crime of attacking civilians, Element 3; Schwarz 2017, p. 1315.

179 Additional Protocol I, above n. 114, Articles 51 and 52(1). See ICRC 2009, pp. 69 et seq.

180 In the Kibbutz Nirim case, for instance, there is no information about the existence of a military objective in the surroundings to rebut the 'protected status' presumption. See UNHRC 2015a, paras 21 et seq. See also ICRC 2009, pp. 57, 79.

181 With regard to the prohibition of reprisal in International Humanitarian Law see ICTY, *Prosecutor v. Zoran Kupreškić et al.*, 14 January 2000, IT-95-16-T (*Kupreškić et al.* 2000), paras 527–536.

182 See Elements of Crimes, above n. 108, Article 8(2)(b).

183 UNHRC has reported that 'some Palestinian armed groups made efforts to direct projectiles, especially mortars, at military objectives'. See UNHRC 2015a, para 31.

target.[184] A similar conclusion was reached in the Martić Rule 61 proceedings.[185] In the latter ruling, the Trial Chamber argued that the use of such weapons (in this case, an Orkan rocket with a cluster bomb warhead) is a proof of 'the intent of the accused to deliberately attack the civilian population'.[186] Hence, it could be concluded, on the ground of the reports that brought to light the use of such mortars and rockets and the elements of the crime, those Palestinian armed groups have intentionally targeted civilian and civilian objects.

With regard to the Israeli Defence Force, reports have identified a pattern in targeting civilian objects.[187] Considering the Defence Force's use of 'precision-guided weapons' the total or partial destruction of many residential buildings can be linked with targeting civilians and civilian objects.[188] In the absence of information on why a civilian object, which as a principle is a protected object,[189] has become a military objective, the attack is presumed as intentionally targeting civilians and civilian objects. The fact that many of the attacks on residential buildings were conducted at times when families were in the buildings (dawn and evenings) could show an intention to target civilians or lack of precautions to spare civilians.[190]

There are instances where the Israeli Defence Force targeted civilian buildings after providing warnings or notices for evacuation.[191] Despite the warnings, however, civilians and civilian objects do not lose their protected status for the mere reason that warnings were given. Thus, the conduct qualifies as a war crime given that there is no military necessity or legitimate military purpose in conducting the attack, and if the damage caused is disproportional to the military advantage

---

[184] *Blaŝkić* 2000, above n. 150, para 512. A similar judgment was given by other Trial Chambers as well. See, for instance, ICTY, *Prosecutor v. Stanislav Galić,* Judgment, 5 December 2003, IT-98-29-T, para 57. The Appeals Chamber upheld this decision under para 132; ICTY, *Prosecutor v. Stanislav Galić,* Judgment, 30 November 2006, IT-98-29-A (*Galić* 2006), para 132. With regard to States' choice of weapons the International Court of Justice has also established that 'they must consequently never use weapons that are incapable of distinguishing between civilian and military targets'. See ICJ Advisory opinion 1996, above n. 83, para 78.

[185] ICTY, *Prosecutor v. Matrić*, Decision, IT-95-II-I (Martić Rule 61 Decision), 8 March 1996, paras 23–23; Kalshoven 2007, p. 811.

[186] Martić Rule 61 Decision, above n. 185, paras 23–31. Amongst the weapons used by Palestinian armed groups, it was confirmed that the Fajr-5, J-80 M-75 and R-160 rockets can land as far as 3–6 km away from any intended target. See UNHRC 2015b, para 97; Kalshoven 2016, p. 215.

[187] The commission reached a conclusion on the patterns of strikes on the ground of information gathered by Amnesty International and B'Tselem, which was also corroborated by satellite imagery. See UNHRC 2015a, paras 36 et seq.; B'Tselem 2015, p. 46; and Amnesty International 2014, p. 42.

[188] UNHRC 2015a, para 37.

[189] ICRC 2009, pp. 75 et seq.

[190] This appears to be the case for six incidents the commission selectively examined. See UNHRC 2015a, para 38.

[191] Ibid., paras 44 et seq.

anticipated.[192] However, separate from instances where warnings were given via telephone or text messages, techniques such as the 'roof knock', [193] in most cases, did not give enough time for evacuation or were misunderstood by the residents.[194] Despite the limited effectiveness of the technique apparent in the mounting civilian toll and unprecedented damage to civilian objects, the lack of assessment of the resultant effect and re-examination of the method could indicate a military tactic of targeting those protected or failure to take enough precaution before attacks.[195]

Causing Excessive Death, Injury, or Damage

Unlike the intentional attacks on civilians, Article 8(2)(b)(iv) criminalises excessive incidental death, injury, or damage. In so doing, it reflects the cardinal principles of distinction, military necessity, proportionality and humanity as well as the prohibition on causing superfluous injury or unnecessary suffering.[196] In light of the elements of the crime, for the conduct to be criminal under this provision, the attack shall be 'clearly excessive in relation to the concrete and direct overall military advantage'.[197] Hence, the provision focuses not on the mere existence of collateral damage to civilians and civilian objects, which is an intrinsic element of war, but on the foreseeable, unjustified and disproportionate damage to those protected. The 'clearly excessive' element included in the second element of the crime provides a 'wider margin of appreciation' and allows the Court to use the standard of 'a reasonable commander'.[198]

During Operation Protective Edge, the Israeli Defence Force has targeted civilian buildings, which are the residences of individuals allegedly linked with the

[192] ICRC 2009, pp. 77 et seq.; Solis 2010, pp. 273–275.

[193] This is a technique that the Israeli Defence Force used especially during Operation Protective Edge. It drops a small mortar on the target to warn the residences to flee before the building is attacked. See E. Levy, 'Knock on the Roof': This is How It's Done, YNetNews.com, 11 July 2014; and E. Groll, UN: Israeli 'Roof-knock 'Did not Provide Effective Warning to Gaza Civilians', Foreign Policy, 22 June 2015.

[194] UNHRC 2015a, paras 44 et seq.

[195] Additional Protocol I, above n. 114, Article 57(2)(a)(i); ICRC 2009, p. 74. The commission of inquiry has concluded that such attacks give the impression that targeting civilians was a military tactic reflective of a broader policy. In the view of the commission, the policy could be one 'approved at least tacitly by decision-makers at the highest levels of the Government of Israel'. See UNHRC 2015a, paras 44 et seq. See also Amnesty International 2014, p. 6; FIDH 2014, pp. 29–30. Incidents such as the killing, by a Navy ship fire, of the four children playing soccer on the beach and the strike that killed nine civilians watching world cup games on a beach café in Khan Yunis are hard to justify as a legitimate target. In this regard see Human Rights Watch 2015.

[196] These principles are enshrined under Additional Protocol I, above n. 114, Articles 35, 51, 55 and 85. See ICRC 2009, pp. 77 et seq.; and Triffterer and Ambos 2016, p. 376.

[197] Elements of Crimes, above n. 108, Article 8(2)(b)(iv), Element 2.

[198] The military advantage sought should also be 'substantially and relatively close'. Justifications behind a military attack which have a potential advantage or which only accrue in the long term are not considered 'concrete and direct'. See Triffterer and Ambos 2016, p. 377.

police, Hamas and different armed groups.[199] These cases give rise to the following question: Is a member of an organised armed group who left the 'combat zone' for his residence a lawful military target and if so, are the family members considered as willingly abdicating their protected status by the mere fact of their proximity to the former. The issue is worth considering as Israel has justified the attack on various residential buildings on the basis of the presence of a member of an armed group. For instance, the Al Dali building (33 civilians and one alleged member of the Al Quds Brigade killed), the Al Batsh house (18 civilians and two people allegedly affiliated with the Al Qassam Brigade killed and 50 civilians injured) and the Al Salam tower (11 civilians and one alleged member of Al Quds Brigade killed) were targeted on this ground.[200]

Even if individuals are presumably linked to armed groups, mere membership to an armed group does not make an individual a legitimate target at all times and places.[201] The commission has opined that those persons could be targeted only when they are taking an active part in conflict or if they 'are members of organized armed groups with a continuous combat function'.[202] This is also the case for armed groups of non-State parties to the conflict who are affiliated to a state party to a conflict. Hamas (and its military group), as the governing body of Gaza and on which the Geneva Conventions are applicable,[203] can be grouped as an 'organised armed group belonging to a State party to the conflict' or an armed group with an equivalent degree of organisation as a State's armed force.[204] It is one of the belligerents of an international armed conflict whose members qualify as members of an organised armed group.[205]

The Law of Armed Conflict and the ICRC's clarification on the notion of direct participation in hostilities provide that one of the concomitant effects or downside of membership to a formal or functional armed group is the fact that members are 'continuing lawful target' during an armed conflict.[206] In a situation of armed conflict, they 'may be attacked at any time until they surrender or are otherwise *hors*

---

[199] The attack on the families of those reported to be members of Hamas or other armed groups among many are; the attack on Kwarea family killed Eight people including six children following a brief time after warning was given: the attack against the Hammad residence was conducted without warning and a short time after the family members had gone to sleep resulting in the death of six people and the attack on the Al-Hajj family killed all members of the family except one. See UNHRC 2015a, paras 110 et seq.

[200] Ibid.

[201] ICRC 2009, p. 57; Schwarz 2017, pp. 1310 et seq.

[202] See UNHRC 2015a, paras 39–40.

[203] Palestine signed the Geneva Convention in April 2014.

[204] ICRC 2009, pp. 46 et seq.

[205] Additional Protocol I, above n. 114, Article 43(1); Bothe 2010, p. 200.

[206] Additional Protocol I, above n. 114, Articles 48, 51 and 52; ICRC 2009, pp. 46 et seq.; Melzer 2010, p. 161; Solis 2010, p. 188.

de combat, and not only when actually threatening the enemy'.[207] As the aim is to weaken the military potential of the opposing party, they are legitimate targets while outside the combat zone, while at home on leave or even sleeping. Hence, members of the Al-Qassam Brigade (the military wing of Hamas) are legitimate targets during Operation Protective Edge unless there is proof that they are former combatants who demobilised, are visibly surrendering, wounded or sick. Without prejudice to the issue of proportionality discussed below, targeting of a member of the Al-Qassam Brigade at his place of residence does not constitute a violation of the laws and customs of armed conflict. The same applies to members of other armed groups with continuous combat function whose conducts are attributable to a party to a conflict (to Al-Qassam Brigade) such as the Al-Quds Brigade who may qualify as partisans, guerrillas or volunteer corps.[208] On the other hand, those civilians who take an active part in hostilities, members of an unorganised armed group whose membership is evidenced only by their 'continuous combat function', in general categorised as unlawful combatants could only be targeted—in the sense argued by the commission—while taking an active part in the conflict.[209] Members of the police force are treated as civilians 'unless and for such time' that 'by virtue of an act of their State or through their own decision' they are included in the armed force or are directly participating in the conflict.[210] In the absence these two scenarios, Israel's targeting of residences of Police officers is contrary to the law of armed conflict.

Although the Israeli Defence Force can legitimately target members of organised armed groups and those taking an active part in the conflict, the attacks are required to be in accordance with the principles of armed conflict.[211] Targeting those residences with the hope of killing one or two members of armed groups is not justified, as is the case in many of the above incidents, in view of the unparalleled civilian causalities. In the absence a military necessity that could justify the disproportionate civilian toll or a disproportionately damaging military activity

---

207 Additional Protocol I, above n. 114, Articles 48, 52 and 53; Sassòli and Olson 2008, pp. 605–606; Solis 2010, p. 188.

208 Members of partisans, guerrillas, rebel groups, insurgents and volunteer corps enjoy the privileges of combatancy if they fulfil the following criteria:

a. If they are commanded by a person responsible for his subordinates;
b. Carry a fixed distinctive sign recognisable from a distance;
c. Openly carry arms;
d. Conduct operations in line with international humanitarian law.

See Geneva Convention III, above n. 114, Article 4(A)(2–6); ICRC 2009, p. 22; Melzer 2010, p. 155; Solis 2010, p. 195.

209 UNHRC 2015a, paras 39–40.

210 Additional Protocol I, above n. 114, Article 51(3). In light of this, the ICRC Interpretive Guidance on Direct Participation in Hostilities provides parameters to qualify direct participation in hostilities: first, the activities should satisfy a threshold of harm (or likely harm), second there must exist direct causation (between the act and expected harm) and third belligerent nexus (nexus between the act and the hostilities). See ICRC 2009, pp. 27 et seq.; Ipsen 2008, pp. 79–80.

211 ICRC 2009, pp. 77–79.

emanating from the residences (or dual use of the residence), the attack on those residences is in contravention to the law of armed conflict.

The Rome Statute does not criminalise indiscriminate attacks against civilians *per se*, unless the same conduct could be viewed as intentional attack on civilian population or civilian objects.[212] Thus, at this juncture, the issue that follows is if these disproportionate attacks could qualify as 'intentional' direct attacks in the context provided under Article 8(2)(b) of the Rome Statute. The elements of the crime require knowledge on the part of the perpetrator that the attack would result in excessive damage to civilians and civilian objects.[213] Hence, the challenge is in establishing the evaluation of the commander at the time of the attack.[214] An alleged erroneous evaluation may result in invoking the defence of mistake (Article 32 of the Statute) or may ultimately negate *mens rea*. However, the sequence and similarity of the attacks on the residences, the knowledge that civilians normally inhabit the houses rebuts/negates the 'erroneous evaluation' or 'defence of mistake'. Moreover, the fact that the attacks employed weapons which totally annihilate and destroy could indicate the disregard to the excessive collateral damage on civilian lives and objects.[215] Although the intention may be to take out a legitimate target, one could assert with a reasonable certainty that an attack on a building inhabited by civilians—to target one or two combatants—would result in an excessive damage and a long-term impact on the livelihood of the residents' in the sense provided under Article 8(2)(b)(iv) of the Statute.[216]

5.3.1.2 Use of Human Shields

Article 51(7) of the Additional Protocol I to the Geneva Conventions outlaws the use of protected persons to shield military forces or areas as it violates the cardinal principle of distinction and the obligation to take feasible precautions to separate civilians and military objectives.[217] State practice has also established this prohibition as a norm of customary international law irrespective of the character of the

[212] Rome Statute, above n. 2, Article 8(2)(a). The ICJ in the Nuclear weapons case has equated indiscriminate attacks with that of direct attack against civilians. It stated that States should never target civilians and civilian objects and must not consequently use weapons incapable of distinguishing between legitimate targets and protected objects. See ICJ Advisory opinion 1996, above n. 83, para 78; Dörmann 2003, pp. 345–346.

[213] Elements of Crimes, above n. 108, Element 2 of Article 8(2)(b)(iv).

[214] *Kupreškić et al.* 2000, above n. 181, para 524.

[215] Ibid.

[216] Israeli attacks on civilian infrastructures, especially schools, hospitals and those carrying the emblems of international organizations, could, however, easily fall in this category. See ICJ Advisory opinion 1996, above n. 83, para 78.

[217] ICJ Advisory opinion 1996, above n. 83; Henckaerts and Doswald-Beck 2005, p. 338; Salmón 2015, pp. 1138 et seq.

armed conflict.[218] Though always condemned, the jurisprudence of the *ad hoc* Tribunals or any other Tribunal did not criminalise the use of 'human shields' as an autonomous crime indictable on its own right.[219] The ICTY, for instance, recognised the conduct as a war crime albeit as 'inhuman or cruel treatment'[220] 'an outrage up on personal dignity',[221] or 'hostage taking'.[222]

The Rome Statute formally criminalised the use of human shields for the first time in international law.[223] In the context of the Statute, the use of protected persons as shields in international armed conflict gives rise to criminal liability if a perpetrator 'moved or otherwise took advantage of the location' of protected persons to shield a military objective or to 'shield, favour/impede military operations'.[224]

Be that as it may, there were reports that Palestinian forces stocked their military assets and carried out military operation within the vicinity of protected objects during Operation Protective Edge.[225] The obligation to locate military objectives far from civilian and civilian objects is not absolute and compliance could be difficult due to the small size and high population density of Gaza. Such circumstances, similar to other strategic and tactical necessities, could operate as a mitigating factor, but do not relieve one from the obligation to adhere to the cardinal principles of armed conflict[226] If any of the reported civilian casualties were caused by the armed group's attempt to shield a 'legitimate military objective' within a protected object, the armed groups are responsible for those casualties.[227]

On the other hand, the Independent Commission of Inquiry's report positions that Palestinian armed groups encourage residents to disregard evacuation warnings

---

[218] Henckaerts and Doswald-Beck 2005, p. 337; Salmón 2015, pp. 1138 et seq.

[219] Triffterer and Ambos 2016, pp. 503–594.

[220] See for example *Blaškić* 2000, above n. 150, para 716; *Kordić* and *Čerkez* 2001, above n. 147, para 256.

[221] See for example, ICTY, *Prosecutor v. Aleksovski*, Judgment, 25 June 1999, IT-95-14/1-T, para 229.

[222] Triffterer and Ambos 2016, pp. 503–504.

[223] Schabas 2011, p. 137.

[224] Elements of Crimes, above n. 108, Article 8(2)(b)(xxiii).

[225] The UN fact-finding mission report has indicated that Palestinian armed groups have endangered the lives of civilians by conducting operations 'within or in close proximity' of structures having a protected status. On a public summary of a report of the UN Headquarters Board of Inquiry submitted to the UN Security Council on 27 April 2015 regarding incidents involving facilities of the UN during OPT, the Secretary General has indicated that there were instances in which military maps and weapons were found hidden in UNRWA centres. The details of the report were not made public. See UNHRC 2015a, paras 63–64; and UNSC, Letter dated 27 April 2015 from the Secretary-General addressed to the President of the Security Council, UN Doc. S/2015/286, 27 April 2015.

[226] The principle of distinction, duty to take necessary precautions and the principle of proportionality are still applicable. See Heines 2014, p. 288.

[227] Solis 2010, p. 320.

from the Israeli Force.[228] Depending on the purpose behind the conduct, as the commission rightly concluded, the conduct could amount to taking advantage of the status of protected persons or failure to take necessary precautions to protect civilians. In a case by case analysis, however, in situations where it could be proven that the aim was to use the presence of civilians and civilian objects to shield military assets from attacks, those who perpetrated the conduct could be liable in light of the elements of crimes of Article 8(2)(b)(xxiii).

The detailed report of the commission has also provided purported incidents of the Israeli Defence Force using Palestinian civilians as human shields.[229] The Israeli Military Advocate General has reportedly opened a criminal investigation on an incident in which a civilian was used to check booby traps and to conduct other search operations.[230] There are also reports that the Israeli Defence Force has used human shields in order to deter Hamas forces from returning fire, a state of affairs that has, at the time of writing, yet to trigger an investigation.[231] Notwithstanding other challenges to jurisdiction and admissibility, these alleged incidents could satisfy the elements of crimes for charges of exploiting the status of a protected person so as to render military forces immune from attack.

5.3.1.3 Settlements

Transferring parts of a State's own civilian population into a territory it occupies is prohibited under Article 49(6) of Geneva Convention IV.[232] It is a grave breach of Additional Protocol I (Article 85(4)(a)) and is established as a norm of customary international law applicable in international armed conflicts.[233] The conduct has severe lasting consequence.[234] It changes the demographic composition and political reality of the occupied territory creating a hardly reversible situation and obscuring resolution of conflicts.[235] Transferring or facilitating the migration of own population into occupied territory helps solidify territorial and political claims

---

[228] UNHRC 2015a, para 66.

[229] UNHRC 2015b, paras 320–321.

[230] The Israeli Defence Force MAG Corps, Decisions of the IDF MAG regarding exceptional incidents that allegedly occurred during Operation 'Protective Edge'—Update no. 4, http://www.law.idf.il/1007-en/Patzar.aspx (accessed 13 July 2016).

[231] UNHRC 2015b, paras 322–323.

[232] The fact that Israel occupies the Palestinian territories of the West Bank, the Gaza Strip and East Jerusalem is not disputed. See ICJ Advisory opinion 2004, above n. 83, para 136; UNSC 1967b; UNSC 1973; and ICRC 2002b.

[233] Cryer 2005, p. 273; Henckaerts and Doswald-Beck 2005, p. 462; Tomuschat 2015, pp. 1559–1560, 1566; Triffterer and Ambos 2016, pp. 405–406; Werle and Jessberger 2014, p. 461.

[234] Triffterer and Ambos 2016, p. 405.

[235] Henckaerts and Doswald-Beck 2005, p. 463; Triffterer and Ambos 2016, pp. 405–406; Werle and Jessberger 2014, p. 461.

over the occupied territory.[236] It goes against the established international humanitarian law rule that belligerent occupation must be for limited duration and makes difficult the realisation of the right to return of refugees and restitution of property.[237]

Under Article 8(2)(b)(viii) of the Rome Statute, this particularly controversial crime was coined as 'the transfer, directly or indirectly by the occupying power of parts of its own civilian population into the territory it occupies, or the deportation or transfer of all or parts of the population of the occupied territory within or outside this territory'.[238] The provision constitutes two crimes. The first category is the direct or indirect transfer by the occupying power parts of its population and the second one is 'deportation and transfer' of the occupied population 'within or outside' the occupied land. The following discussion deals with the first category, as one of the most prevalent contentions in the situation at hand falls in that category.

Israel's settlement policy has not only resulted in various Security Council and General Assembly Resolutions[239] but according to Bothe,[240] it was also one of the major 'political targets' behind the inclusion of the provision in the Statute.[241] As discussed under Chap. 2, the first round of settlement construction on the occupied territories was from 1967 to 1977, following the second Arab-Israel war, and the latest plan for new settlements were introduced between January and March 2017.[242] Different from other crimes of concern to the ICC, the factual elements of the Israeli settlements in the Occupied Palestinian Territories, be it the policies behind or the actual existence of the settlements is not disputed, even by Israel.[243] What could possibly be challenging is whether the matter falls within the temporal jurisdiction of the Court.

---

236 Triffterer and Ambos 2016, pp. 405–406.

237 Tomuschat 2015, pp. 1559 et seq.; Triffterer and Ambos 2016, p. 406; Werle and Jessberger 2014, p. 461. With regard to the Human Rights dimension see UN Sub-Commission on Human Rights 1994. See also Spoerri 2014, pp. 183–184.

238 It is the inclusion of this provision that led Israel to vote against the Statute. See Cryer 2005, p. 273.

239 See, among others, UNSC 1980a, b, 1979a, b, which deplore the construction of settlements, call for end of the occupation and reiterate that all measures that change the 'geographic, demographic and historical character' of Jerusalem as null and void. Settlement practices have also been condemned by the General Assembly, among many, in the following resolutions: UNGA 1981, 1982, 1983, 1999. See also Tomuschat 2015, p. 1556.

240 Bothe 2002, p. 413.

241 On the drafting history see Triffterer and Ambos 2016, pp. 407–409.

242 See UN, Meetings Coverage, UNSC 7908th meeting: Israel markedly increased settlement construction, decisions in last three months, Middle East Special Coordinator tells Security Council, 24 March 2017, https://www.un.org/press/en/2017/sc12765.doc.htm (accessed 27 March 2017).

243 See Al Jazeera, Israel announces plans to build 450 new settler homes in West Bank, 30 January 2015, http://america.aljazeera.com/articles/2015/1/30/israel-settlements-politics.html (accessed 16 July 2016); M. Bard, Israeli Settlements: Facts about Jewish Settlements in the West Bank, http://www.jewishvirtuallibrary.org/jsource/Peace/settlements.html (accessed 16 July 2016).

As discussed under Sect. 4.3.1, due to the absolute temporal bar set under Article 11(1),[244] the formal criminal character of a conduct could be given effect only if the conduct subsists after the critical date for the Statute, i.e., 1 July 2002. The temporal scope set for the Palestinian situation goes only as far back as 13 June 2014, thus, there is no jurisdictional challenge for dealing with settlements constructed after this date. As the Statute sets forth no provision on the issue of settlements as continuing crimes, the issue is whether the Court can deal with settlements constructed before 13 June 2014, as well as those constructed before 1 July 2002. Any resolve on prosecution of settlements constructed before 1 July 2002 *mutatis mutandis* resolves the temporal issue for those settlements constructed before 13 June 2014.

The transfer of part of one's own population into an occupied land has the intrinsic element of permanency. The prohibition is included with the aim of protecting the occupied population.[245] Thus, it is not only the mere transfer but the continued expropriation and use of land that is prohibited. Until the time the settlements are disbanded, the occupying power remains in continuous breach of its obligation. It could be argued that as settlements have inter-temporal element that their mere existence, maintenance and sustenance by the occupying power after the time the Court enjoys jurisdiction is a continuous violation. Nonetheless, as the discussion on the temporal jurisdiction of the Court affirmed,[246] for the Court to deal with the direct and indirect transfer of population to the occupied land made between 13 June 2014 and 1 July 2002 or even those that started before 1 July 2002 and continued thereafter, the *actus reus* of the crime need to occur within the temporal scope of the Court.

The *actus reus* of the crime, as provided in the elements of crimes of the Statute, expressly criminalises the direct or indirect 'transfer'.[247] The added footnote on the word 'transfer' only indicates that the word shall be interpreted in light of the rules of international humanitarian law.[248] Although that is the case, provisions dealing with the same issue, namely Article 49(6) of Geneva Convention IV and Article 85 (4)(a) Additional Protocol I, do not provide any further explanation.[249] Nonetheless, as Tomuschat rightly argues, a broad interpretation that aims to serve the purpose of the prohibition (discussed above) shall be adopted.[250]

Action by the occupying power is a necessary element of the *actus reus* as it excludes individual possession of property in private capacity.[251] The action, thus,

---

[244] See Sect. 4.3.1. See also Boot 2002, p. 371.

[245] Dörmann 2001, pp. 481–482; Tomuschat 2015, p. 1560; Triffterer and Ambos 2016, p. 410.

[246] See Sect. 4.3.1.

[247] Rome Statute, above n. 2, Article 8(2)(b)(viii); Elements of Crimes, above n. 108, Article 8(2)(b)(viii), Element 1(a).

[248] See ibid., n. 44. See also Dörmann 2001, pp. 481–482; Triffterer and Ambos 2016, p. 410.

[249] Dörmann 2001, pp. 481–482.

[250] Tomuschat 2015, p. 1563.

[251] Werle and Jessberger 2014, p. 462.

could range from the physical transfer of population by the occupying power to putting in place policies and measures that induce migration into the occupied territory.[252] In light of ICJ's wall opinion, policies and measures that provide economic and financial incentives, tax exemptions and subsidies or other measures that make relocation attractive are considered as 'indirect' efforts to transfer.[253] In view of this opinion, those measures that are aimed to maintain the settlements, such as subsidies, tax exonerations, especial security protections and provision of infrastructures by the Israeli government fall within the 'indirect transfer' category.[254] Such measures and incentives given after 1 July 2002 for those settlements built before and after 1 July 2002 fall within the temporal jurisdiction of the Court. As these *actus reus* of 'indirect transfer' are (re)occurring within the temporal scope of the Court, their prosecution do not contravene the absolute temporal bar of the Statute or the principle of non-retroactivity. If, however, the Court chooses to draw the line on its temporal jurisdiction at 13 June 2014 or 1 July 2002 for any practical reason, settlements constructed before these dates could be used to prove 'background issues' such as motive, intent and knowledge.[255]

Criminal responsibility falls, among others, on government officials and legislative bodies of the occupying power as well as superior commanders who are crucial to maintain the *status quo*.[256] In light of their contribution and without prejudice to gravity and other considerations, corporate executives complicit in the construction and maintenance of settlements could also fall within the purview of the Court.

5.3.1.4 Wilful killing

Wilful killing of protected persons is considered a grave breach of the Geneva Conventions.[257] The law of occupation mutually enforces International humanitarian law and International human rights law for guaranteeing the right to life of the occupied population. Pursuant to Article 43 of The Hague Regulations, the occupying power has the obligation to provide security and maintain public order, which could range from enforcing law to managing civil unrests and disturbances.[258] In the absence of active hostilities in the occupied territory, the law enforcement paradigm sets stricter standards for the respect and protection of

[252] Tomuschat 2015, p. 1563.

[253] ICJ Advisory opinion 2004, above n. 83, para 120. See also Cryer 2005, p. 273.

[254] Concerning such subsidies and grants benefiting settlements see Sect. 2.4.2. See also Tomuschat 2015, p. 1563.

[255] Schabas 2006, p. 136.

[256] Rome Statute, above n. 2, Article 28; Triffterer and Ambos 2016, p. 411.

[257] Henckaerts and Doswald-Beck 2005, p. 311.

[258] Article 43 of Convention (IV) Respecting the Laws and Customs of War on Land and its Annex: Regulation concerning the Laws and Customs of War on Land, signed 10 October 1907, 187 CTS 227 (entered into force 26 January 1910).

human rights of the occupied population, which is especially the case for the elementary and non-derogable right to life.[259]

Wilful killing is specified as a war crime under Article 8(2)(a)(i) the Rome Statute. The Elements of Crimes requires an *actus reus* of killing or causing death to a protected person.[260] Despite the difference in settings, there is no qualitative (substance) variance between wilful killing and murder.[261] Hence, proof for the elements wilful killing could *mutatis mutandis* be used to charge the crime against humanity of murder under Article 7(1)(a) of the Statute.[262]

Arbitrary or excessive use of lethal force against civilians that pose less or no threat to safety amounts to wilful killing.[263] In situations of passive occupation as in the West Bank and East Jerusalem, the law enforcement paradigm[264] allows lethal force in very strict conditions—as an absolute last resort or to pursue legitimate aims proportional to the imminent threat to life.[265] Israeli security forces' alleged use of live ammunitions against protestors and demonstrators in the West Bank and East Jerusalem could amount to unlawful deprivation of life of protected persons. Nonetheless, as a potential case before the ICC, an individual assessment of alleged wilful killings requires examining each use of lethal force and the circumstances surrounding each case. Considering, the quantitative factor[266] and the temporal scope in place, this category may appear to have a relatively lesser gravity than other alleged crimes in the situation. However, wilful killings in the passive occupation setting could satisfy the gravity threshold as crimes committed with low intensity in an extended period of time. Alternatively, the conducts could also qualify as constitutive elements of other crimes.[267]

---

[259] Guilfoyle 2015, p. 1074; Henckaerts and Doswald-Beck 2005, pp. 299–303, 313; Spoerri 2014, p. 198–203.

[260] Triffterer and Ambos 2016, pp. 330–331.

[261] The ICTY Trial Chamber has ruled that 'the elements defining murder under Article 3 of the Statute are identical to those required for 'wilful killing' as a grave breach of the 1949 Geneva Conventions under Article 2 of the Statute and murder as a crime against humanity under Article 5 of the Statute'. See Judgment, *Prosecutor v. Orić,* IT-03-68-T, 30 June 2006, para 345. See similar rulings as *Blaškić* 2000, above n. 150, para 181 and ICTY, *Prosecutor v. Vidoje Blagojević and Dragan Jokić,* Judgment, 17 January 2005, IT-02-60-T (*Blagojević and Jokić* 2005), para 556.

[262] With regard to cumulative charges, see The Possibility of Charging Persecution Cumulatively.

[263] Between 12 June and 26 August 2014 alone, 27 Palestinians, including five children, were allegedly killed and more than 3,100, Palestinians were injured. See UNHRC 2015a, para 70. See also Diakonia International Humanitarian Law Resource Centre 2015, p. 4.

[264] This is in contrast to the hostilities paradigm in which parties have much more freedom to use lethal force. The hostilities paradigm comes into picture in situations of active hostilities. This paradigm does not apply to the West Bank and Eastern Jerusalem, as there is no active hostility.

[265] Diakonia International Humanitarian Law Resource Centre 2015, p. 7; Ferraro 2013, pp. 288–289; Tomuschat 2010, pp. 8 et seq.

[266] With regard to the gravity element on case selection, see the discussion in Sects. 4.4.2 and 5.2.2.1.

[267] See the section "The Possibility of Charging Persecution Cumulatively" above.

A potential case of wilful killing in a hostilities paradigm involves Hamas and other military factions in Gaza. One could take note of Hamas's summary execution of alleged Israeli collaborators during Operation Protective Edge.[268] However, as the prohibitions of war crimes protect civilians and those rendered *hors de combat* of the enemy force, the alleged executions cannot be dealt with under Article 8(1)(a). Even if it could be argued that it satisfies the elements of the crime against humanity of murder, considering the Prosecutor's position on quantitative requirements of gravity,[269] a onetime incident involving execution of 23 individuals may give rise to issues of gravity. However, the fact that the alleged crime is one of the crimes of particular concern to the OTP, the cruelty in its manner of commission, its alleged aim of spreading terror and that it was committed by a party with the duty to protect may increase its seriousness.[270] Hence, despite the highly debated practice of using, among others, numeric calculations to determine gravity, the prosecutor may take into consideration these circumstances in her decision to or not to prosecute the alleged killings.[271]

5.3.2 Cases of Crimes against Humanity

Despite the recurrent invocation of crimes against humanity in contemporary legal discourse, the distinguishing features of the crime were controversial in the post WWII Trials.[272] When the crime was first codified under Article 6(c) of the Nuremberg Charter, the definition required a nexus to war of aggression or war crimes.[273] Control Council Law No. 10 excluded the nexus. However, the Charter of the ICTY reintroduced the nexus element but merely for jurisdictional purposes. Also as a means of restricting the jurisdiction of the Tribunal, the Statute of the

268 Amnesty International, Gaza: Palestinians tortured, summarily killed by Hamas forces during 2014 conflict, 27 May 2015, https://www.amnesty.org/en/latest/news/2015/05/gaza-palestinians-tortured-summarily-killed-by-hamas-forces-during-2014-conflict/ (accessed 29 May 2017).

269 The prosecutor's approach in the Gaza flotilla incident and the decision not to investigate the Iraq situation (2006) indicate that a decision on the gravity of a situation is also based on quantitative numeric calculations. In the Iraq situation, the prosecutor noted in particular wilful killings of 12 individual and inhuman treatment of a limited number of people is not sufficiently serious. See L. Moreno-Ocampo, Letter concerning communication on the situation in Iraq, 9 February 2006, http://www.iccnow.org/documents/OTP_letter_to_senders_re_Iraq_9_February_2006.pdf (accessed 20 May 2017). The decision was not, however, purely motivated by legal considerations, as there were reports regarding an earlier assurance the former prosecutor gave to US diplomats that he would not peruse the Iraq situation. See Bosco 2014, p. 88. See also Schabas 2015, p. 373.

270 Rules of Procedure and Ethics, above n. 2, Rule 145(2); Rome Statute, above n. 2, Articles 8 (2)(b)(iii) and 70; Guariglia and Rogier 2014, p. 360.

271 Ibid.

272 Jalloh 2013, p. 385.

273 Schabas 2006, p. 186.

ICTR provided that the acts should be committed on 'national, political, ethnic, racial or religious ground'.[274] Yet, despite the considerable variations in the definition, criminal responsibility for crimes against humanity has long been affirmed as customary international law.[275]

Notwithstanding the instrument they are found, crimes against humanity are crimes of particularly odious nature constituting serious attacks on human right, peace, security and well-being of the world. They do not constitute isolated or sporadic crimes, but those that are committed as part of a policy or a widespread commission of offences tolerated or overlooked by an authority in charge.[276]

The absence of a comprehensive universal treaty,[277] unlike in the case of war crimes and genocide, has created a normative gap particularly with regard to the context that qualifies a crime as a crime against humanity.[278] In light of Article 7 of the Rome Statute, the commission of one of the prohibited acts listed under Article 7(1) becomes a crime against humanity if committed 'as part of a widespread or systematic attack'. The widespread or systematic scale, among others, catapults what especially gives the crime the essential character of a crime against all of humanity (the mass crime prevention rationale).[279] Article 7(2)(a) clarifies what is meant by an 'attack directed against any civilian population' as 'a course of conduct involving the multiple commission of acts referred to in Paragraph 1 against any civilian population, pursuant to or in furtherance of a State or organizational policy to commit such attack'. This part, in addition to reflecting on the colossal nature and scale of the crime, limits the application to offences that employed State or organizational means (predatory State rationale).[280]

The jurisprudence of the ICTY and ICTR has evolved from requiring a preconceived plan or policy to the exclusion of the requirement.[281] The Rome Statute, however, provides a policy element that applies to (and could be used to prove) the

---

[274] On this provision see Werle and Jessberger 2014, pp. 331–332.

[275] Ibid., p. 330. See also Schabas 2006, p. 186.

[276] Cassese 2002, p. 360.

[277] There is an initiative and a proposal to devise a global Convention on crimes against humanity. The proposed Convention adopts the definition of crimes against humanity of the Rome Statute but adds provisions on mutual legal assistance, extradition and inter-State cooperation. See International Law Commission, Proposed international convention on the prevention and punishment of crimes against humanity, August 2010, http://law.wustl.edu/harris/cah/docs/EnglishTreatyFinal.pdf (accessed 20 July 2016).

[278] Jalloh 2013, pp. 382, 385.

[279] Ibid., p. 385.

[280] Ibid., pp. 408–409.

[281] *Akayesu* 1998, above n. 111, para 580; *Tadić* 1997, above n. 150, para 648. See also *Blaškić* 2000, above n. 150, para 203. The Tribunals did no longer require the policy element since the Appeals Chamber judgment on *Kunarac et al.* The Appeals Chamber in *Kunarac et al.* stated 'neither the attack nor the acts of the accused needs to be supported by any form of "policy" or "plan". There was nothing in the Statute or in customary international law at the time of the alleged acts that required proof of the existence of a plan or policy to commit these crimes'. See *Kunarac* 2002, above n. 133, para 98.

'widespread and systematic' nature of the attack.[282] The inclusion was the result of a compromise during the negotiations and was inspired by earlier definitions, which treated the crime as being a consequence of State policies, incitements, support or tolerance.[283] Nonetheless, the 'State or organizational plan or policy' requirement has been expanded to include those attacks that were 'thoroughly organised' and 'follow a regular pattern'.[284] Pursuant to the Pre-Trial Chamber II, such policy need not be formal and could be made by 'groups of persons who govern a specific territory or by any organisation with the capability to commit a widespread or systematic attack against a civilian population'.[285] However, the perpetrator does not necessarily have to be a member of the 'State or organization'. Any person who commits the prohibited acts in support or to further the policy qualifies as a perpetrator.[286]

For crimes against humanity to qualify as such, the attack should be directed against a civilian population, in contrast to 'attacks against individuals' or 'isolated acts of violence'.[287] Different from war crimes that are committed only in situations of armed conflict, crimes against humanity are committed both in peace and war-times and against civilians of both sides of the conflict.[288] Hence, 'considering the victim's need for protection', the phrase 'civilian population' is interpreted broadly excluding persons who are taking an active part in conflicts.[289]

In light of what is provided under Article 30 of the Rome Statute, to satisfy the mental element of crimes against humanity, a perpetrator has to be aware that his/her conduct is part of the 'widespread or systematic attack on a civilian population'.[290] However, as provided in the Elements of Crimes, the perpetrator is not required to have knowledge of the precise details of the 'plan or policy' or all

---

282 Werle and Jessberger 2014, pp. 340–341.

283 For a critical look on this issue see ibid., pp. 340–346.

284 *Katanga* 2008, above n. 160, para 396; Judge Kaul argued that 'though the constitutive elements of Statehood need not be established those "organizations" should partake of some characteristics of a State'. See ICC, Dissenting Opinion of Judge Hans-Peter Kaul, Situation in Kenya, ICC-01/09, 31 March 2010, para 51. See also Cassese 2002, pp. 375–376.

285 *Bemba* 2009, above n. 111, para 81; *Katanga* 2008, above n. 160, para 396. See also Schabas 2011, p. 113.

286 Werle and Jessberger 2014, p. 346.

287 See ICTR, *Prosecutor v. André Ntagerura et al,* Judgement, 25 February 2004, ICTR-99-46-T (*Ntagerura* 2004), para 698. Werle and Jessberger rightly opine that what is required is 'shared characteristics' that make the specific group a target. The shared feature could be any common feature including factors such as geographically occupying a certain area. See Werle and Jessberger 2014, p. 334.

288 Schwarz 2017, p. 1310; Werle and Jessberger 2014, p. 335. For crimes against humanity, it is only in the crime of persecution that the identity of the victim is taken into consideration. See Cassese 2002, pp. 360–361.

289 ICTY, *Prosecutor v. Martić*, Judgment, 8 October 2008, IT-95-11-A, paras 303 et seq.; Werle and 2014, p. 336.

290 Rome Statute, above n. 2, Article 30.

features of the attack.[291] In the absence of knowledge of the contextual elements, the perpetrator could not be charged for one or more of the crime(s) enumerated under Article 7.[292]

5.3.2.1 Forcible Transfer of Population

Different from the crime of deportation, which has been part of various international legislations,[293] forcible transfer of population was first treated as a crime against humanity in the 1996 ILC Draft Code and later in the Rome Statute.[294] International humanitarian law prohibits forcible displacement of population unless it is conducted for the security of the population or when 'imperative military reasons so demand'.[295] In such exceptional situations, the person should be allowed to return once the situations improve or cease to exist.[296] The UNHCR guiding principles on internal displacement have also called up on all international actors to avoid and 'where no alternatives exist' to minimise displacement of persons.[297] Principle 6 of the document prohibits displacement that, among others, is based on policies and practices that aim to alter the ethnic, religious or racial composition of the population, and one used as a collective punishment.[298] As the ICTY Statute does not include the crime as a self-contained crime against humanity, it has prosecuted forcible transfer of population as a form of inhuman treatment[299] and as one constitutive element of persecution.[300]

---

[291] See Elements of Crimes, above n. 108, Elements of Article 7.

[292] Schabas 2011, p. 114.

[293] The 1919 Peace Conference Report recognised forcible displacement of Armenians within the Ottoman Empire as a Crime against humanity in the form of deportation. Later on the Nuremberg and Tokyo Charters, Control Council Law No. 10 and the Statutes of the Ad hoc Tribunals dealt with the crime as a crime against humanity. See Triffterer and Ambos 2016, p. 195.

[294] Werle and Jessberger 2014, p. 357.

[295] Para 2 of Article 49 of Geneva Convention IV, above n. 123, provides that 'the Occupying Power may undertake total or partial evacuation of a given area if the security of the population or imperative military reasons so demand. Such evacuations may not involve the displacement of protected persons outside the bounds of the occupied territory except when for material reasons it is impossible to avoid such displacement. Persons thus evacuated shall be transferred back to their homes as soon as hostilities in the area in question have ceased'. See Chetail 2015, pp. 1191–1192.

[296] *Blagojević and Jokić* 2005, above n. 261, para 597; Ambos 2014, p. 87; Chetail 2015, p. 1192.

[297] UNHCR 1998.

[298] Ibid., Principle 6.

[299] ICTY, *Prosecutor v. Krstić,* Judgment, 2 August 2001, IT-93-33-T, para 532. See also the following ICTY cases: *Prosecutor v. Tolimir*, Judgment, 12 December 2012, IT-05-88/2-T, paras 802–803; *Prosecutor v. Perišić*, Judgment, 6 September 2011, IT-04-81-T, para 114; and *Prosecutor v. Dordević,* Judgment, 23 February 2011, IT-05-87/1-T, paras 1610–1614.

[300] *Blagojević and Jokić* 2005, above n. 261, para 602.

Article 7(1)(d) of the Rome Statute criminalises forcible transfer of population as a crime against humanity.[301] It defines the crime as 'forced displacement of the persons concerned by expulsion or other coercive acts from the area in which they are lawfully present, without grounds permitted under international law'.[302] The first material element of the crime expands the scope of the coercion to include not only physical force but also any 'threat of force or coercion' including psychological oppression and a coercive environment.[303] The ICTY case law adopted a broader approach to include displacement due to the absence of genuine choice, even when there is consent to 'relocate'.[304]

Be that as it may, the UN's Office for the Coordination of Humanitarian Affairs (OCHA) and the Israeli Committee Against House Demolitions (ICAHD), among others, have reported about what they consider the 'quiet transfer' of Palestinians in the occupied Palestinian territories through forced evictions and house demolitions.[305] Israeli authorities provide various reasons for demolitions of Palestinian houses. The most common are administrative demolitions, punitive demolitions, land-clearing demolitions and demolitions for security/military reasons.[306] Although demolitions of houses belonging to families of alleged attackers, namely punitive demolitions[307] are widely reported, the majority of demolitions are

---

301 The specific provision of the Statute criminalises deportation and forcible transfer of population. Although the Statute does not provide a clear distinction between the two, there is a near consensus that deportation refers to the forced transfer of population across borders while the latter involves a movement within the national frontiers of a country. The first element of the crime indicates that the forcible transfer and forcible displacement could be used interchangeably. See Elements of Crimes, above n. 108, Element 1 of Article 7(1)(d). See also Werle and Jessberger 2014, p. 358; Triffterer and Ambos 2016, p. 196.

302 Rome Statute, above n. 2, Article 7(2)(d).

303 Elements of Crimes, above n. 108, Element 1 of Article 7(1)(d).

304 See ICTY, *Prosecutor v. Krnojelac*, Judgment, 17 September 2003, IT-97-25A, para 229.

305 The ICAHD reports that as of 2009, around 24,000 Palestinian houses have been demolished. Figures provided by OCHA show an increase in the number of demolitions from 50 demolitions per month in 2012–2015 to 165 in January, 235 in February and 591 demolitions in April 2016. See Al Jazeera, Israel ramps up demolitions of Palestinian structures: UN figures show the destruction of homes in the occupied territories has tripled since January, 7 April 2016, http://www.aljazeera.com/news/2016/04/israel-ramps-demolitions-palestinian-structures-160407140314909.html (accessed 09 August 2016); L. Baker, With demolitions, Israel tightens squeeze on West Bank Palestinians, Reuters, 7 April 2016; and B. White, How home demolitions threaten Palestinian Statehood, Al Jazeera, 20 April 2016.

306 ICAHD, Overview of Israel's Demolition Policy, https://icahd.org/wp-content/uploads/sites/1/2017/12/Updated-comprehensive-information-on-demolitions-3-Dec-2017.pdf (accessed 10 November 2017).

307 Around 15 houses from 2015 to March 2016 were demolished on this ground. These demolitions go against the prohibition of collective punishment, the principle of individual guilt/personal culpability and due process of law. See B'Tselem, Statistics on punitive house demolitions, 22 March 2016, http://www.btselem.org/punitive_demolitions/statistics (accessed 10 August 2016); Kremnitzer and Saba-Habesch 2015.

administrative.[308] Orders for administrative demolitions are issued for lack of a permit to build. As more than 94% of Palestinian applications for permits are rejected, in order to meet natural growth, the alternatives are either to build without permit or to relocate to a different part of the occupied Palestinian territories.[309] The question that follows is if those structures that were demolished on the ground of 'illegality' are contrary to the 'lawful presence' envisaged under Article 7(1)(d) of the Statute and whether there is any ground to justify the practice of house demolitions in light of the exception provided under Article 49(2) of Geneva Convention IV.

Various scholars agree that lawfulness of residence is determined by international rather than national law.[310] Leaving aside the fact that East Jerusalem and Area C of the West Bank are considered part of the occupied Palestine, the mere continuous presence of the population as per 'principles of law common to many legal systems' grants a valid right to remain.[311] As Hall and Stahn note, expulsion without a fair judicial decision on the basis of national and international law constitute a forcible transfer.[312] The lack of any other justification for the demolition orders—including the absence of any claim on the part of the Israeli government about the existence of compelling national security and public safety grounds or 'military necessity'—places the legality of the demolition orders in question.[313] Moreover, the absence of the 'permitted grounds' for displacement and its non-provisional nature makes the query whether there is an intent to allow the return of the displaced somewhat futile.[314]

It is also worth noting that the existence of various reasons for demolition of houses and the fact that this prevalent practice is peculiar to the occupied Palestinian territories point to one of the core issues of the conflict, namely the conflicting territorial claims of the two nations. Especially in the Israeli-Palestinian conflict, a house does not only represent one's property. It embodies one's connection to the land, history, identity, tradition and personal belongingness.[315]

Owing to Israel's claim of the 'united Jerusalem', including East Jerusalem as its capital, the urban policies are aimed to maintain the Jewish majority through

---

308 The Israeli Committee against House Demolitions has reported that the zoning policy of Israel do not allow Palestinians to build in more than 85% of East Jerusalem and 99% of Area C of the West Bank. As reported by B'tselem between 2000 and 2004, 60% of the Palestinian homes demolished as part of military 'clearing operations;' 25% for not having permits and 15% as deterrence ('homes belonging to families of people known or suspected of involvement in attacks on Israeli civilian'). See ICAHD 2012, above n. 305.

309 S. Bannoura, 94% of applications for construction permits are rejected by Israel, International Middle East Centre, 22 February 2008.

310 Triffterer and Ambos 2016, p. 267; Werle and Jessberger 2014.

311 Triffterer and Ambos 2016, p. 267.

312 Ibid.

313 For a concurring opinion, see White 2016, above n. 305.

314 The ICTY has a similar stance. See *Naletilić and Martinović* 2003, above n. 119, para 520.

315 Kremnitzer and Saba-Habesch 2015, p. 218.

planning and zoning mechanisms, leaving only 11% of East Jerusalem and 7% of total urban land for Palestinian housing.[316] According to B'tselem, the 'quiet transfer' is effected due to the sever housing shortage in East Jerusalem (a result of expropriation of land and house demolitions among others) that forces individuals to move outside the city, which in turn gives rise to revocation of Jerusalem residency of Palestinians.[317]

In light of the Pre-Trial Chamber II's stance on *Ruto, Kosgey* and *Sang* case, the *actus reus* leading to displacement is an 'open-conduct crime'.[318] That means various conducts could qualify as causes as long as the conduct forces the victim to leave the area. Nonetheless, the Chamber specified that there should be causation or 'a link between the conduct and the resulting effect of forcing the victim to leave the area to another State or location'.[319] Considering the broad approach of the ICTY case law[320] and the first element of Article 7(1)(d)[321] on what amounts to 'coercive acts', the systematic denial of permit and demolition could be considered as coercive acts which have the resultant effect of displacement. Moreover, the motive behind the conduct can be gathered from the fact that new settlements are usually planned in the place of the demolished structures.[322]

5.3.2.2 The Crime of Apartheid

Although the UN General Assembly declared apartheid a crime against humanity in 1965,[323] it was the International Convention on the Elimination of All Forms of

---

316 HSRC 2009, pp. 205–207.

317 Ibid., pp. 206–207.

318 ICC, *Prosecutor v. William Samoei Ruto, Henry Kiprono Kosgey and Joshua Arap Sang*, Decision on the Confirmation of Charges Pursuant to Article 61(7)(a) and (b) of the Rome Statute, 23 January 2012, ICC-01/09-01/11-373 (*Ruto, Kosgey and Sang* 2012), para 244.

319 *Ruto, Kosgey and Sang* 2012, above n. 318, para 245.

320 The ICTY Trial Chamber in the *Milosević*, *Naletilić* and *Martinović* have, for instance, held that the 'prohibition of physical and moral coercion' includes 'pressure that is direct or indirect, obvious or hidden' and that the term 'forcible' should not be restricted to physical coercion'. See ICTY, *Prosecutor v. Milošević,* Judgment, 12 December 2007, IT-98-29/1-T, para 75 and *Naletilić and Martinović* 2003, above n. 119, para 519.

321 The first element of Article 7(1)(d) has defined 'forcible' as 'not restricted to physical force, but may include threat of force or coercion, such as that caused by fear of violence, duress, detention, psychological oppression or abuse of power against such person or persons or another person, or by taking advantage of a coercive environment'. See Elements of Crimes, above n. 108, Element 1 of Article 7(1)(d).

322 For instance the escalation of demolition of Palestinian structures from January to April 2016 in Area C were matched with the simultaneous approval of 72% of the planned new settlements on the same piece of land. See White 2016, above n. 305; and Middle East Eye, Israel accelerates settlement construction, as Palestinians urge UN resolution, http://www.middleeasteye.net/news/israel-accelerates-settlement-construction-palestinians-urge-un-resolution-1100281775 (accessed 10 August 2016).

323 UNGA 1966.

Racial Discrimination that first proscribes the practice of apartheid. As such crime, it was also included in the Apartheid and the Non-Statutory Limitations Conventions.[324] The crime is also framed as one of the grave breaches of the Geneva Conventions in Additional protocol I, when committed in armed conflict.[325]

Article 7(2)(h) of the Rome Statute refers to apartheid as an act committed:

> … in the context of an institutionalized regime of systematic oppression and domination by one racial group over any other racial group or groups and committed with the intention of maintaining that regime.

It is the fact that 'the conduct was committed in the context of an institutionalised regime of systematic oppression and domination by one racial group' over other racial group' that forms the core aspect of the elements of the crime of apartheid.[326] The uniqueness of the crime is derived from the 'systematic and institutionalised' nature of the discrimination.[327] The crime is particularly offensive as the system is sanctioned, maintained and enforced by law and legal institutions, and its general legalistic nature.[328] Hence, the Statute criminalises a system which is either legal or permitted in the domestic legislation or *de facto* policy of the respective State.[329]

The term 'inhumane acts of a character similar to those referred to in Paragraph 1' read in line with the elements of the crime, includes acts referred under Article 7(1)(a)−(i) and (k) of the Statute and acts of a similar character as composite *actus reus*

[324] Convention on the Non-Applicability of Statutory Limitations to War Crimes and Crimes against Humanity, opened for signature 16 December 1968, 754 UNTS 73 (entered into force 11 November 1970); and International Convention on the Suppression and Punishment of the Crime of Apartheid, opened for signature 30 November 1973, 1015 UNTS 243 (entered into force 18 July 1976) (Apartheid Convention). See ICJ, Advisory Opinion: Legal Consequences for States of the Continued Presence of South Africa in Namibia (South West Africa) notwithstanding Security Council Resolution 276, 21 June 1971, ICJ Reports 1971 at p. 16, paras 117–127. The ICJ advisory opinion on Namibia calls the practice a 'flagrant violation of the purpose and principles of the (UN) Charter'. In the Apartheid Convention, the prohibition of the crime of apartheid gives rise to universal jurisdiction reflecting the gravity of the crime and the commitment of the international community to eradicate the act. Nonetheless, unlike the prohibition of apartheid, it is doubtful if the crime of apartheid is already established as a rule of customary international law. See Cryer 2005, p. 259; Dugard and Reynolds 2013, p. 883; Triffterer and Ambos 2016, p. 234.

[325] Additional Protocol I, above n. 114, Article 85(4)(c).

[326] Elements of Crimes, above n. 108, Article 7(1)(j).

[327] The elements of crimes for the crime of apartheid provide a dual systematic requirement. As per Paragraphs 4 and 6 of the elements of crime, the 'inhumane act' should be 'committed in the context of an institutionalized regime of systematic oppression and domination' and 'as part of a widespread or systematic attack'. See Elements of Crimes, above n. 108, Article 7(1)(j).

[328] Triffterer and Ambos 2016, pp. 283–284.

[329] Ibid., p. 384.

of apartheid.[330] Pursuant to Hall and van den Herik,[331] many of the conducts listed under Article 2 of the Apartheid Convention, which are not expressly included under Article 7(1) of the Statute, could be read into the 'inhumane acts' category of the crime.[332] As Article 2 of the Apartheid Convention uses the word 'inhuman', which carries a higher degree of severity, in contrast to the 'inhumane acts' used under the Statute, other crimes such as the crime of denying members of a racial group's fundamental rights and freedoms which consist of the right to work, education, right to leave and return to their country, freedom of movement and residence, peaceful assembly and freedom of expression could be included.[333] The same applies *inter alia* to 'legislative measures that divide the population along racial lines by the creation of separate reserves and ghettos' or 'the expropriation of landed property belonging to a racial group' as provided under Article 2(d) of the Apartheid Convention.[334]

The crime of apartheid is a composite conduct as it inculcates 'a series of acts or omissions defined in aggregate as wrongful'.[335] It is a continuous breach 'which extends in time from the commission of the first of the actions or omissions in the series of acts making up the wrongful conduct'.[336] So long as the act is repeated or remains in breach of the prohibition, in principle, no temporal limitation could bar its prosecution. The inherently repetitive, systematic and protracted nature of the breach may require the Court to deal with 'inhumane acts' committed before the specific temporal limit for Palestine, i.e., 13 June 2014. Nonetheless, since all the elements of the alleged composite crimes of apartheid are present or persist after 13 June 2014, the matter still falls within the temporal scope of the Court.[337]

Be that as it may, to establish the commission of the crime of apartheid, the following three basic elements need to be proved: the existence of two racially distinct groups, the commission of 'inhumane acts' in the context provided under the first element of the crime,[338] and the institutionalised and systematic nature of the domination.

The legal contents of the crime of apartheid, especially the repeated reference to racial groups, is known to be highly influenced by the apartheid past of Southern

---

330 Elements of Crimes, above n. 108, Article 7(1)(j); Rome Statute, above n. 2, Article 7(1)(j); Triffterer and Ambos 2016, p. 283; Werle and Jessberger 2014, p. 384.

331 See the commentary in Triffterer and Ambos 2016, p. 283. See, in general, Bradley 2016.

332 For a concurring opinion see Werle and Jessberger 2014, p. 384.

333 Apartheid Convention, above n. 324, Article 2.

334 This approach could however give rise to issues of legal uncertainty. See Ambos 2014, p. 114.

335 International Law Commission, Draft articles on Responsibility of States for Internationally Wrongful Acts, with Commentaries, 2001, International Law Commission, 2001, vol. II (part 2), pp. 62–63.

336 Dugard and Reynolds 2013, p. 912; Draft Articles on Responsibility of States for Internationally Wrongful Acts, above n. 335, pp. 62–63.

337 With regard to the composite crime nature of the crime of apartheid see Grover 2014, pp. 191–192.

338 Elements of Crimes, above n. 108, Element 1, Article 7(1)(j).

Africa (South Africa and Namibia). Although that is the case, the relevance of the prohibition has universal application and has gained currency in international law on its own merits—mainly as a 'species of crimes against humanity'.[339] As Falk notes, 'each situation has its originality', and that there are resemblances and dissimilarities between the situation in Palestine and apartheid South Africa.[340] The following analysis, therefore, considers the issue of apartheid on its own merits, in light of the Rome Statute and the Apartheid Convention. It, nonetheless, greatly benefits from a comparative outlook between the Palestinian situation and Apartheid South Africa. It adopts the approach employed by the Human Sciences Research Council of South Africa (HSRC). Yet, it takes precaution to avoid using the discrete cases in apartheid South Africa as a yardstick to qualify conducts as amounting to the crime of apartheid.[341]

Existence of Distinct Racial Groups

Before establishing whether inhumane acts are perpetrated against one racial group over another, the crucial question that must be addressed is whether Palestinians and Jews constitute independent and separate racial groups for the purpose of the crime of apartheid and in sense provided in the Rome Statute. On the ground of the traditional colour categories of races, both Palestinians and Jews are comprised of different 'races' as both groups contain members with European, Asian and African origins.[342] These may give rise to the argument that in the absence this clear distinction on race, it cannot be asserted that Israel discriminates based on race.

Neither the Apartheid Convention nor the Rome Statute provides a definition of the term 'race', requiring resort to other Conventional law.[343] Dugard rightly opines that race is a 'social construct rather than a scientific reality' which is 'falling out of technical usage except in the context of racial discrimination'.[344] Due to this, he

339 Dugard and Reynolds 2013, p. 870.

340 C. Balsam, Israel guilty of war crimes; Palestinians are winning the legitimacy war, an interview with UN Special Rapporteur Richard Falk, *Alternatives International,* 17 March 2009.

341 Regarding the risks of employing apartheid South Africa as a benchmark to measure if a regime qualifies as an apartheid regime See ESCWA 2017, pp. 14–17. This ESCWA report, which was commissioned and approved by the UN has not obtained an official endorsement from the Secretary General of the UN. Hence, it does not represent the views of the UN. Following the publication of the report and strong criticism from Israel and the US and call for its withdrawal, the Secretary of the Commission resigned from the post. See T. Perry, Israel is imposing 'apartheid regime' on Palestinians, UN agency says, The Independent, 16 March 2017; Text of Resignation Letter by ESCWA Executive Secretary Rima Khalaf, http://www.globalresearch.ca/israels-crime-of-apartheid-text-of-resignation-letter-by-escwa-executive-secretary-rima-khalaf/5580624 (accessed 28 March 2017).

342 Chetrit 2010, pp. x et seq. See generally Spangler 2015; Likhovski 2005, p. 78.

343 Rome Statute, above n. 2, Article 21.

344 Dugard and Reynolds 2013, pp. 885–886. Similar to Dugard, Triffterer and Ambos in the commentary on the Rome Statute have noted that race, as a term and concept, has become almost obsolete and further suggest that the meaning of race, in the context of apartheid, could include 'other types of discriminatory denomination'. See Triffterer and Ambos 2016, p. 285.

states, international human rights law defines race in a broader scope. Similar to the Apartheid Convention, the Convention on the Elimination of All Forms of Racial Discrimination defines 'racial' in 'racial discrimination' to mean 'race, colour, descent, national or ethnic origin'.[345]

The jurisprudence of the ICTR dealing with the crime of genocide, particularly in the *Akayesu* case, has established that the meaning of race depends on 'local perceptions and shall be assessed in light of a particular political, social and cultural context'.[346] In the *Jelisic case*, the ICTY used the perspective of the perpetrator in targeting the group.[347] In light of the judgment, the determining factor is the fact that the perpetrator identified or singled out the targeted group because of the differing characteristics it possess.[348] The concept of race is rather fluid that relies on the local setting and environment.[349] Hence, for the purposes of applying Article 7(2)(h) of the Rome Statute and based on any of the above views, Jewish-Israelis and the Arab-Palestinians are considered as possessing distinct racial identities in the Israeli-Palestinian setting.[350]

Consequently, Palestinian identity, as specified in the Charter of the Palestine Liberation Organisation,[351] is intergenerational that passes down from father to son and comprises of Arab Palestinians in the occupied Palestinian territories and those refugees of the Arab-Israel wars residing in neighbouring States.[352] On the Israeli side, Jewish identity as per the Law of Return (1950 as amended in 1970)[353] consists of one born from a Jewish mother or has converted to Judaism, or as per the Declaration of Independence of Israel (1948) one that claim to have the 'lineal descent from antiquity' or has the 'unbroken bloodline' tracing ancestry to ancient Palestine.[354]

---

[345] Article 1(1) of International Convention on the Elimination of All Forms of Racial Discrimination, opened for signature 21 December 1965, 660 UNTS 195 (entered into force 4 January 1969) (Convention on the Elimination of All Forms of Racial Discrimination).

[346] *Akayesu* 1998, above n. 111, paras 512–515. See also Dugard and Reynolds 2013, p. 887.

[347] ICTY, *Prosecutor v. Jelisic*, Judgement, IT-95-10, 14 December 1999, para 70.

[348] Ibid. See also Dugard and Reynolds 2013, p. 888.

[349] See ESCWA 2017, p. 21.

[350] The two groups have different historical, national, social and cultural identities. Although both groups have a dominant religion (Judaism for Israel and Islam for Palestine), religion is not a main defining feature for identifying oneself as part of the group. Although being a Jew has links with Judaism, the term is considered as indicating ethnic and national origins. Similarly, as there are varieties of religion practiced in Palestine, one is identified as a Palestinian mainly based on the roots of his/her ancestry. For more on this see Dugard and Reynolds 2013, p. 890.

[351] Article 5 of the Charter of the Palestinian Liberation Organisation states 'The Palestinian personality is a permanent and genuine characteristic that does not disappear. It is transferred from father to sons'. See Palestinian National Charter of 1964, http://www.palwatch.org/main.aspx?fi=640&doc_id=8210 (accessed 21 March 2017).

[352] ESCWA 2017, pp. 4, 23.

[353] Law of Return 5710–1950, http://www.mfa.gov.il/mfa/mfa-archive/1950-1959/pages/law%20of%20return%205710-1950.aspx (accessed 21 March 2017).

[354] ESCWA 2017, p. 25.

Constitutive 'Inhumane Acts'

As there are readily available detailed reports[355] regarding laws and alleged practices that constitute the alleged 'inhumane act' element of the crime of apartheid in the Occupied Palestinian Territories, this section does not aim to replicate all details of the reports. It is, however, important to provide some of the manifestations of the alleged breaches of the prohibition of apartheid. To establish the alleged commission of 'inhumane acts' as provided under Article 7(1)(j) of the Rome Statute, the discussion uses the acts illustrated under Article 2 of the Convention against apartheid as a governing outline. It first discusses Article 2(a) of the Convention namely the 'denial to a member or members of a racial group or groups of the right to life and liberty of person' followed by Article 2(b) 'deliberate imposition on a racial group or groups of living conditions calculated to cause its or their physical destruction in whole or in part'. Conducts provided under Article 2(d) namely those dealing with 'measures designed to divide the population along racial lines' and those under Article 2(c) particularly 'measures preventing participation in political, social, economic and cultural life, and preventing full development' are covered thereafter.

Denial of members of a racial group's right to life and liberty of person is one of the prominent human right violations in an apartheid regime. The Report published by the Truth and Reconciliation Commission of South Africa (TRC) has documented violations of the right to life and liberty of blacks and other ethnic groups in 1960–94 in South and southern Africa. Apartheid, as the TRC reported, was enforced, amongst other methods, through State-sanctioned murder and the death penalty against those who were designated as adversaries to the system.[356] The opponents, who were conveniently labelled terrorists, 'their supporters and hosts' were targeted through extra-judicial killings, assassinations and cross-border raids.[357] Unlawful detention was 'apartheid's big gun' in maintaining the system, where more than 80,000 people were subjected to this 'form of neutralisation'.[358] Detentions occurred mainly for the purposes of interrogation, as a 'preventive measure' and as a means of intimidating opponents.[359] Official records for 1987, for

---

[355] Among others, the Committee on the Elimination of Racial Discrimination, several UN Special Rapporteurs and fact-finding mission, the HSRC have pointed out various policies and practices of Israel that amount to a *prima facie* breach of the prohibition of apartheid. See Committee on the Elimination of Racial Discrimination 2012, paras 10–26; UNHRC 2007, para 50; UNGA 2010, paras 3 et seq.; UNHRC 2009b, paras 198–209; and HSRC 2009, pp. 174 et seq.

[356] Truth and Reconciliation Commission 1998, vol. 6, Sect. 3, p. 192.

[357] Ibid., vol 1., p. 799. The Terrorism Act, no. 83 (1967) was the stated aim of combating terrorism in South West Africa (Namibia). A year after it came into force, it was used to charge South Africans. It allowed indefinite detention without trial in solitary confinement for the aim of conducting interrogation. Parties opposing apartheid such as the Pan Africanist Congress and the African National Congress were banned under the Internal Security Act 44 of 1950 later known as the Unlawful Organizations Act 37 of 1960. See Coleman 1998, p. 44; and Dugard and Reynolds 2013, p. 875.

[358] Coleman 1998, p. 43.

[359] Truth and Reconciliation Commission 1998, vol. 4, Chap. 7, para 13.

instance, reveal that of the total detainees 34% were between 12 to 18 years of age.[360] Most frequently, torture was used against detainees to extract confessions, obtain convictions or to simply 'soften' 'stubborn' detainees.[361]

The Israeli Defence Force has authorisation to 'liquidate' Palestinian 'terrorists' even where they are not on the verge of committing an attack or when they could be arrested and brought before a Court.[362] Israel justifies the conduct as 'self-defence', pre-emptive strike or prevention of terror while Palestinians categorise it as 'assassination' or 'extra-judicial execution'.[363] Palestinian resistance to the Israeli occupation is labelled as 'terrorism' and those who allegedly lead and participate in the resistances are targeted in or outside hostilities. Targeted killings are practised against these individuals despite the often disproportionate 'collateral damage'.[364] Amnesty international, among others, has also reported on alleged excessive use of force against Palestinian demonstrators in the West Bank, which has reportedly killed thousands of Palestinians to date.[365] Israeli political leaders and senior police officers have publicly supported the extra-judicial killings of those suspected of attacking or attempting to attack Israeli soldiers and civilians.[366] In addition, the recurrence of purported deliberate and indiscriminate killing of civilians in Israeli operations in Gaza, as reported by the UN Fact-Finding Mission[367] display, partly, a pattern aimed at intimidating dissenters and, at worst, a disregard to Palestinian lives.

Administrative detention is reported to be widely used by Israel to repress dissent.[368] Detention without trial is justified in an armed conflict if only 'imperative

---

[360] Coleman 1998, p. 51.

[361] Truth and Reconciliation Commission 1998, vol. 4, para 13. See also Coleman 1998, pp. 47 et seq.; and HSRC 2009, p. 173.

[362] A. Benn and A. Harel, Kitchen Cabinet okays expansion of liquidation list: IDF warns of rise in violence shortly, Haaretz, 17 July 2001.

[363] Kendall 2002, p. 1072.

[364] Dugard and Reynolds 2013, p. 891. See UN Human Rights Committee 2010, para 10.

[365] This is most notable during the two intifadas. Hundreds of Israelis have also lost their lives during the two Intifadas. See Amnesty International 2015; Amnesty International, Press release: Israel/OPT: Pattern of unlawful killings reveals shocking disregard for human life, 28 September 2016, https://www.amnesty.org/en/press-releases/2016/09/israel-opt-pattern-of-unlawful-killings-reveals-shocking-disregard-for-human-life-1/ (accessed 17 October 2016). See also Human Rights Watch, Israel: killing of children apparent war crime, 9 June 2014, https://www.hrw.org/news/2014/06/09/israel-killing-children-apparent-war-crime (accessed 17 October 2016).

[366] B'Tselem, Press release: Human rights organizations in Israel: Politicians' calls to police and soldiers to shoot rather than arrest endorse the killing of Palestinians', 14 October 2015, http://www.btselem.org/press_releases/20151014_summary_execution_joint_Statement (accessed 17 October 2016)

[367] UNHRC 2009b, paras 653 et seq., 704–885.

[368] Administrative detention, as employed by Israel, is detention for indefinite period without charge or trial and renewable every six months. Even if the procedure is often used to detain Palestinians from the occupied territories, foreigners and Israeli citizens could also be detained. So far nine Israeli citizens have been in administrative detention. See Addameer Prisoner Support and Human Rights Association, Administrative detention, December 2015, http://www.addameer.org/israeli_military_judicial_system/administrative_detention (accessed 17 October 2016).

security reasons' so require. The detainee must also be released as soon as the grounds for detention cease to exist.[369] Article 285 of Military Order 1651, Military Order No. 132, Internment of Unlawful Combatants Law and Emergency Powers (Detentions) Law of Israel are used to base administrative detention. It is estimated that around 40% of male Palestinians have been detained at some point in their lives.[370] At the time of writing, around 16 members of the Palestine Parliament also called the Palestinian Legislative Council are under administrative detention.[371] The military Courts try an average of 500 to 700 Palestinian children every year[372] mostly for stone throwing which results in a sentence of six months up to 20 years' imprisonment.[373] Under Military Order No. 132, Palestinian children above the age of 12 could be sentenced to prison terms while the Israel criminal law sets the limit on 14, which is adhered to for Israeli children.[374] Despite the prescriptions of the Youth Bill,[375] it is alleged that Palestinian minors are usually arrested during late nights, interrogated in the absence of parents, denied access to consult lawyers and

---

[369] Geneva Convention IV, above n. 123, Article 78.

[370] B'Tselem, Statistics on administrative detention, 20 March 2013, www.btselem.org/english/Administrative_Detention/Statistics.asp (accessed 5 May 2016); Addameer Prisoner Support and Human Rights Association, Administrative detention, above n. 368.

[371] Sputnik News, Palestine envoy to Russia slams Israel for arresting Palestinian lawmaker, 9 April 2015, https://sputniknews.com/middleeast/201504091020683095/ (accessed 17 October 2016).

[372] Children from Eastern Jerusalem are tried based on civil law as they are residents of Israel. UNHRC 2009b, paras 207 et seq. HSRC reported that Israeli military officers chair military Courts. The average hearing lasts less than 4 minutes, with 0.3% of acquittal rates and 95–97% of convictions. Conviction could also be based on 'secret evidence' not available to the accused. See HSRC 2009, pp. 116 et seq.

[373] Law imposing a mandatory minimum sentence on convicted stone-throwers Enacted by the Knesset on 2 November 2015 as Amendment no. 120 to the Israeli Penal Code, available (in Hebrew), http://fs.knesset.gov.il/20/law/20_lsr_315852.pdf (accessed 4 March 2016). Under Military Order no. 378, throwing stones against immovable things such as the separation wall could result in a sentence up to ten years and if against a vehicle, it results in a sentence up to 20 years See also UN Committee Against Torture 2002, para D (6)(d); Dugard and Reynolds 2013, p. 893; HSRC 2009, p. 181. Human Rights Watch has reported that children detained have reported abuse and ill-treatment. Defense for Children International-Palestine has documented 66 cases of solitary confinement between 2012 and 2015. See Human Rights Watch 2016; Committee on the Rights of the Child 2013, paras 35–36, 73–74.

[374] Although any Palestinian below the age of 17 is considered a minor, under Military Order No. 132, a Palestinian is considered a child if he/she is 11 year of age or below. That is to mean that minors of 12 years of age and above receive a similar treatment to an adult under the military order. Israeli children below the age of 14 are not 'subject to prison sentences'. See UN Committee Against Torture 2002, para D (6)(d). See also Dugard and Reynolds 2013, p. 893; HSRC 2009, p. 181.

[375] L. Dearden, Israel approves new law to jail child 'terrorists' as young as 12, Tej Independent, 3 August 2016; The Knesset, Press release: Knesset gives final approval to bill allowing imprisonment of terrorists under the age of 14, 3 August 2016, https://www.knesset.gov.il/spokesman/eng/PR_eng.asp?PRID=12206 (accessed 24 April 2017).

conjugal visits. Although, Military Order 1745 (2014), requires interrogations to be recorded and conducted in a language the child understands, the order states, such rights do not apply to those suspected of security offences, such as stone throwing.[376]

As per the reports of the committee against torture and the Special Rapporteur on the promotion and protection of human rights, administrative detentions involve a high possibility of torture and ill-treatment.[377] Israeli Security Agency reportedly uses particularly severe interrogation technics against 'security prisoners'. As B'Tselem documented, among other methods, the Agency allegedly employs solitary confinement, cuffing in a *Shabah* position[378] for a protracted period, deprivation of sleep and beatings during interrogation.[379]

The deliberate imposition of living conditions with the aim of causing the physical destruction of the racial group is the second category of conducts in the list of the composite crimes of apartheid. Article 2(b) of the Apartheid Convention borrows one of the acts that constitute the crime of Genocide from the Convention on the Prevention and Punishment of the Crime of Genocide. Minus its designated focus on racial groups—in contrast to 'a national, ethnical, racial or religious group' of the Genocide Convention—Article 2(b) of the Apartheid Convention is a direct replica of Article 2(c) of the Genocide Convention. Hence, without prejudice to its focus on race and racial groups, Article 2(b) of the Apartheid Convention is interpreted and applied in the same way as Article 2(c) of the Genocide Convention, which, consequently, requires the inclusion of the strict intent element for the crime of Genocide.

Apartheid South Africa had (its remnant still has) a dire impact on the lives of the black population in particular.[380] Many have lost lives in varieties of ways and

---

376 United Nations International Children's Emergency Fund 2015, p. 2. See also The Association for Civil Rights in Israel 2014, pp. 68–69; and Addameer Prisoner Support and Human Rights Association, Administrative detention in the Occupied Palestinian Territory: between law and practice, https://www.oceansofinjustice.com/resource/addameer-administrative-detention-2010.pdf (accessed 20 August 2016), p. 38.

377 The absolute prohibition of torture is not included in the Israeli laws. Israeli High Court of Justice has allowed the use of 'pressure and discomfort' to extract information. This decision is further re enforced by the General Security Service Law (2002) which states that any Security Service Agent 'shall not bear criminal or civil responsibility for any act or omission performed in good faith and reasonably by him within the scope and in performance of his function.' See Supreme Court of Israel, *The Public Committee Against Torture in Israel v. The Government of Israel*, Motion for an Order, 18 September 1994, HCJ 5100/94. See also UN Committee Against Torture 2001; UNHRC 2007; UN Human Rights Committee 2003; UNHRC 2009b, para 209; HSRC 2009, pp. 181–183; and Amnesty International 2008, pp. 5 et seq.

378 This position is where one sits on a small chair tilted forward or where hands and legs are tied together under a chair. It could also take other forms. See Carey 2012, p. 105; and Human Rights Watch 2008, p. 42.

379 B'Tselem 2007, pp. 67 et seq.; Carey 2012, p. 116; HSRC 2009, pp. 181–182; Kadman 2015, pp. 52 et seq.

380 Arellano et al. 2006, p. 399.

have undergone 'wide-scale suffering'.[381] But as the TRC puts it, the then South African government did not harbour the intent to cause the destruction of the black population in whole or in part. All the more, the main aim of the system was to maintain the population as a source of cheap labour.[382]

Pappé argues that 'a historical evaluation and contextualisation' of Israel's military operations in Gaza depicts what he calls 'Israel's genocidal policy' and its overall strategy towards Palestinians.[383] As reported by the UN Fact-Finding mission, among others, 'attacks on Gaza's industrial infrastructure, food production, water installations, sewage treatment plants and housing' have devastating results on the lives of Palestinians.[384] The operations, coupled with the blockade, has *inter alia* made 80% of the population aid recipient, 90% of the water unfit for consumption, unemployment rate of about 38% and an increasing poverty, environmental degradation and reducing physical and mental health of residences.[385] Nonetheless, contrary to Pappé's stance, 'genocidal intent' cannot be derived from the blockade of Gaza, the large number of causalities and destruction of structures and infrastructures.

Proving 'specific intent' for genocide, as Werle and Jessberger noted,[386] requires evidence on the fact that 'the accused acted within the framework of an overarching plan or policy to commit genocide'.[387] The ICJ, in the case *Bosnia v. Serbia* has also recognised that one cannot establish the specific intent (*dolus specialis*) merely based on the tactics used. In the Bosnian case, tactics such as a siege, 'shelling of population centres' and cutting off food supplies were used to force ethnic Croatians and Muslims to flee.[388] Similar to the ICJ's cautious approach regarding inference of specific intent, in *Prosecutor v. Omar Al Bashir*, the ICC has held that 'specific

---

[381] HSRC 2009, p. 192.

[382] Norval 1996, p. 229; Rothenberg 2010, p. 250.

[383] Pappé 2015, p. 148

[384] UNHRC 2009b, pp. 913–1031.

[385] Gilbert 2014, p. 3.

[386] Werle and Jessberger 2014, p. 320.

[387] In addition to the contextual element, knowledge of the perpetrator about the crime and his opinion about the objects of the attack is necessary. With regard to establishing the 'specific intent' for one of the accused named *Ljubiša Beara* the ICTY Trial Chamber noted 'there is no direct explicit evidence that *Beara* had the requisite specific intent for genocide. Therefore, the Trial Chamber must look at all of the surrounding circumstances, including *Beara*'s words and acts, as well as the inferences to be drawn, to determine whether genocidal intent has been established'. See ICTY, *Prosecutor v. Popović, Beara & et al*, Judgment, 10 June 2010, IT-05-88-T, para 1311.

[388] ICJ, Application of the Convention on the Prevention and Punishment of the Crime of Genocide (*Bosnia and Herzegovina v. Serbia and Montenegro*), Judgment, 26 February 2007, ICJ Reports 2007 at p. 43, paras 327–328; *Galić* 2006, above n. 184, paras 107–109, 335, 386–390; The Special Rapporteur of the United Nations Commission on Human Rights Report, 28 August 1992, para 17.

intent should not be inferred from the factual circumstances'.[389] In the absence of any proof on the existence of 'an overarching plan or policy to commit genocide', as in the situation in Gaza and the Occupied Palestinian Territories, it is submitted that the conducts of Israel do not constitute conducts committed with the intention to cause the physical destruction of Palestinians in whole or in part.

The other group of conducts prohibited under Article 2 of the Anti-apartheid Convention are measures that aim to divide the population along racial lines. Segregation on the basis of a group's racial identity is a legally and morally condemned conduct. It contravenes the right to equality and violates the principle of non-discrimination enshrined in numerous international instruments.[390] Despite the motive, if a conduct has the outcome of creating 'distinction, exclusion, restriction or preference based on race, colour, descent, or national or ethnic origin' it is deemed as 'racial discrimination'.[391]

Reserves are sections of land allotted or apportioned for the exclusive use of a specific group. Even if reserves could also be created for preserving cultural heritages of a group, in the apartheid context they are aimed to exclude a group from another and to confine one into specific areas of land. In Apartheid South Africa, the Group Areas Act 41 of 1950, among others, divided the country into fragments whose inhabitation was contingent on the race of the individual.[392] The uprooting of blacks and the immense suffering caused in the process of creating the separate reserves or Bantustans was justified by the government as the only means to eliminate racial conflict, and prevent the disaster that could result from 'multiracialism, multinationalism and multiculturalism'.[393]

Jewish settlements in the West Bank and East Jerusalem are primarily aimed to secure Israel's control of the territory. At times, they are justified on 'security' grounds. Despite the motive or justification behind, the infrastructures—supporting the settlements and connecting them to other Israeli highways in Israel proper and the West Bank—have created fragmented Palestinian enclaves. The infrastructures constituting for more than 40% of the West Bank comprise the settlements, military

---

[389] ICC, *Prosecutor v. Omar Al Bashir*, Decision on the Prosecution's Application for a Warrant of Arrest against Omar Hassan Ahmad Al Bashir, 4 March 2009, ICC-02/05-01/09 (*Al Bashir* 2009), para 194.

[390] See, among others, the International Covenant on Civil and Political Rights, opened for signature 16 December 1966, 999 UNTS 171 (entered into force 23 March 1976); Convention on the Elimination of All Forms of Racial Discrimination, above n. 345.

[391] Convention on the Elimination of All Forms of Racial Discrimination, above n. 345, Article 1. See also The Association for Civil Rights in Israel 2014, p. 124.

[392] The Glen Grey Act (1874); The Bantu Land Act (1913); The Native Trust and Land Act (1936) and The Prevention of Illegal Squatting Act (1952) were used to enforce the segregation and separate enclaves amongst the blacks and whites of South Africa.

[393] O'Meara 1996, p. 69; Commission for the Socio-economic Development of the Bantu Areas within the Union of South Africa 1955, pp. 103, 196 et seq. See also HSRC 2009, pp. 253–254.

areas, outposts, nature reserves and the separation wall. Consequent to the separation of the Palestinian enclaves due to the Israeli infrastructures and the closure regime, a permit and ID system and about 460 roadblocks and 96 checkpoints (on top of hundreds of surprise checkpoints) are created, and are applicable only on Palestinians.[394] As a result, the Israeli and Palestinian populations in the West Bank especially are allocated different 'physical spaces' in which entry into the different reserves depends on identity. Accordingly, there are significant variations in the standard of living, quality of infrastructure, public services and allocation of resources.[395] The Jewish-only highways are prohibited and inaccessible to Palestinians.[396] The myriad of restrictions on movement, as well as residence and family reunification in the West Bank are applied mainly based on one's identity.[397] The policy of segregation is formally known in Israel as *hafrada* (Hebrew for 'separateness').[398]

Two separate systems of law applicable to the two groups help maintain the segregation.[399] Most laws distinguish between Jews (Israeli residents and citizens, as well as those Jews who benefit from the Law of Return) on the one hand and Palestinians on the other. The Order Concerning Security Provisions (Judea and Samaria) No. 378, for instance, orders the closure of Israeli settlements in the West Bank to any non-Israeli excluding anyone who is not a resident or citizen of Israel, 'any person who is not a resident of the area and holds a valid entry permit to Israel'.[400] The seam zone permit also closes entry to Palestinians.[401] In addressing the two-tier legal system, the UN Fact-finding mission mandated to investigate the implications of Israeli settlements on the rights of Palestinians in Occupied Palestinian Territories has concluded that:

---

394 As per the UN report, the closure and the movement restrictions in the Gaza and the West Bank have respectively resulted in 50–74 and 30–50% unemployment rate. See UNHRC 2009b, para 204. See also B'Tselem, Checkpoints, physical obstructions, and forbidden roads, 20 May 2015, http://www.btselem.org/freedom_of_movement/checkpoints_and_forbidden_roads (accessed on 19 October 2016).

395 Braverman 2013; Davis and Coffman 2014, p. 31; Zunes 2009, p. 147.

396 The Association for Civil Rights in Israel and B'Tselem reported: 'as of May 2015, 'Israel designates 60.92 kilometers of West Bank roads for the exclusive, or almost exclusive, use of Israelis, and first and foremost – West Bank settlers'. See The Association for Civil Rights in Israel 2014, p. 105; and B'Tselem 2015, above n. 394.

397 HSRC 2009, pp. 206, 257–260, 271.

398 UNHRC 2014, para 70.

399 UNHRC 2011, paras 20–22; UNHRC 2014, para 70.

400 Government of the State of Israel, Order Concerning Security Provisions (Judea and Samaria) (No. 378), 5730–1970 and Proclamation Concerning the Closure of a Territory (Israeli Settlements) (Judea and Samaria), 5757–1997.

401 Government of the State of Israel, General Permit for Entering the Seam Zone and Staying Therein (Judea and Samaria), No. S/2/03, 5764–2003. See The Association for Civil Rights in Israel 2014, pp. 124–125.

> The legal regime of segregation operating in the Occupied Palestinian Territory has enabled the establishment and the consolidation of the settlements through the creation of a privileged legal space for settlements and settlers. It results in daily violations of multitude of the human rights of the Palestinians in the Occupied Palestinian Territory, including, incontrovertibly, violating their rights to non-discrimination, equality before the law and equal protection of the law.[402]

The blockade of Gaza has also alienated the residents from the rest of the Palestinian territories and the world as entry and exit is difficult to impossible depending on the will of Israeli officials.[403] Israelis are not allowed to enter Gaza and residents of Gaza cannot travel to the West Bank without a special permit. Gaza qualifies as a complete compulsive ghettoization or enclaving of people on a justification similar to what is given by the apartheid South African government, i.e., eliminating (racial) conflict. Hence, despite the justifications Israel gives in creating the facts and reality on the ground, the resultant effect has brought about enclaving Palestinians in separate reserves where entry and exit is determined by the permit they carry. It has created a scenario in which race, particularly, the national and ethnic origins of an individual, is the determining factor in how the State deals with the residents.

Although the ICC lacks personal jurisdiction regarding those Israeli citizens of Palestinian origin (20% of the general Israeli population), the distinction in treatment between those of Palestinian and Jewish origin backs the above claim. Israeli law distinguishes between Israeli citizens (which includes Israeli citizens of Palestinian origins) and Israeli nationals (mainly Jewish) and is employed to provide legally sanctioned distinct treatments. There are also informal restrictions regarding, among others, the provision of social services, budget allocations, economic opportunities and areas of residence.[404] The distinction and preferential treatment based on race is even further evidenced by the refusal of Israel to allow the return of 3.4 million UN registered Palestinian refugees with ancestral origins in Palestine and their designation as a 'demographic threat' when it allows any person with a 'Jewish' claim to return regardless of the person's ancestral lineage.[405]

Article 2(c) of the Apartheid Convention prohibits measures such as those that prevent certain groups 'from participation in the political, social, economic and cultural life' of their country and the 'deliberate creation of conditions preventing the full development of such group'. As this category contains second generation rights, it may give the appearance that violations of these rights may not be of 'the same nature' and gravity as those crimes against humanity under Article 7(1) of the Rome Statute.[406] Nonetheless, the linkage and overlap of violations of these rights

[402] UNHRC 2013, para 49.

[403] HSRC 2009, pp. 199–203.

[404] ESCWA 2017, p. 39.

[405] On the Right to Return of Palestinian refugees see UNGA 1948 and UNSC 1967a. See also ESCWA 2017, p. 48.

[406] Triffterer and Ambos 2016, p. 284. See Elements of Crimes, above n. 108, Element 2 of Article 7(1)(j).

with first generation rights, their inclusion in other crimes against humanity as in the case of persecution, and the long term and adverse impact on the alleged victims grants them the required gravity.[407] This, however, does not mean that all violations within this category deserve consideration for the crime of apartheid. Due to their overarching impacts, those alleged violations against freedom of movement and economic rights and access to resources are discussed hereunder.

Freedom of Movement: Human rights instruments guarantee freedom of individuals to move freely within their own State, to leave and return to their country, as well as to choose their place of residence. It is regarded as a natural law and integral to one's 'personal liberty'.[408] One of the core features of apartheid South Africa was the severe restriction on freedom of movement and its essential components. The apartheid master plan, which preserved some urban centres for the white race, was enforced through, among others, the Native Urban Areas Amendment Act of 1955 and the Pass Law. A black person has to obtain a permit from the authorities to be able to travel from a rural to an urban zone.[409]

In the occupied Palestinian territories, in particular the West Bank and East Jerusalem, Palestinians are required to carry permits to pass checkpoints and roadblocks. Permits are required for entry to settlement areas in occupied Palestinian territories, Israel, East Jerusalem, special permits for the Seam Zone,[410] the Jordan valley and the Nablus District of the West Bank and permits to travel from the West Bank to Gaza which are nearly impossible to obtain. The permit regime exceedingly obstructs the movement, economy and personal life of Palestinians.[411]

Israel justifies the regime on security grounds. The majority of these checkpoints and roadblocks, nonetheless, are located far from the Israeli border that, further, is enclosed by the wall.[412] The UN Special Rapporteur on the occupied Palestinian territories pronounced that the more likely explanation for the permit regime is 'to facilitate the travel of settlers through the West Bank and to impress upon the Palestinian people the power and presence of the occupier'.[413] The Special

[407] See Triffterer and Ambos 2016, p. 284.

[408] McAdam 2011, pp. 6.

[409] Amnesty International 1986, pp. 2 et seq.; Horrell 1960, pp. 1 et seq.

[410] The Seam Zone is the land between the Green line and the separation wall. Following the construction of the wall, individuals living there are required to hold a personal permit or a seam zone residence permit to live, work or move through the Zone. The permits are granted for limited periods, which require application for renewal by providing justification regarding the individual's connection to the land. Such requirement is levied only on Palestinians. See Government of the State of Israel, General Permit for Entering the Seam Zone and Staying Therein (Judea and Samaria), No. S/2/03, 5764-2003. See also The Association for Civil Rights in Israel 2014, p. 109.

[411] A special permit is also required to use 'second category roads' which are different from roads reserved for exclusive use of settlers and other roads for Palestinians.

[412] UNHRC 2008, para 35.

[413] Ibid.

Rapporteur also made a comparison between the pass law of apartheid South Africa and the permit regime in the occupied Palestinian territories, as both require the locals to demonstrate proof for 'permission to travel or reside anywhere'.[414] The permit system is premised on the conviction that all Palestinians are a security threat,[415] as it is only Palestinians, in contrast to settlers and other Israel citizens, who are subjected to such restrictions. Such racial profiling[416] constitutes racial discrimination in the sense provided under Article 2(c) of the Apartheid Convention and results in violation of the right to movement.

Economic Rights and Access to Resources: This section covers those legal principles in light of the International Covenant on Economic, Social and Cultural Rights which establish economic equality and allows sustainable and equitable economic growth and development. In apartheid South Africa, the right to work, among other economic rights, was highly controlled and restricted on the basis of one's race. The pass laws and the 1963 Job Reservation Act enforced work segregation.[417]

The overall Israeli policy on the occupied Palestinian territories, namely, the closures, roadblocks, curfews, and checkpoints as well as the permit regime has reportedly affected the right to work and economy of Palestinians. The closure has resulted in, among others, in one of the highest unemployment rates and reduction in the annual GDP.[418] Direct physical damage on cultivated land[419] and the denial of permit to access cultivated land has greatly affected the livelihood.[420]

On the other hand, Israel has declared part of the West Bank 'State land'. In accordance with Israeli laws, State lands are designated for the exclusive use of Jewish people and are administered based on the land policies of Israel.[421] The fact

---

414 Ibid.

415 HSRC 2009, p. 203.

416 Racial profiling is the prohibited use of race and other personal characteristics of an individual by law enforcement agents 'in determining which individuals to stop, detain, question, or subject to other law enforcement activities'. See The Leadership Conference 2011, p. 7.

417 African National Congress, *South Africa Freedom News,* 1962, p. 22; Amnesty International 1986, pp. 2 et seq.; Horrell 1960, pp. 1 et seq.

418 UNCTAD 2016. See also Oxfam, 20 facts: 20 years since the Oslo Accords, https://www.oxfam.org/sites/www.oxfam.org/files/oxfam-oslo-20-factsheet.pdf (accessed 28 March 2017).

419 Between 2006–2007, for instance, the Israeli military destroyed 12,900 dunums of cultivated land, 2,775 fruit trees and 332 green houses in the West Bank.

420 UNOCHA has reported that after the construction of the separation wall and the introduction of the permit regime around 80% of farmers who used to cultivate their lands in the Seam Zone are denied permit to do so. See UNOCHA-OPT 2007, p. 2. About 95% of the access to groundwater in the West Bank is closed off by the Separation Wall. According to UN report, Palestinians in the West Bank obtain up to 60 litres of water per day while settlers obtain up to 450 litres. See Israel's violations of the International Covenant on Economic, Social and Cultural Rights with regard to the human rights to water and sanitation in the Occupied Palestinian Territory, https://unispal.un.org/DPA/DPR/unispal.nsf/0/25404F8138A8FEA5852578FC0050F939 (accessed 1 September 2016).

421 See ESCWA 2017, pp. 34–35.

that agencies such as the Jewish Agency and World Zionist Organization are authorized to administer such lands and other 'Jewish-national affairs' does not relieve the State from responsibilities.

Freedom of opinion and expression: Although not absolute, freedom of opinion, expression and assembly, as established in various international instruments, envelops freedom of choice, conscience, religion, association, political identification and protest. It is one of the main beacons of a functioning democracy. In the apartheid South African context, censorship, banning and restrictions on publications and broadcasts were used as a means of social control and a method to maintain the apartheid regime.[422]

Reporters without Borders have ranked Israel at 101th country on the World Press Freedom Index of 2016 with a significant ranking disparity within and outside the occupied Palestinian territories.[423] There is, reportedly, direct censorship regarding news published in the occupied Palestinian territories or about Palestine published in Israel. A series of military orders require the military censor to pre-approve publications of Palestinian newspapers. Military permits have to also be obtained beforehand.[424] There is also a purported suppression of opponents of the occupation through arbitrary arrest, detentions, extra-judicial killings and travel bans.[425] Following the arrest and torture of a Palestinian journalist after receiving the Martha Gellhorn Prize for Journalism, the UN special Rapporteur has stated that the incident is a 'part of a broader pattern of Israeli punitive interference with independent journalistic reporting on the occupation'.[426]

The mere construction of the State of Israel as a Jewish State tends to result in conflating opposition to racial distinction and discrimination with an attack on the mere existence of the State. The Basic Law of Israel (the constitution) deems illegal any opposition to the construction of the State as Jewish and lists it in the same

---

422 See Chaps. 2 and 4 of Drewett and Cloonan 2016; and Green and Karolides 2005, p. 530.

423 Reporters Without Borders, Reporting constrained by terror in the Middle East and North Africa, https://rsf.org/en/reporting-constrained-terror-middle-east-and-north-africa (accessed 25 October 2016). See also Reporters Sans Frontières—Reporters Without Borders, Annual Worldwide Press Freedom Index: statistics, https://rsf.org/en/world-press-freedom-index (accessed 09 April 2016).

424 Dugard and Reynolds 2013, p. 897; Human Rights Watch 2010; Tilley 2012, pp. 216–218.

425 Al-Haq, Right to life of Palestinian Children disregarded in Ni'lin as Israel's policy of wilful killing of civilians continues, http://www.alhaq.org/advocacy/topics/right-to-life-and-body-integrity/190-right-to-life-of-palestinian-children-disregarded-in-nilin-as-israels-policy-of-wilful-killing-of-civilians-continues (accessed 01 September 2016); B'Tselem reports that there are State-sanctioned policies on extra-judicial execution of oppositions to the occupation. See B'Tselem, Activity of the undercover units in the occupied territories, May 1992, http://www.btselem.org/Download/199205_Undercover_Units_Eng.doc (accessed 13 October 2016); Middle East Watch 1993. See also HSRC 2009, pp. 174–175.

426 UNHRC 2008b, paras 19–20.

category as incitement to racism and support of terrorist organisation.[427] When a State makes the opposition of racial preference and distinction illegal instead of the act of racial discrimination and preferential treatment,[428] it is, in fact, curtailing freedom of opinion and expression.

The Institutionalised or Systematic Nature of the 'Inhumane Acts'

Both the Apartheid Convention and the Rome Statute criminalise the distinct inhumane acts as apartheid only if committed in an institutionalised form with intent and purpose of racial domination. Isolated conducts of discrimination are not in essence composite constitutive acts of the crime unless they form part of the systematic and institutionalised 'oppression and domination'. Most of the distinct acts, as discussed above, could strongly suggest the *actus reus* for the crime of apartheid. However, in the absence of a proof that the acts are perpetrated 'in the context of an institutionalised regime of systematic oppression and domination', it would be wrong to assert the commission of the crime of apartheid.

One has to note that in a situation of occupation, other factors such as security and military reasons could justify some of the imposed rules and 'separateness' as necessary and justifiable. However, a necessary distinction has to be made between 'justified discrimination' on the one hand and a pattern of unjustified discrimination as provided in the prohibition of apartheid. Moreover, it is imperative to mention the fact that the commission of the 'inhumane acts' discussed above is continuous and also grounded on Israeli military orders and other State legislations gives the system a policy base, hinting on its systematic nature.[429] The alleged 'inhumane acts' do not appear as random incidents. They are adequately grounded in law, State policy and are enforced by formal State institutions so as to describe them as sufficiently 'institutionalised'.[430]

The 'Specific Intent' Element for the Crime of Apartheid

Establishing individual criminal responsibility requires linking evidences for specific acts committed to specific individuals, which necessitates detailed forensic investigation and interrogation of the applicable Israeli laws and policies on Palestinians. To establish the objective elements of the composite crime, for instance, the Prosecutor has to prove the existence of an institutionalized regime of systematic oppression. Following the results of investigation and analysis of the

427 Article 7(a) of the Basic Law: The Knesset (1958) states that a person that negates 'the existence of the State of Israel as a Jewish and Democratic State' shall not be a candidate for the Knesset.

428 A similar idea is indicated in the ESCWA Report. See ESCWA 2017, pp. 20, 32–33.

429 On the 'systematic' element of the crime, see Triffterer and Ambos 2016, p. 170; Werle and Jessberger 2014, pp. 337 et seq. For texts and descriptions of active laws and pending bills that are supposedly discriminatory, see the Discriminatory Laws Database, http://www.adalah.org/en/content/view/7771 (accessed 12 August 2016).

430 A similar conclusion is also reached by, among others, UNHRC 2014, para 77. See also HSRC 2009, p. 275.

various reports and the elements of the crime, the Prosecutor has to show that those members of the Israeli government, at least, at the top of the hierarchy are in *prima facie* violation of the prohibition of apartheid.

In light of the elements of crimes, in addition to having knowledge that the conduct is part of a 'widespread or systematic attack', there must be proof that the perpetrator intended to 'maintain such regime by that conduct'.[431] The general mental element provided under Article 30 of the Statute and the special intention requirement under Article 7(2)(h) requires knowingly causing the particular result. Hence, the element is not established if the accused did not contemplate the result.[432] While committing the crime of apartheid, the perpetrator, therefore, must act with the aim and purpose of bringing about or maintaining the regime of apartheid.[433]

The difficulty of proving the specific intent could make apartheid, as Ambos argued, 'a *de facto* leadership crime'.[434] The specific intent required for the crime of apartheid appears as specific as that of 'intent to destroy in whole or in part' of the crime of genocide.[435] Similar to the crime of genocide, perpetrators whose conducts satisfy the *actus reus* of the crime but who do not harbour the required specific intent fail to meet the elements of the crime of apartheid.[436] Hence, with regard to the situation in Palestine, the most crucial issue is whether one can assert that the systematic oppression and domination through the instrumentality of the constitutive inhumane acts are perpetrated with the specific intent to maintain an overall system of Jewish domination over Palestinians.

As can be inferred from the discussion on settlements (see Sect. 5.3.1.3), forcible transfer of population (see Sect. 5.3.2.1) as well as the refusal of Israel to allow the return of Palestinian refugees, the main objective of the system in place is maintaining a Jewish majority demographic balance.[437] The ultimate aim is preserving the 'Jewish character' of Israel in as much of the territory of ancient Palestine as possible. Notwithstanding the legality or illegality of demographic engineering, which is beyond the scope of this section, the constitutive inhumane acts are committed to facilitate these goals of preserving the Jewish character of the State

[431] Elements of Crimes, above n. 108, Element 5 of Article 7(1)(j).

[432] Rome Statute, above n. 2, Article 7(2)(h); Dubber and 2014, pp. 291 et seq.

[433] Werle and Jessberger 2014, p. 385.

[434] Rome Statute, above n. 2, Article 25(3)(c). In the event, the commission of the 'inhumane acts' could form part of the element of crime for other crimes against humanity, it could be charged for crimes against humanity. Rome Statute, above n. 2, Article 7. See Ambos 2014, pp. 27 et seq. This view is also taken again in Triffterer and Ambos 2016. Triffterer and Ambos state that even if, in principle, apartheid is not limited to high level perpetrators, i.e., organisers and leaders, it is 'impossible to prove the specific intent for individuals other than the leaders'. See Triffterer and Ambos 2016, p. 285; Werle and Jessberger 2014, p. 385.

[435] Rome Statute, above n. 2, Article 6. On the specific intent required for the crime of genocide see Werle and Jessberger 2014, p. 314.

[436] Rome Statute, above n. 2, Article 7(2)(h); Elements of Crimes, above n. 108, Article 7(1)(j). Concerning the specific intent criterion for the crime of genocide and crime of apartheid see, respectively, pages 314 and 385 of Werle and Jessberger 2014.

[437] Ismael et al. 2016, pp. 419 et seq.

and building a greater Israel. These acts are not, thus, committed with the intent to maintain a regime of apartheid but rather to attain the above stated goals.[438]

It is imperative to note here that the principal goals of apartheid South Africa, in contrast to the system in the Palestine, was to 'maintain white domination while extending racial segregation'.[439] It was a system of class exploitation premised on the superiority of the white race over the others. The white race was viewed as the only civilized race deserving of absolute political power.[440] Apartheid officials, therefore, legislated and enforced laws to maintain the system of white domination over others. It is this specific intent to maintain an institutionalized system of racial domination that is absent in the situation in Palestine.

Conclusion on the Commission of the Crime of Apartheid

Despite the existence of a *prima facie* evidence on the commission of the constitutive inhumane acts (*actus reus*), in the absence of the specific intent to maintain a regime of apartheid one cannot charge a crime of apartheid. Therefore, in light of Article 7 (2)(h) of the Statute and the elements of the crime under Article 7(1)(j),[441] it is concluded that the crime of apartheid is not committed in the situation in Palestine.

5.3.2.3 Persecution

Apart from the Nuremberg Tribunal dealing with the persecution of Jews,[442] the *Tadić* case is the most notable case in which an international Tribunal dealt with persecution in detail.[443] Despite the inclusion of the crime in the Nuremberg Charter, Control Council Law No 10, the Tokyo Charter and the Statutes of the *ad hoc* Tribunals, by the time of the *Tadić* Trial and the negotiations of the ICC Statute, the crime was not clearly defined. The *Tadić* precedent established that, for persecution to exist there should be 'some form of discrimination that is intended to

---

[438] Rome Statute, above n. 2, Article 30(2). Concerning the general 'intent' criterion, the jurisprudence of the ICC, particularly in *Bemba* and *Katanga* decisions gravitate towards requiring a substantial probability of occurrence of the result as satisfying the 'intent' element. See *Bemba* 2009, above n. 111, paras 352–369; Judgement, *Prosecutor v. Katanga*, ICC-01/04-01/07-3436, 7 March 2014, para 774.

In regard to *dolus directus* or the 'concept of a desire for the occurrence of consequences' applicable to crimes of the Rome Statute as provided under Article 30 of the Statute see ibid.; Triffterer and Ambos 2016, pp. 1122–1123; Werle and Jessberger 2014, pp. 175 et seq.

[439] Arellano et al. 2006, p. 399; Southall 2012, p. 375.

[440] Beck 2014, pp. 135 et seq.; Congressional Quarterly Inc., The concise encyclopedia of democracy, 2000, p. 357; Marx 1998, p. 198.

[441] Elements of Crimes, above n. 108, Element 5 of Article 7(1)(j); Werle and Jessberger 2014, p. 385.

[442] The Nuremberg Trial focused more on the non-technical matters of the crime of persecution mainly referring to figures. See Nuremberg Trial Proceedings, above n. 83, 30 September 1946, vol. 22, paras 421, 491–496. See also Zahar and Sluiter 2008, pp. 211–212.

[443] *Tadić* 1997, above n. 150, paras 694 et seq.

be and results in an infringement of an individual's fundamental rights'.[444] The emphasis of the *Tadić* approach to persecution rests on the existence of a discriminatory intent than the inhumane nature of the crime.[445]

A more explicit definition for the crime against humanity of persecution is provided under Article 7(1)(h) of the Rome Statute. Different from the jurisprudence of the *ad hoc* Tribunals and in what the ICTY Trial Chamber in the *Kupreškić et al* case considered 'not consonant with customary international law',[446] the Statute sets underlying or peripheral acts of persecution in connection with the crimes within the jurisdiction of the Court. Hence, in light of the ICC Statute, the persecutory conduct committed against the 'identifiable group or community' must be connected with one or more crimes contained in the Statute.[447]

Although persecution requires a specific discriminatory intent,[448] there is no need to prove the *mens rea* for the underlying acts.[449] The attacker, however, has to have knowledge that his conduct forms part of the widespread and systematic attack against a civilian population.[450] Hence, despite what appears to be a restrictive approach, the list of acts that can be characterised as persecution is extensive due to the broad range of crimes under Article 7(1) and other core crimes within the Court's jurisdiction.[451] As Ambos notes, the connection criterion, thus, only helps to limit the focus of the Court to forms of persecution with a similar 'elevated objective dangerousness' as other crimes within the Statute.[452] In addition to the general threshold set by the 'widespread and systematic attack' requirement, the aforementioned is also confirmed by the requirement set under Article 7(2)(g) and Element 1 of Article 7(1)(h). Accordingly, the persecutory conduct has to be a 'severe deprivation of fundamental rights contrary to international law'.[453]

Acts that satisfy the severity threshold while contravening fundamental rights qualify as persecution. The jurisprudence of the *ad hoc* Tribunals extends the forms of persecution to include not only those that cause physical injury but also to 'acts rendered serious by the discrimination they seek to instil within humankind'.[454] Hence, it encompasses persecutory policies and discriminatory laws against an identifiable group to the detriment of their social, political and economic rights. In

---

444 Ibid., para 697.

445 Zahar and Sluiter 2008, pp. 211–212.

446 *Kupreškić et al.* 2000, above n. 181, para 580; *Kordić* and *Čerkez* 2001, above n. 147, para 197. See also Ambos 2014, p. 105.

447 Werle and Jessberger 2014, p. 373.

448 Ibid. pp. 347, 377.

449 Ambos 2014, p. 105.

450 See ICTR, *Prosecutor v. Muhimana*, Judgement, 28 April 2005, ICTR-95-1B-T, paras 529–530; and *Ntagerura* 2004, above n. 287, para 698.

451 In a similar vein, see Elements of Crimes, above n. 108, Element 4 of Article 7(1)(j); and *Kordić* and *Čerkez* 2001, above n. 147, para 197.

452 Ambos 2014, p. 106.

453 Ibid.

454 *Blaškić* 2000, above n. 150, para 227.

addition, as Werle and Jessberger note, acts that target property have also been included as persecutory so long as the other criteria, such as the severity and persecutory intent, are met.[455]

Applying the above analysis, one could argue that the alleged severe economic and social restriction on the population of Gaza imposed due to the blockade may satisfy the requirements of persecution. The same point could be raised concerning other alleged crimes discussed in this chapter that are committed with a specific discriminatory intent. However, as the unique legal issues the Gaza blockade gives rise to do no allow a categorical conclusion, it necessitates a special consideration.

The Blockade of Gaza as a Crime of Persecution

In spite of the question of Israel's right to impose the blockade[456]—which is a purely international humanitarian law matter—one could separately analyse the nature of the blockade and its lawfulness. Hence, despite the treatment of Gaza as besieged or occupied, any severe deprivation of fundamental rights, as provided in the Statute, could constitute persecution as Israel is bound by the legal obligations arising from human rights law.[457] The law of armed conflict requires States to meet certain humanitarian standards while imposing blockades.[458] Among the duties, the occupying power has an unconditional obligation to allow relief supplies for the needy population. Any measure where the damage to the civilian population is disproportional to the alleged concrete and direct military advantage anticipated from the blockade could be characterised as over-restrictive.

The policy of total closure implemented following the electoral victory of Hamas, restricts all goods and people from entering and leaving Gaza unless there is consent obtained from Israeli authorities.[459] Israel controls the air, maritime and land entries to Gaza. On the basis of the blockade, it restricts activities on the Mediterranean Sea and has severely restricted entry of goods.[460] The continuing

---

455 *Kupreškić et al.* 2000, above n. 181, para 631; *Blaškić* 2000, above n. 150, para 233; Werle and Jessberger 2014, p. 375.

456 The right to impose a blockade is reserved for international armed conflict. Considering the stance of Israel that it is not occupying Gaza after the 2005 disengagement, it cannot claim that it has the right to enforce the blockade. On the other hand, if one views Gaza as an occupied territory, as the UN and most States do, the occupying power is not only bound by the obligation of Geneva Convention IV but has also the right to impose a blockade if other requirements of the law of armed conflict are met.

457 See ICRC 1958.

458 See ibid.

459 UNHRC 2009b, paras 311 et seq.

460 Before Israel decided to ease the restrictions in 2010, imports were limited to 'humanitarian minimum'. Goods it designated as 'luxury' (e.g, crayons, notebooks), 'dual-use (e.g, many raw materials for agriculture and production and construction materials) or banned (e.g, industrial equipment, types of wood) did not gain access. See Al-Haq, Al-Mezan Centre for Human Rights, Palestinian Centre for Human Rights et al. 2016, pp. 27 et seq. See also Gisha, Dark grey lists, http://gisha.org/UserFiles/File/publications/Dark_Gray_Lists/Dark_Gray_Lists-en.pdf (accessed 8 August 2016).

restriction on imports of building materials coupled with the repeated military operations, which cause significant damage on lives and infrastructure, has aggravated the already deteriorating situation.[461] Amongst its impact on infrastructure, the damage on power supplies is a case in point. Through the military operations conducted since the year 2000, Israel has damaged 244 water wells and all the six transformers making Gaza dependent on Israel for water and electricity.[462] As part of the policy of closure, Israel has decided to cut power and fuel supplies and imports to renovate grid lines and power plants resulting in power outage that lasts up to 20 hours a day. The outage severely hampers, among others, hospitals, water pumps, schools, industries and businesses.[463]

The Israeli government has openly stated that the closure is a means of economic warfare aimed to put pressure on the regime in Gaza.[464] The policy has, nonetheless, proved its devastating impact on the lives of the civilian population as it has resulted in unprecedented higher rates in food insecurity, aid dependency and unemployment, and the 'de-development' of the region.[465] The dire situation of the residents is evidenced, *inter alia*, on the fact that 96% of the population is said to suffer from psychological problems[466] and about 80% of the population is dependent on international aid. If current trends continue, the UN report of 2015 has indicated that Gaza could become uninhabitable by 2020.[467] This indicates that the State policy of closure passed by top Israeli State officials and enforced through its State machineries collectively targets the civilian population of Gaza. The policy omits making a distinction between Hamas and the civilian population as official Israeli position designates Gaza, as a whole, a 'hostile entity'.[468]

The grave restrictions that undermine the economic and social fabric of Gaza, its effect on the realisation of fundamental rights of the residents and the grave humanitarian situation resulted qualify as a severe deprivation.[469] This deprivation, in the sense provided under Article 7(2)(g) of the Statute, amounts to commission

---

461 Al-Haq, Al-Mezan Centre for Human Rights, Palestinian Centre for Human Rights et al. 2016, pp. 29–38.

462 Li and Lein 2006, pp. 4 et seq. See also UNCTAD 2015, paras 20 et seq.

463 Human Rights Watch, Gaza: widespread impact of power plant attack, 10 August 2014, https://www.hrw.org/news/2014/08/10/gaza-widespread-impact-power-plant-attack (accessed 29 May 2017).

464 Supreme Court of Israel, *Al-Bassiouni v. The Prime Minister*, Judgment, HCJ 9132/07, 30 January 2008, paras 43–44. See also Al-Haq, Al-Mezan Centre for Human Rights, Palestinian Centre for Human Rights et al. 2016, p. 30.

465 P. Beaumont, Gaza could soon become uninhabitable; UN report predicts, The Guardian, 27 September 2015.

466 UNHRC 2009a, para 8. See also P. Beaumont P, above n. 465.

467 UNCTAD 2015.

468 ICRC, News release: Gaza closure: not another year!, 14 June 2010, https://www.icrc.org/eng/resources/documents/update/palestine-update-140610.htm (accessed 29 May 2017). See also Al-Haq, Al-Mezan Centre for Human Rights, Palestinian Centre for Human Rights et al. 2016, p. 109.

469 UNOCHA-OPT 2015.

of the crime of persecution. Such is the case as restriction on, for instance, access of people to agricultural land and fishing waters could not be argued as having any clear 'concrete and direct military advantage'.

The Possibility of Charging Persecution Cumulatively

Unlike in the case of Gaza's blockade, crimes such as forcible transfer of population or wilful killing could also be charged as persecution. This is provided they satisfy the specific discriminatory intent required for the crime of persecution. Hence, the next issue is whether these crimes should be charged cumulatively or charges on these specific crimes exclude a charge on persecution.[470]

In the case *Prosecutor v. Bemba*, crimes against humanity and war crime charges were made based on the same set of facts/conduct.[471] In response to the Prosecutor's argument, the Pre-Trial Chamber I, during the confirmation of charges, ruled that only distinct crimes justify cumulative charges as such practice is 'detrimental to the rights of the defence'.[472] On what appears to be an evolution from the latter precedent, in the *Prosecutor v. Al Bashir*, the Chamber accepted a cumulative charge for murder and extermination as crimes against humanity.[473] It followed the same reasoning in the *Prosecutor v. Ruto* and the stance of the ICTY from the *Kupreskić* judgment and argued that cumulative charging for the same conduct is permitted given each charge contains a materially distinct element.[474] The part of the ruling reads:

> The definition of persecution contains materially distinct elements not present in the definition of murder, namely the requirement of proof that a particular group was targeted on the basis of certain discriminatory grounds described in Article 7(l)(h) of the Statute. Murder, by contrast, requires proof that the accused caused the death of one or more persons, regardless of whether the act or omission causing the death discriminates in fact or was intended as discriminatory. The same holds true with respect to persecution and deportation or forcible transfer; the former requires, as "materially" distinct elements not included in the definition of deportation or forcible transfer, proof of intent to discriminate. On the contrary, deportation or forcible transfer requires, inter alia, proof that the perpetrator displaced one or more persons, regardless of whether the conduct was intended as discriminatory. Accordingly, the practice of cumulative or multiple charging as to these crimes on the basis of the same conduct is permissible.[475]

---

[470] Stuckenberg 2015, p. 847.

[471] The same conduct (rape) was used to charge crimes against humanity of torture and rape and war crime of rape and outrages against personal dignity. See *Bemba* 2009, above n. 111, para 199.

[472] The Chamber argued that such practices place an undue burden on the defence and affects the fairness and expeditiousness of the proceedings. See *Bemba* 2009, above n. 111, para 202. See Kuczyńska 2015, pp. 131–137.

[473] *Al Bashir* 2009, above n. 389, paras 95–96.

[474] *Ruto, Kosgey and Sang* 2012, above n. 318, paras 279–281. See also Kuczyńska 2015, pp. 131–137.

[475] *Ruto, Kosgey and Sang* 2012, above n. 318, paras 280–281.

In regard to what amounts to 'a materially distinct element', the *Blockburger* test, named after the case *Blockburger v. United States,*[476] at the Supreme Court of the US offers a solution. The test follows a similar approach as *Čelebići,* which established that 'an element is materially distinct from another if it requires proof of a fact not required by the other'.[477] Even if the same conduct is used to charge, as the Chamber argued, 'each provision requires proof of an additional fact which the other does not'.[478]

Recording a conviction on persecution may show a violation of a different legal standard or help capture the extent of perpetration the specific crimes do not.[479] Moreover, in the same vein as the ruling of the Special Tribunal for Lebanon,[480] it could be argued that the cumulative charges may address a substantially different value than addressed by the specific crimes.[481] Despitethe technicality, the Prosecutor could take practical considerations, mainly availability of evidence and possibility of obtaining a conviction in choosing which charge to pursue (*Čelebići* test). Nevertheless, any choice of charge would still be prone to re-characterization by the Trial Chamber in light of Regulation 55 of the Court.

5.4 Chapter Summary

There are numerous challenges to dealing with case selection and prioritisation. In dealing with the situation in Palestine, justifying the prosecution of one case over another is a bigger challenge, which necessitates a clearer and more elaborate case selection policy and strategy. It is apparent that the tremendous loss of lives and destruction of civilian objects as well as alleged systematic and perpetual crimes indicated in various reports require the Court's attention. Amongst the numerous cases, the Prosecutor has to apply the principles of case selection and prioritisation to determine which cases deserve the Court's attention. While much progress has been made with regard to the case selection framework, coming up with a more

[476] US Supreme Court, *Blockburger v. United States*, Judgment, 4 January 1932, 284 US 299 (1932), para 304.

[477] ICTR, *Simba v. Prosecutor*, Judgment, 27 November 2007, ICTR-01-76-A, para 277; ICTR, *Prosecutor v. Ntagerura, Bagambiki & Imanishimwe,* Judgment, 7 July 2006, ICTR-99-46-A, para 425. See also Sedman 2010, p. 265; Stuckenberg 2015, p. 847; Trechsel and Summer 2005, p. 398.

[478] Stuckenberg 2015, p. 847.

[479] For a similar view see *Akayesu* 1998, above n. 111, paras 468 et seq. See also ICTY, *Prosecutor v. Jelisić*, Judgment, Partial Dissenting Opinion of Judge Shahabuddeen, 5 July 2001, IT-95-10-A, para 34. The judgment stated 'to record the full criminality of his conduct, it may be necessary to convict of all the crimes, overlapping in convictions being adjusted through penalty'.

[480] Special Tribunal for Lebanon, Interlocutory Decision on the Applicable Law: Terrorism, Conspiracy, Homicide, Perpetration, Cumulative Charging, 16 February 2011, STL-11-01/I, para 299.

[481] Stuckenberg 2015, p. 855.

elaborate and transparent mechanism becomes even more significant in dealing with situations that could test the limits of the Court.

The determination on the crimes committed and the possible charges that could be brought before the Court depend on various factors among which availability and access to evidences take bigger shares. In light of a *prima facial* analysis, it could, however, be argued that there is a reasonable ground to believe that the war crimes of attack on civilians and civilian objects, use of human shields and transfer of parts of the population of the occupied power into occupied territory have been committed.

In regard to crimes against humanity, there is also reasonable ground to believe that the crime of forcible transfer of population and persecution were or are being committed in the situation. Concerning the crime of apartheid, although there is a *prima facie* evidence to show that the constitutive inhumane acts are committed, there is no specific intent to maintain a regime of apartheid in the Palestine situation. The crimes are committed to facilitate other aims such as maintaining a Jewish majority demographic balance and building a larger Israel.

In its 2016 report, the OTP has identified the possible commission of all of the war crimes discussed above. The report has identified alleged systematic and institutionalised ill-treatment of Palestinians. However, it has not categorised it as the crimes against humanity of persecution. Rightly, the report of the OTP did not raise the alleged crime of apartheid in the context at hand.

Although not peculiar to the situation in Palestine, each case will have its own specific jurisdictional and procedural challenges. As discussed in this chapter, the political arrangement of the States and the nature of the crimes as well as availability and access to evidence would pose a great challenge. However, considering its contribution to creating a foundation of justice for peace settlements and redressing the many wrongs, prosecution of alleged crimes in the situation in Palestine cannot be oversold.

References

Al-Haq, Al-Mezan Centre for Human Rights & Palestinian Centre for Human Rights et al (2016) Situation of Palestine: Closure of Gaza. Al-Haq, Ramallah.

Ambos K (2013) Treatise on international criminal law, vol 1. Oxford University Press, Oxford.

Ambos K (2014) Treatise on international criminal law, vol 2. Oxford University Press, Oxford.

Ambos K, Stegmiller I (2013) Prosecuting international crimes at the International Criminal Court: Is there a coherent and comprehensive prosecution strategy? Crime Law Social Change 59:391-413.

Amnesty International (1986) South Africa, imprisonment under the Pass Laws. Amnesty International, New York.

Amnesty International (2008) Israel and the Occupied Palestinian Territories (OPT): Briefing to the Committee Against Torture. Amnesty International Publications, London.

Amnesty International (2014) Families under the rubble – Israeli attacks on inhabited homes. Amnesty International Publications, London.

Amnesty International (2015) Israel/OPT: No justification for deliberate attacks on civilians, unlawful killings by Israeli forces, or collective punishment of Palestinians. https://www.amnesty.org/en/documents/mde15/2633/2015/en/. Accessed 17 October 2016.

Aranburu X (2010) Prosecuting the most responsible for international crimes: Dilemmas of definition and prosecutorial discretion. https://www.academia.edu/2571646/Prosecuting_the_most_Responsible_for_International_Crimes_Dilemmas_of_Definition_and_Prosecutorial_Discretion Accessed 2 September 2016.

Arellano N, Chigona W, Moore J et al (2006) ICT-based community development initiatives in South Africa. In: Marshall S, Taylor W, Yu X (eds) Encyclopedia of Developing regional communities with information and communication technology. Idea Group Reference, Hershey, Pennsylvania, pp. 399–404.

The Association for Civil Rights in Israel (2014) One rule, two legal systems: Israel's regime of laws in the West Bank. The Association for Civil Rights in Israel, Jerusalem.

Beck R (2014) The history of South Africa, 2nd edn. ABC-CLIO, Santa Barbara, California.

Bedi S (2007) The development of human rights law by the judges of the International Court of Justice. Hart Publishing, Portland, Oregon.

Boot M (2002) Nullum crimen sine lege and the subject matter jurisdiction of the International Criminal Court: Genocide, crimes against humanity and war crimes. School of Human Rights Research, Utrecht.

Bosco D (2014) Rough justice: The International Criminal Court in a world of power politics. Oxford University Press, Oxford.

Bothe M (2002) War crimes. In: Cassese A, Gaeta P, Jones J (eds) The Rome Statute of the International Criminal Court: A Commentary. Oxford University Press, Oxford, pp. 379–426.

Bothe M (2010) The status of captured fighters in non-international armed conflict. In: Tomuschat C, Lagrange E, Oeter S (eds) The right to life. Martinus Nijhoff Publishers, Leiden, pp. 195–214.

Bouchet-Saulnier F (2007) The practical guide to humanitarian law. Rowman and Littlefield Publishers, Lanham, Maryland.

Bradley C (2016) Custom's future: International law in a changing world. Cambridge University Press, New York.

Braverman M (2013) A wall in Jerusalem: Hope, healing, and the struggle for justice in Israel and Palestine. Jericho Books, New York.

Brown B (2011) International criminal law: Nature, origins and a few key issues. In: Brown B (ed) Research handbook on international criminal law. Edward Elgar Publishing Limited, Gloucestershire, pp. 3–16.

Brubacher M (2004) Prosecutorial discretion within the International Criminal Court. JICJ 2:71–95.

B'Tselem (2007) Absolute prohibition: The torture and ill-treatment of Palestinian detainees. Israeli Information Center for Human Rights in the Occupied Territories, Jerusalem.

B'Tselem (2015) Black flag: The legal and moral implications of the policy of attacking residential buildings in the Gaza Strip. Israeli Information Center for Human Rights in the Occupied Territories, Jerusalem.

Carey H (2012) Reaping what you sow: A comparative examination of torture reform in the United States, France, Argentina and Israel. Praeger, Santa Barbara, California.

Cassese A (2002) Crimes against humanity. In: Cassese A, Gaeta P, Jones J (eds) The Rome Statute of the International Criminal Court: A Commentary. Oxford University Press, Oxford, pp. 353–378.

Chetail V (2015) The transfer and deportation of civilians. In: Clapham et al (eds) The 1949 Geneva Conventions: A Commentary. Oxford University Press, Oxford, pp. 1185–1214.

Chetrit S (2010) Intra-Jewish conflict in Israel: White Jews, black Jews. Routledge, Oxon.

Coleman M (ed) (1998) A crime against humanity: Analysing the repression of the apartheid state. David Philip Publishers, Cape Town.

Commission for the Socio-economic Development of the Bantu Areas within the Union of South Africa (1955) Summary of the Report on the Commission for the Socio-Economic Development of the Bantu Areas within the Union of South Africa. The Government Printer, Pretoria.

Committee on the Elimination of Racial Discrimination (2012) Concluding observations of the Committee on the Elimination of Racial Discrimination, UN Doc. CERD/C/ISR/CO/14-16.

Committee on the Rights of the Child (2013) Concluding observations on the second to fourth periodic reports of Israel, adopted by the Committee at its sixty-third session (27 May - 14 June 2013), UN Doc. CRC/C/ISR/CO/2-4.

Côte L (2005) Reflections on the exercise of prosecutorial discretion in international criminal law. JICJ 3:162–186.

Cryer R (2005) Prosecuting international crimes: Selectivity and the international criminal law regime. Cambridge University Press, Cambridge.

Davis W, Coffman P (2014) From 1967 to the present - The triumph of revisionist Zionism. In: Wagner D, Davis W (ed) Zionism and the quest for justice in the Holy Land. Lutterwork Press, Cambridge, pp. 28–62.

DeGuzman M (2012) Choosing to prosecute: Expressive selection at the International Criminal Court. Michigan Journal of International Law 33:265–320.

Diakonia International Humanitarian Law Resource Centre (2015) Law enforcement under occupation: The case of wilful killings in the West Bank. Diakonia IHL Resource Center, Jerusalem.

Dinstein Y (2000) The initiation, suspension and termination of war. In: Schmitt M (ed) International law across the spectrum of conflict: Essays in honour of Professor L.C. Green on the occasion of his eightieth birthday. Naval War College, Newport, Rhode Island, pp. 134–146.

Dinstein Y (2004) The Conduct of Hostilities Under the Law of International Armed Conflict. Cambridge University Press, Cambridge.

Dörmann K (2001) Preparatory Commission for the International Criminal Court: The Elements of War Crimes, Part II: Other serious violations of the laws and customs applicable in international and non-international armed conflicts. ICRC 83:461–487.

Dörmann K (2003) War Crimes under the Rome Statute of the International Criminal Court, with a Special Focus on the Negotiations on the Elements of Crimes. Max Planck UNYB 7:341–407.

Drewett M, Cloonan M (eds) (2016) Popular music censorship in Africa. Routledge, London.

Dubber M, Hörnle T (2014) Criminal law: A comparative approach. Oxford University Press, Oxford.

Dugard J, Reynolds J (2013) Apartheid, international law and the occupied Palestinian territory. EJIL 24(3):867–913.

ESCWA (2017) Israeli practices towards the Palestinian people and the question of apartheid, UN Doc. E/ESCWA/ECRI/2017/1.

Ferraro T (2012) Determining the beginning and end of an occupation under international humanitarian law. International Review of the Red Cross 94:133–163.

Ferraro T (2013) The law of occupation and human rights law: some selected issues. In: Kolb R, Gaggioli G (eds) Research handbook on human rights and humanitarian law. Edward Elgar Publishing, Cheltenham, pp. 273–293.

FIDH (2014) Trapped and punished: The Gaza civilian population under Operation Protective Edge. FIDH, Gaza.

French S (2003) Murderers, not warriors: The moral distinction between terrorists and legitimate fighters in asymmetric conflicts. In: Sterba J (ed) Terrorism and international justice. Oxford University Press, Oxford, pp. 31–46.

Gilbert M (2014) Brief Report to UNRWA: The Gaza Health Sector as of June 2014. University Hospital of North Norway, Tromsø.

Green J, Karolides N (2005) Encyclopedia of censorship. Facts on File, Inc., New York.

Greenwood C (2008) Scope of application of humanitarian law. In: Fleck D (ed) The handbook of international humanitarian law, 2nd edn. Oxford University Press, Oxford, pp. 45–78.

Grover L (2014) Interpreting crimes in the Rome Statute of the International Criminal Court. Cambridge University Press, Cambridge.
Guariglia F, Rogier E (2015) The selection of situations and cases by the OTP of the ICC. In: Stahn C (ed) The law and practice of the International Criminal Court. Oxford University Press, Oxford, pp. 350–364.
Guilfoyle D (2015) The use of force against pirates. In: Weller M, Solomou A, Rylatt JW (eds) The Oxford handbook of the use of force in international law. Oxford University Press, Oxford, pp. 1057–1076.
Guilfoyle D (2016) International criminal law. Oxford University Press, Oxford.
Hayes N (2015) La lutte continue: Investigating and prosecuting sexual violence at the ICC. In: Stahn C (ed) The law and practice of the International Criminal Court. Oxford University Press, Oxford, pp. 801–839.
Heines S (2014) The developing law of weapons: Humanity, distinction and precautions in attacks. In: Clapham A, Gaeta P (eds) The Oxford handbook of international law in armed conflict. Oxford University Press, Oxford, pp. 273–295.
Henckaerts J, Doswald-Beck L (2005) Customary International humanitarian law, vol. 1. Cambridge University Press, Cambridge.
Horrell M (1960) The 'Pass Laws'. South Africa Institute of Race Relations, Johannesburg.
HSRC (2009) Occupation, colonialism, apartheid? A re-assessment of Israel's practices in the occupied Palestinian territories under international law. HSRC, Cape Town.
Human Rights Watch (2008) Internal fight: Palestinian abuses in Gaza and the West Bank. Human Rights Watch, New York.
Human Rights Watch (2010) Separate and unequal: Israel's discriminatory treatment of Palestinians in the Occupied Palestinian Territories. Human Rights Watch, New York.
Human Rights Watch (2015) World Report 2015: Israel/Palestine events of 2014. https://www.hrw.org/world-report/2015/country-chapters/israel/palestine. Accessed 16 June 2016.
Human Rights Watch (2016) Extreme measures: Abuses against children detained as national security threat. https://www.hrw.org/report/2016/07/28/extreme-measures/abuses-against-children-detained-national-security-threats. Accessed 17 October 2016.
ICRC (1958) Commentary of 1958: Article 59 of Geneva Convention IV. https://ihl-databases.icrc.org/applic/ihl/ihl.nsf/COM/380-600066?OpenDocument. Accessed 14 August 2016.
ICRC (2002a) Elements of war crimes under the Rome Statute of the International Criminal Court: Sources and Commentary.
ICRC (2002b) Implementation of the Fourth Geneva Convention in the occupied Palestinian territories: History of a multilateral process (1997–2001). Article, International Review of the Red Cross, No. 847. https://www.icrc.org/eng/resources/documents/article/other/5fldpj.htm. Accessed 20 November 2016.
ICRC (2009) Interpretive guidance on the notion of direct participation in hostilities under international humanitarian law. International Committee of the Red Cross, Geneva.
Ipsen K (2008) Combatants and non-combatants. In: Fleck D (ed) The handbook of international humanitarian law, 2nd edn. Oxford University Press, Oxford, pp. 79–113.
Ismael T, Ismael J, Perry G (2016) Government and politics of the contemporary Middle East: Continuity and change, 2nd edn. Routledge, London.
Jalloh C (2013) What makes a crime against humanity a crime against humanity? American University ILR 28:381–441.
Kadman N (2015) Backed by the system: Abuse and torture at the Shikma Interrogation Facility. B'Tselem and HaMoked, Jerusalem.
Kalshoven F (2007) Reflections on the law of war: collected essays. Martinus Nijhoff Publishers, Leiden.
Kendall N (2002) Israeli counter-terrorism: 'targeted killings' under international law. North Carolina Law Review 80:1069–1088.
Kittrie O (2106) Lawfare: Law as a weapon of war. Oxford University Press, New York.
Kremnitzer M, Saba-Habesch L (2015) House demolitions. Laws 4:216-228.

Kuczyńska H (2105) The accusation model before the International Criminal Court: Study of convergence of criminal justice systems. Springer, New York.
Li D, Lein Y (2006) Act of vengeance: Israel's bombing of the Gaza Power Plant and its effects. B'Tselem, Jerusalem.
Likhovski A (2005) Law and identity in Mandate Palestine. The University of North Carolina Press, Durham, North Carolina.
Marx A (1998) Making race and nation: A comparison of South Africa, the United States and Brazil. Cambridge University Press, Cambridge.
Materu S (2015) The post-election violence in Kenya: Domestic and international legal responses. T.M.C. Asser Press, The Hague.
Maxwell C (2012) Rebutting the civilian presumption: Playing whack-a-mole without a mallet? In: Finkelstein C, Ohlin J, Altman A (eds) Targeted killings: Law and morality in an asymmetrical world. Oxford University Press, Oxford, pp. 31–59.
McAdam J (2011) An intellectual history of freedom of movement in international law: The right to leave as a personal liberty. Melbourne Journal of International Law 12:1–30.
Mégret F (2015) The universality of the Geneva Conventions. In: Clapham, Gaeta, Sassóli (eds) The 1949 Geneva Conventions: A Commentary. Oxford University Press, Oxford, pp. 669–688.
Melzer N (2010) The ICRC's clarification process on the notion of direct participation in hostilities under international humanitarian law. In: Tomuschat C, Lagrange E, Oeter S (eds) The right to life. Martinus Nijhoff Publishers, Leiden, pp. 151–166.
The Leadership Conference (2011) Restoring a national consensus: The need to end racial profiling in America. http://cdm266901.cdmhost.com/cdm/ref/collection/p266901coll4/id/3486 . Accessed 30 May 2017.
Mettraux G (2011) Trial at Nuremberg. In: Schabas W, Bernaz N (eds) Routledge Handbook of international criminal law. Routledge, London, pp. 5–16.
Middle East Watch (1993) A license to kill: Israeli undercover operations against 'wanted' and masked Palestinians. Human Rights Watch, New York.
Moreno-Ocampo L (2013) The place of sexual violence in the strategy of the ICC Prosecutor. In: de Brouwer A, Ku C, Römkens R, van den Herik L (eds) Sexual violence as an international crime: Interdisciplinary approaches. Intersentia, Cambridge, pp. 151–155.
Norval A (1996) Deconstructing Apartheid Discourse. Verso, London.
Öberg M (2009) The absorption of grave breaches into war crimes law. International Review of the Red Cross 91:163–183.
Olasolo H (2008) Unlawful attacks in combat situations: from the ICTY's case law to the Rome Statute. Martinus Nijhoff Publishers, Leiden.
O'Meara D (1996) Forty lost years – The Apartheid state and the politics of the National Party 1948–1994. Ravan Press, Randburg.
OTP (2015) Strategic plan: 2016–2018. https://www.icc-cpi.int/iccdocs/otp/EN-OTP_Strategic_Plan_2016-2018.pdf. Accessed 16 November 2016.
OTP (2016) Policy paper on case selection and prioritisation. https://www.icc-cpi.int/itemsDocuments/20160915_OTP-Policy_Case-Selection_Eng.pdf. Accessed 16 December 2016.
Pappé I (2015) A brief history of Israel's incremental genocide. In: Barat F (ed) On Palestine: Noam Chomsky and Ilan Pappé. Haymarket Books, Chicago, pp. 147–154.
Peschke K (2011) The ICC investigation into the conflict in northern Uganda: Beyond the dichotomy of peace versus justice. In: Brown B (ed) Research handbook on international criminal law. Edward Elgar Publishing Limited, Gloucestershire, pp. 178–205.
Pictet J (1952) Commentary on the Geneva Convention for the amelioration of the condition of the wounded and sick in armed forces in the field. ICRC, Geneva.
Rothenberg M (2010) The USSR and Africa: New dimensions of Soviet global power. Indiana University Press, Indiana.
Salmón E (2015) Who is a protected civilian? In: Clapham et al. (eds) The 1949 Geneva Conventions: A Commentary. Oxford University Press, Oxford, pp. 1135–1154.

Sassòli M (2015) The concept and the beginning of occupation. In: Clapham et al. (eds) The 1949 Geneva Conventions: A Commentary. Oxford University Press, Oxford, pp. 1389–1420.
Sassòli M, Olson L (2008) The relationship between international humanitarian and human rights law where it matters: Admissible killing and internment of fighters in non-international armed conflicts. International Review of the Red Cross 871:599–627.
Schabas W (2006) The UN international criminal tribunals: The former Yugoslavia, Rwanda and Sierra Leone. Cambridge: Cambridge University Press.
Schabas W (2008) Prosecutorial discretion v. judicial activism at the International Criminal Court. JICJ 6:731–761.
Schabas W (2011) An introduction to the International Criminal Court. Cambridge University Press, Cambridge.
Schabas W (2015) Selecting situations and cases. In: Stahn C (ed) The law and practice of the International Criminal Court. Oxford University Press, Oxford, pp. 365–380.
Schwarz A (2017) War crimes. In: Lachenmann F, Wolfrum G (eds) The law of armed conflict and the use of force. The Max Planck encyclopaedia of public international law. Oxford University Press, Oxford, pp. 1302–1319.
Sedman D (2010) Should the prosecution of ordinary crimes in domestic jurisdictions satisfy the complementarity principle? In: Stahn C, van den Herik L (eds) Future perspectives on international criminal justice. T.M.C. Asser Press, The Hague, pp. 259–266.
Shany Y (2005) Faraway, so close: the legal status of Gaza after Israel's disengagement. Yearbook of International Humanitarian Law 8:1–20.
Solis G (2010) The law of armed conflict: International humanitarian law in war. Cambridge University Press, Cambridge.
Southall R (2012) South Africa. In: Isakhan B, Stockwell S (eds) The Edinburgh companion to the history of democracy. Edinburgh University Press, Edinburgh, pp. 373–384.
Spangler E (2105) Understanding Israel/Palestine: Race, nation, and human rights in the conflict. Sense Publishers, Rotterdam.
Spoerri P (2014) The law of occupation. In: Clapham A, Gaeta P (eds) The Oxford handbook of international law in armed conflict. Oxford University Press, Oxford, pp. 182–205.
Stegmiller I (2011) The pre-investigation stage of the ICC: Criteria for situation selection. Duncker & Humblot, Berlin.
Steinke R (2012) The politics of international criminal justice: German perspectives from Nuremberg to The Hague. Hart Publishing, Oxford.
Stigen J (2008) The relationship between the International Criminal Court and national jurisdictions. Martinus Nijhoff Publishers, Leiden.
Stuckenberg C (2015) Cumulative charges and cumulative convictions. In: Stahn C (ed) The law and practice of the International Criminal Court. Oxford University Press, Oxford, pp. 840–858.
Tilley V (ed) (2012) Beyond occupation: Apartheid, colonialism and international law in the occupied Palestinian territories. Pluto Press, London.
Tomuschat C (2010) The right to life: Legal and political foundations. In: Tomuschat C, Lagrange E, Oeter S (eds) The right to life. Martinus Nijhoff Publishers, Leiden, pp. 1–18.
Tomuschat C (2014) Human rights: Between idealism and realism, 3rd edn. Oxford University Press, Oxford.
Tomuschat C (2015) Prohibition of settlements. In: Clapham et al. (eds) The 1949 Geneva Conventions: A Commentary. Oxford University Press, Oxford, pp. 1551–1574.
Trechsel S, Summer S (2005) Human rights in criminal proceedings. Oxford University Press, Oxford.
Triffterer O, Ambos K (eds) (2016) The Rome Statute of the International Criminal Court, 3rd edn. Hart Publishing, Munich.
Truth and Reconciliation Commission (1998) Report of the South African Truth and Reconciliation Commission. Truth and Reconciliation Commission, Cape Town.
UN Committee Against Torture (2001) Conclusions and Recommendations of the Committee Against Torture: Israel. 23/11/2001, UN Doc. CAT/C/XXVII/Concl.5.

UN Committee Against Torture (2002) Report of the Committee Against Torture, UN Doc. A/57/44.
UNCTAD (2015) Report on UNCTAD assistance to the Palestinian people: Developments in the economy of the Occupied Palestinian Territory, UN Doc. TD/B/62/3.
UNCTAD (2016) Report on UNCTAD assistance to the Palestinian people: Developments in the economy of the Occupied Palestinian Territory, UN Doc. UNCTAD/APP/2016/1.
UNGA (1948) Resolution 194 (III), UN Doc. A/RES/194 (III).
UNGA (1966) Resolution 2002, UN Doc. A/RES/2202.
UNGA (1981) Resolution 36/147, UN Doc. A/RES/36/147.
UNGA (1982) Resolution 37/88, UN Doc. A/RES/37/88.
UNGA (1983) Resolution 38/79, UN Doc. A/RES/38/79.
UNGA (1999) Resolution 54/78, UN Doc. A/RES/54/78.
UNGA (2003) Resolution 58/163, UN Doc. A/RES/ 58/163.
UNGA (2010) Report of the Special Rapporteur on the situation of human rights in the Palestinian territories occupied since 1967, UN Doc. A/65/331.
UNHCR (1998) Guiding principles on internal displacement. UN Doc. ADM 1.1, PRL 12.1, PR00/98/109.
UNHRC (2007a, 29 January) Report of the Special Rapporteur on the situation of human rights in the Palestinian territories occupied since 1967, John Dugard, UN Doc. A/HRC/4/17.
UNHRC (2007b, 28 November) Report of the Special Rapporteur on the promotion and protection of human rights and fundamental freedoms while countering terrorism, Martin Scheinin, addendum, Mission to Israel, including visit to occupied Palestinian territory, UN Doc. A/HRC/6/17/Add.4.
UNHRC (2008a) Human rights situation in Palestine and other occupied Arab territories: Report of the Special Rapporteur on the situation of human rights in the Palestinian territories occupied since 1967, John Dugard, UN Doc. A/HRC/7/17.
UNHRC (2008b) Report of the Special Rapporteur on the situation of human rights in the Palestinian territories occupied by Israel since 1967, Richard Falk, UN Doc. A/63/326.
UNHRC (2009a, 11 February) Report of the Special Rapporteur on the situation of human rights in the Palestinian territories occupied since 1967, A/HRC/10/20, 11 February 2009.
UNHRC (2009b, 25 September) Human rights in Palestine and other occupied Arab territories: Report of the United Nations Fact-Finding Mission on the Gaza Conflict, UN Doc. A/HRC/12/48.
UNHRC (2011) Report of the Special Rapporteur on the situation of human rights in the Palestinian territories occupied since 1967, Richard Falk, UN Doc. A/HRC/16/72.
UNHRC (2013) Report of the independent international Fact-Finding mission to investigate the implications of the Israeli settlements on the civil, political, economic, social and cultural rights of the Palestinian people throughout the Occupied Palestinian Territory, including East Jerusalem, UN Doc. A/HRC/22/63.
UNHRC (2014) Report of the Special Rapporteur on the situation of human rights in the Palestinian territories occupied since 1967, Richard Falk, UN Doc. A/HRC/25/67.
UNHRC (2015a) Report of the Independent Commission Of Inquiry Established Pursuant To Human Rights Council Resolution S-21/1, UN Doc. A/HRC/29/52 (22 June).
UNHRC (2015b) Report of the detailed findings of the independent commission of inquiry established pursuant to Human Rights Council resolution S-21/1, A/HRC/29/CRP.4 (24 June).
UN Human Rights Committee (2003) Concluding observations of the Human Rights Committee: Israel, UN Doc. CCPR/CO/78/ISR.
UN Human Rights Committee (2010) Concluding observations of the Human Rights Committee, UN Doc. CCPR/C/ISR/CO/3.
UN International Children's Emergency Fund (2015) Children in Israeli military detention observations and recommendations. United Nations International Children's Emergency Fund, Occupied Palestinian Territories.
UNOCHA-OPT (2007) The barrier gate and permit regime four years on: humanitarian impact in the northern West Bank. UNOCHA, East Jerusalem.

UNOCHA-OPT (2015) The Gaza Strip: the humanitarian impact of the blockade. UNOCHA, East Jerusalem.
UNSC (1967a) Resolution 237, UN Doc. S/RES/237.
UNSC (1967b) Resolution 242, UN Doc. S/RES/242.
UNSC (1973) Resolution 338, UN Doc. S/RES/338.
UNSC (1974) Resolution 3236 (XXIX), UN Doc. A/RES/3246 (XXIX).
UNSC (1979a) Resolution 446, UN Doc. S/RES/446.
UNSC (1979b) Resolution 452, UN Doc. S/RES/452.
UNSC (1980a) Resolution 465, UN Doc. S/RES/465.
UNSC (1980b) Resolution 476, UN Doc. S/RES/476.
UN Sub-Commission on Human Rights (1994) Progress report prepared by the Special Rapporteur on the human rights dimensions of population transfer, including the implantation of settlers, UN Doc. E/CN.4/Sub.2/1994/18.
UN War Crimes Commission (1949) Law reports of trials of war crimes. United Nations War Crimes Commission, London.
Van der Wilt H, Braber I (2014) The case for inclusion of terrorism in the jurisdiction of the International Criminal Court. Amsterdam Centre for International Law Research Paper 1–22.
Werle G, Jessberger F (2014) Principles of international criminal law, 3rd edn. Oxford University Press, Oxford.
Zahar A, Sluiter G (2008) International criminal law. Oxford University Press, Oxford.
Zunes S (2009) Peace Process. In: Looney R (ed) Handbook of US-Middle East Relations. Routledge, Oxon, pp. 544–560.

Chapter 6
Perspectives on the Intervention of the ICC in Palestine

Contents

Abstract Peace and justice are no longer viewed as mutually exclusive. Establishing sustainable peace requires addressing injustices and combatting the culture of impunity. The proper application and sequencing of transitional justice tools enable peace and justice to augment each other. This chapter discusses this inherent connection between peace and justice in light of the intervention of the International Criminal Court in the Israeli-Palestinian conflict. It is difficult to categorically measure and conclusively assert the impact the International Criminal Court's investigations and prosecutions could have on the conflict before the Court finalizes the intervention. In comparison with other situations the Court has dealt with, this chapter addresses potential impacts of the Court's intervention on combating impunity, the statehood question of Palestine, the stability of the two nations and the credibility of the Court itself. Taking note of the often raised claim that prosecution of alleged crimes committed in the conflict would disrupt peace settlements, the chapter also examines the pros and cons of establishing accountability on peace efforts.

© T.M.C. ASSER PRESS and the author 2019

S. H. Adem, *Palestine and the International Criminal Court*,
International Criminal Justice Series 21,
https://doi.org/10.1007/978-94-6265-291-0_6

Keywords Peace negotiation · Transitional justice · Combating impunity · Prosecution · Situation in Palestine · International Criminal Court

6.1 Introductory Remarks

Establishing accountability, as a means of transitional justice,[1] is believed to further peace efforts in conflict-ridden nations.[2] Delivering justice is no longer said to be an afterthought. Although the tools befitting a particular transition are applied in a particular context, in most transitions what is important is to ensure that there is legal accountability for the gross human rights perpetrated. This is necessary to deter similar acts being perpetrated and to allow a country to strive towards the goal of establishing enduring peace.[3] On the other hand, there exists an on-going debate whether prosecutions, as a transitional justice accountability mechanism, have just the opposite effect of creating tension within society and rekindling civil conflict. The question is whether such consequences can be tolerated at the cost of establishing justice.[4]

The preamble of the Rome Statute has recognised the inherent connection between countering impunity for grave crimes on the one hand and peace on the other.[5] The tension between peace and justice is an on-going phenomenon. On the one side of the spectrum there is the view that sustainable peace cannot be established in a society where the official truth is not established and where perpetrators of gross violations enjoy impunity. The opposing view holds that prosecution could make it difficult to achieve a negotiated settlement between or among the parties that were in conflict with each other. The failure to reach a negotiated settlement could re-open previous wounds and re-trigger conflict resulting in egregious crimes

---

[1] Transitional justice refers to various judicial and non-judicial mechanisms to deal with human rights violations. Although transitional justice normally refers to those means to establish truth, justice and reconciliation in post-conflict situations, its mechanisms are also applicable before transition. In this sense, the transition refers to the State's or the chosen organization's recognition of the gross violations and application of the transitional justice mechanisms to redress the injustices—rather than transition in the sense of regime change. See Stan and Nedelsky 2013, p. xli; UNSC 2011, para 17.

[2] Be it in the national and international context, establishing accountability has been used as one of the tools of transitional justice since the 1990s. See Porter 2015, pp. 10–18; Stan and Nedelsky 2013, p. 27.

[3] Corradetti et al. 2015, pp. 59 et seq.; Dezalay 2012, p. 79; Olsen 2017, p. 153; Sriram et al. 2013.

[4] Hayner 2009, pp. 5–8; Rodman 2014, p. 20; Kritz 1995, pp. xxi–xxvi.

[5] Paragraph 3, Preamble of the Rome Statute of the International Criminal Court, opened for signature 17 July 1998, 2187 UNTS 90 (entered into force 1 July 2002) (Rome Statute). See also Méndez and Kelley 2015, p. 479.

being perpetrated. In contrast to this sharp divide is a via media, an integrated approach, one which could be regarded as more acceptable. This would entail an approach that enforces prosecution, establishes truth, guarantees reparations and institutional reforms. The notion of making peace and justice mutually exclusive has lost ground to an approach which sees the two approaches as complementary.[6]

But what makes the peace-justice divide an essential subject of discussion in the ICC's context is the fact that the Court, unlike other regional criminal Tribunals, is predisposed to intervening in on-going conflicts.[7] The Court's mandate and its institutional architecture enable or require it to start judicial proceedings before the end of conflicts. This, in turn, gives rise to debates on the effects of international criminal accountability on conflict resolution and 'just outcome'.

Similar to its investigations in Uganda, the Democratic Republic of Congo, the Central African Republic, Darfur/Sudan, Côte d'Ivoire, Libya and Mali, the ICC's involvement in the on-going Israel-Palestine conflict gives rise to the unavoidable peace-justice debate and its various impacts.[8] Supporters of the ICC's examination of the Palestine situation have argued on the one hand that the Court's intervention helps to reduce conflict, the commission of crimes and helps the parties to make concessions during negotiations.[9] Critics, on the other hand, suggest that holding individuals accountable, in the context at hand, would cause a stalemate in the peace negotiations.[10] Although analysing the consequences of the ICC's involvement prior to the completion of investigations and prosecutions is challenging, the issues at hand are too vital to overlook.

The impact of the Court's intervention on the legitimacy and credibility of the Court itself is another issue examined in this chapter. Considering the Court would not remain unaffected by the situations it chooses to intervene in and that the stakes are higher when it intervenes in on-going conflicts, the Palestine situation would bring its inevitable challenges. The chapter also briefly addresses other routes to deal with the alleged crimes committed in the Palestine situation, such as universal jurisdiction and a special Tribunal. If these other routes are pursued, be they as alternatives or parallels to a prosecution before the ICC, crimes committed within the jurisdiction of the ICC and those outside its scope could be dealt with.

---

6 See Ambos et al. 2009, p. v; Shimko 2016, p. 235; Stegmiller 2011, p. 393.

7 Kersten 2016, p. 3. See also Olasolo 2005, p. 39.

8 The intervention in the DRC, Uganda, the CAR and Mali are the result of self-referral by the respective States and started in 2004, 2003, 2004 and 2012, respectively. On the other hand, the situations in Darfur in 2005 and Libya in 2011 were the results of Security Council referrals. See Mendes 2010, pp. 132–133; Kersten 2016, pp. 5–6.

9 For an overview of the various views on the intervention of the Court in Palestine, see M. Masri et al., Palestine and the ICC, Middle East Research and Information Project, 8 January 2015, https://www.merip.org/palestine-icc (accessed 20 May 2017), items 1–4.

10 Ibid.

6.2 Possible Impacts of the ICC's Intervention in the Palestine Situation

Measuring the impact of the ICC's intervention before the conclusion of proceedings is generally difficult. The effect differs from situation to situation as every situation has its unique context and originality. It also depends on the level of peace negotiation, the trigger mechanism for the Court's intervention, the timing of investigation and indictments, the political atmosphere surrounding the situation, the stages of the conflict or the parties targeted by the Court.

As witnessed, for instance, in the situations in Kenya[11] and Colombia[12] the effects of the Court do not emanate only from judicial rulings. Prosecutorial decisions and the activities of the OTP have, in addition, shaped the effects of the Court on situations.[13] This section addresses the possible impacts of the Court's intervention in the fight against impunity, the peace process and stability in Israel and Palestine. It further reviews the impacts of dealing with the Palestine situation on the credibility and legitimacy the Court.

It has to be emphasised that the analysis that follows does not conclude on the importance of combating impunity through the ICC based on its outcome and its potential to contribute to other ends. The inherent value of justice makes it non-interchangeable with other tools such as peace settlements, sanctions and military interventions.[14] This is valid even if justice cannot effectively result in peace and stability compared to other measures. Although the pursuit of justice should not be judged on its outcomes, it would, however, be unfeasible not to deal with the effect establishing justice has on facts on the ground.

6.2.1 *Combating Impunity*

Recognising that impunity in respect of grave crimes threatens peace, security and the well-being of the world, the preamble of the Rome Statute affirms that the 'most serious crimes of concern to the international community… must not go unpunished'.[15] The Statute envisages accountability to be established not only through the ICC but also through national prosecutions and international cooperation. As the jurisdiction of the Court is complementary to the jurisdiction of national Courts, it encourages and assists the respective national jurisdictions to investigate and

[11] Materu 2015, pp. 254–255.

[12] Mendes 2010, pp. 135 et seq.; Nicholas 2015, pp. 41–42.

[13] Kersten 2016, p. 12.

[14] Vinjamuri 2015, p. 26.

[15] Rome Statute, above n. 5, Preamble, paras 3–4.

prosecute grave crimes of concern to the international community.[16] It, however, could be difficult to measure the effects of ICC investigation in the overall fight against impunity, especially if the assessment, as in the case of Palestine, is one before the fact and one that may vary depending on the time in question. The impact of the Court in contrast to other accountability or alternative dispute resolution mechanisms could also be assessed only in a counter-factual outlook.

The effects of the Court on various situations have differed depending on, among other things, the type of trigger mechanism leading to the intervention.[17] For instance, Security Council referrals have principally targeted State officials while rebel groups are primarily the subject of investigation in self-referred situations.[18] As State cooperation to collect evidences and execute warrants relies on the referring body, the resultant 'asymmetrical attribution of accountability' should not come as a surprise.[19] Except in the situation of Uganda, the other two situations that are the result of *ad hoc* declarations, namely, Côte d'Ivoire and Ukraine, enjoyed symmetrical investigations of alleged perpetrators. Hence, these prior records make any conclusive insight on the resultant impact of the ICC's intervention in Palestine difficult. Thus, the analysis that follows explores the ideal or potential effects of the Court's intervention in contrast to what could be the actual effect.

6.2.1.1 Individualising Guilt and Challenging Narratives

As established in the Judgment of the International Military Tribunal at Nuremberg, grave crimes of concern to the international community are not committed by 'abstract entities' but by men.[20] The Nuremberg trials and other post WWII precedents have established that international law can effectively be enforced by individualising guilt and punishing those perpetrators.[21] In the context of transitional justice, individualising guilt is critically important in establishing the truth and in helping society deal with past injustices.[22]

In a situation of on-going conflict as in the case of Palestine, it is easy to lay the blame on part or a significant section of the population. It is a conflict which is narrated in an 'us versus them' manner, namely, as the Israelis versus Palestinians,

---

[16] Ibid., Article 17.

[17] Kersten 2016, pp. 185, 189.

[18] Burke-White 2005, p. 565; Rodman 2014, p. 14.

[19] M. Kersten, The ICC and its impact: more known unknowns, *OpenGlobalRights*, 5 November 2014, https://www.openglobalrights.org/icc-and-its-impact-more-known-unknowns/ (accessed 20 May 2017).

[20] International Military Tribunal, *United States et al. v. Hermann Wilhelm Göring et al.*, Judgment, 14 November 1945–1 October 1946, in Trial of the Major War Criminals before the International Military Tribunal, vol. 1, p. 223.

[21] Ibid.

[22] Szekely 2014, pp. 103 et seq.

the occupier versus the occupied or the Jews versus the Arabs.[23] The fact that responsibility for commission of atrocities is individually allocated to the organisers and architects of the crimes assists in paving the way to reconciliation amongst the societies. It counters the notion of collective guilt and helps the two parties come to terms with the history of the conflict.[24]

The ICC, however, is restricted to prosecution of specific cases with the required gravity against those most responsible and those that satisfy the criteria of the Statute. Due to its structural capacity, the Court focuses mainly on those who orchestrated, incited, supported or perpetrated grave crimes at the highest level or in the gravest manner.[25] It is not, on its own, capable of writing the history of the conflict, investigate and rule on the causes of the conflict, nor to take individual statement of every victim, as a truth commission would do.[26] It, nonetheless, makes an indispensable contribution towards that end as it assembles Court verified (official) facts. It is such facts that help challenge myths or 'fabrications of knowledge', which could be used to stir new or justify enduring conflicts in the future.[27]

6.2.1.2 Responding to the Needs of Victims

The prosecutorial policy of the ICC, among other things, is expected to be well appreciative of the needs of victims within the situation under its scrutiny.[28] From preliminary examination to reparations, the Prosecutor has to be cognisant of the needs of victims as they constitute one of the main stakeholders in the proceedings.[29] The interests of victims in the interventions of the Court could range from justice to security and protection.[30] The physical and psychological well-being of victims and their right to privacy and dignity also have to form part of the equation.[31] As the OTP's Policy Paper on Interest of Justice provides, in light of Article 53 of the Rome Statute, the Prosecutor is empowered to discontinue investigations and prosecutions on the ground that its tasks endanger the interest of victims.[32] The difficulty is, however, in establishing the needs of victims.

The challenge of establishing a victim's need arises from the divergent views on what is best for the victims, their families and the broader community. One has to conduct the proper survey and sampling to reach a conclusion on the perspectives

23 Said 1995, p. 143.
24 Lindenmann 2007, p. 327.
25 Ralston and Finnin 2008, p. 48.
26 Lindenmann 2007, p. 325.
27 Ibid., p. 319.
28 Unger and Wierda 2009, p. 274.
29 Ibid., pp. 274–275.
30 Rome Statute, above n. 5, Articles 54(1)(b) and 68; OTP 2007, p. 6.
31 Ibid., p. 5; Mnookin 2012, p. 154.
32 OTP 2007, pp. 5–6.

of the victims, which could be obtained from religious, tribal and political leaders, as well as local and international governmental and non-governmental organisations.[33] One could, still, easily assume that it is in the interest of the victims of gross human rights violations to see justice done against perpetrators of those violations. Nonetheless, in the context of the Israel-Palestine conflict, an on-going century old conflict, the intervention brings about greater expectations and possibly different priorities.[34] Although, as established above, the ICC is a judicial body which could not make or break peace on its own, its intervention has the possibility of tipping the balance of the conflict, giving rise to even more divergent views on victim perspectives.[35]

The duration and intensity of the conflict also affects the choices of the players. Political compromise could be one of the prominent choices, especially when, in the view of the victims, the costs of accountability and judicial actions are rather higher, as was the case when Palestine considered joining the ICC.[36] On the other hand, the prolonged nature of the conflict has created countless victims, making waver of 'accountability options' more precarious.[37]

The impact of the duration of the conflict and the desperate desire for a political compromise is evidenced in the Palestinian leadership's use of the Court as a bargaining chip for political compromises[38]—rather than employing the avenue to combat the prevalent impunity. Despite the leadership's view of the move, various voices ranging from those of Palestinian academics to those of youth movements pressured the Palestinian leadership to go to Court.[39] Be it to establish accountability, to shape narratives of the conflict or to obtain legitimacy and international

---

[33] Stegmiller 2011, p. 384.

[34] Masri et al. 2015, above n. 9; Stegmiller 2011, p. 386.

[35] Victims of conflict have shown different priorities than justice, for instance, in the Uganda Situation. See Pham et al. 2007, pp. 7 et seq.; Stegmiller 2011, p. 386.

[36] The cost of pursuing justice through the ICC is higher for the Palestinian side. The US has warned the PLO that bringing cases before international Courts would result in closing PLO's office in the US, end of foreign aid to Palestine and the possible restoring of the PLO into the terrorist groups list. See Kittrie 2016, p. 209; Palestinian Officials Say U.S. Threatens 'Severe Steps' if Leaders Sue Israel in World Court, http://www.haaretz.com/middle-east-news/palestinians/.premium-1.769034 (accessed 2 February 2017).

[37] Sriram 2004, p. 26.

[38] That was evidenced by the temporal scope provided in the *ad hoc* declaration and the fact that the declaration was lodged immediately after Palestine's UN bid in the Security Council failed to accrue the necessary votes. Another instance is where the threat of joining the ICC was used for a negotiation in Cairo to obtain compromises from Israel during Operation Protective Edge. See J. Borger and I. Black, Palestinian leaders poised to join ICC in order to pursue Israel for war crimes, *The Guardian*, 5 August 2014; Kittrie 2016, pp. 210–211; C. McGreal, Palestinians warn: back UN statehood bid or risk boosting Hamas, *The Guardian*, 27 November 2012; J. Reed, Palestinians push for UN deadline on Israeli withdrawal, *Financial Times*, 16 December 2014.

[39] D. Spiegelfeld, Can Kerry keep the Palestinians out of the ICC? *The Daily Beast*, 27 March 2013.

attention to the Palestinian cause, the intervention of the Court appears favourable to the diverse interests of the victims.

On the Israel side, the prevailing view is that the ICC is a disruption to peace processes and a Palestinian 'law fare' through a 'biased' judicial system.[40] Some Arab legislators of the Knesset and Israeli human rights organizations have, however, supported the indictment of senior Israeli leaders for violations of international law. A member of the Knesset, Haneen Zoabi, in particular, has strongly argued that as legitimacy of Israel is a sensitive matter, any measure that delegitimises Israeli policies would send a strong message to the Israeli public and pressure for change in *status quo*.[41] Regarding its benefits to Israeli victims, the contingency of the materialization of an ICC prosecution, the likelihood of a Security Council deferral and the effects of possible diplomatic pressure on the Court may not invite victims to look up to the Court for victim redress. Especially considering the possible damaging effects of this 'law fare' to the status quo, it appears that the Israeli leadership prefer to employ their own devices to serve the needs of Israeli victims.

6.2.1.3 Deterrence and Retribution

Retribution and deterrence are the main traditional purposes of punishment which, *inter alia*, give international criminal law its required legitimacy.[42] Imposing sentences through the ICC aims to, among others, deter the accused (special deterrence) as well as future offenders (general deterrence) from committing similar crimes.[43] In addition to its preventive effect, it establishes that crimes of such nature would not go unpunished. The punishment also serves the demands of 'elementary justice', which requires and morally justifies proportional punishment as

---

[40] BBC News, Will ICC Membership Help or Hinder the Palestinians' Cause? 1 April 2015, http://www.bbc.com/news/world-middle-east-30744701 (accessed 31 May 2015). See Kontorovich 2014. See also Kittrie 2016, pp. 209–220.

[41] B. Lynfield, Zoabi Offers to Help the ICC Indict Netanyahu over Settlement Law, Jerusalem Post, 17 February 2017.

[42] This is established in the jurisprudence of the ICTY and the ICTR. See, for instance, the following ICTY cases: *Prosecutor v. Dragan Nikolić*, Sentencing Judgement, 18 December 2003, IT-94-2-S, para 140; *Prosecutor v. Kupreškić et al.*, Judgement, 14 January 2000, IT-95-16-T, para 848; *Prosecutor v. Dlacić et al.*, Judgment, 16 November 1998, IT-96-21-T (*Dlacić* et al. 1998), paras 1231–1234; *Prosecutor v. Erdemovic*, Sentencing Judgement, 24 December 1996, IT-96-22-T, para 64; *Prosecutor v. Furundžija*, Judgement, 10 December 1998, IT-95-17/1-T, para 288. For ICTR cases, see the following: *Prosecutor v. Kambanda*, Judgement and Sentence, 4 September 1998, ICTR 97-23-S, para 28; *Prosecutor v. Akayesu*, Sentence, 2 October 1998, ICTR-96-4-S, para 19; *Prosecutor v. Serushago*, Sentence, 5 February 1999, ICTR-98-39-S, para 20; *Prosecutor v. Rutaganda*, Judgement and Sentence, 6 December 1999, ICTR-96-3-T, para 456; *Prosecutor v. Musema*, Judgement and Sentence, 27 January 2000, ICTR-96-13-T, para 986. See also Werle and Jessberger 2014, pp. 36–37.

[43] ICC, *Prosecutor v. Thomas Lubanga Dyilo*, Decision on the Prosecutor's application for a warrant of arrest Article 58, 10 February 2006, ICC-01/04-01/06-8, paras 54, 60. See also Vinjamuri 2015, p. 16; Van der Wilt 2010, pp. 52 et seq.

consequential to the pain inflicted/wrongful acts.[44] The punishment of those guilty of the crimes, even if it does not aim to fulfil the victims' desire for vengeance, duly represents the 'outrage and condemnation of the international community'.[45]

It is impossible to causally connect and conceptually measure a certain punishment's deterrent effect on a crime that was not committed.[46] One can therefore not assert conclusively that a certain crime would have been committed had it not been for the deterrent effect of a punishment or its threat thereof.[47] Though one can point out the individuals who are not deterred, it is hardly possible to identify those who are.[48] However, this does not challenge the well-established preventive effect of punishments.[49] It is not the specific punishment (*per se*) but the likelihood of such punishment that has a significant deterrence. The effect of possible punishment could be considered as directly proportional to the predictability of the punishment.[50]

In situations where the OTP announced that it has jurisdiction or provides information on its activities, as in the case of Côte d'Ivoire, Kenya, Georgia or Guinea, the threat of prosecution has helped reduce violence and limit the scope and extent of new commissions.[51] In Kenya, for instance, after the Prosecutor asserted jurisdiction on the 2007 post-election violence, all actors expressed their commitment to address and prevent political violence. This commitment has contributed in the decline of violence.[52] The arrest of rebel leaders in the DRC for the recruitment and use of child soldiers had a deterrent and educational impact in the sense that the legal response showed that the acts are wrong and prosecutable.[53] For the situation of Darfur, however, despite the imminent threat of prosecution before the ICC, there was no such deterrent effect given the policy of impunity maintained by the Al-Bashir government.[54] The Darfur case, therefore, shows that extraneous factors can have a significant impact on the deterrent effect of punishment or its threat.

---

[44] *Dlacić* et al. 1998, above n. 42, paras 1231–1234; A. Walen, Retributive justice, *Stanford Encyclopedia of Philosophy*, https://plato.stanford.edu/entries/justice-retributive/ (accessed 30 September 2016), items 1–2; Werle and Jessberger 2014, pp. 36–37; Van der Wilt 2010, p. 51.

[45] Special Court of Sierra Leone, *Prosecutor v. Charles Ghakay Taylor*, Sentencing Judgment, 30 May 2012, SCSL-03-01-T, para 13; ICTY, Judgement in Sentencing Appeals, *Prosecutor v. Dusco Tadić*, 26 January 2000, IT-94-1-A, paras 48–56; ICTY, *Prosecutor v. Aleksovski*, Judgment, 24 March 2000, IT-95-14/1-A, para 185.

[46] Kersten 2016, p. 26.

[47] Ibid.

[48] Schabas 2011a, p. 61.

[49] Kelley and Méndez 2015, p. 489.

[50] Ibid.

[51] Dancy et al. 2015; Kelley and Méndez 2015, pp. 490–491.

[52] Ibid. See also Dancy et al. 2015.

[53] Hayner 2009, p. 17.

[54] Human Rights Watch 2009, p. 74.

Although one could simply make the assumption that the intervention of the Court in Palestine prevents commission of war crimes,[55] there are reports indicating that there is a significant increase in commission of certain alleged crimes within the jurisdiction of the Court. This is particularly the case for alleged crimes of constructing settlements, house demolitions[56] and unlawful killings by Israeli forces, and violent attacks by Palestinian assailants.[57] Various factors could cause an escalation of crimes perpetrated, but it also reflects the limited preventive effect of the judicial process in the Palestine situation as compared to other situations. Undeniably, the Palestinian situation is unique, a factor which possibly results in distinct impact and reaction to the Court's intervention. One has to assess the reasons behind the escalation in some of the State-sponsored alleged crimes such as those stemming from the construction of the settlements.

The predictability of prosecution, as established above and the time consumed in the investigatory process have roles to play in the effectiveness of the preventive force and deterrence. Where the prospect of prosecution appears to be remote, or where the long-standing tradition of impunity has undermined public confidence in the belief that justice will be seen to have been done,[58] and in instances where ICC trials do not have the effect of causing the government's tight control of the political situation, the deterrent effect of a criminal sanction could be minimal. As criminological research has shown, 'those in positions with more at stake to risk are more likely to desist and or refrain from crime'.[59] Rothe and Collins rightly argue that in situations of conflict, the law can be viewed as negotiable, ineffective or inapplicable given the circumstances. Such is particularly possible in situations where 'individual morality is influenced by the on-going situation' or the 'ideology guiding the behaviour'.[60]

Israel views its occupation of Palestine, particularly the Gaza blockade, as the only means to advance the interest of Israel and to defend itself from what it considers to be a security threat.[61] Such views make the situation or the alleged crimes committed to maintain the *status quo* appear necessary. On the other hand,

---

[55] UNHRC 2009, para 1966; Azarova 2013, p. 260.

[56] After Palestine made an *ad hoc* declaration, in particular after 2015, around 15,300 acres of the West Bank was declared Israeli State land, which is reportedly one of the largest land appropriations since 2005. Between January and August 2016, 2,623 new units are planned to be built in the occupied territories. In 2015 and 2016, respectively, around 688 and 889 Palestinians were displaced due to house demolitions. See OTP 2016, pp. 29–30.

[57] Regarding the increase in 'lone wolf' attacks in the West Bank and Jerusalem see Y. Bob, Intel report: West Bank terror stays heated, Gaza rockets quietest year, The Jerusalem Post, 05 February 2017.

[58] UNHRC 2009, para 1964.

[59] Rothe and Collins 2013, p. 195.

[60] Ibid., p. 196.

[61] B. Ravid, Netanyahu: security blockade on Gaza will only get stronger, Haaretz, 6 February 2017; G. Sher and D. Wolf, Recognizing that Israel is not an occupying power in Gaza is good for everyone, War on the Rocks, 8 July 2016.

Hamas and its affiliated armed groups justify any armed resistance against Israel as justified and necessary as the groups claim that such acts are the integral part of their right to self-determination and self-defence. Hence, the perception towards the alleged crimes could be said to have affected the aims of deterrence and retribution as the State sanctioned alleged crimes are not viewed as 'crimes'.[62]

It is, however, difficult to ignore the impact of 'judicial stigmatization', 'social deterrence' or the 'extra-judicial impacts of prosecution' in contrast to the prosecutorial deterrence. As Jo and Simmons argue, parties more concerned with the legitimacy of their cause in the view of the international community are likely to be deterred.[63] According to the social deterrence theory put forward by Jo and Simmons, rebels and secessionist groups are 'deterrable' as they aim to foster their domestic and international legitimacy.[64] In this sense, even if prosecution is not a real risk, the extra-judicial impact would still matter.[65] In light of this, Hamas and its affiliates are more likely to consider prosecution through the ICC a real risk and as having a far-reaching impact than that of the Israeli Defence Force.[66] A case in point is the fact that, in more than a decade, the lowest number of rockets was fired from Gaza in 2016.[67] Hence, although the ICC does not solve the conflict on its own, it seems to have contributed to the reduction of active military engagement between the two parties.

6.2.1.4 Promoting National Judicial Reforms

The ICC is established with the purpose of prosecuting the most serious crimes of concern perpetrated mainly by senior leaders and officials. The ICC relies on the premise that lower ranked culprits are investigated and prosecuted by national Courts.[68] The norms underlying the principle of complementarity were conceived to maintain this parallel arrangement.[69] It is, therefore, one of the main aims of the Court to call up on and to assist national Courts to function in compliance with the required international standards.[70] The Court provides training to judges and encourages States to incorporate the Rome Statute crimes into their respective domestic criminal law. Implementation of the Statute in a State's national law, as in

[62] Rothe and Collins have also argued similarly regarding the factors that affect the individual behavior in committing crimes and the ideologies justifying such acts. See Rothe and Collins 2013, p. 196.

[63] Jo and Simmons 2014, pp. 12–15.

[64] Ibid.

[65] Ibid., p. 20.

[66] Kittrie 2016, pp. 215 et seq.

[67] Bob 2017, above n. 57.

[68] Azarova and Weill 2012, pp. 934–935; Kleffner 2008, p. 288; Stone 2015, p. 288.

[69] Schabas 2011b, p. 155.

[70] ASP 2011. See also Azarova and Weill 2012, pp. 934–935. See also Mendes 2010, p. 133.

the case of Germany[71] and South Africa,[72] promotes reform of domestic penal laws.[73] Similar initiatives have also occurred, for instance, in Uganda where Chambers are established for Statute crimes and in the Democratic Republic of Congo where the crime of rape has been included into the penal code's list of war crimes.[74]

On the other hand, the mere existence of the Court could potentially encroach on the traditional sovereign prerogatives of a State to deal with issues concerning the State and its citizens.[75] That is particularly the case when the State has to but is unwilling or unable to exercise its national criminal jurisdiction.[76] By making sure that the national judicial system functions complementary to the Court and in light of the necessary standards, a State could avoid the 'intrusion' of the ICC.[77] Hence, considering successful domestic prosecutions could obviate the Court's intervention, it serves as an incentive for States to reform and capacitate their investigatory and prosecutorial infrastructures at the domestic level.[78] The threat of prosecution or the 'shadow effect' of the prosecutor, thus, plays an indispensable role.[79] In this regard, the activities of the Sudanese government between 2005 and 2008 provide a practical example. Following the decision of the Prosecutor to open an investigation into the situation, the Sudanese government announced the establishment of a special criminal Court to deal with events in Darfur. In an attempt to avoid the intervention of the Court, additional measures to improve the national accountability mechanisms were also made. Based on these improvements, the Sudanese government argued that as it has the capacity to handle prosecutions domestically the intervention of the Court is unwelcomed.[80]

Following the publication of the Goldstone Report, which—in the absence of good-faith investigations—calls for a Security Council referral of the Situation in Palestine to the ICC, the Israeli legislative and judicial system has also shown some improvements.[81] Amongst the significant reforms that have been considered, as discussed under Sect. 4.4.1.1, are the modification of the manner in which the Israeli Defence Force conducts armed conflict and its willingness to collaborate

[71] Act to Introduce the Code of Crimes Against International Law (Völkerstrafgesetzbuch) of 26 June 2002.

[72] Implementation of the Rome Statute of the International Criminal Court Act 27 of 2002 as amended by Judicial Matters Amendment Act 22 of 2005.

[73] Werle and Jessberger 2014, pp. 128 et seq.

[74] Wegner 2015, p. 30. See also Dancy et al. 2015.

[75] DeGuzman 2012, pp. 54–55.

[76] The principle of complementarity recognizes that national criminal jurisdiction is both the right and duty of a sovereign State. See OTP 2003, p. 5. See also Schabas 2011b, p. 156.

[77] Jo and Simmons 2014, p. 18.

[78] Stahn 2010, p. 678.

[79] Mnookin 2012, p. 156.

[80] Human Rights Watch 2009, pp. 102–103; Nouwen 2013, pp. 276 et seq.

[81] UNHRC 2009, paras 1970–1971.

with human right organisations critical of its actions.[82] The examination of the Gaza flotilla incident by the ICC has also brought attention to the issue of domestic investigations and prosecution, which gave rise to a two volume investigatory report named the Israeli Turkel Report. The second volume of the Report has listed out areas of the Israeli judicial system in need of reform. In light of the report, the system of investigation, 'war crimes' legislation, the 'dual hat' of the Military Advocate General and transparency of proceedings are amongst some of the main areas mentioned as necessitating a reform.[83] Following the opening of preliminary examination in the situation of Palestine, Israel has also attempted to improve its judicial system further. Although there are reports asserting that the inherent structural deficiencies apparent in the system in place are relatively unaffected by the minor alterations made,[84] one has to take note of the intention to reform the system as a step in the right direction in the road to effective reforms.

In addition, the intervention of the Court and the resultant promotion of international criminal justice, demonstrates 'a symbolic social function that spreads the rule of law by example'.[85] Trials of gross crimes are beacons of hope that symbolise a moral authority common to all of humanity. It is this moral appeal that facilitates the acceptance of and compliance with rule of law.[86] Promotion of the rule of law is, in addition, institutionally enforced through the principle of complementarity. The standards or the 'rules of the road' that national Courts need to maintain to investigate crimes domestically, in effect, formalise this value and inspire States to maintain such standards through legal capacity building.

6.2.2 *Fostering Palestine's Statehood*

The failure of the Israel-Palestine peace process has, arguably, led the Palestine Authority to resort to measures to internationalise the 'Palestinian cause'.[87] After the UN 'upgraded' Palestine's status to a non-member observer State, Palestine has signed more than 20 international treaties including the Rome Statute. Israel views Palestine's engagement with the ICC as 'an act of unilateralism and aggression' and

---

[82] K. Heller, Israel's changes in response to the Goldstone Report, http://opiniojuris.org/2011/04/17/israels-changes-in-response-to-the-goldstone-report/ (accessed 30 November 2016).

[83] Turkel Commission 2013, pp. 425 et seq. See also Weill 2012, p. 110.

[84] UNHRC 2015, para 610; Israeli human rights organizations B'Tselem and Yesh Din: Israel is unwilling to investigate harm caused to Palestinians http://www.btselem.org/press_releases/20140905_failure_to_investigate (accessed 21 March 2016).

[85] Vinjamuri 2015, p. 18.

[86] Ibid.

[87] Kittrie 2016, pp. 210–211.

the US has asserted that it is an unproductive unilateral move, which significantly damages the peace process.[88]

The bilateral talks mostly mediated by the US have repeatedly failed. The lack of compromise on core issues and trust on implementing the 'road maps' to peace as well as the disruptive actions of both sides have also impeded attempts to revive the peace deals.[89] Thus, the Palestine authorities' unilateral move to internationalise the Palestine cause, at least from the Palestinian perspective, allows a more promising multilateral approach to address the cause. It could be argued that internationalising the Palestinian cause could help cement support for self-determination and to implement details of future peace deals. The ultimate goal is to transform and crystallise the support towards a 'tangible international framework for statehood' and 'recognition as a legitimate actor' in the international arena.[90]

As discussed in Sect. 6.2.1.2, the temporal scope provided in the Palestinian *ad hoc* declaration, among other things, indicates that the move is not purely inspired by the pursuit of international justice. The political and rhetorical profits, as Huber and Kamel rightly note, are implicit in or are components of the resort to a judicial organ.[91] As such, the recourse to the ICC to benefit not only from the explicit pursuit of justice but also from the implicit benefits does not make the move necessarily wrong. Although a judicial forum, the ICC is also an institution composed of States parties, which are at best political entities. Accession to the Statute grants Palestine all the rights and obligations of a State party and the intervention of the Court in Palestine affirm this position. The treatment of Palestine similar to any other State party and the recognition of this status by members of the Assembly of States Parties helps consolidate the status of Palestine under international law, which consequently gives Palestine a better standing in future negotiations.[92]

However, these gains for Palestine could give rise to the assertion that the ICC is being exploited for political gains.[93] Yet, one has to distinguish between resort to the Court for mere political benefits on the one hand, and a resort to the Court that has both legal and political implications on the other. International law and its enforcement carry a stronger significance and impact when it also affects political interests. In light of its general substantial impact relating to the fight against

---

[88] Collins 2016, p. 149; Israel Ministry of Foreign Affairs, FM Lieberman: Security Council should deal with world threats, not Palestinian gimmicks, 18 December 2014, http://mfa.gov.il/MFA/PressRoom/2014/Pages/FM-Liberman-Security-Council-should-deal-with-world-threats,-not-Palestinian-gimmicks-18-Dec-2014.aspx (accessed 17 November 2016).

[89] Kelman 2007, p. 287; Oberschall 2007, pp. 142–143. See also A. Ben-Meir, Why have past Israeli-Palestinian negotiations failed? The World Post, 18 November 2015; and BBC News, History of Mid-East peace talks, 29 July 2013, http://www.bbc.com/news/world-middle-east-11103745 (access 31 May 2017).

[90] Huber and Kamel 2015, pp. 2 et seq.; Kearney and Reynolds 2013, p. 420.

[91] Huber and Kamel 2015, p. 13.

[92] Ibid.

[93] Kontorovich 2014; Kittrie 2016, pp. 210–212.

impunity, the affirmation on the international personality of Palestine could be considered as an extraneous consequence of the resort to the Court. More importantly, it is an effect that is not the direct result of diverting the mandate and competence of the Court.

6.2.3 *Peace Negotiations*

The dichotomous approach that treats peace and justice as excluding one another has transcended to an approach that argues that the two are intractably linked and complementary.[94] Inherent in this approach is that there need not be a trade-off between peace and justice. Undeniably, peace could reinforce justice and vice versa. Depending on the reality on the ground, prosecution and peace-making could take place parallel to each other. However, considering the various difficulties of peace making, it would be too idealistic to resort to the convenient assertion that the divide no longer exists or to suggest that the two are necessarily mutually reinforcing.[95]

The level of the Court's involvement and the stages of the peace process (pre-negotiation, negotiation and post negotiation) determine the impact of the ICC's intervention on the Israeli-Palestinian peace process.[96] The following assessment, however, deals with the overall impact of the Court on the conflict and does not assume that the peace efforts and the need for justice are incompatible. It thus explores the instances where there is a possibility of tension between the two by analysing the pros and cons of both sides.

6.2.3.1 Promoting Peace Negotiations

Accountability provides a firm background to a sustainable peace and is viewed as one element in any comprehensive effort to resolve conflicts. Peace and justice could be viewed as complementary and mutually reinforcing. A prevalent impunity is supposed to undermine peace-making efforts as it increases the possibility of repetition of violations. Establishing justice is, therefore, one of the instruments to solve conflicts peacefully and a means to further peace efforts.[97] Unless the structure that allowed the violations is dismantled and the cycle of impunity is broken, a lasting peace may be hard to achieve.[98]

---

[94] Grono and O'Brien 2008, p. 13.

[95] Ibid.

[96] Kersten 2016, p. 13.

[97] Mendes 2010, pp. 132–133; Wegner 2015, pp. 288–289.

[98] Méndez and Kelley 2015, pp. 482–484; Unger and Wierda 2009, p. 265.

As an international accountability mechanism, the ICC could be used both as an instrument of justice and peace.[99] The intervention of the Court could be an incentive for peace efforts. It could revive peace negotiations and may require parties to the conflict to redouble their efforts at reaching settlements. The threat of prosecution may reduce the option of maintaining power through arms and increase the political costs of supporting the targeted party thereby leading parties to engage in peace talks.[100] By undermining their legitimacy and weakening their support, indictments marginalise perpetrators. To maintain their standing perpetrators may be coerced or incentivised to negotiate.[101]

In the case of Darfur, for instance, renewed negotiations between President Al-Bashir and the rebels occurred following the issuance of an arrest warrant against Al-Bashir. The judicial intervention (even if controversial) is said to have fostered rather than hampered the peace process as it cornered the incumbent head of State to appear constructive in the eye of the UN-AU Mediator.[102] Human Rights Watch and other scholars have noted that the effect of the ICC's action is also evident in the decision of the Lord's Resistance Army to negotiate with the government of Uganda in 2006.[103] Prosecutions could also make peace deals possible by removing spoilers from negotiations. Political deals were made possible, for instance, in the case of Sierra Leone and the former Yugoslavia due to the indictment of Charles Taylor and Radovan Karadzic and Ratko Mladic, respectively.[104]

Investigation and possible prosecution of the ICC in Palestine could undermine the legitimacy of parties to the conflict, draw the attention of the international community to the situation and strengthen (or weaken depending on the reaction) support to one's cause. By doing so, the Court could help in coercing the parties to take peace negotiations seriously.[105] Although establishing accountability in on-going conflicts as in the case of Libya may not on its own be sufficient to end conflicts and establish peace, in situations where narratives and international support play a significant role, as in Palestine, criminal justice makes gross violations of law politically risky and costly.

However, it would be credulous to argue that the ICC intervention would transform the protracted moribund negotiations in the Israel-Palestine conflict into a negotiation that fruitfully finds a solution to the conflict. The intervention could help shape the context in which peace settlements are dealt with. As any ICC

---

99 Méndez and Kelley 2015, p. 484.

100 Human Rights Watch 2009, p. 28.

101 Vinjamuri 2015, pp. 16–17.

102 It has to be noted that, in the Darfur case, although the ICC intervention helped to revive the mediation, the marginalizing effect of the indictment did not last in the domestic political arena as the indicted incumbent president run for office and succeeded. See Méndez and Kelley 2015, p. 488; and Vinjamuri 2015, p. 17. See also Nouwen 2013, pp. 276 et seq.

103 Vinjamuri 2015, p. 16; Hayner 2009, p. 17; Human Rights Watch 2009, p. 28.

104 Hayner 2009, p. 17.

105 Azarova 2013, p. 260.

intervention, the Court may help challenge the dominant conflict narratives, establish the cause of the conflict and identify those most responsible.[106] The binary narratives of the conflict portraying one side as good and another as bad has played a great role on how peace deals are shaped and negotiated. In the event where an impartial judicial institution investigates and helps shape this dominant narration and establish the responsibility of parties to the conflict, both parties would be more likely to take negotiations seriously and invest in a more genuine effort to change the *status quo*.

It bears mentioning that the proceedings of the ICC on the situation in Palestine could give rise to an Article 16 deferral. The provision grants the Security Council power to defer a commencing or proceeding investigation and prosecution for a renewable 12 months. To obtain the unanimous votes required for the deferral, an alternative peace deal for the Israel-Palestine conflict could be presented before the members of the Council that needs not only to be endorsed but also driven by the major allies of Israel.[107] If that is the case, once again, the treat of enforcing individual criminal liability through the ICC could prompt conclusive peace negotiations and increase the cost of maintaining the inaction and *status quo ante*.[108]

Unless the possible peace deal contains accountability measures, this may, in the end, result in trading justice for peace. Permitting justice to be compromised and side-lined for the benefits of peace deals risks the significant developments so far achieved on the fight against impunity. Alternatively, one could argue that as reaching a peace deal helps prevent the perpetual commission of crimes, the Court would still achieve one of its overarching goals, namely, prevention of crimes. Therefore, in either case, the intervention of the Court could be construed as promoting peace in the region.

6.2.3.2 Hindering Peace Negotiations

Opponents of the ICC's intervention in on-going conflicts argue that the Court impacts peace negotiations by leading perpetrators to commit crimes so as to increase their influence in peace deals. As peace talks are quoted in light of international judicial intervention after the Court gets involved, it either marginalises or includes one party over another. So far, in the majority of situations, the Court has viewed conflicts as having a prosecutable one side and an innocent cooperative side on the other. The intervention of the Court in Northern Uganda

[106] M. Kersten, The ICC in Palestine: changing the narrative, rattling the status quo, 7 April 2015, https://justiceinconflict.org/2015/04/07/the-icc-in-palestine-changing-the-narrative-rattling-the-status-quo/ (accessed 15 November 2016).

[107] J. Hudson and C. Lynch, From Tel Aviv to Turtle Bay, Foreign Policy, 18 March 2015; M. Kersten, Palestine and the ICC: a piece of justice or a peace for justice? 1 April 2015, https://justicehub.org/article/palestine-and-icc-piece-justice-or-peace-justice (accessed 20 January 2017).

[108] Kersten 2015, above n. 107.

that targeted the Lord's Resistance Army but not the Government of Uganda, and the situation in Libya which framed only Gaddafi and his officials to the exclusion of the member States of the NATO and the Libyan opposition forces are exemplary.[109] Such conflict framing could create a marginalized party with little to no incentive to negotiate and a cooperative side that refuses to negotiate with an international 'criminal' sought by the Court.[110] Hence, an actual or potential prosecution may help convince parties to refuse or ploy around peace settlements.[111]

The intervention of the Court also makes amnesty or pardon through peace deals unfeasible as bilateral agreements do not bind the Court, and the agreements cannot be extended to the Court.[112] In the absence of a possible amnesty or general pardon for those most responsible, the intervention of the Court, among other factors, could further reduce the incentive to reach settlements, thus creating stalemates.[113] Similar to the approach employed by the Lord's Resistance Army, parties could also aim to use peace deals to shield themselves from prosecution thereby protracting negotiations and conflicts.[114]

Be that as it may, as discussed in Chap. 2, various efforts to conclude peace deals were made in an attempt to resolve the Israel-Palestine conflict. None of the efforts made have produced a reliable solution.[115] It is this lack of solution and absence of accountability for alleged crimes that, among other causes, stirs new or maintains the enduring conflict. In the Palestine context, therefore, establishing accountability is not only justified but is required to address the concerns for peace. In the absence of any worthwhile peace effort and when parties are unwilling or unable to reach peace deals, alleging that the Court's intervention stalls peace settlements[116] is unjustified. Even assuming, for the sake of argument, that the intervention of the Court stalls peace settlements, the vitality of establishing justice does not arise from its instrumentality to other ends, be they peace, stability or

109 Kersten 2016, pp. 185, 189.

110 This was one of the justifications given by the National Transitional Council of Libya to reject negotiations with Gaddafi. However, this does not mean that peace deals would have been made had it not been for the intervention of the ICC. Other extraneous factors have also played a significant role. See ibid., p. 191.

111 Guembe and Olea 2006, p. 121.

112 The practice of granting amnesties and pardons to perpetrators who committed gross human right violations is also no longer in line with international legal standards. The precedents of Inter-American Court and Inter-American Commission on Human Rights establish this practice. See, for instance, the following IACHR judgments: *Almonacid-Arellano et al. v. Chile*, 26 September 2006, IACHR Series C No. 154; *Barrios Altos v. Peru*, 30 November 2001, IACHR Series C No 87; *"Las Dos Erres" Massacre v. Guatemala*, 24 November 2009.

113 As witnessed in Sierra Leone and the DRC, the non-recognition of amnesties and pardons has a direct impact on peace deals. See Guembe and Olea 2006, p. 121; Hayner 2009, p. 8.

114 Kersten 2014, above n. 19.

115 BBC News, History of Mid-East peace talks, 29 July 2013, http://www.bbc.com/news/world-middle-east-11103745 (accessed 31 May 2017).

116 Collins 2016, p. 149.

legitimacy.[117] Though it may ultimately complement peace and peace efforts, justice is an end in itself that should be pursed independent of other goals. Hence, establishing justice through the ICC is not only justified because diplomacy and peace negotiations have proved futile—'last resort rationale'[118]—but also because of its positive contribution to the prospects and sustainability of peace in the region.

6.2.4 Stabilising the States

The pursuit of justice in conflict may have both positive and negative implications on stability and ending conflicts. On the positive side, one could assert that removing key individuals central to the perpetration of the crimes helps to defuse violence. It places the blame on the main perpetrators and away from the general public, thereby helping to halt the cycle of violence.[119] On the other hand, investigations and prosecutions have the potential to shame the targets that may in turn resort to measures to maintain and consolidate power. Possible judicial conviction of the 'political violence' used to further a political community's cause may appear as insolence and a disregard of the 'plight' of the respective community. This may result in violent reprisals, retaliation and (re)commitment to violence to further the cause.[120]

The resultant effects of the ICC's intervention in instigating violence are hard to underestimate as the jurisdictional and resource limitations do not enable the Court to deal with all alleged injustices.[121] The Court does not deal with, among others, the root causes of the Israeli-Palestine conflict unless it happens to be a 'continuing crime' within the jurisdiction of the Court. In principle, it does not address all alleged injustices committed before 13 June 2014 and those crimes that may possibly be excluded for reasons of lack of the required gravity or considered out of the jurisdictional demarcation of the Court. An example would be Hamas's rockets and the Israeli blockade of Gaza. Hamas justifies firing rockets into Israel based on the right to self-defence in response to and in retaliation for the military occupation of Israel and the crippling blockade that holds the people of Gaza in siege. The blockade, which started following the coming into power of Hamas back in 2007, may not be within the potentially prosecutable cases of the Prosecutor unless it is addressed as a continuing crime falling within the ambit of the Court.[122] Hamas's firing of rockets on the other hand are easy to prosecute as this conduct is within the

[117] Kelley and Méndez 2015, p. 488.

[118] Vinjamuri 2015, p. 21.

[119] Ibid., p. 17.

[120] Kersten 2016, p. 27.

[121] Ibid.

[122] The Preliminary Examination Reports of 2015 and 2016 did not cover the blockade as a potentially prosecutable case. See OTP 2015, pp. 11 et seq.; OTP 2016, pp. 25 et seq.

jurisdiction of the Court and it does not appear that the Prosecutor may lack evidence to pursue the charge. Hence, the prosecution of a conduct (rocket attacks) which has been championed as a right to self-defence or a reaction to the 'injustices' of the blockade in the absence of prosecution for what Hamas considers is the cause (blockade) may lead Hamas to recommit and instigate violence.[123]

The Palestinian population, in particular, views the intervention of the ICC as a panacea. The Palestinian leadership also approached the recourse to the ICC as 'a last resort' to obtain the international community's attention to the 'Palestinian cause'.[124] As was witnessed in the case of the *ad hoc* Tribunals, international criminal justice has arguably been employed as veneer for inaction.[125] Similarly, parties to the conflict and the international community as a whole could use the intervention of the Court as a substitute to taking action on the ground (e.g., peace-keeping mission), thereby burdening the Court with an increased expectation about what it could achieve. In such cases of 'incautious optimism', there is a great disparity between expected and actual results, which leads to frustrations. Such frustrations could result in resort to more violent individual actions. Resort to individual action was witnessed during the intifada following the failure of the much-acclaimed Oslo Accords that gave rise to an increasing number of 'lone wolf' attacks against Israeli civilians.

The impact of the Court's intervention on stability could, therefore, be both positive and negative. To achieve and maximise on the positive impacts, the Court needs to advocate and publicise its aims, purpose and what it could or could not achieve.[126] As resort to a judicial organ is a novel un-used route to deal with the Israel-Palestine conflict, it is difficult to conclusively and boldly forecast its impacts on stability. Nonetheless, considering its contribution to establish accountability, the consequent deterrent effect the Court's action would bring as well as its weighing positive impact on peace deals, thus tilting the scale towards the positive impact of the Court's intervention on stability.

In an attempt to find an immediate solution, one may find it easy to undervalue the impact of justice and forgo accountability for other alternatives.[127] Nonetheless, in the long run, as a Human Rights Watch study of cases of the 1990s and 2000s indicates, decisions that enforce the culture of impunity have carried a much higher

---

[123] Retaliation to the Court's action, albeit in a different context, has been witnessed following the issuance of an arrest warrant against the incumbent head of State of Sudan, Omar Al-Bashir. Subsequent to the campaign of shaming and marginalizing that followed the arrest warrant for war crimes, crimes against humanity and genocide, around 13 humanitarian agencies were expelled from Sudan despite the dire need of the victims of violence and it risked a violent cycle of conflict. See Kersten 2016, p. 28.

[124] Collins 2016, p. 149; S. Maupas, Palestine engages International Criminal Court as last resort, *JusticeInfo.Net*, 26 June 2015, https://www.justiceinfo.net/en/truth-commissions/925-palestine-engages-international-criminal-court-as-last-resort.html (accessed 20 May 2017).

[125] Chesterman 2001, p. 8; Kersten 2016, p. 28; Peskin 2008, p. 36.

[126] Mendes 2010, p. 133.

[127] Ibid., pp. 132–133.

cost.[128] Hence, despite some of the short-term negative effects of the intervention on stability, in the long run, the Court's actions would contribute to the stability of the region in question. Noting this positive impact and considering there are various causes to the conflict besides the prevalent impunity, it has to be emphasised that establishing accountability through the Court should not be viewed as a sole causal factor to create stability in the region.

Although it is imperative to take note of the ICC's effect on stability, it has to be noted that the impact of the Court on conflict and conflict resolution efforts should not be the principal measurement of the Court's effectiveness. As a judicial institution solely mandated to establish individual criminal accountability, its contribution should, principally, be evaluated based on its ability to achieve criminal justice.[129] The stance of the Prosecutor of the Court has so far claimed to distinguish between the interests of justice and the interest of peace. Interest of peace is often enunciated in the context of political rhetoric, if not *realpolitik*. Prosecutor Bensouda and her predecessor have noted that it is outside the remit of the Court to take into consideration conflict resolution efforts as that is the task of other institutions such as the Security Council. Nonetheless, one could argue that as most crimes of concern to the Court are basically crimes of political nature, the Court could not ignore the implications of its actions on the political atmosphere and the impact of politics on its proceedings.[130] To attempt to emancipate the laws and practices of the Court from politics—though in line with the ideals of legalism—is, in the words of Rodman, 'neither possible nor desirable'.[131] Despite the non-recognition, the Court plays a role in conflict resolution when it intervenes in on-going conflicts. Hence, it should take into account its effect on conflict resolution efforts and, as Kersten rightly argues, re-imagine its impact[132] not only to maximise the effects of investigations and prosecutions but also to help the legitimacy and credibility of the Court.

6.2.5 Promoting the Credibility of the Court

Similar to any organisation, the ICC has institutional interests it endeavours to protect and advance. Among other interests, maintaining the viability, vitality, legitimacy and reputation of the Court and obtaining State cooperation to collect

[128] The price of including alleged perpetrators in administration and government positions, for instance in Afghanistan, the DRC and Bosnia and Herzegovina, and the lack of effective prosecution in Sudan proved counterproductive. See Human Rights Watch 2009, pp. 3, 35, 43, 54 and 68 et seq.

[129] Kersten 2016, p. 33.

[130] Vinjamuri 2015, p. 20; Kersten 2016, p. 34.

[131] Rodman 2014, p. 3.

[132] Kersten 2016, pp. 35–36.

evidences and enforce arrest warrants are the main interests of the Court.[133] The upholding of these interests is, however, constrained by, *inter alia*, diplomatic pressure, dependence on States for annual budgets and the lack of a police force.[134] These constraints, coupled with the political atmosphere surrounding each situation has, for instance, given rise to one of the serious challenges the Court has faced since its establishment, namely the 'African bias' allegation.

Up to the time of writing, the ICC's prosecutions have exclusively focused on Africa while situations such as Afghanistan and Colombia are still under investigation for almost a decade.[135] In the absence of a coherent data on public opinion, it is hard to conclude that this has damaged the Court's legitimacy.[136] However, the declaration of intent to withdraw from the Statute by South Africa and Burundi is largely attributed to the alleged 'African bias' of the Court.[137] Although this repeatedly raised assertion is rather flawed and at best simplistic,[138] it has so far been exploited for political reasons, and in the process has compromised the reputation of the Court. Hence, the issue at hand begs the question whether the reputation of the Court could endure the tribulations the Israel-Palestine conflict brings. On the contrary, one may wonder if the situation is to the reputational advantage of the Court given the potential of prosecutable non-African cases.

Certainly, the situation potentially produces non-African cases, which could help dispute the 'African bias' claim. Considering the interests at stake in the Israel-Palestine conflict, the ICC's action in the situation could indicate that the Court is not swayed by the tides of politics and does not shy away from cases for fear of super power disapproval. The intervention of the Court in this highly politicised situation tips on the vitality of the Court as an important stake holder in the international arena.

On the other hand, in the absence of cooperation from the respective State, the Court cannot conduct searches and seizures as the Statute does not endow the Court such powers.[139] The Court depends on the State to, for instance, enter a certain territory and collect evidence, to obtain protection for the safety of its staff or compel witness to appear before the Court.[140] In the absence of State cooperation, it

[133] Ibid., pp. 168–172.

[134] Mnookin 2012, p. 151.

[135] See OTP 2016.

[136] Materu provided surveys conducted in relation to the Kenyan situation before the ICC. The public opinion poll of Kenyans indicates that the support for the Court generally remained above 50% during the Court's interaction with Kenya. However, such surveys are not the continental scale. See Materu 2014, pp. 222–225.

[137] L. Miyandazi et al. Why an African mass withdrawal from the ICC is possible, Newsweek, 2 November 2016. See also Kittrie 2016, p. 220.

[138] Regarding the main flaw of the 'Africa bias' claim which is the attribution of blame on the ICC rather than that of the Security Council, see Okoth 2014.

[139] Kittrie 2016, p. 213; Stone 2015, p. 288; Swart 2002, p. 1589.

[140] Ibid.

is also difficult to enforce the rulings of the Court including arrest warrants.[141] Attaining State cooperation has been relatively easier in situations of self-referrals. In all cases of self-referrals, non-State actors were the subject of the Court's investigation and prosecution.[142] Situations in which both sides to the conflict are simultaneously targeted or in which the party in power is the subject of investigation did not enjoy State cooperation. The situation in Darfur and the Kenyan situation provide practical examples. In situations, as in the case of the DRC and Uganda, where both sides to the conflict allegedly committed crimes, the Prosecutor has conveniently chosen to prosecute non-State actors.[143] By doing so, the Office was able to secure State cooperation and to see an end to the proceedings.

In the Palestine situation, however, the Preliminary Examination and the reports that followed have focused on both parties to the conflict. This symmetric approach, albeit ideal, creates practical difficulties to execute investigatory tasks. In addition, Israel, which is a non-party State, claims that the Court lacks jurisdiction to deal with the situation and as a result it will not cooperate with the Court.[144] Despite Palestine's willingness to cooperate, the Prosecutor does not have access to most parts of the territory in the absence of Israel's cooperation. Even if the Prosecutor could still rely on submissions from other States and NGOs, as was the case in the Darfur situation, lack of State cooperation is detrimental to the Court's tasks, particularly when it comes to enforcing arrest warrants. The stalemate or paralysis that may result—'no one being prosecuted, no one being surrendered to The Hague, and no justice being served'—affects the credibility and legitimacy of the Court.[145]

Considering the powers at play in the region, pragmatic factors should be taken into consideration. The prosecutorial strategy should incorporate the impacts of contextual factors on the consequences and vice versa. Prosecutorial discretion in timing investigations and prosecutions as well as in interpreting the principle of complementarity and interest of justice could be used to manage situations.[146] The manner and the timing of the OTP's actions and their publications should be evaluated in light of their impact on the behaviour of local actors. Decisions on questions such as the type of arrest warrants (public or sealed), to stay or open investigations or to wait on reforms or criticise national prosecutions have to be made in light of the context at hand.[147]

However, despite the approach the prosecutor adopts, allies of Israel would not see investigations and prosecutions targeting Israeli officials favourably. Bearing in

141 Kittrie 2016, p. 216; Rodman 2014, p. 5.

142 Ibid.

143 Burke-White 2005, p. 565; Rodman 2014, pp. 14 et seq.

144 M. Newman, Israel announces it won't cooperate with UN Gaza probe, The Times of Israel, 12 November 2014.

145 Kersten 2016, p. 169.

146 Mnookin 2012, p. 145.

147 P. Hayner, Does the ICC advance the interests of justice? *Open Democracy,* 4 November 2014, https://www.opendemocracy.net/openglobalrights/priscilla-hayner/does-icc-advance-interests-of-justice (accessed 20 May 2017).

mind the abstinence of the US and the wide support for the UN Security Council Resolution 2334, which reiterated the illegality of the Israeli settlements, one may anticipate that proceedings before the ICC may not cause the previously anticipated outrage. Nonetheless, unlike the UN Resolution, which only has a normative value and which the then US administration, to the surprise of many, decided not to veto, prosecution before the ICC, as discussed above, has greater connotations. Also considering the stance of the Trump administration and the disproportionate support Israel enjoys from the United States, prosecution before the Court may cause a stronger reaction.[148] Even so, it is an outcome one can forecast when dealing with a situation as sensitive as Palestine.

Although the intervention of the Court on Palestine may help to refute the 'African bias' claim, it is likely that it opens a door for an 'Israel bias' claim, a claim repeatedly raised against UN bodies investigating the situation.[149] Yet, it is not the 'suicidal mission' some made it appear to be. This is also partly because the criticisms do not challenge the basic tenets of the principle of justice and accountability but the Court's proceedings and the decisions surrounding it. Despite the challenges, however, the manner the Prosecutor handles not only the possible cases in the situation but also its public relations regarding the situation could help endure the possible turbulence and shape its ramifications.[150]

6.3 Alternative and Parallel Options to the ICC

Although the ICC, at present, is the most viable option to establish accountability in the Israel-Palestine conflict, there are judicial options that could arguably operate as an alternate or parallel to the Court. These options, namely prosecutions on the ground of universal jurisdiction and prosecutions through a special tribunal may not be as constrained by jurisdictional limitations, as is the case with the ICC. They could deal with the crimes discussed in the previous chapter even if their scope could be limited and their occurrence uncertain for contextual/*sui generis* reasons. This section discusses whether these options are in fact options in the practical sense of the term.

---

148 Haaretz, Palestinian officials say U.S. threatens 'severe steps' if leaders sue Israel in world court, 1 February 2017, http://www.haaretz.com/middle-east-news/palestinians/.premium-1.769034 (accessed 2 February 2017).

149 See M. Bard, United Nations: The UN Relationship with Israel, Jewish Virtual Library, 2017, http://www.jewishvirtuallibrary.org/the-u-n-israel-relationship (accessed 5 April 2017); Collins 2016, p. 149; L. Harkov, Netanyahu: UN anti-Israel bias hasn't changed since 'Zionism is racism' libel', The Jerusalem Post, 5 January 2016. See also J. Muravchik, The UN and Israel: a history of discrimination, World Affairs, December 2013.

150 Rodman similarly asserts that this approach should be adopted for the general operation of the Court and in dealing with situations in ongoing conflict. According to Rodman, the Court needs to adopt 'a politically grounded legalism' so as to conduct consensus building activities amongst other stakeholders. See Rodman 2014, pp. 27, 30.

6.3.1 *Prosecutions Through Universal Jurisdiction*

Regardless of the place of commission, the nationality of the perpetrator of the crime or the victim, certain international crimes (universal wrongs) trigger universal jurisdiction as they are considered to be directed against the international community as a whole.[151] The principle of universal jurisdiction allows any national jurisdiction to prosecute such crimes due to the international nature of the violations.[152] Customary international law recognises the application of universal jurisdiction for grave breaches of the Geneva Conventions, the crime of genocide and crimes against humanity.[153] State practice, however, has developed certain limitations on what was seen as an 'absolute universal jurisdiction' or the 'deterritorialization of criminal justice'.[154] Various domestic laws have provided that universal jurisdiction shall be exercised when the jurisdiction with the traditional links (territorial, active and passive personality) to the crime is unwilling or unable to prosecute. The other most notable (developing) limitation is the criterion that the defendant shall be available within the territory of the Forum State.[155]

Domestic Courts and special Tribunals have exercised universal jurisdiction most notably over the war criminals of Bosnia, Rwandan *Génocidaires*,[156] Pinochet of Chile and Argentinian torturers, as well as in the most prominent case of Hisséne Habré.[157] In the Israel-Palestine context there were attempts to investigate international crimes against, among others, Israeli former and current State officials namely Ariel Sharon, Benjamin Netanyahu, Avigdor Lieberman, Benny Begin, Moshe Yaalon, Ehud Barak, Eli Yishai, and Eliezer Marom and former Palestine Liberation Organization leader Yassir Arafat.[158] The issue, therefore, is whether prosecution on the ground of universal jurisdiction is an alternate or a parallel to proceedings before the ICC.

---

[151] Ambos 2016, p. 240; Bassiouni 2001; Reydams 2011, p. 337; Werle and Jessberger 2014, pp. 73–74.

[152] The Eichmann case is viewed as one of the groundbreaking applications of the principle of universal jurisdiction. That is even though the Court employed the 'protective principle of nationality' instead of universal jurisdiction. The prosecution was conducted in the absence of any territorial and personal links between the prosecuting State and the accused. See Supreme Court of Israel, *Attorney General v. Adolf Eichmann*, Judgment, Supreme Court of Israel 336/61, 29 May 1962; ICJ, Case Concerning the Arrest Warrant of 11 April 2000 (*Democratic Republic of Congo v. Belgium*), Judgment, 14 February 2002, ICJ Reports 2002 at p. 3, para 41. See also Alvarez 2009, p. 27; Hanna 2008, pp. 323–324; and Kleffner 2008, pp. 283, 286.

[153] Werle and Jessberger 2014, p. 75.

[154] Reydams 2011, p. 338; Werle and Jessberger 2014, pp. 74 et seq.

[155] Alvarez 2009, p. 27; Werle and Jessberger 2014, p. 77.

[156] Van den Herik 2009, pp. 1117–1131. The term *génocidaires* is widely used in Rwanda to refer to those who were involved in the Rwandan genocide or who have 'blood on their hands'.

[157] Jessberger 2014, pp. 168–70.

[158] C. Silver, Top Israeli officials face arrest in Spain, South Africa, The Electronic Intifada, 17 November 2015.

With no statutory limitation, international crimes committed in any State are, in principle, prone to prosecution through universal jurisdiction, which makes universal jurisdiction a readily accessible leeway to a wider deterrence. Nonetheless, most virtual cases ranging from Pinochet (in 1998) to Benjamin Netanyahu (in 2015)–in between Fidel Castro, George Bush, Paul Kagame, Ariel Sharon, Amos Yaron, Donald Rumsfeld—produced very little. Except the case of Pinochet, cases having no possible link with the Forum State, namely, purely universal jurisdiction cases, were subverted by diplomatic efforts. Due to this they have not gone beyond making headlines.[159] States, namely, the US, Israel and China have put pressure on Belgium[160] and Spain, known for their wide use of universal jurisdiction. These States were influenced or convinced to amend or repeal their Statutes on universal jurisdiction and its use.[161] The United Kingdom has also amended the use of universal jurisdiction following the unsuccessful arrest warrant issued against former Israeli foreign minister Tzipi Livni.[162]

Universal jurisdiction could be both an alternative and a parallel to a proceeding before the ICC and prosecutions in Israel and Palestine. For that to exist, however, one has to assume unanimity in establishing accountability despite the nationality of the victim or the offender. Reydams argues, and rightly so, that in the face of politics and diplomacy, universal jurisdiction does not grant the absolute right to prosecute international crimes.[163] Where the use of universal jurisdiction against alleged perpetrators is successfully averted through diplomacy, it would show, in the words of Reydams, a 'self-imposed political blindness' to argue that universal jurisdiction is an easily available alternate to prosecute crimes in the Israel-Palestine conflict.[164] It is, nonetheless, an alternative but an inconvenient, toilsome and obscure one.

The other matter worth considering is whether the ICC could prosecute a person when the same person is being prosecuted by a third State on the ground of universal jurisdiction. Similar to various international instruments, the Rome Statute, under Article 20, provides for the principle of *ne bis in idem*. Article 20 read with the principle of complementarity do not allow the Court to assert jurisdiction when a competent national Court has tried or is trying the person in question

159 Reydams 2011, p. 348. See also Jessberger 2014, p. 166.

160 Belgium reportedly limited the application of Universal jurisdiction in its jurisdiction following the suggestion by Donald Rumsfeld that if it does not do so there would be pressure for NATO to withdraw from Belgium. See Human Rights Watch, Belgium: universal jurisdiction law repealed, 1 August 2003, https://www.hrw.org/news/2003/08/01/belgium-universal-jurisdiction-law-repealed (accessed 31 May 2017). See also Alvarez 2009, p. 28; Cryer et al. 2014, p. 62; L. King, On learning lessons: Belgium's universal jurisdiction law under threat, The Electronic Intifada, 24 June 2003.

161 Reydams 2011, pp. 348–349. See also Jessberger 2014, p. 167.

162 Ministry of Justice (UK) and Kenneth Clarke QC, Press release: Universal jurisdiction, https://www.gov.uk/government/news/universal-jurisdiction (accessed 12 December 2016).

163 Reydams 2011, p. 350.

164 Ibid.

for the same conduct.[165] In the event where a national legal system has already tried the person *bona fide*, i.e., to serve the ends of justice, the proceeding bars the ICC from prosecuting the person concerned for the same conduct.[166] However, considering the limited scope of ICC's jurisdiction on the Palestine situation and the wide ranging crimes committed in the situation, there is a slight chance for such overlap. Hence, as long as prosecutions on the ground of universal jurisdictions do not contravene the principle of *ne bis in idem*, they could be conducted parallel to prosecutions in the ICC.

6.3.2 A Special Tribunal

In the spirit of the Special Tribunal for Lebanon, Cambodia, Senegal or Sierra Leone, and the *ad hoc* Tribunals,[167] among others, a special Tribunal could be contemplated for the Israeli-Palestinian situation. The UN has been involved in the establishment of various international Tribunals. In agreement with the respective States, as in the case of, East Timor, Cambodia, Sierra Leone, Bosnia-Herzegovina and Lebanon, it has (helped to) establish(ed) special Tribunals to prosecute international crimes.[168]

The Security Council acting under authority vested in it by Chapter VII could determine that the Palestine situation poses a threat to international peace and security and decide to establish an international criminal Tribunal. Although a case could be made to the detrimental effect of the situation at hand to international peace and security, a Security Council Resolution to that effect may not gain the favour of all veto wielding powers. Most arguments for the case against international criminal accountability for the conflict could *mutatis mutandis* apply for prosecution through an international Tribunal, even so for hybrid Courts composed of experts from both sides to the conflict. However, if there is the political will to do so, the Charter allows the General Assembly of the UN to create 'subsidiary organs as it deems necessary'.[169] Article 11(2) read with Article 22 of the UN Charter authorises the General Assembly to establish such Tribunals. The Assembly could also establish a body mandated to investigate and collect evidence on crimes allegedly committed in the situation.

---

[165] El Zeidy 2008, pp. 283–285.

[166] Ibid.

[167] The ICTY and the ICTR were the result of Security Council Resolutions 827 and 955, respectively. See UNSC 1993 and 1994.

[168] Stan and Nedelsky 2013, above n. 1, p. 44.

[169] K. Iliopoulos, Will anyone be held accountable for war crimes in Gaza? *Crimes of War*, http://www.crimesofwar.org/commentary/will-anyone-be-held-accountable-for-war-crimes-in-gaza/ (accessed 13 December 2016).

Such Tribunals could be designed to fill the gaps of impunity the ICC fails to address. Crimes committed before 13 June 2014 and those not technically within the territorial scope of the two States (e.g., Golan Heights) or within the gravity threshold of the ICC could be adjudicated through a special Tribunal. Although, currently, it is a mere theoretical option, if such a Tribunal is established, it can operate as an alternative or parallel to the ICC.

6.3.3 *Non-judicial Measures*

In addition to the judicial avenue open through the ICC and the slim possibilities of prosecution through universal jurisdiction and a special Tribunal, alternative law enforcement and military cooperation measures are particularly vital. Gross human right violations committed during apartheid South Africa, for instance, were not adjudicated upon by using judicial avenues. Although it does not serve the need for justice of victims in the strictest sense, efforts that aim to impose embargoes, curtail multinational deals on sales of arms, military training, financial supports and restriction on travel of officials have proved effective. When large-scale and systematic crimes are allegedly committed as in the case of the situation in Palestine, judicial intervention and prosecution of certain individuals do not on their own shift the balance of power or enable change in regime or scenery. In such settings, international criminal accountability could achieve a broader goal if it is complemented by non-judicial tools and the cooperation and intervention of external forces.[170]

Up to the time of writing, many of the third party measures in relation to the Israeli-Palestinian conflict significantly focus on Israel. For instance, the EU's relation with Israel has experienced a significant change following the decision for divestment of Israeli products from settlements and other dealings with entities engaged in alleged illegal acts.[171] These measures could be coordinated with judicial actions so as to pressurise parties to transform policies and systems in place internally. As the Palestinian government is dependent on foreign assistance, financially and materially supported social sanctions could help ensure compliance with international law.[172] The impact of international and domestic human rights organisations and civil societies cannot also be overstated.

170 Rodman 2014, pp. 6, 8.

171 Azarova 2015; S. Westbrook, Israel excluded from Italy military exercises after protests, BDS, 20 October 2014.

172 Jo and Simmons 2014, p. 19.

6.4 Chapter Summary

The intervention of the ICC in situations has both a positive and negative impact on peace, justice and stability. The impact differs from situation to situation and on the side of the conflict investigated and prosecuted. Out of ten situations the Court has dealt with, all self-referrals by State parties resulted in the investigation and prosecution of rebels or non-government forces to the exclusion of the referring party. The preliminary examination on Palestine has so far focused on both parties to the conflict although Palestine requested the intervention of the Court. Accordingly, in the Palestine case, the impact of the Court and the reaction to it may depend on which crimes and individuals are indicted by the Court. Nonetheless, one has to critically consider the 'contextual dynamics' of the Israeli-Palestinian conflict and the peace deal efforts to explain the events that unravel. It is misleading to attribute to the Court developments that would not have otherwise been attributed to the Court for the mere reason that the Court is intervening in the situation. A particular example would be to ascribe a possible failure of peace deals (one of the presumed effects) to the intervention of the Court when parties have been neither willing nor able to reach deals since the Oslo Accords.

Despite the anticipated negative impact of the Court's intervention in the conflict, establishing justice does not necessarily call for an end to peace deals or a renewed conflict. Justice is an indispensable element to establish sustainable peace. It is not only the implications of conviction and punishment of perpetrators through the Court but also its non-judicial social and political implications that make the intervention of the Court particularly crucial for the Palestine situation.

Generally, in the long run, the intervention of the Court may have positive impact on peace, justice and stability in the region. The stakes of the intervention are, however, higher as it is one of the longest and most politicised on-going conflicts. The Court could maximise its effect if it recognizes and acknowledges that it has an impact on the elements of peace, and stability and sequence its activities to achieve a more positive impact.

References

Alvarez J (2009) Alternatives to international criminal justice. In: Cassese A (ed) The Oxford companion to international criminal justice. Oxford University Press, Oxford, pp. 25–38.

Ambos K (2016) Treatise on international criminal law: International criminal procedure, vol. III. Oxford University Press, Oxford.

Ambos K, Large J, Wierda M (eds) (2009) Building a future on peace and justice. Springer, Göttingen.

ASP (2011) Report of the Bureau on Complementarity, ICC-ASP/10/24.

Azarova V (2013) Tell it to the judge: Palestine's UN bid and the International Criminal Court. In: Qafisheh M (ed) Palestine membership in the United Nations: Legal and practical implications. Cambridge Scholars Publishing, Newcastle, pp. 252–267.

Azarova V (2015) Palestine's day in court? The unexpected effects of ICC action. https://al-shabaka.org/briefs/palestines-day-in-court-the-unexpected-effects-of-icc-action/. Accessed 28 May 2017.
Azarova V, Weill S (2012) Israel's unwillingness? The follow-up investigations to the UN Gaza conflict report and international criminal justice. International Criminal Law Review 12:905–935.
Bassiouni M (2001) Universal jurisdiction for international crimes: Historical perspectives and contemporary practice. Virginia Journal of International Law 42:1–62.
Burke-White W (2005) Complementarity in practice: The International Criminal Court as part of a system of multi-level global governance in the Democratic Republic of Congo. Leiden Journal of International Law 18:557–590.
Chesterman S (2001) No justice without peace? International criminal law and the decision to prosecute. In: Chesterman S (ed) Civilians in war. Lynne Rienner Publishers, Boulder, Colorado, pp. 145–164.
Collins A (2016) Contemporary security studies, 4th edn. Oxford University Press, Oxford.
Corradetti C, Elsikovits N, Rotondi JV (eds) (2015) Theorizing transitional justice. Routledge, London.
Cryer R, Friman H, Robinson D et al. (2014) An introduction to international criminal law and procedure, 3rd edn. Cambridge University Press, Cambridge.
Dancy et al. (2015) The ICC's deterrent impact – What the evidence shows. https://www.openglobalrights.org/iccs-deterrent-impac/. Accessed 20 May 2017.
DeGuzman M (2012) How serious are international crimes? The gravity problem in international criminal law. Columbia Journal of Transnational Law 51:18–68.
Dezalay S (2012) Lawyering war or talking peace? On militant usages of the law in the resolution of internal armed conflicts: A case study of international alert. In: Dezalay Y, Garth B (eds) Lawyers and the construction of transitional justice. Routledge, Oxon, pp. 60–83.
El Zeidy M (2008) The principle of complementarity in international criminal law: Origin, development and practice. Martinus Nijhoff Publishers, Leiden.
Grono N, O'Brien A (2008) Justice in conflict? The ICC and peace processes. In: Waddell N, Clark P (eds) Courting conflict? Justice, peace and the ICC in Africa. Royal African Society, London, pp. 13–20.
Guembe M, Olea H (2006) No justice, no peace: Discussion of a legal framework regarding the demobilization of non-state armed groups in Colombia. In: Roht-Arriaza N, Mariezcurrena J (eds) Transitional justice in the twenty-first century: Beyond truth versus justice. Cambridge University Press, Cambridge, pp. 120–142.
Hanna M (2008) A historical overview of national prosecution for international crimes. In: Bassiouni M (ed) International criminal law: International enforcement, vol. III. Martinus Nijhoff Publishers, Leiden, pp. 297–328.
Hayner P (2009) Negotiating justice: Guidance for mediators. Center for Humanitarian Dialogue, Geneva.
Huber D, Kamel L (2015) The multilateralisation of the Israeli-Palestinian conflict: A call for an EU initiative. Istituto Affari Internazionali Working Paper 15–02.
Human Rights Watch (2009) Selling justice short: Why accountability matters for peace. Human Rights Watch, New York.
Jessberger F (2014) 'On behalf of Africa': Towards the regionalization of universal jurisdiction? In: Werle G, Vormbaum M (eds) Africa and the International Criminal Court. T.M.C. Asser Press, The Hague, pp. 155–178.
Jo H, Simmons BA (2014) Can the International Criminal Court deter atrocity? https://www.ipinst.org/wp-content/uploads/2015/03/Simmons_Paper.pdf. Accessed 20 May 2017.
Kearney M, Reynolds J (2013) Palestine and the politics of international criminal justice. In: Schabas W, McDermott Y, Hayes N (eds) The Ashgate research companion to international criminal law: Critical perspectives. Routledge, Oxon, pp. 407–434.

Kelley J, Méndez J (2015) Peace making, justice and the ICC. In: De Vos C, Kendall S, Stahn C (eds) Contested justice: The politics and practice of International Criminal Court interventions. Cambridge University Press, Cambridge, pp. 479–495.
Kelman H (2007) The Israeli-Palestinian peace process and its vicissitudes insights from attitude theory. American Psychologist 63 (4):287–303.
Kersten M (2016) Justice in conflict: The effects of the International Criminal Court's interventions on ending wars and building peace. Oxford University Press, Oxford.
Kittrie O (2016) Lawfare: Law as a weapon of war. Oxford University Press, New York.
Kleffner J (2008) Complementarity in the Rome Statute and national criminal jurisdictions. Oxford University Press, New York.
Kontorovich E (2014) Politicizing the International Criminal Court. http://jcpa.org/politicizing_the_international_criminal_Court/. Accessed 5 April 2014.
Kritz N (ed) (1995) Transitional justice: How emerging democracies reckon with former regimes. United States Institute of Peace Press, Washington, DC.
Lindenmann J (2007) Transitional justice and the International Criminal Court: Some reflections on the role of the ICC in conflict transformation. In: Kohen M (ed) Promoting justice, human rights and conflict resolution through international law. Martinus Nijhoff Publishers, Leiden, pp. 315–338.
Materu S (2014) A strained relationship: Reflections on the African Union's stand towards the International Criminal Court from the Kenyan experience. In: Werle G, Vormbaum M (eds) Africa and the International Criminal Court. T.M.C. Asser Press, The Hague, pp. 211–228.
Materu S (2015) The post-election violence in Kenya: Domestic and international legal responses. T.M.C. Asser Press, The Hague.
Mendes E (2010) Peace and justice at the International Criminal Court: A court of last resort. Edward Elgar Publishing, Cheltenham.
Méndez J, Kelley J (2015) Peace making, justice and the ICC. In: De Vos C, Kendall S, Stahn C (eds) Contested justice: The politics and practice of International Criminal Court interventions. Cambridge University Press, Cambridge, pp. 479–495.
Mnookin R (2012) Rethinking the tension between peace and justice: The international criminal prosecutor as diplomat. Harvard Negotiation Law Review 18:145–174.
Nicholas L (2015) The International Criminal Court and the end of impunity in Kenya. Springer, New York.
Nouwen S (2013) Complementarity in the line of fire: The catalysing effect of the International Criminal Court in Uganda and Sudan. Cambridge University Press, Cambridge.
Oberschall A (2007) Conflict and peace building in divided societies: Responses to ethnic violence. Routledge, Oxon.
Okoth J (2014) Africa, the United Nations Security Council and the International Criminal Court: The question of deferrals. In: Werle G, Vormbaum M (eds) Africa and the International Criminal Court. T.M.C. Asser Press, The Hague, pp. 195–210.
Olasolo H (2005) The triggering procedure of the International Criminal Court. Martinus Nijhoff Publishers, Leiden.
Olsen J (2017) Democratic accountability, political order and change. Oxford University Press, Oxford.
OTP (2003) Paper on some policy issues before the Office of the Prosecutor. https://www.icc-cpi.int/nr/rdonlyres/1fa7c4c6-de5f-42b7-8b25-60aa962ed8b6/143594/030905_policy_paper.pdf. Accessed 10 February 2017.
OTP (2007) Policy paper on the interests of justice. https://www.icc-cpi.int/NR/rdonlyres/772C95C9-F54D-4321-BF09-73422BB23528/143640/ICCOTPInterestsOfJustice.pdf. Accessed 10 February 2017.
OTP (2015) Report on preliminary examination activities. https://www.icc-cpi.int/iccdocs/otp/OTP-PE-rep-2015-Eng.pdf. Accessed 10 February 2017.
OTP (2016) Report on preliminary examination activities. https://www.icc-cpi.int/iccdocs/otp/161114-otp-rep-PE_ENG.pdf. Accessed 20 June 2017.

Peskin V (2008) International justice in Rwanda and the Balkans: Virtual trials and the struggle for state cooperation. Cambridge University Press, New York.
Pham P, Vinck P, Stover E et al. (2007) When the war ends: A population-based survey on attitudes about peace, justice, and social reconstruction in Northern Uganda. Harvard Humanitarian Initiative, Cambridge.
Porter E (2015) Connecting peace, justice and reconciliation. Lynne Rienner Publishers, Boulder, Colorado.
Ralston J, Finnin S (2008) Investigating international crimes: A review of international law enforcement strategies: Expediency v effectiveness. In: Blumenthal D, McCormack T (eds) The legacy of Nuremberg: Civilising influence or institutionalised vengeance? Martinus Nijhoff Publishers, Leiden, pp. 47–68.
Reydams L (2011) The rise and fall of universal jurisdiction. In: Schabas W, Bernaz N (eds) Routledge handbook of international criminal law. Routledge, London, pp. 337–354.
Rodman K (2014) Justice as a dialogue between law and politics embedding the International Criminal Court within conflict management and peace building. JICJ 437–469.
Rothe D, Collins V (2013) The International Criminal Court: A pipe dream to end impunity? In: Rothe D, Meernik J, Ingadóttir T (eds) The realities of international criminal justice. Martinus Nijhoff Publishers, Leiden, pp. 191–209.
Said E (1995) Peace and its discontents: Essays on Palestine in the Middle East peace process. Knopf Doubleday, New York.
Schabas W (2011a) An introduction to the International Criminal Court. Cambridge University Press, Cambridge.
Schabas W (2011b) The rise and fall of complementarity. In: Stahn C, El Zeidy M (eds) The International Criminal Court and complementarity: From theory to practice, vol. I. Cambridge University Press, Cambridge, pp. 150–164.
Shimko KL (2016) International relations: Perspectives, controversies and readings, 5th edn. Cengage Learning, Boston.
Sriram CL (2004) Confronting past human rights violations: Justice vs peace in times of transition. Frank Cass, New York.
Sriram CL, García-Godos J, Herman J et al. (eds) (2013) Transitional justice and peacebuilding on the ground: Victims and ex-combatants. Routledge, London.
Stahn C (2010) Arrest and surrender under the ICC Statute - A contextual reading. In: Stahn C, Van den Herik L (eds) Future perspectives on international criminal justice. T.M.C. Asser Press, The Hague, pp. 655–666.
Stan L, Nedelsky N (eds) (2013) Encyclopedia of transitional justice, vol. 1. Cambridge University Press, Cambridge.
Stegmiller I (2011) The pre-investigation stage of the ICC: Criteria for situation selection. Duncker & Humblot, Berlin.
Stone C (2015) Widening the impact of the International Criminal Court: The prosecutor's preliminary examinations in the larger system of the international criminal justice. In: Minow M, True-Frost CC, Whiting A (eds) The First Global Prosecutor: Promise and Constraints. University of Michigan Press, Ann Arbor, pp. 287–308.
Swart B (2002) General problems. In: Cassese A, Gaeta P, Jones J (eds) The Rome Statute of the International Criminal Court: A Commentary. Oxford University Press, Oxford, pp. 1589–1605.
Szekely O (2014) The costs of avoiding transitional justice: Lessons from Lebanon. In: Fisher K, Stewart R (eds) Transitional justice and the Arab Spring. Routledge, New York, pp. 94–111.
Turkel Commission (2013) Israel's mechanisms for examining and investigating complaints and claims of violations of the laws of armed conflict according to international law (2nd report). Turkel Commission, Israel.
Unger T, Wierda M (2009) Pursuing justice in ongoing conflict: A discussion of current practice. In: Ambos K, Large J, Wierda M (eds) Building a future on peace and justice. Springer, Göttingen, pp. 263–302.

UNHRC (2009) Human rights in Palestine and other occupied Arab territories: Report of the United Nations Fact-Finding Mission on the Gaza Conflict, UN Doc. A/HRC/12/48.

UNHRC (2015) Report of the detailed findings of the independent commission of inquiry established pursuant to Human Rights Council resolution S-21/1, UN Doc. A/HRC/29/CRP.4.

UNSC (1994) Resolution 955, UN Doc. S/RES/955.

UNSC (1993) Resolution 837, UN Doc. S/RES/827.

UNSC (2011) Report of the Secretary-General: The rule of law and transitional justice in conflict and post-conflict societies, UN Doc. S/2011/634.

Van den Herik L (2009) A quest for jurisdiction and an appropriate definition of crime: Mpambara before the Dutch courts. JICJ 7:1117–1131.

Van der Wilt H (2010) Why international criminal lawyers should read Mirjan Damaška. In: Stahn C, Van den Herik L (eds) Future perspectives on international criminal justice. T.M.C. Asser Press, The Hague, pp. 44–57.

Vinjamuri L (2015) The ICC and the politics of peace and justice. In: Stahn C (ed) The law and practice of the International Criminal Court. Oxford University Press, Oxford, pp. 13–29.

Wegner P (2015) The International Criminal Court in Ongoing Intrastate Conflicts: Navigating the Peace-Justice Divide. Cambridge University Press, Cambridge.

Weill S (2012) The follow up to the Goldstone Report and its legal impact in Israel and beyond. In: Meloni C, Tognoni G (eds) Is There a Court for Gaza? A Test Bench for International Justice. T.M.C. Asser Press, The Hague, pp. 105–120.

Werle G, Jessberger F (2014) Principles of international criminal law, 3rd edn. Oxford University Press, Oxford.

Chapter 7
Conclusions and Recommendations

Contents

7.1 General Remarks

This book relies on two foundations. One, impunity regarding gross human rights violations should not be tolerated and those who bear the greatest responsibility should not go unpunished. Two, in the absence of a concerned domestic judicial system willing and able to investigate and prosecute crimes of international concern, the ICC has the purpose and institutional capacity to adjudicate such crimes that fall within its jurisdiction. On the basis of these premises, the study had the objective of examining the jurisdictional and procedural challenges for the ICC to investigate and prosecute the crimes committed in the Israeli-Palestinian conflict; to analyse, within the spectrum of the Rome Statute, the justiciability of the crimes allegedly committed in the conflict; and to explore the possible significance, impact and contribution of the involvement of the ICC in the Israeli-Palestinian conflict and jurisprudence of the Court. In light of these objectives and on the basis of the discussion, this concluding chapter reiterates the main findings and draws institutional lessons for the ICC to deal with the Palestine situation and situations of a similar nature.

7.2 Conclusions

The interaction between Palestine and the ICC, be it the 2009 or the 2014 *ad hoc* declaration, is triggered by, among other causes, active military engagements between Israel and armed Palestinian groups. Nonetheless, the history of the Israeli-Palestinian conflict attests to the commission of international crimes in

© T.M.C. ASSER PRESS and the author 2019

S. H. Adem, *Palestine and the International Criminal Court*,
International Criminal Justice Series 21,
https://doi.org/10.1007/978-94-6265-291-0_7

various contexts. It is a conflict that originates from clashing territorial claims over the same piece of land that through time interwove elements of politics, race, religion and economic interests. In the absence of a final settlement between the two parties, the intervention of the ICC, as shown in this book, is neither a panacea nor an avenue to pursue *in lieu* of peace deals.

Scholars remain divided on the question pertaining to the international organ mandated to rule on the statehood of Palestine and Palestine's capacity to conduct juridical acts with international institutions in general and the ICC in particular. However, following Resolution 67/19 of the General Assembly, the Prosecutor of the ICC as well as other organs in charge of depositing accessions of international instruments have treated Palestine, and rightly so, as an entity enjoying international personality. Out of the Palestine situation, a question on the capacity of the entity making an *ad hoc* declaration has emerged. This study has shown that the competence to determine on the capacity of the entity remains within the Court. As one organ of the Court, the Office of the Prosecutor is duty-bound to satisfy itself on issues relating to pre-conditions on the exercise of jurisdiction. In matters dealing with *ad hoc* declarations, regarding the capacity of the entity making the declaration or issues dealing with jurisdiction and admissibility, the book outlines a practical and plausible route to follow. It contends that the prosecutor has to decide on the matter and request a ruling by the Pre-Trial Chamber.

Although the study adopted the functional approach to answer the question regarding the capacity of Palestine to lodge the declaration, in response to the approach employed by the prosecutor to resolve the issue, it has provided a discussion of the statehood issue of Palestine in the abstract. On the basis of the history of the creation of the State of Palestine, the criteria of the Montevideo Convention and the theories of State recognition, one could conclude that a Palestinian State exists. Nonetheless, due to the absence of an established criterion and the multitude of ways States come into existence, the satisfaction of the elements does not guarantee a conclusive answer. Be it a State or a quasi-State, the purpose of the Rome Statute strongly gravitates towards a flexible approach that does not allow for the existence of a legal void. Adoption of a functional approach, as argued in this book, helps serve the aims and purposes of the Statute and gives the Statute wider application.

The pre-investigation considerations of the Statute require an examination of jurisdiction, admissibility and interest of justice. In light of the 2014 Palestinian *ad hoc* declaration, the temporal scope of the Prosecutor's investigation is limited to crimes committed after 13 June 2014. Nonetheless, the situation in Palestine covers crimes of a continuous nature that have been allegedly committed before 13 June 2014 and continued thereafter. The study has consulted the jurisprudence surrounding permanent and continuous crimes and has concluded that the temporal jurisdiction of the Court also covers continuing crimes, such as settlements and the forcible transfer of the population as long as the *actus reus* of the crime was committed or continues to be committed within the temporal scope of the Court. Within the territories recognised as occupied Palestinian territories, crimes committed by Israelis in Palestine and crimes committed by Palestinians anywhere fall within the Court's jurisdiction. The unsettled border of Palestine and Israel as well as the need to delimit the territorial scope of the Court could, however, cause the Court to look into the history of the conflict and the various claims over the territory. In any case, UN Resolutions, the ICJ wall opinion and various State recognitions endorse a State of Palestine comprising of the West Bank, the Gaza Strip and East Jerusalem.

The admissibility considerations of the Statute comprise two of the crucial elements that should be fulfilled for a preliminary examination to proceed to investigation. In light of the established principle of complementarity, the book has dealt with the judicial systems of both Israel and Palestine to investigate grave crimes of international concern. Structural, substantive and procedural limitations have incapacitated the Israeli judicial system to investigate and prosecute crimes under international law. In regard to institutionalised and policy based crimes such as construction of settlements, house demolitions and certain policies dealing with Palestinians, the State of Israel does not view such crimes as violations of international law. In an instance where the system in place is evidently flawed and where certain crimes within the jurisdiction of the Court are not domestically criminalised and are enforced through state machineries, the accountability mechanism in place could not be viewed as complementary. The case is no less different for the Palestinian accountability mechanism. The installed judicial system is not only ill equipped to deal with certain crimes, in cases such as rocket and mortar attacks against Israeli civilians, but there is also an obvious indisposition to address the conducts.

Once a situation graduates from examination to investigation, the Prosecutor deals with the sensitive and procedural process of case selection and prioritisation. The study provided the criteria for case selection based on the Rome Statute, the policy paper on case selection and prioritisation and the strategy of the Prosecutor. In light of the gravity of the crimes, their reoccurrence and relative uniqueness, war crimes and crimes against humanity have been discussed.

Based on scholarly analysis and various reports, the book has established that there is a reasonable ground to believe that both parties to the conflict have committed war crimes. As discussed in Chap. 4, impunity for crimes under international law prevails in respect of alleged war crimes committed by the Israeli Defence Force. The alleged war crimes range from those committed during Operation Protective Edge, the construction of settlements and wilful killing in the context of the military occupation in the West Bank.

In an active hostility setting, alleged attacks on residential buildings and the disproportionate civilian toll and civilian damage coupled with the absence of accountability within the military give rise to questions on the military policy in place. In this regard, the military policy and the role played by senior military officials could be of special interest to the Prosecutor. This focus satisfies the established case selection criteria by guiding the investigation to focus on faulty State policies, those most responsible and those cases most practical to prosecute.

Impunity also prevails with regard to direct attacks against Israeli civilians and civilian objects. The use by Palestinian armed groups of weapons incapable of discriminate targeting, as argued in the book, amounts to the intention to target civilians. The alleged tolerance and support of Hamas of these acts is a violation of the basic international humanitarian law principles that could result in the prosecution of senior officials of the governing entity.

With regard to settlements, there is no challenge proving the existence of the settlements or State policies behind the settlements. The main issue, therefore, is whether the matter falls within the Court's jurisdiction, particularly within the temporal jurisdiction of the Court. Settlements, unlike other war crimes, are argued as having the character of permanency. This continuing nature of the crime helps extend the temporal jurisdiction of the Court to those settlements built before the temporal scope for Palestine. Most indirect efforts to transfer Israelis to the settlements do not only fall within the material element of the crime but are committed within the temporal jurisdiction of the Court.

To the exclusion of other crimes against humanity, the study dealt with the forcible transfer of the population, the crime of apartheid and persecution. In regard to the crime of the forcible transfer of the population, it has shown that there is a reasonable ground to believe that the systematic denial of permission to build, the strict criteria for Jerusalem residency and the lack of possibilities for relocation within the same area indicate an overall policy aimed at maintaining a Jewish majority demographic balance in Jerusalem. When it comes to the other areas under occupation, the purpose of house demolitions, however, amounts to the forceful take-over of land and other resources.

Coupled with the conducts examined for the crime of the forcible transfer of the population and other policies, and conducts that constitute the composite elements of the crime of apartheid, the book has dealt with the alleged crime of apartheid in the Palestine context. The discussion relied, among others, on the Anti-apartheid Convention and the Rome Statute. As the main purpose of the analysis is a scholastic inquiry, international human rights law instruments and authoritative reports were employed. In light of these instruments and taking stock of South Africa's apartheid experience, the study has concluded that inhumane acts that constitute the crime of apartheid are committed in Palestine. However, in light of Article 7(2)(h) and Article 30, one cannot assert with a reasonable degree of certainty that there is a specific intent to impose and maintain a regime of apartheid in Palestine. The constitutive conducts of the crime are committed to facilitate and enforce aims such as maintaining the Jewish nature of Israel and building a greater Israel. Therefore, the study concludes that although there is *prima facie* evidence to believe that the material elements for the crime of apartheid are being committed in the situation, there is no specific intention to impose and maintain a regime of apartheid in Palestine. In the absence of this crucial intention element, one cannot conclude that the crime is committed in the Palestine situation.

Concerning the crime of persecution, the study specifically focused on the Gaza blockade. In this regard, the book has detailed the significant socio-economic impact the policy of blockade has on the civilian population. The effect of the blockade has resulted in a severe deprivation in the sense provided by the Statute. Based on available jurisprudence, therefore, it is concluded that there is *prima facie* evidence to prove the commission of the crime of persecution in Gaza. As the conducts that amount to persecution could also be charged as, for instance, forcible transfer of population, the study further explored the possibility of charging persecution and other crimes cumulatively. In light of other crimes within the Court's jurisdiction, a charge of persecution serves a different legal purpose and requires proof of a materially distinct element. Thus, the study concluded that a charge of persecution, based on the same set of facts, can be pursued cumulative to other charges. Then again, the potential charges to be pursued depend on the legal and pragmatic challenges at hand, among which availability and access to evidence play a defining role.

One of the most debated issues regarding Palestine and the ICC is the implication of the intervention on matters such as peace, domestic prosecutions, Palestine's statehood and the credibility of the Court. Cognisant of the fact that the situation is an on-going conflict and that investigation is still underway, the assertions reached remain anticipative and contingent on forthcoming factors. Undeniably, however, the intervention of the Court helps in the overall fight against the culture of impunity in the region. Though not entirely, it helps respond to the needs of victims for justice and redress. It also plays a significant role to promote domestic investigations and prosecutions. In regard to its effect on deterrence of possible crimes, the study has looked into other situations and the manner events unravel in the Palestine situation after the Prosecutor opened an investigation. On these bases, it is concluded that the deterrence impact of the Court's intervention depends on other extraneous factors such as the ideology behind the commission of the crimes and predictability of prosecution. Emphasis is, however, given to the often-overlooked significance of judicial stigmatisation or the extra-judicial impacts of prosecution in shaping conducts of parties to the conflict.

Opponents of the Court's intervention in the Israeli-Palestinian conflict have often asserted that establishing accountability through the ICC would deter peace efforts. In the absence of any worthwhile peace efforts since the Oslo Accords, the study has argued that the assertion fails to create any causal link between establishing justice and its negative impact on peace efforts. As managing the peace vs. justice dilemma should not necessarily result in an either or approach, the study has indicated that the prosecutor could, in such scenarios, employ her discretion to broadly interpret 'interest of justice'. This approach does not only help to take peace settlements into consideration, it also broadens the interpretation of justice and 'needs of victims' to include restorative and preventive measures.

7.3 Recommendations

Establishing accountability for the Israeli-Palestinian conflict through the ICC is a novel, uncharted and propitious option. The Court, nonetheless, is not a panacea. It is an institution mandated to establish individual criminal accountability. As such, its effectiveness should be measured in light of the enforcement of criminal justice within the scope of the Statute. Undeniably, it is matters extraneous to the main aims and purposes of the Court that cause controversy about the Court's intervention in the situation in Palestine. If, however, the Court is viewed for what it is, an institution established to prosecute the 'most serious crimes of concern to the international community', it would help increase the effectiveness of the Court. For this to happen, the Court needs to establish effective institutional responses to queries from States parties, misleading reports and approaches to its tasks.

The interpretation and application of the Statute also plays a substantial part. Concerning its impact on peace efforts in particular, the Prosecutor has the authority to redefine the application of 'interest of justice' and the 'principle of complementarity' to take into consideration peace efforts. Bearing in mind the political ramification of its activities, the interpretation of Article 53(1)(c) and 53(2) should not only focus on interest of justice in the strict sense of prosecution. As justice should not be viewed as only synonymous with prosecution, peace should not also be seen as only synonymous to negotiated peace. The office should be able to take into consideration alternative justice mechanisms of States and other tools that serve, *inter alia*, the peace, reconciliation and stability interests of victims.

Furthermore, the Court should recognise and acknowledge the fact that it has a notable impact on peace and stability and assert a clear stance in this regard. It has to make efforts to match and sequence its activities with the realities on the ground. This in turn increases the effectiveness of the Court as well as helps elevate its credibility and reputation. Taking principled pragmatic considerations in strategising its work is also in the interest of the institution. Doing so is vital to obtain and further State cooperation that is crucial for the Court's success as well as the legitimacy and preservation of the institution.

A case in point could be the manner in which the Office of the Prosecutor dealt with the 2009 *ad hoc* declaration of Palestine. As many, including the then Prosecutor, have viewed the delegation of jurisdiction as a political statement, the 'decision not to decide' by outsourcing the duty to interpret the word 'State' under Article 12(3) to political organs has resulted in inauspicious reviews. As a judicial organ aimed to maximise prevention and deterrence for the commission of gross crimes, the study has underlined that the befitting interpretation of the Statute should be the one that principally furthers the purpose of the Court.

In light of the principle of complementarity, domestic investigations and prosecutions have to also be conducted. Both States, Israel and Palestine, as recommended by various UN bodies and other institutions, are required to take measures to capacitate and make available effective, independent and impartial judicial organs to address the gross crimes committed. Other States parties to the Statute also have responsibility not only to assist the Court in its investigation and prosecution, but also in conducting their own domestic prosecutions through the instrumentality of universal jurisdiction. The role the Security Council could play in this regard cannot also be overstated. It can urge parties to act in line with international humanitarian law and human rights law principles and assist parties to include the pursuit of justice as a crucial element of any sustainable peace effort.

Index

© T.M.C. ASSER PRESS and the author 2019

S. H. Adem, *Palestine and the International Criminal Court*,
International Criminal Justice Series 21,
https://doi.org/10.1007/978-94-6265-291-0

FSC
www.fsc.org
MIX
Papier | Fördert
gute Waldnutzung
FSC® C083411

Kolibri 360 GmbH
Ferdinand-Jühlke-Straße 7
99095 Erfurt, Deutschland
produktsicherheit@kolibri360.de